OCR PE A2

PHYSICAL EDUCATION

Dave Carnell • John Ireland • Ken Mackreth • Sarah Powell • Sarah van Wely

Revision Guide

Heinemann

Heinemann is an imprint of Pearson Education Limited, a company incorporated in England and Wales, having its registered office at Edinburgh Gate, Harlow, Essex, CM20 2JE. Registered company number: 872828

www.heinemann.co.uk

Heinemann is a registered trademark of Pearson Education Limited

Text © Dave Carnell (Chapters 16–19), John Ireland (Chapters 6–10), Ken Mackreth (Chapters 20–21), Sarah Powell (Chapters 11–15), and Sarah van Wely (Introduction and Chapters 1–5) 2010

First published 2010

14 13 12 11 10
10 9 8 7 6 5 4 3 2 1

British Library Cataloguing in Publication Data
A catalogue record for this book is available from the British Library

ISBN 978 0 435466 89 3

Typeset by Tek-Art
Cover design by Wooden Ark Studios
Picture research by Harriet Merry and Lindsay Lewis
Cover photo/illustration by Claus Andersen/Masterfile
Printed in the UK by Scotprint.
Illustrated by Harriet Stares/Nb illustration

Acknowledgements

The author and publisher would like to thank the following individuals and organisations for permission to reproduce photographs:

Topham/Fotomas p41. Hulton Getty p50. Corbis/Hulton Deutsch p51. Topham p52. PA Photos/John Birdsall p53. Getty Images/Hamish Blair p127. PA Photos p159. Photodisc/Lawrence M. Sawyer p204. Alamy/Ace Stock Ltd p204.

We would like to thank the following for permission to reproduce copyrighted material:

Page 165 Fig 16.3 Breakdown of PC coupled to ATP resysnthesis during sprinting Reprinted with permission from J Wilmore and D Costill (1999) Psychology of Sport and Exercise, 2nd edn, (Champaign, IL: Human Kinetics), p121. Page 220 Fig 18.4.8 Exercise intensity linked to fat usage graph adapted from Peak Performance, Issue 263

The authors and publishers would also like to thank Brian Mackenzie for kind permission to reproduce copyright materials from his website Brian Mac Sports Coach.

Every effort has been made to contact copyright holders of material reproduced in this book. Any omissions will be rectified in subsequent printings if notice is given to the publishers.

Table of Contents

INTRODUCTION

This book has been produced specifically for students revising for OCR's A2 Physical Education specification. It follows the same structure as the student book OCR A2 Physical Education and so you can trust that it includes essential information that you need to know, understand and be able to apply in order to achieve A2 exam success – all in a student friendly, thorough and engaging style. Topics within each of the following five sections of the theory Unit G453 are included.

Unit G453 - principles and concepts across different areas of Physical Education
- Historical Studies
- Comparative Studies
- Sports Psychology
- Biomechanics
- Exercise and sports physiology

There is also information on the coursework/practical Unit G454.

Unit G454 - the improvement of effective performance and the critical evaluation of practical activities in Physical Education
- Performance
- Evaluation, appreciation and the improvement of performance (E&A)

This book contains the following features to help you with your revision:

KEY TERM

Key terms – Ensure that you know the meaning of these key terms – most of which are directly lifted from the specification and could feature in examination questions.

EXAM TIP

These are designed to give you essential exam advice and guidance and so maximise success.

Need to know more? These provide cross references to chapters/pages in the main student text (*OCR A2 Physical Education*) where you will find more detailed information.

CHECK

At the end of each chapter you will find an overview section with tick boxes. Use these to help review your revision as well as to check your progress. If you are not satisfied with your knowledge and understanding of a particular topic or chapter, then revisit those areas.

TRUE OR FALSE?

These are at the end of each chapter to provide you with a quick activity to check your progress and hopefully to give you confidence.

EXAM PRACTICE

At the end of each chapter you will find a section of exam-style questions, similar to those used by examiners. Outline mark schemes/answer grids for these questions are at the end of the book.

The next section on exam strategies gives you lots of useful information on how to best prepare for the exam.

EXAM STRATEGIES FOR THEORY UNIT G453

Peak exam performance needs knowledge, application of knowledge and skillfully applied exam technique. Adopting techniques and strategies for exam success is just like learning tactics and strategies for success in sport (e.g. set plays for free throws or kicks).

Here we look at techniques and tactics that will help you succeed. We will also point out how to avoid pitfalls that regularly cause problems and underachievement by candidates.

We'll start by looking at what you need to do on the day and the **rubric** (rules/instructions) from the front of your G453 theory exam paper.

Instructions / information to candidates:

- Write your name clearly in capital letters and your Centre Number and Candidate Number in the spaces provided.
- Use black ink. Pencil may be used for graphs and diagrams only.
- The number of marks is given in brackets at the end of each question or part question.

- Answer three questions: one from section A, one from section B, and one other from any section.
- Read each question carefully and make sure that you know what you have to do before starting your answer.
- The quality of your written communication will be assessed in questions that are indicated (*).

Let's review some particularly important instructions/information:

1. By this stage in your exam-sitting career you are hopefully aware of the significance of **the number of marks given in brackets at the end of each question or part question** – and are able to make the correct number of points/write an appropriate length answer.

2. The instruction **to answer three questions** – one from section A one from section B plus one other (from either section) is also key to exam success. Each year a number of candidates do too few or (more commonly) too many questions while others answer at least one question from a section that they have not even studied! Each of these mistakes will adversely affect your time management, quality of response and ultimately your result. Table 1 shows requirements.

		% value of A2 alone	% value with AS/A2 combined
• The G453 theory exam is 150 minutes or 2½ hrs • Each full question on the G453 paper has 35 marks. • Each has four parts (a – d). • Parts a – c total 15 marks (normally 4 – 6 marks each) • Part (d) is a 20-mark question			
A2 Theory Unit G453	**3 questions:** **1 from section A** Option A1 Historical studies Option A2 Comparative studies **1 from section B** Option B1 Exercise physiology Option B2 Biomechanics Option B3 Sports psychology **Plus one other question from section A or B**	70%	35%
A2 course-work Unit G454	**1 practical activity** and oral (E&A)	30%	15%

1. *Table 1 A visual review of exam requirement*

3. The instruction to **read each question carefully and make sure that you know what you have to do before starting your answer** is also crucial to success. Each year, candidates who have revised effectively wade in to an answer before reflection or planning and so badly affect their result. This mistake should be avoided at all costs.

Some thinking and planning (particularly of your 20-mark answers) is not only valuable but positively essential and an integral part of the examination process. A2 question setters and examiners are looking for 'thinking' candidates who can adapt learned information to the exact question that has been set, and to which candidates may not have considered in that format before. More thinking/evaluating rather than straight forward regurgitation of knowledge is needed at A2 than was needed at AS.

So, just as for AS Level, it is important that you spot and stick to not only the **command word** (e.g. *discuss or critically evaluate*) and the **subject** being examined (e.g. energy systems for Exercise and sport Physiology or public school athleticism for Historical Studies) but also, and perhaps most importantly, the **exact aspect of the subject** that will get you marks. So don't just write everything you know about a topic but adapt your knowledge to the exact question set.

Remember to check/focus on:
- the command word
- the subject
- the specific aspect of the subject that is being examined.

At A2 level there is a greater emphasis on the more demanding commands than at AS (where there was a greater emphasis on the more straightforward

commands) and so for the top grades you need to do more thinking, reasoning, analysis and evaluation as seen near the top of Table 2 (below).

4. It is critical that you understand the instruction that **the quality of your written communication will be assessed in questions that are indicated (*) which is the 20-mark questions.**
- **Quality of written communication**: this is just one of five criteria that examiners will consider when awarding your mark out of 20 in the extended (part d) questions.

The other criteria are:
- Knowledge and understanding
- Analysis/critical evaluation
- Independent opinion, judgment and use of relevant practical examples
- Use of technical and specialist vocabulary.

More about the 20-mark question

The extended (part d) questions are challenging opportunities for you to show how good you are! You will have been building on your extended writing skills and practiced several extended answers during your A2 course. Just as for your AS G451 10-mark questions, the A2 20-markers will be assessing with a '**levels of response**' mark scheme. This gives examiners opportunity to credit the variety of skills listed above. The **quality** of your answer is probably more important than the **quantity** you write.

For each of the 20-mark questions examiners will have a list of facts/points (**indicative content**) that candidates are likely to include in their answers. Examiners also have **levels descriptors** to help them judge the quality of your answers. At A2 level there are four levels which are described as follows:

Evaluation and synthesis of knowledge	Critically Evaluate	Analyse	Justify	These more demanding commands require you to 'play with' your knowledge: to think about, apply and perhaps link information from different parts of the specification. You should include examples and context and perhaps some independent opinion.
	Discuss	Assess	To what extent ...	
Application of knowledge	Contrast	Explain	Describe	These are discursive commands that require thought and development of key words, phrases or statements.
	Compare	Identify differences between ...	Give reasons for ...	
Knowledge and understanding	Define	List	State	These are straightforward 'recall' commands requiring knowledge. Your AS PE exam paper will have some of these.
	Identify	What ...	Outline	

INCREASING DEMAND

Table 2 Command words have different levels of demand and need different levels of analysis/evaluation.

Level 4: *a comprehensive answer* (18–20 marks)

- detailed knowledge & excellent understanding;
- detailed analysis/critical evaluation and excellent critical evaluation;
- well-argued, independent opinion and judgments which are well supported by relevant practical examples;
- very accurate use of technical and specialist vocabulary;
- high standard of written communication throughout.

Level 3: *a competent answer* (13–17 marks)

- good knowledge & clear understanding;
- good analysis and critical evaluation;
- Independent opinions and judgments will be present but may not always be supported by relevant practical examples;
- generally accurate use of technical and specialist vocabulary;
- written communication is generally fluent with few errors.

Level 2: *a limited answer* (8–12 marks)

- limited knowledge & understanding;
- some evidence of analysis and critical evaluation;
- opinion and judgment given but often unsupported by relevant practical examples;
- technical and specialist vocabulary used with limited success;
- written communication lacks fluency and contains errors.

Level 1: *a basic answer* (0–7 marks)

- basic knowledge & little understanding;
- little relevant analysis or critical evaluation;
- little or no attempt to give opinion or judgment;
- little or no attempt to use technical and specialist vocabulary;
- errors in written communication will be intrusive.

So when you are answering practice questions, and during the actual exam, reflect on the following:

- **Knowledge & understanding** – have I made a number of relevant points?
- **Analysis / critical evaluation** – have I stayed relevant but built on, developed or 'picked apart' some of my points?
- **Independent opinion & judgment with practical examples** – have I tried to add my own view or to judge accepted wisdom (with evidence) at times? Have I included regular, relevant links to practical performance?
- **Technical / specialist vocabulary** – have I consistently used vocabulary that illustrates my understanding of and engagement with the subject?
- **Quality of written communication** – is my spelling, punctuation, grammar and answer structure at the highest quality I can manage?

What about revision?

You've probably devised your own revision style by now and if it works well for you that's great. Most people find that they need a varied, active approach. Diagrams and mind maps often help as many find it easier to remember things when they are visual. Notepads and cards are also useful for jotting down key points.

Reminder of essential exam strategies:

- Make a note of key points, definitions, acronyms, mnemonics, data/values/ formulae that you think you might need but might forget.
- Skim-read the whole paper before you start to write.
- Read each question slowly and carefully to check exactly what you need to do.
- Perhaps underline or highlight the key components of each question (command word, subject and the exact aspect of the subject that is being examined).
- Remember – thinking time is essential.
- Keep your eye on the clock and pace yourself.
- Make your writing easy to read.
- Obey the command word/s in the question.
- Be specific, not vague in your answers.
- Keep to the point – avoid irrelevance.
- Develop answers where the command word requires it e.g. critically evaluate or explain.
- Use examples to support points wherever you can.
- Plan – especially the 20-mark answers, but avoid over planning.
- Read through, check and edit your work at the end if possible.

If you know, understand and are able to apply the material to a variety of questions, you have every chance of hitting the top grades!

Good luck in your exam and for the future!

Sarah van Wely

CHAPTER 1
Popular recreation in pre-industrial Britain

CHAPTER OVERVIEW

By the end of this chapter you should be able to demonstrate knowledge and understanding of:

- the characteristics of popular recreation
- how social and cultural factors shaped popular recreation
- how popular recreation affected the physical competence and health of participants
- different opportunities for participation in pre-industrial Britain
- the impact of popular recreation on contemporary participation and performance.

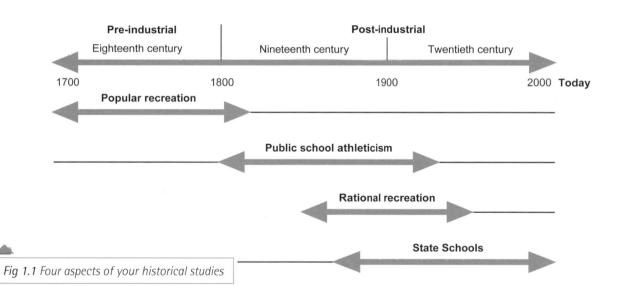

Fig 1.1 Four aspects of your historical studies

Popular recreation in the United Kingdom

Popular recreations were pre-industrial sports and pastimes mainly associated with the peasant or lower class. The term could also refer to the most popular pastimes of the day.

Pre-industrial popular recreation reflected the society, life and time in which it existed. The activities were often colourful and lively and were supported by a strict class system.

- Different classes sometimes shared activities, for example cock fighting.
- Sometimes different classes took part in different activities, such as mob football for the lower class peasants and real tennis for the upper class/gentry.
- Sometimes different classes had different roles within the same activity. For example, a pedestrian – race walker or runner – was often lower class while his patron, or sponsor, was upper class.

EXAM TIP

Ensure that you:
- know the characteristics of popular recreation
- understand the social (or societal) reasons for the characteristics

- can discuss the extent to which each case study activity 'fits' with the typical characteristics of popular recreation.

Natural/simple
Lack of: technology, purpose-built facilities and money for the masses

Wagering
A chance to go from rags to riches (for poor) or to show off (for rich)

Local
Limited transport and communications

Occupational
Work often became the basis of sport

Characteristics of popular recreation
and cultural factors that influenced their development

Simple, unwritten rules
Illiteracy, no NGBs, only played locally

Rural
Before the Industrial Revolution, Britain was agricultural and rural

Cruel/violent
Reflecting the harshness of eighteenth-century rural life

Courtly/popular
Pre-industrial Britain was predominantly a two-class society, based on the feudal system

Occasional
Free time for recreation on Holy Days and annual holidays – e.g. Shrove Tuesday

Fig 1.2 Characteristics of popular recreation and influential social and cultural factors

Popular recreation – its effects on skill and health

	Upper class	Lower class
Bathing and swimming	Likely to increase skill and health	As for upper class; key functional role for hygiene
Athletics	Pedestrianism required skill and would need and increase physical fitness and thus health	Pedestrianism – as for upper class; rural sports – predominantly for recreation
Football	Involvement unlikely so no impact	Mob football was forceful rather than skilful; could be harmful with severe injuries and even fatalities
Cricket	Outside and active during summer months, so a skilful game with potential to improve health	As for upper class
Real tennis	A skilful, potentially health-enhancing game for the elite	Not available to lower class, who played simple hand and ball games (perhaps skilfully) for recreation

Table 1 The impact of popular recreations on the physical competence and health of participants with reference to the five case study activities

Varying opportunities for participation

In pre-industrial Britain, just like today, class and gender were key factors affecting opportunities for participation.

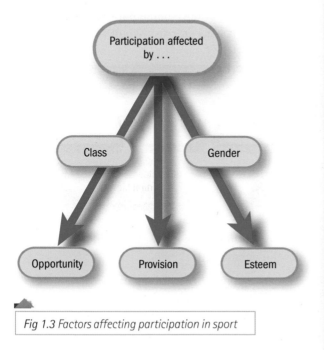

Fig 1.3 Factors affecting participation in sport

Gender	• In pre-industrial Britain, upper-class women pursued elitist pastimes, such as hawking. Lower-class women participated in less sophisticated, more uncouth activities such as smock races. • The Victorian era brought new attitudes, especially for middle-class women for whom physical activity was thought to be unsuitable, undignified and even dangerous. • Nineteenth-century women were later constrained by social attitudes and by lack of opportunity and provision.
Class	• Pre-industrial Britain was predominantly a two-class society. The upper class (also called the gentry or aristocracy) dominated the peasant (or lower) class. • There was also a merchant, trading or commercial class from whom the middle class later emerged. • The upper class had money for facilities, equipment and transport; time to become skilful; and societal status, which increased their self-worth or esteem.

Table 2 Class and gender – key factors affecting opportunities for participation in sport

Activities of the upper class were often...	Activities of the lower class were often...
sophisticated and expensive, e.g. real tennis	simple, accessible and inexpensive, e.g. mob football
rule-based with a dress code and etiquette	simple with unwritten rules and were often violent and/or uncivilised
linked with patronage/ acting as an 'agent', e.g. in pedestrianism	linked with occupation e.g. pedestrianism
distant, due to opportunity to travel	local, due to lack of opportunity to travel

Table 3 How the sporting activities of the gentry (upper class) compared with those of the peasants (lower class) in pre-industrial Britain

The role and attitude of the Church

Popular recreations were subject to periodic Church interference since medieval times.

- Henry VIII broke with the Catholic Church in Rome in 1534. He had no desire to change people's religious, social or sporting habits.
- Change came as a result of the English Reformation (a religious movement which called for the reform of the Roman Catholic Church).
- Puritanism emerged. Puritans opposed the excess, unruliness, spontaneity, swearing and drinking associated with contemporary recreations. They believed that idleness and playfulness were sinful and that salvation could only be earned through a life of prayer, self-discipline and moderation.
- This was a bleak time for popular sports and pastimes.
- The Puritan ethic gave way to the work ethic and spreading Protestantism, whereby leisure pursuits were acceptable only in that they restored people for work.

Eighteenth-century peasant life

- Life was tough for the lower class or agricultural worker in the eighteenth-century; sports and pastimes reflected this harshness.
- The drinking house or pub was central to village life and the focus for community leisure activities.

- The pub hosted bear and badger baiting, dog fighting and prize (bare-fist) fighting as well as less barbaric games such as billiards, quoits, bowls and skittles.
- Landlords often provided prizes for sporting matches and primitive equipment for ball games in order to stimulate interest and, perhaps more importantly, boost profit.
- Many late-eighteenth- and early-nineteenth-century sports clubs used the public house as their base, most famously the Hambledon cricket club at the Bat and Ball Inn, Hampshire, where the game of cricket was nurtured between 1750 and 1780.

Impact on and links to sport today

You need to consider the impact of popular recreation on participation and performance in physical activity today. (In Chapter 2 you will consider the same for rational recreation and in Chapter 3 for public schools.) The impact or link can be either direct or indirect (developmental).

- A direct link is something such as a pre-industrial festival that still occurs today.
- An indirect or developmental link is one that goes to or has come from a previous stage.

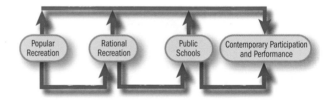

Fig 1.4 Direct and indirect (developmental) impacts of past to present

Your exam questions may ask for either direct or developmental links.

Arguably, popular recreations had some limited direct links to today, but their impact is mainly indirect as they were the starting point of each activity on its developmental journey.

Direct links include:

- illegally-staged bare-fist fights
- blood sports such as badger baiting and dog fights.

Both of these declined as law and order increased (in the nineteenth-century) but they did not completely die out.

Contemporary newspaper articles still occasionally report on bloody activities with betting as a central feature. Fox hunting continues amid ongoing debate.

Need to know more? For more information on pre-industrial popular recreation see Chapter 1, pages 1–13, in the OCR A2 PE Student Book.

EXAM TIP

Remember the importance of links forward to the next stage and/or directly to today. Exam questions will ask for knowledge and understanding of both *then* and *the next stage of development* or *now*.

Case study	Examples of direct links
Swimming	There are links with lake-based swimming clubs or continued motives such as health, recreation and survival/safety.
Athletics	In April 2002 five British athletes (sponsored by Flora) repeated the unique feat of Captain Robert Barclay Allardice who ran 1000 miles in 1000 hours for a wager of over 1000 guineas at Newmarket Heath 200 years ago. That is, a mile an hour, every hour, every day and night for six weeks (see Chapter 4, page 61 in the OCR A2 PE Student Book). Also, rural sports including races and tests of strength continue at some summer fetes and fairs; along with Traditional Olympics – Much Wenlock and Dover Games, for example.
Football	Surviving ethnic sports such as the Ashbourne football game. Occasional violent behaviour by players or spectators in the modern game is another unwelcome direct link.
Cricket	In pre-industrial times the game was for all classes – the English Cricket Board (ECB) stresses that this is the same today.
Tennis	In pre-industrial times the game of real tennis was exclusive and today it is largely the same.

Table 4 Examples of direct links from popular recreations today

CHECK

If you are satisfied with your knowledge and understanding, tick off the sections that you have revised so far. If you are not satisfied then revisit those sections and refer to the pages in the *Need to know more?* features.

☐ Identify the characteristics of popular recreation.

☐ Describe how social and cultural factors shaped popular recreation.

☐ Explain how popular recreation affected the physical competence and health of participants.

☐ Distinguish between different opportunities for participation in pre-industrial Britain.

☐ Access the impact of popular recreation on contemporary participation and performance.

TRUE OR FALSE?

1. Popular recreations are associated with pre-industrial Britain.

2. We can consider everything before 1800 as pre-industrial.

3. Pre-industrial sports and pastimes are mainly associated with the upper class.

4. In pre-industrial times, different classes sometimes shared activities, sometimes took part in different activities and sometimes had different roles within the same activity.

5. Popular recreations usually had the following characteristics: they were regular, with written rules and took place in towns.

6. You need to consider the impact of popular recreation on participation and performance in physical activity today.

7. Britain was a three class society in pre-industrial times – upper, middle and working class.

8. Lower-class women in pre-industrial Britain had more freedom to play than middle-class women in post-industrial Britain.

9. Due to limited transport and communications at the time, popular recreations were usually local.

10. Both the upper and the lower class would wager on activities.

EXAM PRACTICE

1. Describe and explain two characteristics of popular recreation. To what extent are these characteristics evident in physical activity today?   *(4 marks)*

2. Explain how two pre-industrial societal factors impacted on the characteristics of popular recreation and the extent to which your two chosen factors impact on participation and performance in physical activity today.   *(4 marks)*

See page 247 for answers

CHAPTER 2
Rational recreation in post-industrial Britain

CHAPTER OVERVIEW

At the end of this chapter you should have knowledge and understanding of:

- the characteristics of rational recreation

- how to compare the characteristics of popular and rational recreation

- how the following social and cultural factors influenced the nature and development of rational recreations: the industrial revolution; the middle class; changing work conditions; free time and transport; the views of the Church; amateurism and professionalism; the status of women

- how to contrast pre- and post-industrial social and cultural factors relating to popular and rational recreation

- how rational recreation had an impact on the physical competence and health of participants

- the varying opportunities for participation during the nineteenth century

- the impact of rational recreation on participation and performance today, comparing participation then and now

- the five case study activities as rational recreations (you will do this in more detail in Chapter 4).

In post-industrial Britain the new middle class became a dominant social and sporting force. Meanwhile, the rural peasants who had migrated to towns to find factory work became known as the working class, and their opportunity and provision fell way below that of their social superiors. In the space of 100 years, sport and recreation in England was to change from a free-ranging rural activity for participants to an enclosed, urban display for spectators.

EXAM TIP

You need to be able to contrast:
- the characteristics of popular and rational recreation
- pre- and post-industrial social and cultural factors relating to popular and rational recreation.

A good way to remember some of the characteristics of rational recreation is to think of the letter 'R'. They were: rule-based, regular, regional, restrictive (by class and gender), refined, respectable, and with clearly defined roles, such as centre forward in a football or hockey team.

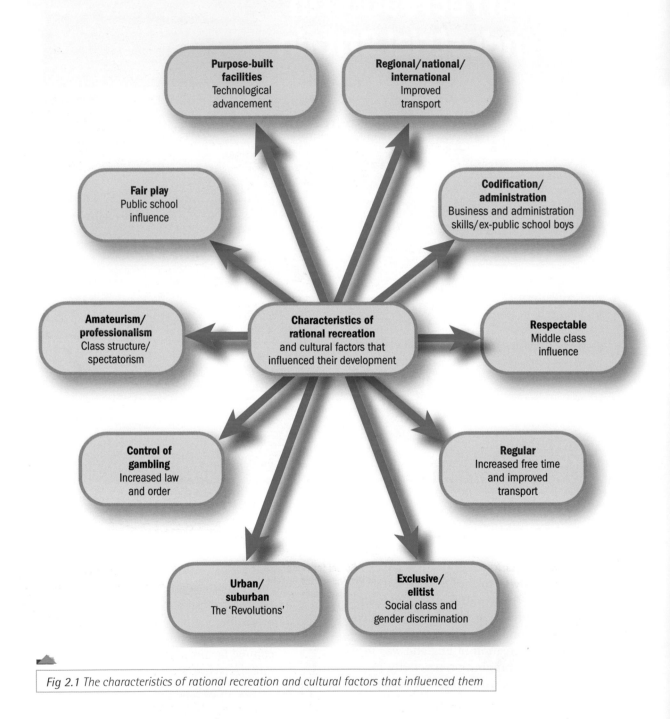

Fig 2.1 The characteristics of rational recreation and cultural factors that influenced them

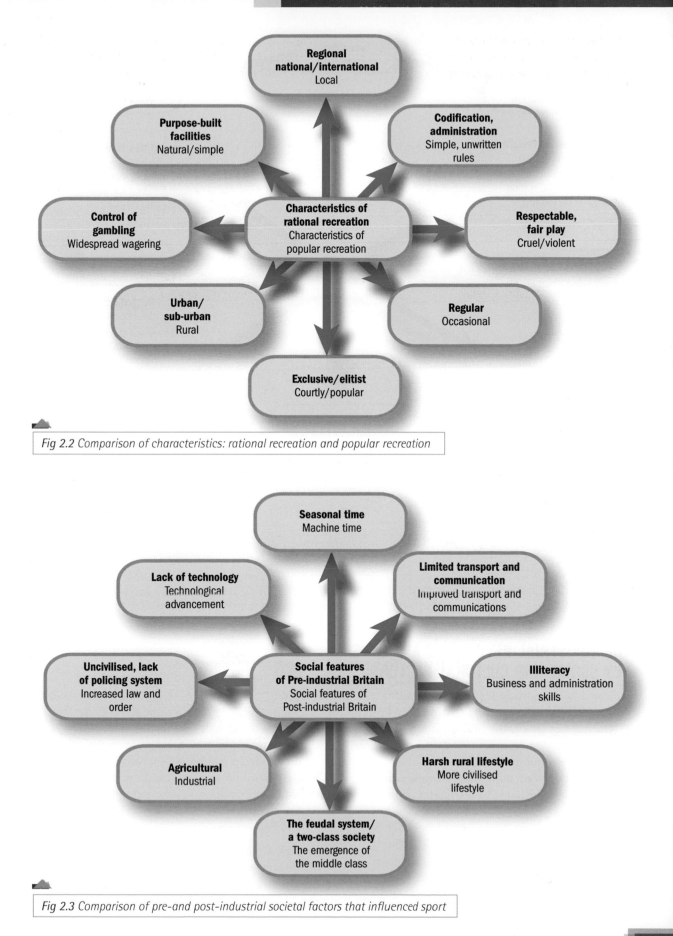

Fig 2.2 Comparison of characteristics: rational recreation and popular recreation

Fig 2.3 Comparison of pre-and post-industrial societal factors that influenced sport

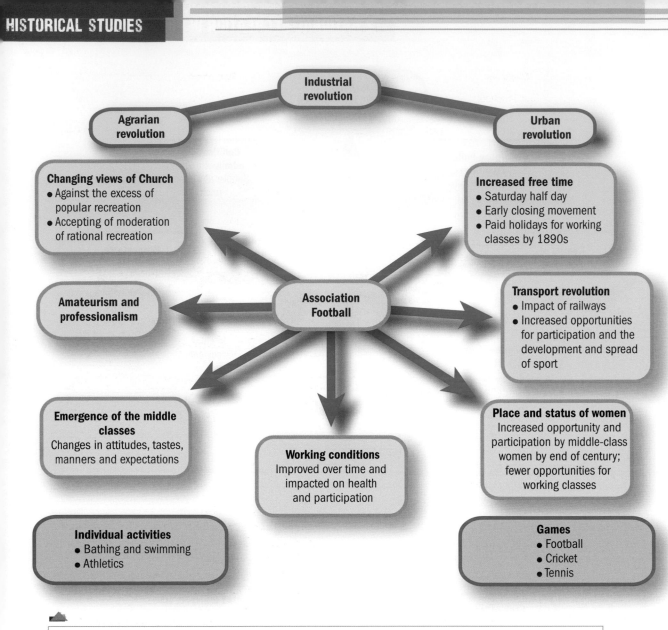

Fig 2.4 Social and cultural factors influencing the development of rational recreation, e.g. Association Football

THE INDUSTRIAL REVOLUTION AND OTHER KEY SOCIAL AND CULTURAL FACTORS:

- The British sporting scene of 1900 was completely different from that in 1800 or 1850.
- During the 1800s, the Industrial Revolution and associated agrarian and urban revolutions spread throughout Britain.
- The process took more than a century to unfold and consisted of a complex series of technological and cultural changes.
- The industrial revolution (sometimes referred to as the onset of the 'machine age' due to the widespread use of steam-powered machines), went hand-in-hand with other massive changes such as new technology, farming and transport methods, urbanisation and a new class structure.

Figure 2.5 shows that:

- when rural peasants initially moved from countryside to towns, opportunities decreased
- life was bleak as they became slaves to the factory system, to machine time and to their employers, but those out of work faced a life on the streets of decay, gloom and hopeless poverty
- the formation and organisation of an effective workforce became a fierce struggle to lift the urban working classes from both oppression and depression.

In these circumstances, the last thing on the minds of the industrial working class in the first half of the century was sport or recreation.

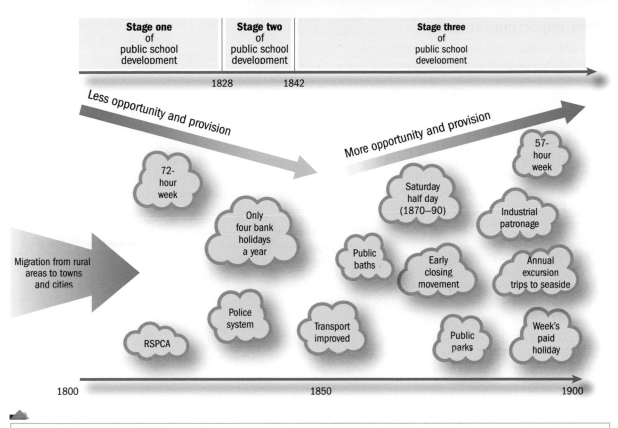

Fig 2.5 Changes in nineteenth-century working-class opportunity and provision as a parallel process to public school developments

By contrast, the second half of the nineteenth-century offered increased opportunity and provision for the working class. This was due to:

- **industrial patronage**
- increased free time
- more public facilities such as parks.

Now let's review the century in more detail.

KEY TERM

Industrial patronage – The provision of social, recreational and sporting opportunities by wealthy industrialists for their workers.

THE FIRST HALF OF THE NINETEENTH CENTURY – THE FIRST EFFECTS OF INDUSTRIALISATION

- Industrialisation resulted in the emergence of a powerful, wealthy group of middle-class industrialists who needed to employ a large workforce to make the mills, factories and foundries profitable.
- Farm worker wages were comparatively low. Rural jobs became harder to find as the use of new agricultural machinery became more extensive.
- Thousands of agricultural workers and their families migrated to cities in the hope of regular work and pay.
- Cities were not ready for the great influx of people and became overcrowded.
- Rooms were rented to whole or perhaps several families while many stayed in lodging houses.
- Living space was cramped and unhygienic, and malnutrition and disease were widespread.
- Urbanisation caused a cholera epidemic which killed 31,000 Britons in 1832.
- Poor living conditions, regular work patterns and excessive work hours took hold as people's space, energy and time were eroded.
- Twelve-hour working days (72-hour working weeks) were common.
- The violent, pre-industrial festival games were unsuitable for urban environment.
- This was a time of social decay and radical change, and a difficult time for sport.
- If the recreations of the lower class were going to survive, they would have to conform to their new surroundings.

Other impacting factors

- Social attitudes, tastes and expectations were changing alongside a growing respectability within society. The middle classes started to shape how things should be done.
- Industrialists and the Church wanted to change the behaviour, bad language and excesses of the old, traditional festivals and the people who had enjoyed them.
- As the new culture of respect and moderation began to take hold, new laws were passed.
- The RSPCA was in existence by 1824 and the Cruelty to Animals Act declared baiting sports illegal in 1835.
- The seasons became less meaningful and a daily cycle of fixed time became the norm.
- By 1834 the number of official holidays had been reduced from 47 in 1761 to just four, with obvious effects on sporting opportunity.
- By the early 1830s stage coaches were out of business. The opening of the Manchester to Liverpool Railway in 1830 marked the beginning of a dramatic new age for sport.

THE SECOND HALF OF THE NINETEENTH-CENTURY

Improved opportunity and provision

- Reform, improvement and increased freedom for the working man shaped the second half of the century.
- Earnings improved, hours at work were reduced and industrial patronage became more widespread.
- Reform by groups such as the Evangelicals, Social Christians and trade unionists became both possible and desirable, with industrialists wanting a healthy and contented as well as a disciplined workforce.
- Some factory owners began to offer opportunities for social, recreational and sporting activity. Some industrialists had genuine motives and were keen to improve the health and morale of the workforce, while others mainly wanted to win loyalty and increase work output.
- The annual excursion trip to the seaside was part of working-class culture by the end of the century.
- The nature and scale of sport in Britain continued to evolve and change.
- Codified games such as rugby football came from Oxford and Cambridge universities.
- Rational games such as lawn tennis were invented by middle-class entrepreneurs.

- Municipal parks became features of enlightened towns and created much needed space, while urban swimming baths were built to wash manual workers.

The transport revolution

Improved transport and communications were the greatest cause of change to sport, and the railways were the most significant mode of transport. Road transport was still slow, canals were for goods and services and air transport had not yet developed.

The railways:

- significantly increased the chance to take part in and to watch sport
- were the main factor that spread sport throughout Britain
- took people further in a shorter time – so distant teams could play each other and take supporters
- caused a standardised set of rules to be needed
- speeded the development of leagues, cups and competitions
- enabled people to get to the countryside – perhaps taking their (newly invented and acquired) bicycle with them
- meant kindly factory owners could lay on excursion trips to the seaside.

The class system

A strict class system still underpinned and operated in British society. Class determined income, housing, lifestyle and sporting opportunities. It also determined your status as an amateur or professional.

Free time: Saturday half-day and the early closing movement

- The early closing movement was a series of Bills through parliament that sought to reduce working hours, particularly in shops.
- Excessive working hours were increasingly thought to be damaging to the health and well-being of workers.
- Between 1870 and 1890 most workers had been granted their half-day of freedom on a Saturday afternoon. This created a nationwide timeslot for watching or playing sport.
- By 1870 some workers had two to three days of paid holiday per year. By the 1890s a week of paid holiday was common.

The first half of the nineteenth-century	The second half of the nineteenth-century
This was a period of decline and limited opportunity due to: • loss of space • the shift from seasonal to machine time • 12-hour days and no time to 'play' • poverty and low wages • loss of rural patronage • sudden urbanisation, overcrowding and poor living conditions • poor working conditions • increased law and order with organisations such as the police force and RSPCA.	Reforms resulted in a period of improved opportunity and provision due to: • more space to play, e.g. public parks • shorter working day and week including free Saturday afternoons (Wednesday for shop keepers) and paid annual holiday • improved wages • increased industrial patronage – opportunities for social, recreational and sporting activity, including the annual excursion trip to the seaside by the end of the century • improved living and working conditions as a result of government 'factory acts' • improved hygiene as a result of public baths • improved transport and communications • changing social attitudes • increased law and order • support from the Church.
Summary: Industrialisation was a multi-dimensional process which, though uneven in speed and geography, completely changed sport in England between 1800 and 1900.	

Table 1 A comparison of life in the first and second halves of the nineteenth-century.

• Meanwhile, wages for the industrial worker had increased and more third-class rail fares had become available.
• Increases in free time were part of a process that started to give a healthier, balanced and potentially active lifestyle to the urban working class.

EXAM TIP

When an exam question asks you to compare two things (e.g. mob football and association football), don't just talk about one *or* the other. It is best to make the comparisons as you go along, e.g. 'mob football was occasional whereas association football was regular'.

Changing views of the Church

The medieval period and Puritanism	• The Church opposed many popular sports at this time. • The Puritans of the 1600s were against the spontaneity and freedom of traditional sports and pastimes, believing that only the prayerful, sober, quiet and hard working would be saved.
From 1700 to 1850 and Protestantism	• In the 1700s the Church provided feast days and space for community gatherings. • By 1800, however, they criticised the drunken excess, violence and mischief linked with popular recreations and withdrew their support. • This resulted in a decline in community participation. • During the nineteenth-century Christianity and the Protestant work ethic became established.
The 1850s, evangelism and social Christianity	• By the mid-nineteenth century newly ordained ex-public school and university men started to promote sports and games in their parishes. • The YMCA (an athletic and religious organisation) encouraged participation in rational sports by young clerks.

Table 2 The Church had different opinions about the status and value of sport throughout time.

RATIONAL RECREATION – ITS EFFECTS ON SKILL AND HEALTH

	Upper and middle classes	Working class
Bathing and swimming	Increased skill and health for middle class as they took to and developed rational swimming in urban baths	Initially functional to combat urban disease – 'penny baths' provided in towns
Athletics	• Opportunities to increase skill and health for both classes as their respective governing bodies were formed • Note the ongoing existence of some early rural sports and the beginnings of urban athletics meetings for both classes, which would impact on health and skill	
Football	Amateur involvement, often in exclusive teams such as the Corinthian Casuals	• Mainly as spectators, so no physical health or skill development • Opportunities for a few very skilful players to become professional
Cricket	Skilful, with potential to increase health as a summer outdoor active game	
Lawn tennis	Skilful and potentially health-enhancing for middle class; new opportunities for women	Limited access for lower class until club and park provision developed

Table 3 *The impact of rational recreations on the physical competence and health of participants*

Amateurism and professionalism

- Amateurism and professionalism influenced the nature and development of rationalised sports and pastimes.
- Class decided your status as an amateur or a professional.
- Middle-class gentlemen amateurs took part for the love of the game and intrinsic rewards.
- Working-class men who could not afford to play games for enjoyment sometimes had a chance to earn money as a professional.

Women in Victorian Britain

- In early Victorian Britain it was thought inappropriate for a middle-class lady to exercise, sweat or display her body.
- This meant that physical activity was effectively outlawed.
- In addition, over-exertion was thought to be medically harmful for women.
- The invention of lawn tennis in the 1870s became a route to social and physical emancipation (freedom) for women.
- Those who continued to object on the grounds of immodesty and bad taste increasingly had to counter the new argument of good health through exercise.
- As physical exercise gradually became more acceptable among middle-class women, appropriate clothing was designed which encouraged freer movement and a gradual relaxation of traditional Victorian stuffiness.

- Working-class women had a different set of rules to live by and they had neither the opportunity nor provision for leisure time physical activity.

Varying opportunities for participation

Class and gender continued to affect participation along with the three variables: opportunity, provision and esteem.

- The emergence of the middle-class was particularly significant. Without access to horses they invented the bicycle and without access to real tennis they invented lawn tennis. In this way the middle class drove the rationalisation and development of most sports.
- The working class had to wait for opportunities to participate at community level, perhaps via factory or local authority public park provision.

IMPACT ON AND LINKS TO TODAY

- You need to consider the impact of rational recreation on participation and performance in physical activity today. You also need to compare participation then with now and think about reasons for differences.
- We still have a mainly decentralised, amateur and voluntary way of organising and administering sport in the UK, particularly at the lower levels.

- This is a direct result of the formation of most NGBs and many sports clubs by keen individuals over 100 years ago.
- Only quite recently have we started moving towards a more professional approach to sport at all levels. For example, this is reflected in the focused and centralised formula adopted by the sport of cycling in the run up to the Beijing Olympics (2008), which resulted in phenomenal success.
- Ethics of sportsmanship are also linked to rational recreations.

▶ **Need to know more?** For more information on rational recreation see Chapter 2, pages 18-29, in OCR A2 PE Student Book.

SPORT ENGLAND ACTIVE PEOPLE SURVEY, 2006

- 21 per cent of adults take part regularly in sport and active recreation with regular participation defined as at least three days a week at moderate intensity for at least 30 minutes.
- Participation ranged from 22.6 per cent in the South East to 19.3 per cent in the West Midlands.
- Walking is the most popular recreational activity in England, with over 20 per cent of adults aged 16 years and over walking recreationally for at least 30 minutes in the last four weeks.
- 13.8 per cent swim at least once a month and 10.5 per cent go to the gym.
- 25.1 per cent of the adult population are members of a club where they take part in sport.
- Regular participation in sport and active recreation varies across different groups – for example, male participation is 23.7 per cent and female participation is 18.5 per cent.

EXAM TIP

Remember that historical studies questions will always relate forward to the next stage, (e.g. popular recreation to rational recreation), or to today. It is therefore important to consider the impact of the past on the present, e.g. working patterns, employment and unemployment, free time, transport and the place and status of women.

CHECK

If you are satisfied with your knowledge and understanding, tick off the sections that you have revised so far. If you are not satisfied then revisit those sections and refer to the pages in the *Need to know more?* features.

☐ Describe the characteristics of rational recreation.

☐ Compare the characteristics of popular and rational recreation.

☐ Explain how the following social and cultural factors influenced the nature and development of rational recreations: the industrial revolution, the middle class, changing work conditions, free time and transport, views of the church, amateurism and professionalism, the status of women.

☐ Contrast pre- and post-industrial social and cultural factors relating to popular and rational recreation.

☐ Discuss how rational recreation had an impact on the physical competence and health of participants.

☐ Outline the varying opportunities for participation during the nineteenth century.

☐ Consider the impact of rational recreation on participation and performance today, comparing participation then and now.

Activity	Percentage of adult population taking part at least once a month	Number of adults taking part at least once a month
Swimming	13.8	5,625,539
Football	7.1	2,910,684
Tennis	2.1	874,040
Cricket	0.9	380,366
Athletics (track and field)	0.6	244,281

Table 4 Sport England Active People Survey, 2006

TRUE OR FALSE?

1. By the early-nineteenth century, Britain was a fully industrialised society and this period is associated with rational recreation.

2. Rational recreations were usually regular, respectable and regional.

3. You need to be able to contrast the characteristics of popular and rational recreation as well as the social conditions that prevailed.

4. The industrial revolution went hand in hand with urban and agrarian revolutions.

5. When the peasant class migrated to towns they enjoyed immediate opportunity and provision for sports and pastimes.

6. Rational recreation can be studied in isolation – it had nothing to do with public school athleticism.

7. The railways had a minor impact on the development of rational recreations.

8. In terms of increased free time, the early closing movement had little impact on the spread or development of sports and recreations.

9. Amateurism and professionalism had more to do with class than with whether someone was paid to play.

10. Middle-class and working-class women had different opportunities for physical activity in the late-nineteenth century.

EXAM PRACTICE

1. Contrast *three* characteristics of popular recreation with *three* characteristics of rational recreation and explain why the change occurred. Take one societal factor and explain the extent to which it continues to impact on participation in sport and physical activity today.   *(6 marks)*

2. Describe and explain two characteristics of rational recreation. To what extent are these rational characteristics evident in physical activity today?   *(4 marks)*

3. Contrast *three* societal factors that impacted on popular recreation with the equivalent factors that impacted on rational recreation. Take *two* post-industrial factors and explain the extent to which each of them continues to impact on participation in sport and recreation today.   *(5 marks)*

See page 249 for answers

CHAPTER 3
Nineteenth-century public schools and their impact on the development of physical activities and young people

CHAPTER OVERVIEW

By the end of this chapter you should have knowledge and understanding of:

* the characteristics of nineteenth-century public schools
* the impact of the public schools on physical activities in general and on the five case study activities in particular (this will be covered in more detail in Chapter 4)
* the relevance of the Clarendon Report
* how nineteenth-century public schools went through three stages of development
* the development of sports and games in each stage
* the impact of the three stages on physical activities and on young people and on participation both in the nineteenth-century and now
* the reasons for the slower development of athleticism in girls' public schools compared with boys' public schools.

CHARACTERISTICS OF PUBLIC SCHOOLS

The characteristics of public schools shaped the development of team games as shown in Figure 3.1.

EXAM TIP

A frequently asked question is *'How did the characteristics of the public schools impact on the development of team games?'*

THE CLARENDON REPORT (1864)

The Clarendon Commissioners task was:

> '...to enquire into the nature and application of the endowments, funds, and revenue belonging to or received by the colleges, schools and foundation... to enquire into the administration and management of the said colleges, schools and foundations... into the system and course of studies pursued therein... into the methods, systems and extent of the instructions given to the students.'
> (Clarendon Report)

Fig 3.1 Characteristics of nineteenth-century public schools and their impact on sports and games

The Clarendon Report: key points

- Queen Victoria appointed the commission to examine all aspects of the nine leading public schools of England following complaints about the finances, buildings and management of Eton College.
- The report was an account of public school life researched by the Earl of Clarendon and his team of commissioners (officials).
- The report was published in 1864.
- It included many criticisms and both general and specific advice for each school.
- It gave a detailed picture of life in the nine schools and attempted to enrich day-to-day academic and residential life for the pupils.

- It concluded that while each school was somewhat different, the status of games (in comparison to academic work) in most of the nine schools was extremely high.
- It was arguably the prototype Ofsted inspection report.

The three developmental stages of athleticism

- The schools were institutions in their own right, often out in the countryside and with their own rules and customs.
- Yet the public schools did not exist in isolation. They reflected changes that were happening in society.

- It could also be argued that they caused social change – certainly in terms of sport and recreation.

By the mid-nineteenth century:

- the RSPCA was successfully reducing cruelty against animals
- the police and changing tastes and manners were reducing the number of bare-fist fights
- in the schools, many headmasters were keen to be seen as enlightened. They wanted their schools to be more refined and cultured and less primitive and wild. This was part of what sociologists call the **civilising process**.

KEY TERM

Civilising process – Improvements relating to more refined or sophisticated behaviour and social organisation and relationships.

EXAM TIP

You need to be able to explain the evolving nature, status and organisation of games through the stages as well as the:

- **Technical developments:** related to rule structure, equipment, facilities, spectatorism, level of skilfulness, etc.
- **Social relationships:** influences of societal change, e.g. improved transport and communications as well as changing social relationships within the schools such as level of bullying, Headmasters' attitudes, interaction between boys, masters and locals.
- **Values linked to sports and games in each stage:** benefits, ethics and morals that build character and become guidelines for living such as teamwork, manliness, loyalty, honour, respect for opponents etc.

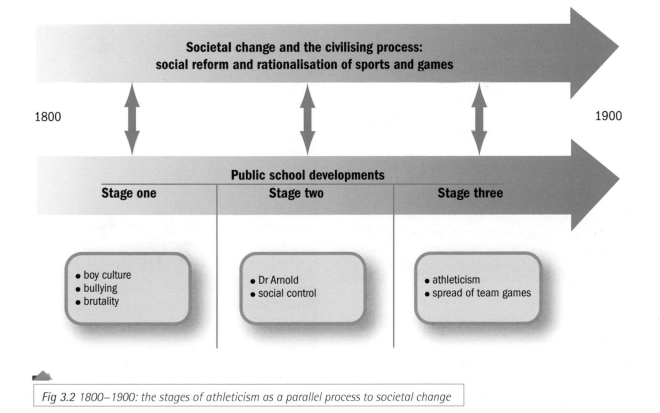

Fig 3.2 1800–1900: the stages of athleticism as a parallel process to societal change

STAGE ONE: (c 1790-1824): BOY CULTURE, BULLYING AND BRUTALITY

- At the end of the eighteenth-century, English society contrasted the high culture of the Regency period fashion with the low culture and apparent brutality of blood sports and bare-fist fighting. Both ends of this social spectrum were mirrored in the public schools.
- This was a time of 'boy culture', when the confrontational behaviour of the French and American revolutions was copied by public schoolboys if things didn't go their way.
- The absence of a police force meant any unrest was controlled by the army.
- All recreational activities were organised by the boys for pure enjoyment and to relieve the boredom of academic work, which consisted solely of the classics (Latin and Greek).
- Masters 'ruled with the rod' in lessons but had no influence or interest outside of the classroom.
- Boys took part in all sorts of mischief including trespass, truancy, poaching and fighting.
- In both society at large and in individual public schools, control was lost and tyranny and chaos resulted.
- This was also a time of public school expansion. An increasing number of upper-class boys enrolled at **preparatory schools**, bringing with them customs and recreations from all over the country.

KEY TERMS

Preparatory Schools – Junior-level schools for younger boys who then advance to the public schools.

Public school expansion and the first 'melting pot'

- These customs and games from a variety of areas were mixed and moulded into schoolboy games that were to become future traditions.
- In this way the sporting culture of each school began to be established along with a need for increased housing (expansion of the

house system) and more **social control** (the establishment of order, stability and good behaviour).

- Games and sports would ultimately provide the medium for social control, but meanwhile severe, imposed discipline by masters and resentful rebellion and hooligan behaviour by boys shaped the norm.
- This was a time of 'institutionalised popular recreation', with activities ranging from the childlike to the barbaric – hoops, marbles and spinning tops were in the playground alongside bare-knuckle fights and mob football.
- The wall at Eton and the cloisters at Charterhouse were the birthplaces of unique and ferocious mob football games.
- Cricket, the rural game already **codified** and played by both classes was immediately adopted by the schools while fox hunting was adapted to **hare and hounds**.
- Boys would also hire boats from local boatyards, play '**fives**' and other ball games against suitable walls, swim in natural bathing places such as rivers and ponds and explore the countryside.

KEY TERMS

Codify – To collect together and organise rules and procedures.

Hare and hounds – An adaptation of fox hunting whereby one boy runs ahead of the pack dropping a trail of paper as 'scent', which is then followed by the chasing crowd.

Fives – A hand and ball game against a suitable wall or (later) in a purpose-built court. Similar to squash, the game was called fives because of the five digits on one hand.

Social control – The establishment of order, stability and good behaviour.

Cult – A craze or obsession with the playing of team games (stage 3).

Assistant masters – Junior masters without the responsibility of a house. Taught an academic subject, but fully involved in the games programme.

Nature of games	• Institutionalised popular recreation; a reflection of society; activities ranged from the childlike to the barbaric.
Status of games	• No official rank, position or status for sports and games. • Informal games were important to most boys while largely ignored by teachers.
Organisation of games	• Activities were organised by and for the boys themselves with no master involvement outside of the classroom. • Unplanned, informal or limited levels of organisation characterised most activities.
Technical development	• There were simple, naturally occurring facilities and limited 'local' rules with simple equipment.
Social relationships	• Widespread bullying and brutality with distrust and poor relationships.
Values	• 'Every man for himself" and survival of fittest with no specific values linked to games.

Table 1 Summary of stage one

STAGE TWO: (1828-1842): DR THOMAS ARNOLD AND SOCIAL CONTROL

- The mid-nineteenth century was a time of change, both in society at large and in the English public schools.
- Parliament and criminal laws were changing, for example laws banning cruelty to animals.
- Transport and communications were dramatically improving, notably due to the railways.
- Queen Victoria was crowned in 1837.
- With life and society becoming more orderly, the freedom and wild escapades of stage one became more and more out of place.

Factfile: Dr Thomas Arnold

- Headmaster of Rugby school from 1828 until his death in 1842.
- Widely regarded as one of the key reformers of the English public school system at a time when it was out of control.
- An ordained clergyman.
- Became obsessed by the immorality and sinfulness of boys and was determined to reform them, their attitudes and their school lives.

Arnold used games as a vehicle for establishing social control:

- He made the Chapel the school's spiritual and symbolic centre. This established a new moral code, which was better suited to the increasingly civilised society.
- He established a more trusting and sympathetic relationship with the sixth form. Masters gradually adopted roles of mentor and guide, rather than 'judge' and 'executioner'.
- He raised the status of the sixth form and increased their discipline. He required them to be positive role models and his 'police force' around the school – the link between masters and boys.
- This enabled Arnold's primary objective of delivering the Christian message to be achieved.
- As a by-product, the status, regularity and organisation of games also increased.
- The house system grew as schools expanded. Houses became the focus of boys' personal, social, recreational and sporting existence.
- Games of inter-house cricket and football/rugby kept boys out of trouble in the daytime and sent them to bed exhausted.
- Thus 'the playground' became a central feature of public school life.

Aspects of public school life reformed by Dr Thomas Arnold and other liberal headmasters of the mid-nineteenth century:

- the behaviour of boys
- the severity of punishments imposed by masters
- the role of the Sixth form
- the academic curriculum
- Muscular Christianity.

Muscular Christianity

Arnold's main aim was to produce Christian gentlemen and to preach good moral behaviour. Muscular Christianity was a combination of godliness and manliness, or the belief in having a strong and fit body to match a robust and healthy soul. It was fine to play sport and to play hard, but always for the glory of God – not for its own sake or for any extrinsic values that could be achieved.

Nature of games	• Games were reformed along with the schools in which they existed.
	• The phases saw the transition from popular recreation to rational recreation.
Status of games	• Both the schools and their games grew in status as they opened themselves up to the reforms that were happening in society at large.
Organisation of games	• Schools and games became more organised especially with the growth of the House system.
Technical development	• More regular play on inter-house basis.
	• Games became more structured with specialist kit, equipment and facilities.
Social relationships	• Improving relationships and restrictions on bullying and brutality.
Values	• Games used to achieve social control.

Table 2 Summary of stage two

EXAM TIP

Dr Arnold did not value games as an end in themselves – he used games as a vehicle for achieving social control in Rugby School.

STAGE THREE: (1842-1914): THE 'CULT' OF ATHLETICISM

The conventional image of a late-nineteenth-century English public school is of mellow stone buildings, magnificent games fields, colours, caps and cricketers. These were all symbols of athleticism – the combination of physical endeavour (or trying hard) with moral integrity (a mix of honour, truthfulness, sportsmanship). Athleticism became a 'cult', or a craze – and here the craze was for team games and the values they allegedly ensured.

- From 1850 team games were increasingly made compulsory and became formally assimilated into the curriculum of public schools.
- Specialist facilities, for example squash courts, were constructed.
- Land was bought and schools re-located purposely to acquire more space for team games, for example Charterhouse School moved from London to Godalming, Surrey in 1872.
- Games earned exceptionally high status in all of the leading public schools – no longer as a vehicle for establishing social control but as a vehicle for developing the character or the boys who played them.
- The aim of team games now was to develop qualities such as honour, leadership, loyalty, courage and manliness.
- The second melting pot was beginning to operate, that is the mixing of games and traditions from a variety of schools up to University. This resulted in a standardised game or system of play.
- The role and impact of games-playing Oxbridge graduates returning to their schools as **assistant masters** was important. They would be employed as an academic teacher but often as a result of their games playing prowess.
- What had been an embarrassment to public school headmasters – games and athletic pursuits – became their pride.

Nature of games	• Games rationalized and respectable.
Status of games	• Games played obsessively at 'cult' proportions by many boys and masters. They were often compulsory each day.
Organisation of games	• Highly organised and fully codified at a time when many NGBs were being established.
Technical development	• Fully technically developed with kit and specialist facilities, skill rather than force and specialist coaching in some sports, for example cricket.
Social relationships	• More friendly between boys and masters and less bullying among the boys.
Values	• Games played for the development of character (loyalty, teamwork, honesty, etc.).

Table 3 Summary of stage three

Influence of ex-public school boys

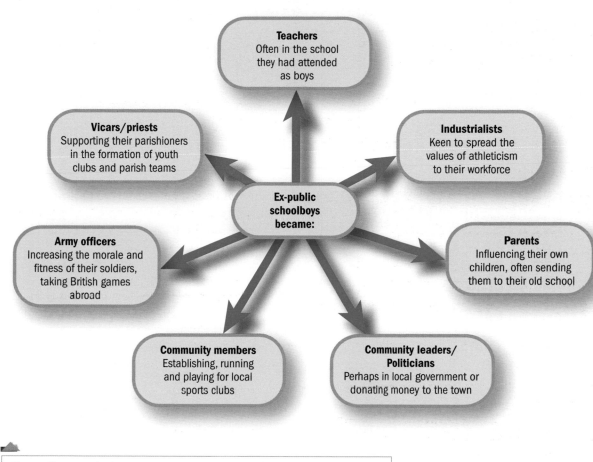

Fig 3.3 *The spread of team games throughout Europe and the British Empire*

Note the influence of public schools on:

- other schools (which copied the Clarendon 'nine')
- universities (as a 'melting pot' for the standardisation of rules)
- organisations (formations of governing bodies)
- regularity of play (which increased standards of performance)
- building of specialist facilities (for example, swimming baths and gymnasia)
- festival days (for example, sports day which rivalled speech day in the school calendar)
- fields (extensive playing fields created and proudly maintained).

Athleticism in girls' public and private schools

While athleticism was reaching **cult** proportions in boys' public schools, there was a delay in the development of opportunities for upper- and middle-class girls. The reasons for this were:

- the traditional role of women – education of females was regarded as a threat to the behavioural norms of society
- anxiety over the wearing of revealing clothing for physical exercise
- the status of women in society – girls' schools concentrated mainly on music, dancing and posture; it was not considered necessary to give girls the same opportunities as boys
- it was thought inappropriate (unladylike) for women to be competitive or exuberant
- medical concerns – it was believed that strenuous physical activity was medically dangerous and could complicate or even prevent child-bearing
- there were concerns that girls would not be able to cope with strenuous physical activity due to their perceived physical inferiority
- there were fewer prominent personalities to match boys' school heads such as Dr Thomas Arnold.

Impact of Stage 1 on:	Then	Now
Physical activity (technical development)	The impact was informal and unofficial rather than structured or planned. Many activities became institutionalised and took place both in school grounds and surrounding countryside, in free time outside of lesson time. Activities usually casual and/or spontaneous and both adopted (such as cricket, football and fighting) and adapted (such as hare and hounds and steeplechase). Also invented to suit natural facilities in schools.	Limited direct impact of Stage 1 today. Examples include maintenance of traditional football games such as the Wall Game at Eton College.
Young people (social relationships and values)	On the positive side, young people had opportunities to develop independence and self-sufficiency. On the negative side there was institutionalised bullying linked with hooligan behaviour and the prefect/fagging system, poor relationships and severe punishments.	Limited direct impact – more indirect impact as a stage on route to athleticism.

Impact of Stage 2 on:	Then	Now
Physical activity (technical development)	As part of the process of social control, sports and pastimes became more controlled and less violent and/or spontaneous. Played more regularly and in school grounds with trespass reduced. A growing programme of games and individual activities played on an inter-house basis.	The house system still central to organisation in many schools today particularly independent boarding schools many of which are modelled on the nineteenth century format.
Young people (social relationships and values)	Games were used to establish social control in Rugby School. Dr Arnold required Christian attitudes and better behaviour especially from the sixth form to whom he gave responsibility. Arnold also keen to change the behaviour of the boys, the severity of punishments imposed by masters, the role of the sixth form, the academic curriculum, the relationships of boys and masters from mutual antagonism to mutual trust and respect.	Limited direct impact – more indirect impact as a stage on route to athleticism.

Impact of public schools

Impact of Stage 3 on:	Then	Now
Physical activities (technical development)	• Organisation – codification and regular fixtures including establishment of inter-school fixtures, leagues, cups and competitions such as public school championships. • Formation of NGBs by Old Boys. • Encouraged by headmaster. • Time, space and expertise available. • Impact of university melting pot on standardisation of rules.	• Some of the old established competitions still exist. • Participation in physical activities considered important for healthy balanced lifestyles.
Young people (social relationships and values)	Character development: • *Physical* – daily participation increased health and skill levels. • *Intellectual* – development of organisational, administrative and management skills. • *Emotional* – need for both independence and teamwork. • *Social* – loyalty to house, school and ultimately to country. Fixtures with local clubs and other schools giving opportunities for friendships. Also: • Fair play. • Appreciation of value of healthy exercise and fresh air. • Participation helped to develop 'all rounders' who were socially acceptable and respected. • The competitive experience useful in an increasingly competitive society. • Old Boys' societies established – financial generosity.	• PE in National Curriculum still focuses on development of whole child (see Chapter 5 – PE in state schools, page 98). • Life similarly competitive today as competitive sport making a come-back in state schools. • Old Boys' and Girls' societies still in existence.
Participation	• Massive impact – daily participation compulsory in many public schools. • Full staff involvement.	• Similar in some independent schools today. • KS3 focuses on participation and healthy balanced lifestyles.

Fig 3.4 Impact of the three stages of public school development on physical activity, young people and (stage three) participation. This is not an exhaustive list. You are probably able to think of more impacts

EXAM TIP

Exam questions could ask you to focus on one phase or to assess change over the three phases. Remember to read the question carefully to determine exactly what you need to do.

> **Need to know more?** For more information on nineteenth century public schools see Chapter 3, page 32, in the OCR A2 PE Student Book.

	Stage one: Bullying and brutality	Stage two: Social control	Stage three: Athleticism
Bathing and swimming	Informal bathing in natural facilities during summer months (mainly for recreation).	More regular and regulated bathing (for hygiene, safety and recreation); increasingly thought to be beneficial as part of a healthy lifestyle.	Increased technical development with changing huts, diving boards, purpose-built facilities and competitions; swimming masters (attendants) for teaching and to oversee safety.
Athletics	Informal running and exploring the countryside; paper chase (hare and hounds) linked to trespass.	Trespass restricted or banned (gave school bad name, irritated neighbouring landowners; against Christian ethics; need to keep boys on site). Hare and hounds and steeple chase continued in more formal style.	Steeple chase and cross-country running; annual sports day as major sporting and social occasion.
Football	Mob games and the first 'melting pot' of activities from 'home'.	More formalised football rules for individual schools (see page 69 in the OCR A2 PE Student Book). Inter-house competitions.	Formal Football Association (FA) or Rugby Football Union (RFU) rules along with traditional games at individual schools. 'Colours', caps, inter-school fixtures.
Cricket	Cricket – transferred directly into the public schools due to its non-violent nature, rule structure and upper-class involvement in society.	Cricket encouraged with massive inter-house participation.	Continued technical development such as professional coaching, 'colours', caps and inter-school fixtures (for example, annually against MCC).
Tennis	Informal hand and ball games against suitable available walls and buildings were referred to as 'fives' or 'tennis' (note: lawn tennis had not yet been invented).	Some fives courts built though fives still an informal activity; game of racquets developing as more formal alternative; also squash racquets.	Fives continued as recreational game; racquets a more formal game of higher status. Lawn tennis comparatively low status in boys' schools, very popular as summer game in girls' public schools.

Table 4 Technical development of the five case studies

CHECK

If you are satisfied with your knowledge and understanding, tick off the sections that you have revised so far. If you are not satisfied, then revisit those sections and refer to the pagers in the *Need to know more?* features.

- ☐ Describe the characteristics of nineteenth-century public schools.

- ☐ Explain the relevance of the Clarendon Report.

- ☐ Describe how nineteenth-century public schools went through three stages of development.

- ☐ Outline the development of sports and games in each stage.

- ☐ Discuss the impact of the three stages on physical activities and on young people, and on participation both in the nineteenth-century and now.

- ☐ Discuss the reasons for the slower development of athleticism in girls' public schools compared with boys' public schools.

EXAM PRACTICE

1. Explain the delay in the development of athleticism in girls' public schools during stage three of athleticism. Comment on the comparative status of sport for males and females in schools today.　　*(5 marks)*

2. Explain the status and organisation of a striking game other than lawn tennis in Public Schools during stage three of development. Explain why lawn tennis was more popular in society at large than in the boys' public schools at that time.　　*(5 marks)*

3. Nineteenth-century public schools were mainly for *gentry boys* and were *Spartan*. Explain the impact of these *three* characteristics (gentry, boys and spartan) on the development of games in nineteenth-century public schools and the extent to which *two* of these characteristics impact on young people in schools today.　　*(5 marks)*

See page 251 for answers

TRUE OR FALSE?

1. The characteristics of public schools included the following: boarding, boys, Spartan and fee-paying.

2. The Clarendon Report reported on the academic progress of public school boys during the first half of the nineteenth-century.

3. Dr Thomas Arnold was a medical doctor who was head of Rugby School between 1828 and 1842.

4. Public school developments should be studied in three stages.

5. Social relationships within the public schools altered very little from 1800-1900.

6. Stage one was a time of highly organised team games and recreational swimming.

7. Dr Arnold was keen to instil Christian values and social control during stage two.

8. Athleticism is the link between physical endeavour and moral integrity.

9. Ex-public school boys had little influence on the spread of team games throughout the world.

10. The house system in schools today as well as some old established competitions are direct links back to public school of the nineteenth-century.

CHAPTER 4
Case Studies

CHAPTER OVERVIEW

By the end of this chapter you should have knowledge and understanding of:
- the five case study activities – bathing and swimming, athletics, football, cricket and tennis
- how these activities developed to the present day through the following stages: popular recreation, via the public schools and rational recreation.
- how to analyse each activity as a pre-industrial popular recreation
- how to assess the influence of nineteenth-century public schools on each activity
- how to demonstrate knowledge and understanding of each activity as a rational recreation
- participation and barriers to participation in each activity today.

INTRODUCTION

Each of the five case study activities will have at least some of the characteristics shown in Table 1.

As popular recreations:	As rational recreations:
• local	• regional, national or even international
• with simple unwritten rules	• with written (NGB) rules
• cruel and/or violent	• refined and respectable
• occasional	• regular
• divided by class (courtly and popular or high and low)	• divided by status (amateur and professional)
• rural	• urban or suburban
• occupational	• some (working-class) professionals
• wagering	• less wagering

Table 1 Characteristics of popular recreation and rational recreation

EXAM TIP

For each of the five activities in the UK today you need:
- knowledge and understanding of both participation and barriers to participation today
- to be aware of factors that have helped to develop each activity with reference to contemporary participation and performance.

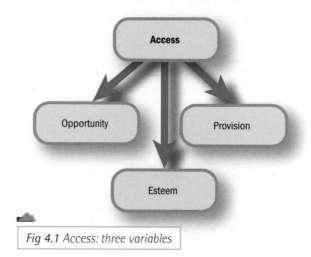

Fig 4.1 Access: three variables

Factors relating to opportunity, provision and esteem that can influence mass participation and sporting excellence	
Mass participation	**Sporting excellence**
OPPORTUNITY – having the chance to take part and/or get to the top	
Disposable income	Funding and financial support, e.g. National Lottery or sponsorship money
Ability, skill, health or fitness or playing standard	Skill level and performance lifestyle
The amount of time available after work and other commitments	Chance to train full time
Do you actually want to take part? Are suitable and appealing activities available?	Whether individuals choose to make the sacrifices and give the all-round commitment needed to get to the top
PROVISION – having the conditions or physical tools to take part and/or get to the top	
The presence or absence of suitable equipment and/or facilities	The availability of world-class facilities and equipment
Access – e.g. for wheelchairs if necessary	The availability of sport science and other 'high tech' support, e.g. modern technological products
Availability of suitable transport – privately owned or public transport	Distance from or access to high performance or National Institute centres, e.g. the National Tennis Centre in Roehampton, southwest London; warm weather or high altitude training venues for athletes
Suitable and available clubs, activities, leagues, competitions or courses nearby	Suitable and regular competitions with and against other high-level performers
The right coaching at the right level by suitably qualified staff	The right highly qualified and experienced coaches
Well-maintained and equipped, private and clean changing and social areas	Performance lifestyle advice and a holistic approach to excellence
ESTEEM – issues to do with respect, admiration, value and appreciation; the perception that society has of an individual or group affects their chances both of taking part and of achieving excellence	
Self-confidence and self-belief – which influences self perception	Self-confidence and self-belief, which impact on performance
Respect from others and social acceptance of everyone's 'right' to take part in any chosen activity	Respect from others – including team mates, opponents and the media
Positive or negative perceptions of certain physical activities	Recent results (good and/or bad) and national and international ranking
Status in society, for example whether from a disadvantaged group	Status in the sporting world

Table 2 Factors relating to opportunity, provision and esteem that can influence mass participation and sporting excellence today

In addition to the contemporary factors shown in Table 2 on page 28, the impact of the following factors on participation can be considered.

Children	• Mini versions of the activities • Children's holiday clubs and parties
Schools	• Positive or negative school experience • Whether the activity is compulsory on the National Curriculum • Strength/success of school club links and work of SSCOs • Passion and commitment of individual teachers • Impact of independent schools boosting local provision as part of their qualification for charitable status; for example, offering times when their tennis courts are available to local schools and clubs
Clubs	• Whether clubs get club mark status; for example, in cricket there are approximately ten focus clubs per county that are responsible for increasing participation locally • The quality of programmes/provision at local clubs or centres
Academies	• Whether the sport has an academy structure (for example, football, rugby, cricket) whereby talented youngsters sign up with clubs and receive the highest quality support • The down side is that the club might then pressure the young person not to play for their school or with their friends
Facilities and equipment	• Improved technology such as Astroturf, clothing or titanium • Cheaper versions of equipment available • The presence or absence of provision for disability sport
Organisation	• Private or NGB campaigns and initiatives • Local authority provision such as ladies-only or novice events • NGB coaching course opportunities and the change in Level One coaching courses, which makes it easier for non-specialists to become coaches. This should help to increase community participation • Provision of competitions, leagues and tournaments for young people
The golden triangle	• Media coverage, for example impact of having netball on Sky TV or the glamorisation of top-level sport particularly with HD televisions • Whether the sport is on Sky TV only, or available to all through the terrestrial channels • Impact of specialist magazines and press coverage • The presence or absence of role models and their success, such as Christine Ohuruogu, Rebecca Adlington and other Team GB athletes • Sponsorship • Lottery funding – both for community provision at the base of the sports development pyramid and for elite performers at the top, some of whom are able to train full-time without the need for a paid job
Additional factors	• Whether the activity is a lifetime sport, such as swimming or tennis, or a sport mainly limited to younger or middle-aged players such as football • Provision and organisation of development for young people such as whether the activity has academies throughout the country • There is a vast number of alternative choices for young people in contemporary Britain other than participation in sport/physical activity

Table 3 Participation and barriers to participation today

BATHING AND SWIMMING AS A POPULAR RECREATION

- In the Middle Ages (c.1200-1500), towns were built at defensive sites and river crossing points. Bathing for pleasure was common, especially on hot summer days.
- As well as a natural playground, the river provided a ready supply of food, a means of transport and a place to wash.
- The river was the commercial centre of the area.
- With work, play and the river so inter-related, learning to swim for safety/survival also became a necessity.
- Just as the Roman nobility had done, the English aristocracy of the Middle Ages considered the ability to swim to be part of their chivalric code, that is, the courteous, gallant and gentlemanly behaviour associated with the upper class.

- The Roman nobility would sometimes sponsor (or 'patronise') outstanding lower class swimmers to represent them in wager races.
- Throughout history, various other sports and pastimes have centred on the riverside, particularly in river loops and adjacent water meadows. These areas of common land had no trees or agriculture so provided a large flat space for casual, informal games, athletic sports, horse racing and shooting.
- They were liable to flooding, so in frozen conditions they also provided a shallow and relatively safe natural facility for sliding and skating.
- Occasionally, the river itself froze, providing a surface for multi-sports festivals called frost fairs or ice fairs. When the Thames froze in 1813 a four-day frost fair was set up, incorporating a variety of fairground stalls, bull baiting, prize fighting, sliding, football and feasting.

EXAM TIP

Consider the extent to which each of your case study activities had the characteristics normally associated with popular recreation – such as in the table below.

EXAM TIP

You need to be able to link bathing with recreation, survival and health. Also note the early development of competitive swimming at this time.

Characteristics of popular recreation	Did early swimming and bathing have this characteristic?
Local	Yes, to a great extent.
Simple unwritten rules	Yes, to a great extent – swimming was functional.
Cruel/violent	To a very limited or no extent.
Occasional/annual	Medium extent – bathing was regular in summer.
Courtly/popular	Both classes would participate, but not together.
Rural	Yes, to a great extent – also in unpolluted urban rivers.
Occupational	Medium extent – there were some swimming teachers who taught for money.
Wagering	Medium extent – not widespread but probably informally.
Simple/natural	Yes, to a great extent in ponds, rivers, lakes. In 1784 the first public swimming bath was created in London.

Table 4 The extent to which swimming and bathing had characteristics of popular recreation

Swimming in the public schools – values and status

	Stage one: Bullying and brutality	Stage two: Social control	Stage three: Athleticism
Bathing and swimming	Informal bathing in natural facilities during summer months (mainly for recreation). In this way, very similar to popular recreation	More regular and regulated bathing (for hygiene, safety and recreation); increasingly thought to be beneficial as part of a healthy lifestyle	Increased technical development with changing huts, diving boards, purpose-built facilities and competitions. Swimming masters (attendants) for teaching and to oversee safety

Table 5 Bathing and swimming in the public schools – nineteenth-century developments

- At the beginning of the nineteenth-century, bathing in public schools was spontaneous and unorganised.
- Boys swam in natural facilities such as local rivers or ponds, which became a place to wash and have fun.
- They brought this culture to school, bathing in their free time with no master input or supervision.
- As the century progressed and athleticism developed, swimming became more structured and regulated. Natural facilities, such as the River Wey at Charterhouse or the Duck Puddle at Harrow, were transformed (often thanks to Old Boys' donations) into major bathing facilities with changing huts, diving boards, swimming instructors and competitions.
- Headmasters increasingly regarded swimming as a necessary athletic, as well as safe and hygienic pursuit and they followed contemporary fashion in believing water immersion to be therapeutic.
- Organised lessons and regular competitions became established in the second half of the century.
- Safety was vital – a well-maintained and safe bathing place gave a good impression at a time of stiff competition between schools. Some schools, such as Charterhouse, invested in purpose-built baths.
- In comparison to major team games, however, the status of swimming and bathing was limited.

Bathing as a rational recreation in urban industrial towns

Public baths in urban industrial towns:

- helped to stop the spread of disease
- were eventually used for washing, recreation and sport.

The development of bathing in industrial towns:

- Towns grew and became overcrowded as a result of industrialisation – hygiene was awful.
- With industrialisation, many rivers and natural water supplies became polluted and unsuitable for washing.
- Two major outbreaks of cholera rampaged through the country in 1832 and 1849, killing thousands and leaving countless families without a breadwinner.
- As only wealthy people could afford bathrooms at home, and rivers became increasingly unsafe for poorer people to use for washing, central government had to take a stand.
- Public baths were built (with loans from central government) to improve public health.
- The Wash House Act of 1846 allowed local authorities to apply for grants to provide public washing facilities.
- Most major towns built a public bath which often included hot and cold water baths and/or plunge baths as well as a public wash-house with laundry and drying facilities.
- Baths had first and second class facilities. This meant that the working class could afford the one penny entrance fee ('penny baths').

- Most of the loans were settled quickly and this attempt to encourage regular bathing, to prevent the spread of disease and to increase labour efficiency, seemed to pay off as work efficiency increased and absenteeism from ill health decreased.
- Plunge baths for swimming recreationally were added later.

> **Need to know more?** For more information on bathing and swimming as a case study, see Chapter 4, pages 53-57 in the OCR A2 PE Student Book.

Factfile: The Amateur Swimming Association (ASA)

- Formed in 1884.
- Middle-class swimmers (like athletes and rowers), were initially determined to exclude the lower class. By the 1880s, however, swimming and water polo clubs were becoming established for the working class with the grudging support of the ASA.

SWIMMING TODAY

Your specification says:	Factors that have helped develop bathing and swimming in the UK and the impact of these factors on contemporary participation and performance
General:	See pages 51 and 52 in the OCR A2 PE Student Book for features relating to opportunity, provision and esteem that might encourage or prevent participation in swimming today
Participation in swimming today:	Recommended and popular since easy on joints as a non-weight-bearing activity and a lifelong physical activity
Factors that have helped develop swimming and might increase participation:	• Pool technology (e.g. hoists for disabled people, modern teaching and learning aids etc.) • Improved material technology for clothing, which increases times, breaks records and increases interest in the sport • Leisure pools offering family entertainment with flumes, wave machines etc. • Blue Flag beaches indicating that water is safer/more pleasant for bathing • Continued awareness of safety – access to pools for families who holiday abroad • Antenatal and parent and baby/toddler classes, aqua aerobics etc • Government targets for more pools, upgrade of existing pools and plans for more Olympic and 50m pools • Growth in number of health clubs and spas with swimming facilities and good changing provision • Government initiative for free entry to pools (initially for U16s and O60s) • Success and inspiration of swimmers such as Michael Phelps (USA), and Rebecca Adlington (Team GB) in the Beijing Olympics 2008 and Eleanor Simmonds (Team GB) in the Beijing Paralympics • Increasing popularity and success of triathlon events (see athletics)
Specific factors that might be a barrier to participation in swimming today:	• Nature of activity (individual and in water) – some people may choose alternative activities that are arguably more sociable • Esteem – embarrassment or limited confidence due to poor body image • Limited media coverage (impact of role models restricted to major world competitions) • Cultural factors/ethnicity – e.g. reluctance to take part by some Asian females • Risk and pollution associated with seas and rivers

Table 6 Swimming and bathing today – factors affecting participation

ATHLETICS AS A POPULAR RECREATION

Community events, rural sports, festivals, commercial fairs and wakes

- A large range of popular games and contests were played in Britain before the advent of modern sports. Many of these can be viewed as seeds from which rationalised (and thus contemporary) athletics grew.
- Organisation was basic, with rules being simple, unwritten and passed on by word of mouth.
- Drinking and play were closely associated.
- The annual village fair, parish feast or Christmas celebration was an important time of community merriment.
- The weekly market was social and sporting as well.
- People needing work would go to the nearest hiring or 'mop' fair and offer their services as maid, cook, shepherd or ploughman.
- Village wakes were associated with praise and worship followed by festivity and feasting. It was a great social occasion, bringing all parts of the community together.
- There were opportunities for men to test their strength, speed and virility in events such as stick fighting, wrestling and running. More playfully they would try to catch pigs with soaped tails and compete in whistling and grinning contests.
- Peasant women would also race.
- Prizes were generally of practical use, for example shirts, smocks, hats, cheeses or joints of meat.
- Other than these gatherings, peasants had little opportunity for sports and pastimes.
- These local events were associated with all kinds of excess such as drinking, blood sports and promiscuity.
- The Reformed Church frowned upon traditional wakes. By the mid-nineteenth-century fetes and tea parties were respectable alternatives.

Pedestrianism: its nature, development and status – a summary

- From the late-seventeenth-century, footmen were employed as messengers or as competitive runners.
- Gentry patrons were their promoters. They looked after the lower-class runners, set up races and provided 'purses'. They also bet on the outcome of their employees.
- Pedestrian contests became huge festival occasions and great spectator attractions that were highly organised and structured (which was not in keeping with most other popular recreations at the time).
- Examples of successful athletes include the Native American Deerfoot and Robert Barclay Allardice.
- Pedestrianism was a simple and cheap activity to take part in and to stage.
- As cheating became common, the activity fell into disrepute. Cheating included match fixing and violence among participants and the crowd.
- Gentlemen amateurs competed to test themselves.
- There was wagering and prizes for participants.
- Associated attractions included horse racing

	Stage one: Bullying and brutality	Stage two: Social control	Stage three: Athleticism
Athletics	Informal running and exploring the countryside; paper chase (hare and hounds) linked to trespass	Trespass restricted or banned. Hare and hounds and steeple chase continued more formally	Steeple chase and cross-country running; annual sports day as major sporting and social occasion

Table 7 Athletics in the public schools – nineteenth-century development

EXAM TIP

Remember that early athletics involved community events, rural sports, festival, commercial fairs and wakes as well as pedestrianism.

Athletics in public schools

- Eighteenth-century public school boys took the sports of their local village wakes and fairs back to school after the holidays.
- Athletics in public schools involved hare and hounds, steeplechase and athletics sports days.
- They played them for fun and to relieve the boredom of early-nineteenth-century school life.

Exeter College, Oxford

In 1850, a group of undergraduates, disappointed by their poor riding in the traditional steeplechase, ran in a 'foot grind' across country, and also staged an Autumn Meeting. This followed the format of a Jockey Club meet, even to the weighing of top runners and the inclusion of a Consolation Stakes for beaten 'horses'.

The idea was soon copied, and by the 1870s athletic sports day had become both a major social occasion and a symbol of a more modern age. Unusually the impact was from the universities back to the schools rather than the other way around (as it was for football and rugby, for example).

Athletic sports days

- School sports day represented an era of technical advancement, more friendly social relationships between boys and masters, and a developing interest in skilfulness over brute force.
- It was also a useful day for the Headmaster to proudly display his school and to tout for financial support.
- Sports days were highly organised with elaborate ribboned programmes, press coverage, large numbers of spectators and often a military band.

The values and status of athletics in public schools

As the century progressed, the character-building values of athleticism, such as teamwork, trust, leadership, loyalty, courage, determination and sportsmanship, so easily linked to football, rugby and cricket, were also considered to be achievable through athletics. Public school boys represented their house – so developing teamwork, leadership and loyalty. Trust, courage and determination could be (and still are) visible in relay events and challenging long distance and cross-country events.

ATHLETICS AS A RATIONAL RECREATION

Opportunities for working–class participation

- The steady urbanisation of England led first to the end of rural fairs and then to professional athletics becoming established in the big industrial cities.
- The lower classes used running as a source of income, even though the winnings were small by pre-Victorian standards (when pedestrianism was still thriving).

- Exploitation was widespread, just as it was with pedestrianism. This included:
  - o 'roping' (holding back in order to lose)
  - o 'running to the book' (disguising one's form to keep a generous handicap)
  - o 'ringing in' (where promoters conspired to size the handicapping unfairly).
- The first purpose-built tracks were constructed in the late 1830s, and by 1850 most major cities had a facility. Carefully-measured tracks led to more stringent timekeeping and the beginning of record keeping, so that by mid-century, up to 25,000 people would watch and wager on a single race.

Amateurism, professionalism and the exclusion clause

Amateurism and professionalism was linked to class and status before the titles were linked to whether a performer was paid or not. Compare the approach to membership adopted by the Amateur Athletics Club and Amateur Athletics Association in Table 8.

The Modern Olympic Games

- Inspired by sport in the English public schools.
- Baron Pierre de Coubertin started the Modern Olympics in 1896.
- The Games aimed to foster patriotism, athleticism and friendship between nations.
- By the time the Games came to London in 1908, de Coubertin's original ideals had largely been crushed. International sport had become both an agent of international peace in a world moving towards war and a means of reviving national morale.
- The public school ideal of playing sport honourably and for its own sake had been lost. The gentleman amateur did not compete for extrinsic rewards, train seriously or aim to win at all costs.

Amateur Athletics Club	Amateur Athletics Association (AAA)
Established in 1866.	Established in 1880
• Set up by ex-university gentleman amateurs, who wanted to compete against one another without having to mix with professionals.	• Responsible for opening up the sport to all levels of society without compromising its respectable image.
• Wanted to dissociate respectable modern athletics from the old corrupted professional form.	• The exclusion clause was withdrawn and a professional became someone who ran for money rather than someone from the lower class.
• Adopted the 'exclusion clause' already used by the Amateur Rowing Association (ARA), which prevented manual workers from joining sports associations.	

Table 8 The early organisation of athletics

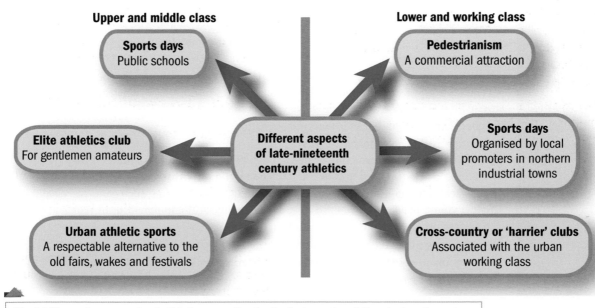

Fig 4.2 The various aspects of athletics operating by the last quarter of the nineteenth-century

> **Need to know more?** For more information on athletics as a case study see Chapter 4, pages 58-66, in the OCR A2 PE Student Book.

EXAM TIP

There is no great need to remember dates. It is important to understand themes such as the development of professionalism and opportunities for working class involvement.

ATHLETICS TODAY

Your specification says:	Factors that have helped develop athletics in the UK and the impact of these factors on contemporary participation and performance
General:	See pages 51 and 52 of the OCR A2 Student Book for features relating to opportunity, provision and esteem that might encourage or prevent participation in athletics today.
Participation in athletics today:	• Jogging or running: cheap, simple and accessible activity. Participation levels are high. It is a popular, fashionable, health-enhancing pastime, despite risks of injury from over-use. • In the much more specialist track and field athletics, participation rates are much lower. • Note success of events such as the London Marathon, Great North Run, Race for Life, Hash House Harriers etc. • Increasing popularity of triathlon events.
Factors that have helped develop athletics and the impact of these factors on participation and performance:	• Technological developments e.g. tracks, clothing, titanium for javelins etc. • Sports hall athletics: indoor athletics for young people. Adapted events use scaled-down versions of mainstream athletics and modified equipment. The aim is for young people to enjoy and develop their athletic capabilities and possibly continue into life-long participation. • Playground athletics: similar to above with a teacher pack for schools showing how athletics can be done safely without specialist equipment • Adequate media coverage to promote role models and make a difference • Competition organisers and development officers who work for county councils and who in some areas run the sports hall athletics programmes • Passion of individual teachers and club members • In September 2008, former Olympic champion Sally Gunnell launched McCain 'Track and Field', a nationwide campaign aiming to make athletics more accessible • Sponsorship, such as from McCain, who in July 2008 announced a five-year £5-million sponsorship deal with UK Athletics • Lottery funding and prize money has meant that the elite can now be career athletes
Specific factors that might be a barrier to participation in athletics today:	• Many events are specialised and linked with risk, so there is a need for specialist coaches and strict, time-consuming health and safety procedures • Many young people get poached by team sports, which are arguably more sociable with less individual exposure; e.g. running an 800m race you are fully exposed, whereas playing at a low-level within a hockey team it is easier to remain unnoticed • Teachers' lack of confidence or fear of legal action • Challenges for schools include: restricted time in summer term; impact of poor weather; expense of equipment; difficulty of getting equipment out (such as hurdles or high jump equipment); lack of throwing cages to reduce risk and increase safety. • Lack of access to top-level clubs where access is determined by trials; such clubs are inaccessible to most young people who will not have seen the specialist equipment until Year 7 at earliest • Athletics is not generally considered to be a lifetime sport • Negative image due to drug scandals may deter young people or their parents • Negative image of some field events as not 'cool' or appealing compared to other events • Indoor facilities very selective and mainly restricted to use by high-performance athletes

Table 9 Athletics today – factors affecting participation

FOOTBALL AS A POPULAR RECREATION – MOB GAMES

- A variety of games involving kicking and throwing a ball were regular features of English pre-industrial society.
- They were sometimes bizarre, always lively and often tragic.
- As a rowdy, violent, locally-coded, occasional encounter between neighbouring villages, mob football is without doubt the best example of a popular recreation.
- Early mob football games were played in restricted city streets as well as in the countryside. They were little more than massive brawls involving brute force between hordes of young men. They caused uproar, damage to property and a perfect setting for anyone attracted to violence.
- Shrove Tuesday became a traditional day for mob games and an opportunity for fun and excitement before the seriousness of Lent.
- Some of the best known games of mob football were in Ashbourne and Derby. Many such games survive today.
- Throughout history, kings, governments and local authorities have frowned on mob games because they caused:
  o damage to property
  o injury to young men (often making them unfit for army training)
  o disrespect for the Sabbath
  o social unrest (which might lead to riot or even rebellion).
- Although successive authorities declared the game illegal, without an effective policing system laws were fairly easy to ignore.

- Mob games can be recognised by their *lack of:*
  o set rules, positions, pitch or boundaries
  o referee or umpire
  o skilfulness (they were forceful and violent)
  o regularity (they were occasional festival games).

Influence of the public schools

- From the earliest days of public school history, impromptu, natural forms of football were played. Boys brought games from their local area which developed into school games dependent on the natural facilities available.
- The first melting pot occurred when boys brought their local games from home during stage one.
- During two stages of public school, with rebellion almost over and fighting on the wane, football became the place to settle disputes and to show courage and determination.
- Thus, football helped the social class that had traditionally tried to kill it off and for the first time in English history it became respectable.
- By the 1860s transport and communications had greatly improved.
- School football had also developed and a variety of internal and external contests were organised.
- The second melting pot involved the mixing of different schools games at university.
- At first most schools were initially unwilling to give up their own codes or to amalgamate with others.
- Disagreement often occurred in inter-school matches, as each school had different rules.

Characteristics of popular recreation	Did mob games have this characteristic?
Local	Yes, to a great extent.
Simple unwritten rules	Yes, due to widespread illiteracy.
Cruel/violent	Yes, very violent, many injuries, some deaths.
Occasional/annual	Usually annual festival occasions.
Courtly/popular	Yes, predominantly lower class (and male).
Rural	Yes, mainly, although there were some town games such as Kingston-upon-Thames.
Occupational	No.
Wagering	Yes, high levels of wagering on outcome.
Simple/natural	Yes, there were no purpose-built facilities so played across fields and between villages or through streets.

Table 10 The extent to which mob games had characteristics of popular recreation

	Stage one: Bullying and brutality	Stage two: Social control	Stage three: Athleticism
Football and rugby	Mob games and the first melting pot of activities from home	More formalised football rules for individual schools; inter-house competitions	Full technical development: Football Association (FA) or Rugby Football Union (RFU) rules along with traditional games at individual schools; 'colours', caps, inter-school fixtures

Table 11 Football in the public schools – nineteenth-century developments

Character building values	How values could be developed through participation in inter-house and inter-school football or rugby
Teamwork	Everyone needed to work together supporting each other for the good of the team.
Leadership	Opportunities available for house and school captains.
Loyalty	To team, to house and to school.
Courage/manliness	These qualities needed to be shown in the face of strong opposition. Boys needed to be able cope with difficult conditions and to show nerve and bravery when injured or losing.
Endeavour, determination and commitment	Players trained and played hard. A boy should never give up no matter what the score or difficult conditions. These qualities were (and still are) shown when coming back from injury, working to get into a team, turning up for training.
Discipline	The need to keep cool under pressure and always obey not only the rules of the referee but also the unwritten rules of sportsmanship and fair play.
Honesty, integrity, Sportsmanship and fair play	Playing to the letter and spirit of the rules was an essential aspect of playing as an amateur or public school boy. Gentlemanly behavior was part of the game which included showing respect for team mates and opponents. Being gracious in victory and defeat was the hallmark of a gentleman.
Trust/acceptance	Needed to be shown in team mates, in decisions of the captain and in selection.

Table 12 Values associated with football and rugby in public schools of the nineteenth-century

FOOTBALL AS A RATIONAL RECREATION

The Football Association (FA) was founded in 1863 and the game became popular very quickly, especially in the northern industrial towns because:

- it was simple, affordable and fitted perfectly into the newly free Saturday afternoon
- it provided a focus for community solidarity and comradeship
- improved transport and communications made travel to away matches and the following of local teams in the press possible

- for professionals, it offered an improved lifestyle and regular wages (but no security)
- it made heroes among the working class.

Amateurism and professionalism

- It soon became clear that the best players could not take unpaid time off work to play.
- When the Football League was founded in 1888 the FA reluctantly accepted professionalism. The first international match between England and Scotland took place in 1870 and by 1885 all the home countries were playing each other.

- Quite quickly, the working class dominance of soccer changed the nature of the game.
- Ex-public schoolboys set up amateur-only leagues, an amateur cup and amateur international fixtures.

Broken time payments and the split between the two codes

- Broken time payments were made to working class players to compensate for loss of earnings. Players could not afford to take unpaid time from work or be unfit for work due to injury.

- They led to professionalism which was looked down on by gentleman amateurs.
- In Rugby Football, meanwhile, there was an increasing need for professional players, particularly in the north of England.
- So, the game split and the Northern Football Union, (having failed to win broken-time payments for players) was formed in 1895.
- With the spread of football across Europe and the Empire, the International Football Federation (FIFA) was formed in 1904 and by 1906 professional football had become the major form of male entertainment in Britain.

Popular recreation – mob games	• Mainly rural and played locally in and around villages • With simple unwritten local rules that were passed on by word of mouth from generation to generation • Violent with severe injuries and even deaths • Based on force not skill • Occasional, often annual events held on festivals or Holy days • Played by lower-class males to show virility and manliness • There were many attempts to stop mob games • Associated with wagering
Public school developments	• Football and/or rugby in public schools was usually compulsory • Inter-house and inter-school matches • Special games afternoons due to the time available • Part of the games cult and often played obsessively • Participation was thought to build character and promote values such as courage, leadership and loyalty • There was a mixing or 'melting pot' of ideas and later codification • Linked with technical developments such as improved facilities, equipment, kit, and so on
Rational recreation – Association Football	• Regional, national and finally international games • Governing body (FA) rules • Respectable and based on skill rather than force, with tactics and strategy and special positions within the team • Played regularly with a 'season' and leagues, cups and competitions • There were gentlemen amateur teams such as Corinthian Casuals, as well as teams for factory workers and opportunities for working-class professionals • Urban purpose-built stadia meant that workers could walk to the ground and spectatorism increased • Spectatorism rather than participation was the norm for the working-class man

Table 13 Summary of football through time

FOOTBALL TODAY

Your specification says:	Factors that have helped develop football in the UK and the impact of these factors on contemporary participation and performance
General:	See pages 51 and 52 in the OCR PE A2 Student Book for features relating to opportunity, provision and esteem that might encourage or prevent participation in football today
Participation in football today:	• Traditionally the national game with history of high participation • Community participation – 'lads and dads' • Boom sport for women and girls, for example at Cramlington Learning Village in Northumberland over 200 girls play football every Saturday morning • Simple, cheap and accessible game that can be modified and played anywhere • Played in majority of schools – curricular, extra-curricular and in playgrounds • Women's World Cup
Factors that have helped develop football and the impact of these factors on participation and performance:	• Spectator game has developed as family entertainment with family enclosures and payment incentives as well as safer, larger stadia; this will all increase spectatorism and arguably could impact on participation • Elite performers as 'rags to riches' icons • Technology and fashionable clothing – kit, boots, balls, turf, stadia (including new Wembley stadium) • Impact of sporting celebrities, for example David Beckham • Academies often provide community football camps • The international game with tournaments such as the African Nations Cup, which includes English and Scottish Premier League players and which thereby attracts interest in the UK • The FAs 'Respect' campaign to combat unacceptable behaviour at every level, both on the pitch and from the sidelines
Specific factors that might be a barrier to participation in football today:	• Less 'street football' due to more cars and/or parental concerns regarding safety • Smaller gardens – less suitable for playing games (decking, etc.) • Reputation of poor behaviour by minority • Selling off of school and municipal playing fields, for example for more profitable housing or supermarkets • Argument of decreasing parental involvement due to work commitments

Table 14 Football today – factors affecting participation

Need to know more? For more information on football as a case study see Chapter 4, pages 67–73, in the OCR A2 PE Student Book.

CRICKET AS A POPULAR RECREATION

• Village cricket was played from the early eighteenth-century, especially in Kent, Sussex and Hampshire.
• Note the *significance of class* on participation – from the start the social classes played together reflecting the feudal or class structure of the village.
• Gentry patrons employed estate workers as gardeners and gamekeepers primarily for their cricketing talents.
• Players could not afford to take unpaid time from work or be unfit for work due to injury.

EXAM TIP

Think of initiatives today that impact on participation/performance of your case studies, e.g. Chance to Shine – rejuvenating cricket in state schools in England and Wales.

• There were also some freelance professionals who played in a servant role to their current employer. Early clubs emerged from these rural village sides.

Figure 4.4 will help you to describe the game of cricket as it existed in pre-industrial Britain. Note the: club-shaped bat, no distinct boundaries, under-arm bowling, 'notching' on wood for keeping score, two stumps, not three.

Factfile:

Interest and patronage by the gentry led to the early standardisation of rules, as follows:

1727 – the first Articles of Agreement were written.
1809 – 'The Laws of the Noble Game of Cricket' were set out by Marylebone Cricket club (MCC).
1835 – round arm bowling legalised.
1864 – over arm bowling legalised.

Fig 4.4 Cricket in pre-industrial Britain, 1743

Cricket was a popular recreation because...	On the contrary...
• it attracted widespread wagering • it was played by both males and females (it took the restricting ethics of Victorianism later in the nineteenth century to restrict women's sporting pursuits) • it was predominantly rural • it was often associated with feasts and festival days • its rules could be locally adapted.	• it was predominantly non-violent • it had an early rule structure • it had national touring sides from the 1840s (see William Clarke XI in rational recreation section, page 75).

Table 15 Arguments for and against cricket being classed as a popular recreation

Cricket in public schools – values, status and organisation

- Already a popular rural game by the mid-1700s, cricket was soon adopted by the public schools.
- Headmasters were happy to accept the game as its standardised rules, lack of violence and involvement by the gentry made it respectable.
- Cricket also occupied boys and kept them out of mischief.
- Changes that occurred during the three stages of development reflected changes in the game at large. During the 1850s and 60s cricket grew

with William Clarke's All England XI touring the country to entertain and inspire; the Lord's festival week being established as a social display of wealth for the Eton, Harrow and Winchester nobility, and the first England team visiting Australia in 1861.

- As a reflection of these developments, cricket in public schools was now highly organised and associated with:
  - o regularity as an inter-house and inter-school game

	Stage one: Bullying and brutality	Stage two: Social control	Stage three: Athleticism
Cricket	Transferred directly into the public schools due to its non-violent nature, rule structure and upper-class involvement in society	Cricket encouraged with massive inter-house participation	Continued technical development such as professional coaching, 'colours', caps and inter-school fixtures (e.g. annually against MCC)

Table 16 Cricket in the public schools – nineteenth-century developments

o compulsory participation
o investment in equipment and groundwork
o the employment of professional coaches
o more time was spent in training
o the appointment of assistant teachers for their cricketing prowess
o the hosting of matches as grand social occasions
o the belief that cricket instilled a range of character-building qualities such as leadership and teamwork.

Fundamentally, though, this was the same game that rural peasants and gentry patrons had played over 100 years before.

Values and status of cricket

The values thought to have been gained through participation in inter-house and inter-school cricket after 1870 included the following:

- physical endeavour, courage and commitment
- physical prowess
- moral integrity and linked qualities such as honesty, fair play and self-discipline
- teamwork, loyalty, leadership and loyal response to leadership
- decision-making, problem solving and organisational skills
- healthy lifestyles and relief from academic work.

The character-building values of athleticism – so easily linked to football and rugby – were also easily achieved through the game of cricket (see Table 17).

CRICKET AS A RATIONAL RECREATION

The William Clarke XI

- William Clarke took advantage of the changing economic and social conditions of the 1840s and helped change cricket from a fragmented localised sport to a national success.
- By the 1840s upper-class patronage of cricket had declined and professionals looked elsewhere for employment.
- Some went to the public schools and universities, while others joined professional touring sides such as the William Clarke XI (established 1847) or the breakaway United XI (formed by unhappy Clarke professionals who complained that they were not being paid enough).
- These sides toured England for many seasons, attracted huge crowds and took on teams of up to 22 opponents.

Class divisions

In the 1870s county cricket took over from the touring elevens as a spectator attraction. This rationalised form of the game had a strict class divide. While the middle-class amateurs needed and respected professionals, they kept them firmly in their social place:

- They had different names - professional versus amateur.
- Their names appeared differently in the programmes for example *A. Mynn Esq.*, for a gentleman and simply *Lillywhite* for a professional.

Character building values	How values could be developed through participation in inter-house and inter- school football or rugby
Teamwork	Everyone needed to work together supporting each other for the good of the team.
Leadership	Captain.
Loyalty	To team, to house and to school.
Courage/manliness	In the face of strong opposition/to cope with difficult conditions/when injured.
Endeavour, determination and commitment	Training hard; not giving up when score or conditions difficult; coming back from injury; working to get into a team; always turning up to practice/having private coaching.
Discipline	The need to keep cool under pressure.
Honesty, integrity, Sportsmanship and fair play	'Walking' when out; admitting you have not made a catch; not cheating; keeping strictly to rules; accepting umpire's decisions; respecting opposition.
Trust/acceptance	Needed to be shown in team mates, in decisions of the captain and in selection.

Table 17 How character building values were developed through inter-house/school football/rugby

- They had different eating arrangements.
- They did not travel together or share a changing room.
- They entered the field of play from a different door.
- The captain and the opening batsman was always an amateur.

The university men (amateurs) looked after 'the lads' while 'the lads' (professionals) arguably respected the gentlemen for their leadership qualities and skills as thinkers and motivators. It was not until 1963 that the distinction between gentlemen and players was finally abolished in English cricket.

EXAM TIP

Remember that the different treatment of working-class players was associated with rational recreation. In pre-industrial times the classes happily played cricket together and on a more equal footing.

Need to know more? For more information on cricket as a case study see Chapter 4, page 73-78, in the OCR A2 PE Student Book.

CRICKET TODAY

Your specification says:	Factors that have helped develop cricket in the UK and the impact of these factors on contemporary participation and performance
General:	See pages 51 and 52 in the OCR A2 PE Student Book for features relating to opportunity, provision and esteem that might encourage or prevent participation in cricket today
Participation in cricket today:	• In its simplest form, a popular beach game • English Cricket Board (ECB) statistics show a 27 per cent increase in participation rates in the twelve months up to October 2008 and a 45 per cent increase in female participation over the same period • 8,000 cricket clubs in England of which 6,500 are affiliated to ECB and 3,700 have junior sections • Summer game in state schools but many constraints, such as need for time, adequate facilities and specialist coaching • Independent schools often able to provide more cricket opportunities than state schools
Factors that have helped develop cricket and the impact of these factors on participation and performance:	• A sophisticated and structured development programme by ECB with development targeted through clubs rather than through schools; programmes are designed and devised locally with regional support form ECB • Strategies and initiatives include adapted games for people with disabilities (blind, deaf, physically or mentally disabled) • The 'club mark' scheme whereby clubs gain a kite mark standard and accreditation as healthy safe places for young people • 'Chance to shine' • Technology for bats, bowling machines, protective clothing and so on • Twenty20, one-day matches • Media hype linked with test matches • Commercialisation of the game at top level – top teams visiting different towns to entertain and inspire (as they did in time of William Clarke) • Asian immigration since 1960s • The England women's victory in the Cricket World Cup in 2009
Specific factors that might be a barrier to participation in cricket today:	• Summer game – limited time available at school level • Kolpak ruling means that less money might be spent on coaching and developing young, home-grown players

Table 18 Cricket today – factors affecting participation

TENNIS AS A POPULAR RECREATION – REAL TENNIS

- Real or royal tennis originated in France and became popular in Britain during the fourteenth-century.
- It was an exclusive, elitist game for kings, nobles and merchants who played on purpose-built, highly-sophisticated courts which varied in size and shape.
- The game had complex rules and required high levels of skill.
- Henry VIII built the court at Hampton Court Palace, which is still used today.

- Most university colleges had a court. For example, Charles I played at Oxford when the city was his stronghold during the English Civil War (1642–6).

EXAM TIP

You need to be able to compare real tennis with mob football. Compare step-by-step thinking about who played, where it was played, rule structure, numbers involved, dress, levels of skill or force, regularity of play and so on.

Characteristics of popular recreation	Did real tennis have this characteristic?
Local	The people who played (upper-class) had the money, time and transport (coach and horses) to allow them to travel.
Simple unwritten rules	No, complex written rules.
Cruel/violent	No, refined and sophisticated.
Occasional/annual	No, those who played had time. The landed gentry were sometimes referred to as the 'leisured class'.
Courtly/popular	Yes, upper-class (and male), though the lower-class peasant would have copied and played hand and ball games against any suitable wall.
Rural	Mixed, remember Henry VIII had a court at Hampton Court.
Occupational	No.
Wagering	Yes, high levels of wagering on outcome.
Simple/natural	No, there were expensive purpose built courts of various shapes and sizes.

Table 19 The extent to which real tennis had characteristics of popular recreation

TENNIS AND OTHER STRIKING GAMES IN THE PUBLIC SCHOOLS – THEIR STATUS AND ORGANISATION

	Stage one: Bullying and brutality	Stage two: Social control	Stage three: Athleticism
Tennis	Informal hand and ball games against suitable available walls and buildings. Referred to as fives or tennis (that is real tennis rather than lawn tennis which had not been invented yet)	Some fives courts built though fives still an informal activity. Game of racquets developing as more formal alternative; also squash racquets	Fives continued as recreational game. Racquets a more formal game of higher status. Lawn tennis comparatively low status in boys' schools; very popular as summer game in girls' public schools

Table 20 Tennis and other striking games in the public schools – nineteenth-century developments

Fives

- Fives is ancient and informal in origin.
- The best-known structured version is Eton fives.
- Fives was hugely popular in the public schools, but failed to become a national game of any repute because:
    - it had a tradition of being played as a recreational game in free time
    - there were different versions of the game (for example, Eton Fives and Winchester Fives)
    - it had limited scope for developing the character
    - the more sophisticated game of racquets was already established.

Racquets

- At first, racquets was played informally by schoolboys on naturally occurring 'courts'.
- By 1850 two standardised courts were built at Harrow at a cost of £850.
- By the time Old boys took the game to University and to their private clubs, it had attained a high social status far beyond its beginnings in a debtors prison.
- As the game became more sophisticated, the court was rationalised with four walls (instead of one) and a roof to guard against bad weather.

Squash

- Many argue that racquets lead to the invention of the more compact and less expensive game of squash rackets, when boys at Harrow who were waiting to play rackets began knocking up outside using a less hard, more 'squashy' ball than for racquets to avoid damage to windows.
- By the 1860s, purpose-built squash courts were common and boys took the game on to university and often back to their country homes.

Lawn Tennis in public schools

Lawn tennis was a social game that became a vehicle for the **emancipation** of women.

Boys' public schools rejected lawn tennis as anything other than an informal social summer game because:

- lawn tennis courts took up a comparatively large space for the number of boys occupied
- the game did not require the courage or physicality of football or cricket
- it could not rival the contemporary status of cricket or football

KEY TERM

Emancipation: liberation linked with new-found freedom. For women in late-nineteenth-century Britain, emancipation meant freedom from the restricting limitations society place on them as women.

- it did not require the teamwork or cooperation of major games
- it had a reputation of being 'pat ball,' and suitable only for girls
- as a new invention it was treated with some suspicion.

TENNIS AS A RATIONAL RECREATION

- The game of lawn tennis was invented, patented and popularised by the middle-class army Major Walter Clompton Wingfield in 1874.
- Wingfield sold the game in a painted box containing a pole, pegs and netting for forming the court, four tennis bats, a supply of balls, a mallet and brush, and a book of the game.
- Originally called 'Sphairistike' (derived from the Greek word for ball) the game was played on an hourglass shaped court, but within a few years the name was changed to lawn tennis and the court was modified to become rectangular.
- Lawn tennis was bought by the most fashionable upper/middle-class families.
- In 1877 the All England Croquet Club introduced lawn tennis at Wimbledon. Twenty-two competitors took part and the finals attracted 200 spectators.
- By 1885, 3,500 spectators watched the men's final.

Summary of the development of lawn tennis

- The middle classes were excluded from real tennis and invented their own alternative.
- The game was perfect for upper/middle-class suburban gardens.
- It was an important social occasion.
- It was patented and became a fashionable status symbol.
- Tennis clubs were formed which allowed social gatherings of the same class of people.

- The lower/middle-class, whose gardens were too small for courts, also frequented these private clubs.
- The working class were excluded – they had to wait for public provision in parks, which delayed their participation.
- The development of tennis reflected the emergence of the urban middle-class.

Lawn tennis – a vehicle for the emancipation/liberation of women

- The game helped to dispel some negative stereotypes of women from earlier Victorian times.
- As a social occasion it was part of family recreation.
- Women could participate in a (mildly) strenuous game for the first time but (crucially) didn't have to over exert themselves and weren't expected to excel.
- They could stay covered up and retain modesty as participation did not require special dress.
- The true social importance of tennis was that it could be played by either sex or by both together.
- The privacy of the garden, with high hedges or walls, provided an opportunity to invite suitable members of the opposite sex for supervised sports.

TENNIS TODAY

Your specification says:	Factors that have helped develop tennis in the UK and the impact of these factors on contemporary participation and performance
General:	See pages 51 and 52 in the OCR A2 PE Student Book for features relating to opportunity, provision and esteem that might encourage or prevent participation in tennis today
Participation in tennis today:	• Focused on clubs with school links important • In spite of initiatives it could be argued that tennis is still predominantly a middle-class game
Factors that have helped develop tennis and the impact of these factors on participation and performance:	• Technology such as Astroturf, titanium racquets, low-compression balls, ball machines and other coaching aids • LTA and other schemes to increase participation in inner cities • Increasing number of indoor courts – David Lloyd and other tennis centres means more are able to play throughout the year, as well as provision in public parks • Regionalisation of LTA • Media coverage – Wimbledon on terrestrial television available to all, so widespread exposure of role models including 2008 junior Wimbledon champion Laura Robson • Retractable roof on the centre court at Wimbledon 2009 • Free or heavily subsidised use of community courts in parks in some areas
Specific factors that might be a barrier to participation in tennis today:	• Public perception that tennis is a game for wealthy people (the cost of hiring a public tennis court can be as much as £9.00 per hour) • Quality of park/public provision – many community courts are neglected and in disrepair; others have been turned into skateboard parks or playgrounds • Summer game – limited time available at school level • Unpredictable British weather • Other challenges at school level, such as specialist coaches needed and 'expensive' space-wise (just as in the boys' public schools) • Courts converted to car parks at many schools/colleges • A comparatively difficult game • Computer alternatives to the 'real thing' such as Wii sports • Prevailing 'stuffy' attitudes at some private clubs

Table 21 Tennis today – factors affecting participation

▶ **Need to know more?** For more information on tennis as a case study see Chapter 4, page 78-83, in the OCR A2 PE Student Book.

CHECK

If you are satisfied with your knowledge and understanding, tick off the sections that you have revised so far. If you are not satisfied, then revisit those sections and refer to the pagers in the *Need to know more?* features.

☐ Discuss the five case study activities – bathing and swimming, athletics, football, cricket and tennis.

☐ Describe how these activities have emerged to the present day through the following stages: popular recreation, via the public schools and rational recreation.

☐ Analyse each activity as a pre-industrial popular recreation.

☐ Assess the influence of nineteenth-century public schools on each activity.

☐ Demonstrate knowledge and understanding of each activity as a rational recreation.

☐ Outline those factors that have helped to develop each activity in the UK today and the impact of these factors on contemporary participation and performance.

TRUE OR FALSE?

1. You need to look at each case study activity in three stages – as a popular recreation, in the public schools and as a rational recreation.
2. Early swimming was important for recreation, survival and health.
3. Post-industrial urban overcrowding and disease lead to the need for Wash and Bath Houses.
4. Pedestrianism is a perfect example of a popular recreation – better than mob football.
5. Amateurs and professionals were happy to run in the same athletics meetings.
6. 'Break-off' payments were made to working-class footballers to compensate for loss of earning and they eventually lead to professionalism.
7. There are no barriers to participation in recreational football today.
8. Early cricket reflected the two class society of pre-industrial Britain – in that the classes were always separate.
9. The fact that cricket is a summer game might be a barrier to participation today.
10. Lawn tennis as a rational game was invented by and for the middle-classes in 1874.

EXAM PRACTICE

1. Discuss the development of athletics from its early pre-industrial roots to the present day. Your answer should include pre-industrial factors; athletics in the public schools; the emergence of amateur athletics as a rational recreation, as well as factors that have helped to develop athletics in the UK today. *(20 marks)*

2. Discuss the development of public baths in late nineteenth-century Britain and how factors continue to impact on participation and performance in swimming today. *(20 marks)*

See page 253 for answers

CHAPTER 5
Drill, physical training and Physical Education in state schools

CHAPTER OVERVIEW

By the end of this chapter you should have knowledge and understanding of:

- how physical activity in state elementary schools progressed from military drill to physical training (PT) and then to Physical Education (PE) between 1900 and 1950
- the ways in which drill, PT and PE in state schools impacted on participation and the promotion of healthy lifestyles
- how to link what happened then to what is happening in schools today
- the objectives, content and teaching methodology of each approach
- how war affected the different approaches
- in what ways and why the 'sporting' experiences of working-class children in state schools differed from that of middle- and upper-class boys and girls in public schools
- the impact of teachers' industrial action in the 1970s and 1980s on participation
- the aims of the National Curriculum for PE and how to critically evaluate its impact.

INTRODUCTION

You need to know *how* and *why* the approach to and teaching of physical skills and activities changed throughout the twentieth-century. Answers to the 'W' questions should help. For each stage you will need to identify:

- *What* was the main aim, e.g. drill, training or education?
- *Who* was doing the teaching and learning (with reference to class, gender and qualifications of instructors or teachers)?
- *When* was it introduced? (You will need to know dates here.)
- *Where* the activity took place, e.g. in the street, playground or a purpose-built gymnasium?
- *Why* the system was introduced, e.g. the effects of war or thanks to particular individuals?
- *How* was it 'taught'?

You need to understand and be able to explain reasons for change over time, which include:

- change in educational philosophy from instructional (1902) to child-centred

(1950s) and choice within a National Curriculum today

- changes from the idealism of the 1950s to increased accountability of teachers today
- changes in standard of living from early poverty to a welfare state system where the government is responsible for assuring basic health and education
- social change from a strict class system to emphasis on equality of opportunity for all
- changes in provision from a playground (at most) to purpose-built facilities and increased availability of equipment today
- changes in teacher training from general class teachers to a graduate PE profession today
- changes due to the effects of war
- reductions in class/group sizes over time
- changes in the needs of society from military readiness to health and combating obesity
- the impact of the National Curriculum and an awareness of initiatives for participation in schools, such as the impact of School Sports Co-ordinators (SSCOs).

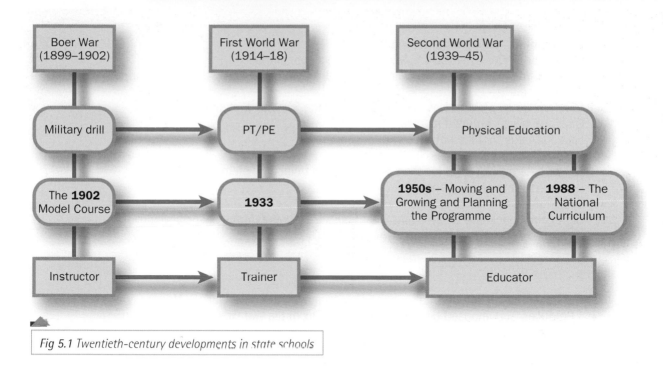

Fig 5.1 *Twentieth-century developments in state schools*

Why was the Model course of 1902 quickly replaced?

- It had been imposed by the War Office.
- Military drill, with its command style, was soon considered unsuitable for young children.
- Educationalists demanded a healthier approach linked to good posture and therapeutic exercises, with children being allowed to play rather than being treated as little soldiers.
- Dr George Newman was Appointed Chief Medical Officer within the Board of Education. Newman stressed the health-giving/therapeutic effects of exercise and the importance of recreational activities for the rehabilitation of injured soldiers.
- Teachers objected to **army non-commissioned officers (NCOs)** in schools and wanted PT to be their responsibility.

EXAM TIP

Remember the important role of Dr George Newman, who oversaw the publication of three Board of Education syllabuses between 1909 and 1933. He was concerned with the health of young people.

Why was the 1933 syllabus replaced in the 1950s?

- A more **holistic** approach to the physical education of young children was sought that incorporated the intellectual, emotional and social development of each individual child.
- There was a desire for less prescriptive 'tables' of exercises and more creativity.
- By the 1950s there were:
  - more female teachers who wanted a different movement style approach to physical activity
  - many new purpose-built gymnasia for gymnastic activity.

KEY TERM

Physical training – A term used between 1880 and 1950 to describe a form of physical exercise for working-class children that consisted of Swedish gymnastics and drill.

Important points/background information
- Military needs became more powerful than educational theory.
- A backward step educationally with Swedish drill, innovation and a therapeutic approach abandoned.
- Condemned by progressives and supporters of the Swedish system.
- Girls and boys instructed together.
- Failed to cater for different ages and/or genders.
- Children treated as soldiers.
- Taught by army NCOs (or teachers who had been trained by them).
- Dull and repetitive – but cheap.
- Large numbers in small spaces.
- Set against backdrop of poor diets, bad housing and other forms of social deprivation.
- It lowered the status of the subject.

Influences
- Imposed as a result of Britain's poor performance in the **Boer War** (S. Africa).
- Produced and imposed by **Colonel Malcolm Fox** of the War Office (not Education Department).

**The Model course
1902**

Massed drill in the school yard around 1902

Also note

❛ It is important therefore that the short time claimed for physical training should be devoted wholly to useful exercises. No part of that time should be wasted on what is merely spectacular or entertaining, but every exercise should have its peculiar purpose and value in a complete system framed to develop all parts of the body. ❜ (*Model Course of Physical Training, 1902*)

Objectives
- Fitness (for military service/war)
- Training in handling of weapons
- Discipline for the working class

Content
- Military drill/marching
- Static exercises, e.g. arm raises
- Weapon training
- Deep breathing

Methodology
- Command-response (for example, 'Attention', ' Stand at ease', 'Marching, about turn'.)
- Group response/no individuality
- In ranks

Fig 5.2 The Model Course, 1902

Important points/background information
- The industrial depression of the 1930s left many of the working class unemployed (no state benefits were yet available).
- A watershed between the syllabuses of the past and the Physical Education of the future.
- This syllabus had one section for the under elevens and one for the over elevens.

Influences
- The Hadow Report of 1926 identified the need to differentiate between ages for physical training.
- Dr George Newman – this was the last syllabus to be published under his direction.

Syllabus of physical training
1933

Emphasis on skills and posture.

Also note
- A detailed, high quality and highly respected syllabus.
- Still set out in a series of 'tables' from which teachers planned their lessons.
- *'The ultimate test by which every system of physical training should be judged [is] to be found in the posture and general carriage of the children'* (1933 syllabus).
- Newman stated that good nourishment, effective medical inspection and treatment and hygienic surroundings were all necessary for good health as well as 'a comprehensive system of physical training ... for the normal healthy development of the body [and] for the correction of inherent or acquired defects.'

Objectives
- Physical fitness
- Therapeutic benefits
- Good physique
- Good posture
- Development of mind and body (holistic aims)

Content
- Athletics, gymnastic and games skills
- Group work

Methodology
- Still direct style for the majority of the lesson/centralised
- Some decentralised parts to the lesson
- Group work/tasks throughout
- Encouragement of special clothing/kit
- Five 20-minute lessons a week recommended
- Used many schools' newly built gymnasia
- Outdoor lessons recommended for health benefits
- Some specialist PE teachers

Fig 5.3 Syllabus of physical training, 1933

Important points/background information
- The (Butler) Education Act 1944 aimed to ensure equality of educational opportunity.
- It also required local authorities to provide playing fields for all schools.
- School leaving age was raised to fifteen years.
- These syllabuses should be viewed in the context of overall expansion of physical activities in schools.
- Intended to replace the under elevens section of the 1933 syllabus.

Influences
- The Second World War, which required 'thinking' soldiers, and the subsequent perceived need for increasingly 'thinking' children.
- Assault course obstacle equipment influenced apparatus design.
- Modern educational dance methods influenced the creative/movement approach.
- An experiment in Halifax, which rehabilitated children with disabilities by encouraging individual interpretation of open tasks, with no pre-set rhythm or timing. This influenced the problem-solving approach.

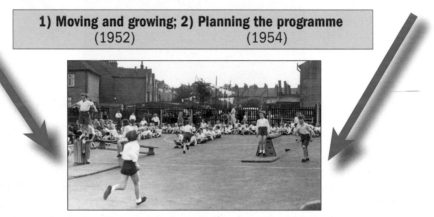

1) Moving and growing; 2) Planning the programme
(1952)   (1954)

An apparatus lesson in the 1950s.

Also note
- The extensive post-war re-building programme lead to an expansion of facilities.

Objectives
- Physical, social and cognitive development
- Variety of experiences
- Enjoyment
- Personal satisfaction/sense of achievement
- Increased involvement for all

Content
- Agility exercises; gymnastics, dance and games skills
- Theme or sequence work
- Movement to music
- Apparatus work

Methodology
- Child-centred and enjoyment orientated
- Progressive
- More specialised PE teachers
- Teacher guidance rather than direction
- Problem-solving/creative/exploratory/discovery
- Individual interpretation of tasks/decentralised
- Using full apparatus (cave, ropes, bars, boxes, mats, and so on)

Fig 5.4 Moving and growing, 1952; 2) Planning the programme (1954)

1) Impact of industrial action by teachers in state schools (1970s and 1980s):
- reduced opportunity and provision
- extra-curricular activities severely restricted or stopped
- participation reduced in schools
- participation shifted to community clubs
- frustration/disappointment for both children and teachers
- negative press for teachers.

❝ My first year of secondary school was great – but from my second year there were no lunchtime or after-school activities – it was really annoying. I just joined clubs outside of school. ❞
(PE Teacher who started secondary school just before the industrial action)

The 1970s and 1980s and the National Curriculum

2) The National Curriculum of Physical Education:
- is one of five subjects which all pupils must pursue from age 5–16 years
- at each Key Stage (KS) children need to show knowledge, skills and understanding in a variety of practical areas.

Potential positive impacts of the National Curriculum include:
- higher standards
- clear national standards
- a broad and balanced PE experience for all
- consistent opportunity and content for all wherever they go to school
- easy transfer between schools
- learners gain the right to learn certain things
- increased likelihood of lifelong participation due to greater variety of activities experienced (especially at KS4)
- as a relatively open framework it can be adapted to the needs of learners
- provides some support, especially to non-specialist teachers of PE
- develops learning, thinking and analytical skills as well as creativity, innovation and enterprise
- develops social skills such as fair play
- helps pupils to manage risk and cope with difficulty
- can develop pupils' integrity and independence.

Potential negative impacts of the National Curriculum include:
- tracking and record keeping can involve large amounts of paperwork for teachers
- lack of assessment experience by some primary teachers can lead to confusion and skewed results at lower KS3
- may reduce creativity of certain teachers who feel constrained – though this may have been addressed with new KS3 curriculum
- can impose pressure on schools with facilities such as tennis courts
- schools are still able to offer an unbalanced programme, for example football and not rugby or avoidance of dance and/or gymnastics by teachers who prefer games
- demanding on teachers (especially at KS1) who may lack support. Partnerships and links between schools are addressing this issue.

Fig 5.5 1970s and 1980s – the impact of industrial action on participation in state schools; 2) the impact of the National Curriculum on PE in state schools today

▶ **Need to know more?** For more information on drill, physical training and Physical Education in state schools see Chapter 5, pages 90-98, in the OCR A2 PE Student Book.

EXAM TIP

It is important to be able to compare the following over time:

- *Objectives* – the aims or intentions of (in this case) a lesson or syllabus, e.g. physical or military fitness.

- *Content* – the subject matter or activities taught in the lesson, e.g. weapons drill or games skills.

- *Methodology* – the teaching style used for delivery, such as command or problem solving.

Remember – exam questions can ask for this information. You also need to compare then (historical) with now (contemporary).

KEY TERM

Army non-commissioned officers (NCO) – low ranking officers with little interest in or knowledge of child development.

Colonel Fox – a long serving army officer appointed in 1902, as a result of the Boer war, to establish and ensure the adoption of a Model course.

Decentralised – the teacher is a guide and children work at their own pace answering tasks in an individual way.

Centralised – the teacher uses an instructive style and the children answer the task in unison.

Holistic – considering the whole rather than separate parts. Holistic approach to PE considers intellectual, emotional and social development of a child, as well as the physical.

Remember

You need to study the past and see how it links forward to the next stage in time or to today, so (among other things) consider:

- improvements in or an increased variety or number of different facilities over time
- increasingly child-friendly or colourful or appropriate equipment today
- a greater emphasis on accountability in schools today in comparison with, for example, the 1950s
- Physical Education now as an all-graduate profession (compare with the NCOs of 1902)
- the impact of the National Curriculum in Physical Education
- initiatives in primary and secondary schools to increased participation and to promote balanced, active and healthy lifelong participation
- the balance between achieving a balanced, active and healthy lifestyles with talent spotting the potential elite
- the need to reduce discrimination and improve opportunities and provision for all.

CHECK

If you are satisfied with your knowledge and understanding, tick off the sections that you have revised so far. If you are not satisfied, then revisit those sections and refer to the pagers in the *Need to know more?* features.

- Describe how physical activity in state schools progressed from military drill to PT and then to PE between 1900 and 1950.
- Explain the ways in which drill, PT and PE in state schools impacted on participation and the promotion of healthy lifestyles.
- Demonstrate links between what happened previously to what is happening in schools today.
- Distinguish between the objectives, content and teaching methodology of each approach.
- Describe how war affected the different approaches.
- Describe in what ways and why the 'sporting' experiences of working-class children in state schools differed from that of middle- and upper-class boys and girls in public schools.
- Outline the impact on participation of teachers' industrial action in the 1970s and 1980s.
- Identify the aims of the National Curriculum for PE and critically evaluate its impact.

TRUE OR FALSE?

1. In terms of state school provision for physical activity, your specification requires knowledge and understanding of 1902, 1933, the 1950s as well as the 1970s and 1980s.
2. The 1902 Model Course was linked with Military drill.
3. The 1902 Model course was taught by specially trained teachers.
4. The 1902 Model Course was brought in by the War Office because Britain lost the Boer War.
5. A lesson based on the 1933 syllabus of physical training had some decentralised parts.
6. There was no group work suggested in the 1933 syllabus.
7. In a 1950s PE lesson, young people were encouraged to be independent decision makers and problem solvers.
8. The 1950s approach was associated with new purpose-built facilities and newly built (post war) gymnasia.
9. Industrial action by teachers in the 1960s lead to decreased opportunity and provision for young people to participate in physical activity in state schools.
10. The National Curriculum for Physical Education has only positive impacts.

EXAM PRACTICE

1. Compare the objectives of the 1950s curriculum for Physical Education in State Schools with the objectives of Physical Education in Sate Schools today. *(4 marks)*

2. Identify **two** differences between the 1902 Model Course and Physical Education in State Schools today. Explain why the Model Course was replaced and the how the 1933 course was different in terms of objectives and content. *(6 marks)*

3. Identify two possible positive and two possible negative impacts of the National Curriculum for PE in state schools today and explain the impact on sport and PE of the 1970s and 1980s teachers' industrial action. *(6 marks)*

See page 256 for answers

CHAPTER 6

Comparative study of the USA and the UK

CHAPTER OVERVIEW

By the end of this chapter you should have knowledge and understanding of:
• the cultural context of sport in the USA and the UK
• PE and school sport in the USA and the UK
• mass participation in sport in the USA and the UK
• sport and the pursuit of excellence in the USA and the UK
• how to critically evaluate the influence of the cultural context on all of the above.

All three countries of study – the USA, Australia and the UK – give high priority to Physical Education in schools, and to sport, both as a mass participation activity, and as a pursuit through which the achievement of excellence is the aim.

HISTORICAL DETERMINANTS

UK	USA
The sociological history of the UK extends much further than USA. E.g. the development of the English nation began a thousand years ago.	The post colonial history of the USA is little more than two hundred years old and is considered therefore to be a young culture.
As a small island the UK did not have a 'frontier' to extend but had a policy of aggressive expansion overseas, giving rise to an empire.	The USA has a history of frontierism. The frontier marked the extent of western expansion into country that was often hostile.
Sport helped to establish UK traditions in the Empire and in turn the Empire influenced the development of sport across the world.	The USA adopted a policy termed isolation and so developed their own sports to suit the culture. Traditional English sports were rejected.
Cricket was played across the entire British Empire. The values of the game reflected the British class system and English values	The slow nature of cricket caused it to be marginalised because it did not reflect the new values of the USA.
The greatest developmental influence on UK sport came from the reformed English Public School system.	In the USA, the traditional universities known as Ivy League Colleges had the greatest impact on sport in America.
The Public School established the view that taking part was more important than winning. This was associated with the notion of the 'Gentleman Amateur' sportsman.	The Ivy League Colleges and American society promoted the 'win ethic' that was later termed Lombardianism. This was later associated with professionalism.
The combination of physical effort and moral integrity associated with good sportsmanship became the dominant ethos in the UK Public Schools.	The ethos of the Colleges represented the 'cult of manliness' that was in keeping with the spirit of frontierism.
The case study sports in the UK embraced commercialism in the late twentieth-century.	The case study sports in the USA looked to develop commercialism in the early twentieth-century.

Table 1 Comparison of historical determinants between the UK and USA

HISTORICAL CONCLUSIONS

The 'Gentleman Amateur' ethic supported by the UK Public Schools in the nineteenth-century may have been more effective than the USA Universities 'win ethic' in developing a sense of fair play and sportsmanship.

GEOGRAPHICAL DETERMINANTS

UK	USA
The population of the UK is approaching 62 million with a relatively high population density of 200 people per square mile.	The population of the USA is approaching 300 million with a population density of 30 people per square mile.
There are remote areas, for example the Highlands of Scotland and areas of Outstanding Natural Beauty. There are no areas of genuine wilderness.	Large unpopulated areas of wilderness sometimes called 'frontier country' have helped to stimulate the US passion for the 'Great Outdoors'.
There is a relatively small group of islands with one type of climate (Western Maritime).	The North American continent has large ranges of latitude and altitude. As a result, the USA has a wide range of climatic zones.
The restricting climate and altitude terrain limits the potential for winter sports pursuits.	High mountain ranges and a suitable winter climate has enabled the USA to stage the Winter Olympic Games on two occasions.
A well-established network of motorways, rail and air routes facilitate good internal communication in both countries and this influences the development of professional sports and pursuits in physical activities.	
The expansion of passenger railways in the UK from the 1850s greatly facilitated the development of organised sport and recreational pursuits in expanding urban areas and the countryside.	Rail links are well established. Trans-American routes were laid down during the period of western expansion during the 'frontier' years. The rapid expansion of professional 'major league' sports like baseball in the 1890's was helped by the railway system.

Table 2 Comparison of geographical determinants between the UK and USA

- Urbanisation and high population densities may not produce the healthiest environmental living conditions, but they do promote social interaction and communication. These factors have been very influential in the development of Physical Education and sport.

- A well-established travel network in the UK provides easy access to areas of Outstanding Natural Beauty. People are encouraged to enjoy active and healthy pursuits in these areas but they are of limited space. Consequently overcrowding is causing erosion and pollution.

- The 'Wilderness' areas of the USA, such as those found in Yosemite National Park, are so vast that visitors make little impact on the natural environment.

COMMERCIALISATION OF SPORT

- In the latter part of the twentieth-century, cricket and both codes of rugby changed from an amateur and semi-professional approach to a commercialised model that dominates the twenty-first-century. (Note that the sports mentioned above are identified as case studies in the syllabus.)
- Association Football at the highest level embraced professionalism shortly after the formation of the Football Association in 1863. It was in the 1990s however, with the creation of BSkyB that UK football became a commercial product.
- All professional sport in the twenty-first-century is strongly associated with the 'Golden Triangle' and at this level sport is considered to be a commodity.
- Association Football is the only UK sport that can match the USA 'Big Four' sports as a commercial product.
- UK sport is copying the USA model which has developed professional sport into an entertainment industry. The copying of an idea from another country is termed 'cultural borrowing'.

GOVERNMENT POLICY

UK	USA
The Monarch is Head of State and the Prime Minister is Head of Government. Overarching power is exercised by the UK Government and the devolved governments of Scotland, Wales and Northern Ireland which are autonomous bodies.	The USA is a Republic with a strong democratic influence. There is no hereditary class privilege that has had the power to determine or influence the opportunity of the people.
The UK is, to an extent, decentralised through local government	The USA has always been committed to a decentralised model of control and this is reflected in each State having autonomy.
Decentralisation is less evident in the Government's National Curriculum in schools model and in the Department for Culture, Media and Sport through which the Government have taken more responsibility for sport.	Decentralisation is strongly evident as there is no National Curriculum in Schools and the Government have little responsibility for sport, e.g. limited funding for Olympic involvement. Sport is largely self funding through commercial enterprise.
UK is inclined toward a mixed economy which restricts commercial enterprise. This has limited the commercialisation of sport.	USA is inclined toward a capitalist economy which encourages commercial enterprise. This economy has encouraged the commercialisation of sport.
Professional sports are becoming increasingly commercialised but are still controlled by sporting governing bodies.	Professional sports are organised as a commercial industry and operate as business cartels to maximise profit.

Table 3 Comparison of government policy between the UK and USA

COMMERCIALISM AND SPORT

Key Factor	UK	USA
Economy	The model of economy although essentially capitalist is inclined towards a mixed model. This model is less favourable to the formation of commercial enterprise.	The capitalist economy enabled professional sports to become a commercial businesses.
Status	The amateur ethic was dominant during the nineteenth and much of the twentieth century.	The early acceptance of professionalism promoted the concept of sport as a consumer commodity.
Ethos	The ethic of participation prevailed in UK sport throughout sporting development of the nineteenth- and twentieth-centuries.	The Lombardian ethos that is associated with professional sport helped to create an image that was reflective of entertainment.
Organisation	Sport continues to have a strong input from the governing bodies. The concept of the business cartel does not operate to the same extent.	Professional sport in the USA is organised as a business cartel for the sole purpose of profit making.
The media	Exclusive coverage was avoided in the 1960s.	Exclusive coverage was encouraged in the 1960s.
The media	In the 1960s, the UK Government and the only available television channels, namely the BBC and ITV agreed, that ten sporting events could be shown by either company.	The media outlet of television became inextricably linked with sport and commercial sponsorship in the 1960s (the Roone Revolution).
The media	Sport was presented in the traditional way.	Sport was presented as an entertainment commodity.
Commercial sponsorship	Commercial sponsorship was evident in some sports in the 1960s but was much slower to be accepted across the major case study sports.	Large businesses sponsor sport as a result of media profile and methods of presentation. The 'Big Four' immediately embraced business opportunities.
Cultural determinants	The nature of the economy and historical determinants like class privilege has prevented a UK equivalent of the 'American Dream'. These factors inhibited the growth of sport as a commercial industry.	The 'Dream' is the keystone of American culture. It draws together and endorses all cultural forces. The Dream can be attained through sport and is driven by the accumulation of wealth.

Table 1 A comparison of commercialism in sport in the UK and USA

- It is likely that sport and commercialism were incompatible in the UK for so long because of the determinants of an old culture. The USA's young culture, together with a desire for 'isolation' encouraged the union of sport and commercialism.
- It could be argued that modern commercial sport is encouraging a dysfunctional culture of gamesmanship, player violence and unethical practice whilst the desirable values of amateur sport are discarded.

Be aware of the following:

- Media finance can be precarious and companies have been known to collapse, for example in 2002 ITV Digital was declared bankrupt whilst owing 200 million pounds to football clubs.

- Financial risk often called 'boom or bust' in the UK, is the underpinning factor of American capitalism.
- The withdrawal of media finance can also occur in the UK because of the traditional system of promotion and relegation.
- Relegation in UK is now a serious business involving the loss of media revenue and a reduced demand for merchandising.
- By contrast, in the USA relegation is not a part of the professional sports scene.
- The RFU was initially reluctant to accept professionalism and the ethos of commercialism. This is because the game had roots in the amateur ethos of the public school system and was regarded as a middle class preserve.

- The RFU is now a highly commercialised sport of national and global significance.
- Rugby League readily accepted professionalism. This is because the game has working class roots in the areas of England formerly associated with heavy industry.
- At the commencement of the 2009 season, the UK based Super League (Rugby League) adopted the American model and abolished the policy of relegation.
- Cricket has adopted a Twenty20 version of the game. This faster, shorter and more intensive form of the game has immediate entertainment appeal and coloured uniforms add to the spectacle.

SOCIAL DETERMINANTS AFFECTING SPORT IN THE UK AND USA

Both in the UK and USA access to sport is determined by three factors;

1. **Opportunity** – the chance to take part or to achieve the highest levels in sport. Chance may be determined by time and money.

2. **Provision** – having the conditions, equipment and facilities to participate or reach the top in sport.

3. **Esteem** – confidence is a determining factor in the decision to participate and to strive for the top levels in sport.

The social values that underpin the organisation of the UK and USA societies are indicated in Table 5. Comparisons have been paired to indicate similarities and differences but sometimes a direct relationship has been difficult to establish.

Social values

- In the western world the notion of democracy is believed to be good and is celebrated both in the UK and USA.
- Arguably, even the most democratic system cannot give a fair and equal opportunity to all people, for example the hierarchical class system of UK and the WASP domination in USA could be linked with opportunity in sport.

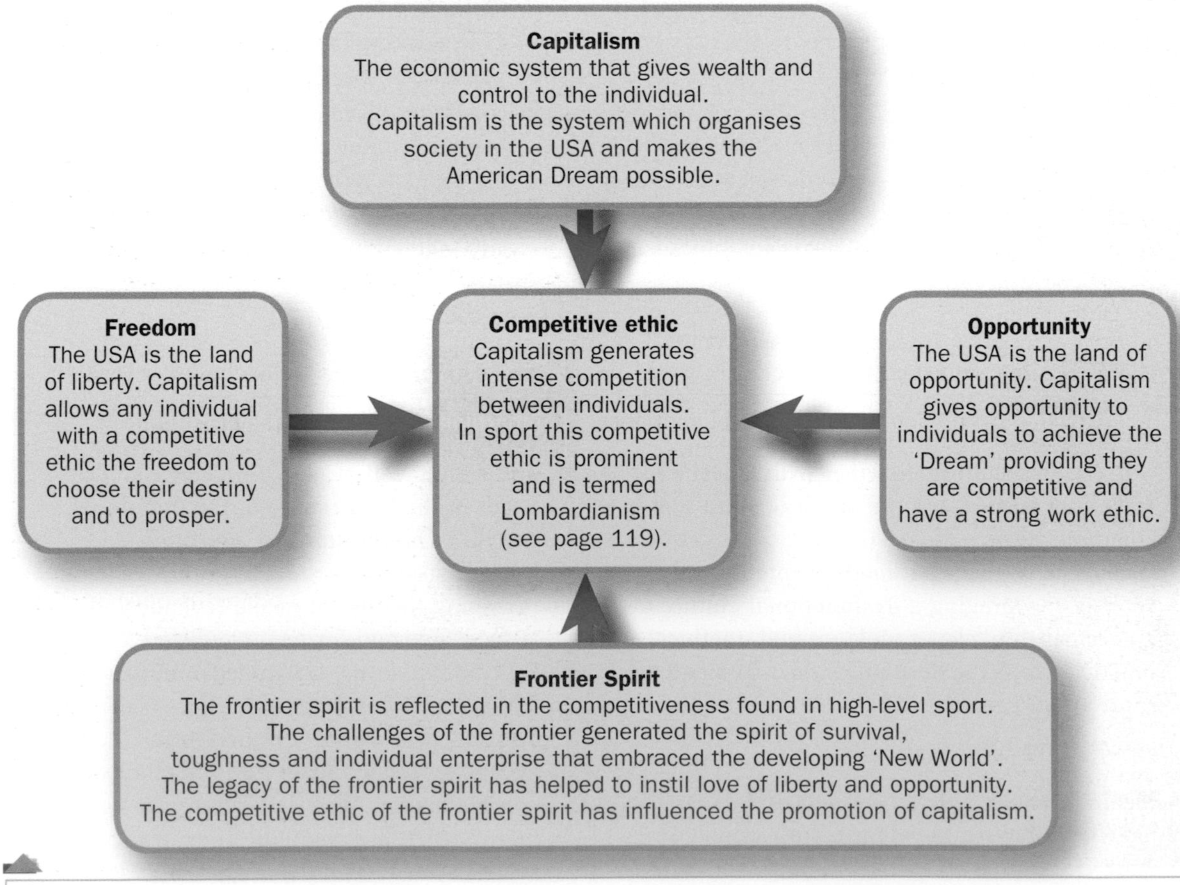

Capitalism
The economic system that gives wealth and control to the individual.
Capitalism is the system which organises society in the USA and makes the American Dream possible.

Freedom
The USA is the land of liberty. Capitalism allows any individual with a competitive ethic the freedom to choose their destiny and to prosper.

Competitive ethic
Capitalism generates intense competition between individuals. In sport this competitive ethic is prominent and is termed Lombardianism (see page 119).

Opportunity
The USA is the land of opportunity. Capitalism gives opportunity to individuals to achieve the 'Dream' providing they are competitive and have a strong work ethic.

Frontier Spirit
The frontier spirit is reflected in the competitiveness found in high-level sport.
The challenges of the frontier generated the spirit of survival, toughness and individual enterprise that embraced the developing 'New World'.
The legacy of the frontier spirit has helped to instil love of liberty and opportunity.
The competitive ethic of the frontier spirit has influenced the promotion of capitalism.

Fig 6.1 Flow chart shows the link between the frontier spirit, the competitive ethic, the American Dream and capitalism

American society, in addition to the hegemonic and pluralistic view, was organised on the basis of ethnic groups. Ethnic minority groups have a place on the hierarchy, as depicted in the list opposite (one being high status, and six being low).

1. WASP
2. Ethnic Europeans
3. African Americans
4. Mexicans & Puerto Ricans
5. Vietnamese
6. Native American Indians

UK		USA	
Value	**Explanation**	**Social Value**	**Explanation**
Democracy	The right to freedom. It involves the right of free speech and expression.	**Land of Opportunity**	The American Dream is associated with individuality and opportunity. Equal opportunity or the chance to achieve is available to all.
Teamwork	Working as part of a team has been a traditional British value since the Empire and the incorporation of team games in the Public Schools system.	**Pluralism**	Describes a group ethos. This group comprises the vast majority of Americans who believe that liberty and justice are equally available to all Americans.
Individuality	The value of the individual is important in the UK and underpins democracy. The mixed economy of the UK places a greater emphasis on teamwork than does the USA capitalist economy.	**Hegemony**	Describes a group ethos. This is the group who has the power to influence and dominate USA society. This group comprises a small minority of the wealthiest people in the USA.
Fair play	A sense of fair play is central to the British sporting ethos and the participation ethic continues to over ride the 'win at all cost' ethic that is the mainstream prevalence in the USA.	**Stacking**	The organisation of society on the basis of mainstream culture and ethnicity.
Centrality	Centrality does not exist as a common term in the UK. The concept however, remains in evidence. Ethnic players now occupy decision making positions in football but rarely appear in this capacity in either rugby code or cricket.	**Centrality**	Refers to the central role in the major American sports that is often given to players from the WASP mainstream culture.
Competitiveness	Winning is of increasing importance at professional level since the advent of commercial sport.	**Lombardian ethic**	Is the win at all cost ethic. It links with competitiveness and capitalism
Participation	Emphasis is placed on participation rather than competitive elitism.	**Counter culture ethic**	This approach has an anti-competitive focus and emphasises the intrinsic benefits which can be derived from participation.
		Radical ethic	A winning outcome is important, as this is a mark of achievement. However the process of arriving at achievement is most important.
Discrimination	Both countries are cosmopolitan societies and both are striving to overcome discrimination.		

Table 5 A comparison of social values between the UK and the USA

- The WASP mainstream culture is the central controlling dominant culture whilst the ethnic minority groups are stacked in order of status and power.
- The terms stacking and centrality are applied to the correlation between racial background and the positions of players in prominent American team sports.
- UK society was at one time organised on a clear structure based on social class. Class barriers are less clearly defined in the twenty first century.
- Both in the UK and the USA the structure and organisation of society is less clearly defined in contemporary society.

The changing structure of USA society has significantly encouraged the sporting success of African American ethnic minority groups.

PHYSICAL EDUCATION AND SCHOOL SPORT IN THE UK AND THE USA

The central support by government in the UK of Physical Education and its consequential place in National Curriculum has increased the status and helped the development of the subject. Conversely, a system given totally to decentralised control allows School Boards of individual schools in the USA to devalue Physical Education and so eliminate it from the curriculum.

Kitemarking for school Physical Education

Kitemarking for School Physical Education involves a scheme to reward schools who are delivering The PE, School Sport and Young People (PESSYP) strategy to a particularly high standard. There are three Kitemark awards:

1. Activemark: an award for Primary Schools
2. Sportsmark: an award for Secondary Schools
3. Sports Partnershipmark: an award for achievement across the School Sport Partnership

Strategies to promote Physical Education in the USA

- Physical Education for Progress (PEP): aims to reverse the decline and improve the quality of Physical Education
- Adapted Physical Programmes: involves Special Needs provision.
- Title IX Government legislation: addresses gender equality in Physical education and Sport

	Physical Education in the UK	Physical Education in the USA
Status	PE is secure as a curriculum subject and is compulsory for all up to the age of 16 years.	Daily PE is an insecure curriculum subject as it is being withdrawn in a significant number of States.
Status	High status.	Questionable status.
Control	The government determines core curriculum.	The School Board controls the curriculum.
Administration	Administration is traditionally decentralised but central government determines the core curriculum. Schools and teachers have retained a degree of autonomy.	Administration is decentralised with the individual States having supervisory control. There is a strong tradition of school and teacher autonomy.
Value	PE is an integral part of the core curriculum and is perceived as an essential educational experience.	PE is considered to have limited educational value. It is furthermore, believed to be financially uneconomic.
Value	PE continues to be a subject of value despite the increased accountability that has been placed on schools to achieve high academic results.	The 'No Child Left Behind' Act has increased the accountability that has been placed on schools to achieve high academic results. This act has had a negative impact on PE.

Table 6 A comparison of Physical Education between the UK and USA

STRATEGIES TO PROMOTE PE AND SCHOOL SPORT IN THE UK

Strand	The strategy promoted by the strand
Sports colleges	Sports colleges receive additional government funding to increase the opportunities for young people to become involved in sport. Sports colleges link with other local schools to form School Sports Partnerships.
School Sports Partnerships (SSPs)	The School Sports Partnerships strategy brings together individual Sports Colleges with groups or 'clusters' of schools. The principle aims of SSPs are to increase participation, promote excellence and develop sporting links in the wider community.
Professional development	The professional development of teachers and coaches involves providing teachers with training to improve the quality of their lesson delivery.
Step into sport	This strategy provides a clear framework to enable young people aged 14–19 years to be involved with sports leadership.
Club links	Club links aim to strengthen the associations between schools and sports clubs.
Gifted and talented	This strategy is designed to help young people with identified ability develop core skills that are the basis of all sports.
Sporting playgrounds	This strategy involves the development of primary school playgrounds to promote play and physical activity.
Swimming	Via this strategy, the teaching of swimming is being increasingly promoted in primary schools, not only as a healthy activity but as part of a healthy lifestyle.
High quality Physical Education and School Sport (PESS)	PESS involves guidance as to how a school can improve the quality of Physical Education.

Table 7 The PE, School Sport and Young People (PESSYP) strategy has nine strands or priorities

OUTDOOR EDUCATION IN THE UK

The term outdoor education implies a formal process of conveying educational values. This takes the form of teaching physical skills and facilitating personal and social development in the outdoor natural environment.

- In the UK outdoor education is a part of the National Curriculum.
- Outdoor education is organised by the school.

In the UK, the benefits for children indicated in Fig 6.2 are believed to arise from outdoor education.

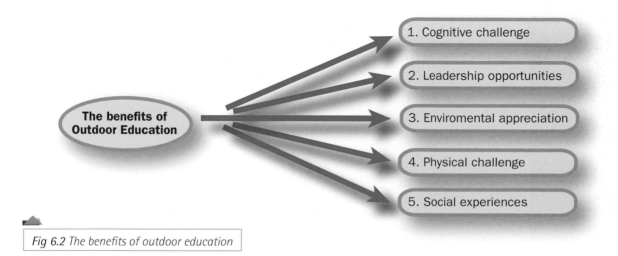

The benefits of Outdoor Education

1. Cognitive challenge
2. Leadership opportunities
3. Enviromental appreciation
4. Physical challenge
5. Social experiences

Fig 6.2 The benefits of outdoor education

There are drawbacks that make it difficult for schools to commit fully to outdoor education. Such drawbacks are identified below:

- **Finance** – the delivery of an outdoor education programme is often expensive.
- **Location** – a suitable natural environment may be a considerable distance from school.
- **Health & safety** – many schools are concerned that outdoor adventure activities present problems relating to health and safety legislation.
- **Pupil absence** – important lessons may well be missed when a pupil is engaged in outdoor adventure activities.
- **Teacher cover** – in their absence teachers supervising outdoor education courses will need to have lessons covered by colleagues.

OUTDOOR EDUCATION IN THE USA

- Since the mid twentieth-century, Summer Camps (sometimes called Camp Schools) for young people have increased significantly.

- Summer Camps take place in the summer vacation for durations of a few days or up to eight weeks.
- Summer Camps are generally not organised by schools.
- There are three classifications of camps.
  1. State sponsored Camps – these enable less wealthy children to enjoy outdoor adventure experiences.
  2. Camps sponsored by business, ethnic and religious groups.
  3. Commercial camps – these can be very lavish and extremely expensive.

Fig 6.3 outlines the benefits of summer camps.

Inter-school sport in the UK and Inter-mural sport in the USA

Table 8 below indicates similarities and differences that exist between the UK and USA on the basis of organisation, status and ethos of school sport.

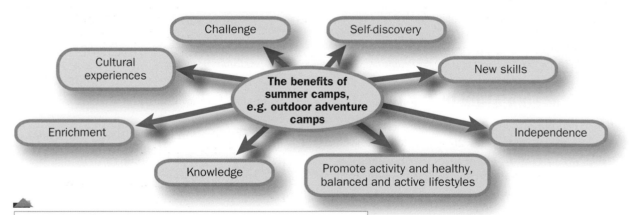

Fig 6.3 The benefits of summer camps, e.g. outdoor adventure camps

	Inter-school sport in the UK	Inter-mural sport in the USA
Organisation	Competitions and leagues are administered by several agencies, for example teachers organising 'friendly' fixtures, local school leagues and NGB competitions.	The State High School Athletic Association (SHSAA), which is a national advisory body, has branches in each state and controls inter-mural athletic competition.
	Frequently organised as extra–curricular activities after school.	Takes place in the evenings to attract spectators.
	Usually takes place on school fields or premises.	Played in the high school stadium.
	There may be some grants or donations from former pupils but schools tend not to be reliant on them.	Alumni donation (financial support from former pupils) helps to finance teams.
	Gate money is not taken and is not a source of income.	'Gate money' is an important source of revenue.

continued

	Inter-school sport in the UK	Inter-mural sport in the USA
Status	Some sponsorship from businesses may be available but sponsorship is not widespread.	Heavy reliance on sponsorship and Alumni donation.
	The PE teacher is often in charge of the organisation and coaching of teams.	The coach is in charge although they may operate below the status of the Athletic Director.
	Some schools and colleges have developed academies of sport but these tend to be associated with professional sports clubs.	USA high schools are perceived as centres of sporting excellence.
	Physical Education is considered to be of higher status to sport.	Sport has high status and is considered to be more important than Physical Education.
	Some University scholarships are awarded but it is not common in UK.	The best players are awarded scholarships from Colleges (Universities).
	School sport is not organised to reflect the professional sports scene.	School sport is a direct reflection of the professional sports scene.
	There is little media attention given to UK inter-school sport.	Considerable media attention.
	Sport in UK schools does not aspire to become a business.	Sport is very expensive with media, sponsorship and large crowds. High school sport is organised as a business.
Ethos	Winning is not of overriding importance. Participation is considered more important than winning.	The Lombardian win at all cost ethic prevails.
	The teacher is employed on what is usually a permanent contract.	The coach is employed on the basis of a contract that is termed 'hire and fire'.
	Sport tends to be inclusive and available to all children.	Sport tends to be exclusive and elitist.

Table 8 A comparison of Inter-school and Inter-mural sport in the UK and the USA

- It could be argued that inter-school sport in the UK carries significant educational value because it aims to provide the individual with a holistic experience as part of the mission of the school.
- Conversely, it may be said that inter-mural sport in the USA is an end in itself, focusing on elitism and the development of the profession athlete.
- It may appear that in the UK standards in the delivery of inter-school sport are erratic and this seriously inhibits the development of young sports talent.
- In the USA, the high-school is perceived as a centre of sports excellence and sporting achievement is an important part of its mission. This approach, it could be argued, is better for the production of elite athletes.

PARTICIPATION RATES IN SPORT IN THE USA AND THE UK

Health, fitness and obesity levels in developed countries are a growing concern. These concerns are global but both the UK and America are experiencing major problems.

Mass participation

- Mass participation rates in the UK are higher than those in the USA.
- Mass participation in sports related physical activity is not high in the USA.
- On both sides of the Atlantic, individual activities (e.g. swimming, keep fit, yoga etc.) show higher participation rates than team games.
- On the whole more men participate in the UK than women and this mirrors the trend in the USA.

HEALTH AND FITNESS

- Participation rates in the UK may be higher than those in the USA because of cultural differences.
- In the UK the ethos of taking part prevails; in the USA winning is important.
- The approach in the UK reflects the traditions of amateur commitment and team involvement which appear to encourage participation.

UK	USA
Statistics indicate that almost 30% of young people are overweight. Of this percentage, 17% of boys and 14% of girls are obese.	15% of American 6-19 year-olds are regarded as clinically obese.
Of all adults in the UK 38% are considered overweight whilst almost 25% have been diagnosed as obese.	In America, 40 million people are considered obese.
UK fitness levels have reached an all time low.	In the total population, 75% of Americans are not reaching basic activity recommendations and 25% of people in this category are completely sedentary.
It would appear that the sedentary lifestyle adopted by the urban population in America during the 1950s, is now taking effect in the UK.	

Table 9 A comparison between sport participation rates in the UK and USA

- Swimming and fitness activities tend to be more popular with women.
- As in the USA, younger people in the UK are more likely to participate in activities. That involvement decreases with age. Participation is significantly reduced after the age of 45.
- In the USA wealth is an important determinant in sports participation.
- The only major game to feature in the top ten sports for participation in the UK was Association Football. In the USA basketball was the only major game represented in the top ten participation sports.
- A 'gym' and 'jogging' culture has been evident in the USA since the 1950s and statistics indicate that engagement in fitness activities is increasing.
- There is a significant increase in gym membership in the UK.
- In 1980 there were fewer than 200 gyms in the UK. In 2008 there were 6,000. The USA 'gym culture' has influenced this trend.

Both countries are aiming to promote mass participation in order to ensure lifelong involvement and healthy lifestyles.

- The tradition of the amateur club as it is understood in the UK does not exist in the USA.
- In the UK a person may elect to join an institutionalised sports club.
- In the USA the emphasis is placed on the individual or groups of friends to form teams.
- These friendship groups can choose to compete in competitions and leagues.
- The Midnight Basketball Leagues are an example of this in operation.

Table 10 below outlines strategies and organisations that promote mass participation in the UK and USA.

Strategy or organisation UK	Explanation
Sportsmatch	Clubs or community facility organisations provide initial investment. The sum raised is then doubled by a grant.
Special interest groups	Groups that tend not to participate in sport are targeted by Sport England.

Strategy or organisation USA	Explanation
Midnight Leagues	The organisation of sports on inner-city asphalt playgrounds during unsociable hours. Basketball is the major game.
Inter-mural sports	School sport that involves schools playing against each other in organised sports competitions. High school sport has high status.

continued

Sport England	This organization, along with other Home Country sports councils such as The Sports Council for Wales, promotes mass participation.	**Intra-mural sports**	Involves recreational sports that take place within the high school. Activities may involve leagues and are open to all students who form their own teams.
National Governing Bodies	These agencies receive central funding to encourage young people to take up sport. E.g. the Rugby Football Union employs local and regional development officers to promote participation.	**Little League**	Takes responsibility for the organisation of junior sports that take place in the community.
Local initiatives	These initiatives are important community sport providers, in the Greater Manchester area 'Sport For All' centres organise basketball, netball badminton and five-a-side football for all abilities and age groups.	**The Amateur Athletic Union**	Takes responsibility for the organisation of sports leagues and competitions. They also administer the National Youth Fitness Programme as a part of the Presidents Challenge.

Table 10 A comparison of strategies and organisations that promote mass participation in the UK and the USA

> **Need to know more?** For more information on the physical education and school sport and mass participation in the USA and UK see Chapter 6, pages 121–141, in the OCR A2 PE Student Book.

PATHWAYS TO PROFESSIONAL SPORT IN THE UK AND USA

The major comparison between the conventional pathways to professional sport in the UK and USA are identified in table 11 below.

UK	USA
Sports identified as case studies, e.g. Association Football, cricket, rugby union and rugby league, tend to have governing body schemes to develop talent.	The major pathway into professional sport in the USA is through the education system.
Individual clubs have development teams and academies to identify and generate potential professional players.	The exception to this pathway defined by the education system is baseball. Baseball tends to have development links associated with the professional clubs.
Olympic performers are developed through the sports institutes of the UK and supported by 'UK Sport'.	Olympic performers are also developed through the education system. There is not an American equivalent of UK Sport.
A performance funding package of £300 million was requested by 'UK Sport' to maximise achievement in the 2012 Olympic Games. Finance is provided by the Government via the National Lottery.	The USA government provides only a small amount of financial support for Olympic excellence.

Table 11 A comparison of pathways to professional sport in the UK and USA

UK Sport

- UK Sport is the organisation with the overall responsibility for producing sporting excellence in the UK.
- The ambition of UK Sport is to achieve fourth place in the 2012 Olympic Games medal table.
- UK Sport has a clear philosophy that Olympic and Paralympic sport can no longer be trusted to enthusiastic and talented amateurs.
- UK Sport ensures that athletic performance, coaching and organisation structure have a professional focus.

Sports Institutes in the UK

- 'Sports Institutes in the UK' are a network of centres that are dedicated to providing support to elite athletes.
- The Sports Institutes have instigated the successes of Team UK in Olympic and Paralympic competition, but not all sports find it necessary to take advantage of the institutes.
- Non-Olympic sports, such as cricket, have their own governing body pathways leading towards professional status.

There are four devolved Home Country Sports Institutes:

- The English Institute of Sport (EIS)
- The Scottish Institute of Sport (SIS)
- The Welsh Institute of Sport
- The Sports Institute of Northern Ireland (SINI).

UK Sport is responsible for the strategic direction of the institute network with a mission to support elite athletes. The supportive services provided by the institutes are:

- sport-specific coaching programmes
- physical conditioning programmes
- sport science and sports medicine
- physiotherapy
- nutrition advice
- performance analysis and planning
- vocational, educational and lifestyle advice.

Pathways to professional sport in the USA

- The high school performer is given a scholarship grant (a financial package) from the College (University).
- Scholarships are available in most major sports and under Title IX legislation women are funded equally to men.
- College sport provides the progressive step into professional and international sport.

Fig 6.4 Pathways to professional sport in the USA

- The 'Big Four' American sports are also successful commercial businesses at collegiate level and make vast profits from sponsors and media interest.
- Talented and well-trained players, often fresh from high school, provide a high standard of sports entertainment to spectators who pay high admission prices
- Three major athletic associations administer collegiate sport. The largest and oldest of these is the National Collegiate Athletic Association (NCAA).

Controversy has always been associated with the sports scholarship system:

- College administrators have enrolled students who are excellent sports performers but academically under-qualified for degree courses.
- Leniency in recruitment enables a college to compete in sport and remain at the highest levels to sustain commercial viability.
- The NCAA has stated that 20 per cent of football and basketball players enter university on 'special admit' programmes.

Pathways to professional sport in the UK and USA

Is it good that 'special admit' programmes allow more people to enter university in the USA? These programmes are difficult to justify as they appear to be an exclusive vehicle for outstanding sports people with low academic ability to access a University education; the USA system may not be serving the best interests of the individual.

- Problems in College sport arise when coaches and directors, in their bid for success, exert excessive control over students.
- When this 'win at all cost' ethos arises, sport loses its educational value.
- When media rights are involved, the academic progress of the student athlete is considered secondary to financial profit.
- Athletic directors, coaches, trainers, publicity directors and support staff make a good living from collegiate sport. Some Athletic Directors and Coaches earn over $500,000 per year and can increase this through sponsorship and TV contracts.
- The student athlete does not get paid. It is against association rules for a player to receive any financial benefits.
- Far from being a 'free ride', a scholarship is in reality a binding contract to play sport for the college teams.
- A student athlete may have to commit to as many as 50 hours of sport per week under a scholarship agreement.

Students remain compliant with this system for the following reasons:

- It is exciting to play in the top flight in front of large crowds. The College Rose Bowl attracts 90,000 spectators.
- There is kudos and social status for the athlete at a major university.

- Most athletes have been conditioned from early high school through the domination of sports leadership. They willingly accept the tough minded, disciplined approach and are dependent on the ethos of team conformity.
- The self-esteem of the athlete grows in direct proportion to athletic prowess.
- College athletes become single minded in their ambition to be successful. This conforming approach is termed 'pragmatic role acceptance'
- The Pro-draft system focuses on selecting the best college players

It would appear that the institutes of sport in the UK make a genuine attempt to help talented athletes to reach their potential and that the best interests of the athlete are central to this mission. There is evidence to suggest that the student athlete at a USA university is subject to exploitation. It is alleged that student athletes are little more than unpaid labourers in a multi-million university sports industry.

Equality and discrimination in UK and USA

The table below outlines key factors that you need to be aware of, as they apply to discrimination of ethnic people in USA sport.

> **Need to know more?** For more information on equality and discrimination and sport and the pursuit of excellence in the UK see Chapter 6, pages 139–141, in the OCR A2 PE Student Book.

Key Factor	Explanation
Centrality	Centrality refers to positions with decision-making responsibilities, for example the pitcher in baseball and the quarter back in grid iron football. These positions are often the preserve of white mainstream players
Stacking	Stacking, in relation to sport (not as it relates to the organisation of USA society), refers to the selection of players belonging to ethnic minority groups into peripheral positions. These positions often require considerable athleticism but minimal strategic influence.
Tokenism	Tokenism is the practice which is less common today, of hiring only a small group of people from ethnic minority groups to give the impression of a non-discriminatory equal opportunities policy. For example, many USA sports teams feel the need to include one ethnic member in the team just to keep the media happy.
White Flight	White players have withdrawn from basketball. The game is increasingly perceived as belonging to African Americans.
Glass Ceiling	This term indicates a division between two layers of society. The people beneath the glass can see their ambition and the position which they wish to occupy.

Table 12 Key factors that apply to discrimination of ethnic people in USA sport

CASE STUDY OF THE 'BIG FOUR' AMERICAN SPORTS

Baseball	
Origins of the game	• Boys played early forms of baseball known as goal ball or rounders during the colonial period. • It became the game of the city in the nineteenth-century and was played mainly by the youth of the working classes. Very few schools and colleges elected to play baseball as adults tended to disapprove of the game.
Nature of the game	• Baseball is a game of impact comprising hard striking and lots of energetic fielding. This results in bursts of action and limitless quick sprinting. There is very little dead time in the game. • Baseball was preferred to cricket, which by contrast lacks the required sensationalism to satisfy the fast pace of American life. • There are no drawn games and this is reflective of a zero-sum ethos.
Sport as an industry	• The scale of Major League Baseball (MLB) as a twenty-first-century business is immense. The MLB is organised as a business cartel. • Eighty million people attend World Series matches averaging 32,000 per game. The commercial status of the game is reflected in the commercial value of the New York Yankees baseball club which is in access of $1 billion.
The relationship between sport, sponsorship and the media ('Golden Triangle')	• Baseball has been known as the 'national pastime' for over a hundred years and is by far the most popular game in the USA. • Baseball was the first USA sport to attract media attention and lucrative sponsorship deals. • The relationship between the sport media and sponsorship was greatly intensified by the 'Roone Revolution' of sport broadcasting in the early 1960s. • The 'World Series' is the major Baseball competition. • The title 'World Series' is a marketing term. It is misleading because the only contestants are American teams.
Gridiron Football	
Origins of the game	• American gridiron football was adapted from English rugby football, which toward the end of the nineteenth-century had a structured club system having been founded in the UK public schools. • The origin of American football lies in the Ivy League Colleges notably Princeton, Colombia, Harvard and Yale.
Nature of the game	• American gridiron football is a high-impact collision game. The rules encourage physical confrontation and play tends to be aggressive. • The protection of a helmet and padding tends to dehumanise the players and encourage physical contact. • The action is sensational and intense. The inclusion of 'time out' periods and tactical substitutions increases the intensity. • There are no drawn games and this is reflective of a zero-sum ethos
Sport as an industry	• The National Football League (NFL) is organised as a profit-making industry and operates as a business cartel. • As a business enterprise the NFL is more lucrative than the Premiership Football League in the UK. E.g. the team value of the Dallas Cowboys who are one of the prominent football teams is $1.1 billion and they were bought in 1989 for $150 million.

continued

Gridiron Football *continued*	
The relationship between sport, sponsorship and the media ('Golden Triangle')	• The reliance of gridiron on the media and sponsorship is exemplified in the 'Superbowl'. This is the show piece event of American football in the twenty-first-century. • With viewing figures of 130 million, the event commands the highest television audience in America. In addition to the spectacle of play, popular singers and musicians perform during pre-game and half-time ceremonies. • Television commercial breaks are numerous and thirty seconds of advertising time costs $2.5 million.
Basketball	
Origins of the game	• Basketball was invented in 1891 by James Naismith at the private Springfield YMCA Training School and was instantly successful in high schools and colleges. • Basketball was rooted in white educational institutions, e.g. schools and colleges.
Nature of the game	• Basketball is a fast game in which play can move quickly from defence to offence. • Action is intense and this is made possible by the small number of players involved on a relatively small playing area. • The inclusion of 'time out' periods and tactical substitutions increases the intensity. • Sensation is evident in quick passing movements and shooting. • Scoring is frequent. • There are no drawn games and this is reflective of a zero-sum ethos.
Sport as an industry	• Basketball teams make up 13% of franchised sport in America. The combined revenue of the thirty National Basketball Association (NBA) teams is approximately $3.5 billion and rising quickly. • The NBA is organised as a business cartel. • The Chicago Bulls business was bought in 1985 for $16 million but now has a team value of $500 million with annual revenue of approximately $140 million.
The relationship between sport, sponsorship and the media ('Golden Triangle')	• Like all 'Big Four' sports basketball has adapted to become part of the sports entertainment industry. • It is fast, exciting and easy to understand. It has therefore considerable media appeal. • Commercial advertising fits easily into the many breaks. Sponsorship is therefore attracted to this spectacle. • Like baseball, basketball is a game of the inner-city. The popularity of the game has been further increased by the creation of 'Midnight Leagues'. Midnight Leagues have spectator appeal and are therefore beginning to attract media attention and commercial interest.
Ice hockey	
Origins of the game	• Ice hockey was adapted from 'ice hurly' by British soldiers serving in Canada in 1850. • The rules were unified by McGill University in Montreal. • The game was adopted by the USA in 1893. • Ice hockey in its contemporary form has origins in the collegiate system and the NCAA inaugurated an ice hockey national tournament for universities in 1948.

continued

Ice hockey *continued*	
Nature of the game	• Ice hockey is a high-impact collision game. The rules encourage physical confrontation and play tends to be aggressive. • The ice rink encourages high speeds and the confined playing areas increases physical contact. • The protection of a helmet and padding tend to dehumanise the players and encourage aggressive play. • The nature of the hockey stick also encourages aggression and violent play. • The action is sensational and intense. The inclusion of 'time out' periods and tactical substitutions increases the intensity. • Scoring is frequent there are no drawn games and this is reflective of a zero-sum ethos.
Sport as an industry	• Ice hockey joined the 'Big Three' in the late 1960's when the 'franchise market' enabled the major Canadian teams to relocate to America. • Further popularity was stimulated by the 1980 Gold medal Olympic success. • Due to the operation of sports franchises twenty of the twenty six National Hockey League (NHL) teams that exist today are located in USA. The remaining six have venues in Canada. • Canadian players in the NHL are 'contracted in' and outnumber American players. • The Carolina Hurricanes were the 2008 holders of the Stanley Cup, the oldest professional trophy in America. • The club was bought in 1994 for $48 million and has a team value of $144 million. The total attendance for all NHL matches is approximately 20 million people.
The relationship between sport, sponsorship and the media ('Golden Triangle')	• Although ice hockey was the last sport to join the 'Big Four' it has developed considerable spectator and media appeal. • The game is therefore attractive to commercial sponsorship. • The commercial operation of Ice Hockey is similar to baseball, gridiron and basketball.

Table 13 Key points of the 'Big Four' American sports

> **Need to know more?** For more information on the Big Four American sports see Chapter 6, pages 143–146, in the OCR A2 PE Student Book.

CHECK

If you are satisfied with your knowledge and understanding, tick off the sections that you have revised so far. If you are not satisfied then revisit those sections and refer to the pages in the *Need to know more?* features.

- ☐ Describe the cultural context of sport in the USA and the UK.
- ☐ Describe PE and school sport in the USA and the UK.
- ☐ Discuss mass participation in sport in the USA and the UK.
- ☐ Discuss sport and the pursuit of excellence in the USA and the UK
- ☐ Consider how to critically evaluate the influence of the cultural context on all of the above.

TRUE OR FALSE?

1. Historically the USA adopted a policy of isolation which influenced their sports culture.

2. Marginalisation of UK sports in the USA meant that sports, like cricket, could only be played in coastal areas.

3. Frontierism (a pioneer spirit, individualism, survival) is reflected in contemporary USA sports.

4. The USA's 'land of opportunity' culture means that everyone has the chance to buy land.

5. The American Dream influences sports. The 'Dream' has roots in frontierism and is made possible through Capitalism.

6. Title IX is the name of the USA schools Physical Education curriculum.

7. In the UK and the USA, Physical Education is higher in status than Inter-mural sport.

8. The American Midnight Leagues encourage community participation in Basketball.

9. Tokenism is the process of paying professional performers in tokens that are cashed when careers end.

10. The 'Golden Triangle' reflects the economic system known as capitalism. It has facilitated the growth of the 'Big Four' USA sports as a commercial business.

EXAM PRACTICE

1. Evaluate the development of one case study sport from the UK and one from the USA. Your answer should include cultural and commercial factors. *(20 marks)*

2. In the UK and the USA strategies are in place to improve national fitness levels of young people by increasing participation in sport and physical activity.
   Outline the opportunities in the USA that enable young people to participate in sport and physical activity. State one similar opportunity in the UK *(4 marks)*

3. Compare the provision for inter-school sport in the UK and in the USA. Your comparison should include the organisation, status and ethos as well as an evaluation of provision of school sport in both countries. *(20 marks)*

4. The UK followed the USA in making professional sport into a commercial business. By referring to historical and social factors, explain why the commercialisation of professional sport was quicker to develop in the USA than in UK. *(6 marks)*

5. Compare the status and value of Physical Education in the UK and USA. *(5 marks)*

See page 258 for answers

CHAPTER 7

Comparative study of Australia and the UK

CHAPTER OVERVIEW

By the end of this chapter you should have knowledge and understanding of:

- the cultural context of sport in Australia and the UK
- PE and school sport in Australia and the UK
- mass participation in sport in Australia and the UK
- sport and the pursuit of excellence in Australia and the UK
- how to critically evaluate the influence of the cultural context on all of the above.

THE CULTURAL CONTEXT OF AUSTRALIA

Australia is believed to have a 'sporting obsession'. The high status given to sport is reflected in the schools Physical Education programmes, commitment to mass participation and pursuit of sporting excellence.

To understand such prolific involvement in sport it is necessary to consider Australia in a cultural context and compare this with the UK.

HISTORICAL DETERMINANTS AS THEY RELATE TO UK AND AUSTRALIA

The sociological history of the UK extends much further than Australia and this difference has strongly influenced the ambitions, values and structure of the respective societies. These factors in turn have impacted on the approach taken by Australia toward sporting activities

> **Need to know more?** For more information on historical determinants of Australia and how they compare with the UK, see Chapter 7, pages 152–154, in the OCR A2 PE Student Book.

UK	Australia
The UK has an old culture which has evolved from ancient origins.	Modern Australia is regarded as a new culture and began as a prison colony in 1788. Free settlement began in the eighteenth-century.
In the nineteenth-century, a clearly defined class system based on hereditary privilege existed in Britain, the legacy of which exists today.	The name 'currency' was given to the children of the convicts. The currency claimed to be the first generation of true Australians. Privilege was not a feature of this society. This was the beginning of the 'social melting pot'.
Class determined income, lifestyle and most significantly, sporting opportunities.	Australia did not have a rigid class structure that determined lifestyle and sporting opportunities. This began the 'land of the fair go' concept.

continued

UK	Australia
The greatest developmental influence on UK sport came from the reformed English public school system. It was largely through the impact of the public schools that in the period 1863 to 1888, sporting traditions and etiquette were reflected throughout the British Empire.	From the outset, sports associated with the UK were readily adopted by the first generation of native born Australians. The 'currency lads' engaged in sports competitions with the 'sterling' who were the colonials or 'free settlers'.
The power and prestige emanating from the British Empire had a global impact. The British empire was the largest in history.	Australia was part of the Empire. The UK was considered the 'Motherland'.
The success of the Empire was the benchmark against which UK national prestige and progress was measured. Sport helped to establish UK traditions in the Empire and in turn, the Empire was to influence the development of sport both in the UK and across the world.	Australian victory against the UK continues to be highly significant. Historically the defeat of the Motherland was regarded as a benchmark against which national progress could be measured.
During the nineteenth-century the UK had clear divisions between amateur and professional players. The English 'gentleman amateur' belonged to the upper-classes. This notion had strong links with the public school system.	The association between social class and sporting status was less rigid in Australia. The values associated with 'land of the fair go' and egalitarianism became dominant. These values were more tolerant of professional sport.
This clear division was evident in all the UK sports identified in the case studies, for example cricket, association football, and both codes of rugby.	Australian sporting traditions, cricket in particular, could not copy or tolerate the class divisions found in English sport.

Table 1 A comparison of historical determinants between the UK and Australia

GEOGRAPHICAL DETERMINANTS OF AUSTRALIA AND HOW THEY COMPARE TO THE UK

	UK	Australia
Size	The UK is a relatively small country and this helped communication and travel during the development of organized sport in the nineteenth-century.	Australia is 32 times larger than the UK. The size of this landmass impeded the initial growth of sport during the nineteenth-century. Travel and communication had to overcome the 'tyranny of distance'.
Topography	The landscape tends to be green and rolling. Mountains do not exceed 4,000 feet and although there are National Parks and areas of outstanding natural beauty there are no areas that constitute 'genuine wilderness'. This restricts the potential for outdoor adventure.	The landscape is varied comprising coastal, scrub land, desert and upland areas exceeding 7,000 feet. There are extensive areas of 'genuine wilderness'. There is considerable potential for outdoor adventure experiences.
Climate	The UK has one climatic type termed Western Maritime. This climate tends to give warm summers and mild winters. The climate can restrict outdoor activities and does impact upon lifestyle.	The Australian climate is diverse. Temperate coastal conditions bring favourable perennial conditions conducive to outdoor participation and lifestyle. Tropical and desert conditions also prevail.

continued

	UK	Australia
Urbanisation	The population of the UK is approaching 62 million with a relatively high population density of 200 people per square mile. Major cities are close together. These urban conditions have helped to stimulate the commercialization of sport.	The population of Australia is 22 million of which 18 million live on the eastern seaboard. The population density of seven people per square mile is misleading. Australia is an urban country, for example South Sydney has 10,000 people in a square mile. These urban conditions have helped to stimulate the commercialisation of sport.
Transport	In the UK, distance did not present a major problem to the development of sporting activities. Easy access to away fixtures through the expanding rail system of the nineteenth-century and sophisticated road and air networks of the twentieth-century have helped to develop and promote commercial sport in the UK.	In Australia distance did present a major problem to sports development. Journeys were undertaken by sea and river. The rail system was begun in the mid-nineteenth-century. Today, Australia has developed a sophisticated transport system. A highly efficient road system incorporating state and urban highways connects all major centres. Airports for internal air travel are accessible and railways link suburbs to the cities. This has helped the promotion of commercial sport in Australia.

Table 2 A comparison of geographical determinants between the UK and Australia

> **Need to know more?** For more information on comparative geographical determinants, see Chapter 7, pages 154–157, in the OCR A2 PE Student Book.

GOVERNMENT POLICIES AS THEY RELATE TO UK AND AUSTRALIA

UK	Australia
The Monarch is head of state and the Prime Minister is head of government. Overarching power is exercised by the UK Government and devolved governments of Scotland, Wales and Northern Ireland are autonomous bodies.	The Monarch of England is Chief of State. Australia remains part of the British Commonwealth but was granted independence in 1901. An elected Prime Minister and a Federal parliament govern Australia.
Through local government, the UK is to an extent decentralised.	The constitution of Australia places local government outside federal jurisdiction. A strong adherence to decentralisation is evident giving autonomy to each state.
Decentralisation is less evident in the Government's National Curriculum in schools model and in the Department for Culture, Media and Sport (DCMS)	There is no National Curriculum in Australia. Decisions about curriculum are taken at state level and to an extent, schools have autonomy.
Although not directly responsible for sports policy, the government has been more involved in sport development through the DCMS. Sport is not perceived as a 'vote catcher'.	Since 1976, the government through the Australian Sports Commission (ASC) has been central in the policies to develop sport. Sport is perceived as a government 'vote catcher'.
The UK is essentially capitalist but inclined toward a mixed economy which restricts commercial enterprise. This has limited the commercialisation of sport.	Australia has adopted a capitalist model of economy which has promoted commercialised sport since the mid 1970s.
Professional sports are becoming increasingly commercialised but are still controlled by sporting governing bodies	

Table 3 A comparison of government policies between the UK and Australia

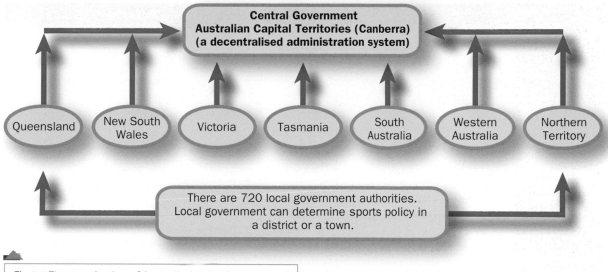

Fig 7.1 The constitution of Australia: levels of government

> **Need to know more?** For more information on comparative government policy, see Chapter 7, pages 157–158, in the OCR A2 PE Student Book.

Government policy as they relate to UK and Australia

- The centrally organised National Curriculum in the UK is good because it ensures that all pupils have the same quality of experience in Physical Education.
- However, it is possible that this framework may inhibit teaching creativity.
- Whilst the government in Australia is active in education policy, schools design their own Physical Education programmes. This autonomy promotes individual innovation.

THE COMMERCIALISATION OF SPORT AS IT RELATES TO THE UK AND AUSTRALIA

- The major professional sports of the UK are, in common with those in Australia, commercialised. They are also, in common with the USA model, part of the entertainment industry.

- Professional sport both in the UK and Australia is regarded as a corporate commodity.
- An irreversible move to commercialisation of sport in Australia began in 1977 when Kerry Packer rivalled the International Cricket Conference by signing the best players in the world to play World Series Cricket exclusively on his own television network channel.
- The Broadcasting Act of 1990 triggered the commercialisation of sport in the UK.
- As in the USA commercial model, professional sport is inseparable from the media and sponsorship from multi-national companies both in UK and Australia.

The factors that have stimulated the commercialization of sport in the UK and Australia are indicated in table 4 below.

> **Need to know more?** For more information on the commercialisation of sport in the UK and Australia, see Chapter 7, pages 159–161, in the OCR A2 PE Student Book.

	UK	Australia
Historical	• A long tradition of sport prevails in the UK. • The UK invented many major sports, e.g. association football, rugby football and cricket. • The evolution of UK sport lies in the nineteenth-century public schools and the traditions of Empire.	• There is a long tradition of sport. • Sport is an indictor of progress and an expression of national pride e.g. the 'Currency sports contests of the nineteenth-century and the Sydney Olympic Games of 2000

continued

	UK	Australia
Geographical	• Society was largely urban prior to the time when sport became fully organised, for example 1850 onwards. • A large spectator base was readily available. • The growth of the railway system from 1830 was the beginning of an efficient transport system that promoted spectator interest in sport. • Sporting venues are easily accessible.	• The society is urban. • There are densely populated cities that can supply a large spectator base. • Transport systems are diverse, efficient and sophisticated. • The tyranny of distance no longer prevails. • Sporting venues are easily accessible.
Socio – economic	• Essentially capitalist with elements of a mixed economy. • Material reward has high status in the UK society. Sport is increasingly perceived as a commodity for the consumer. • The UK is an affluent country and people have disposable income to spend on sport. • Society has access to and can afford a variety of media outlets, for example sky and digital television. • Large amounts of capital are available to build and maintain stadiums. • Naming rights are important for the purpose of sponsorship, for example Emirates Stadium, Arsenal,London and JJB (now the DW) Stadium Wigan.	• A capitalist market economy prevails. • Material reward has high status in society. • Sport is increasing perceived as a commodity for the consumer. • Australia like the UK is an affluent country. • People have disposable income to spend on sport. • Australia has access to and can afford the same media outlets that are available in the UK. • Large amounts of capital are available to build and maintain stadiums. • Naming rights are important for the purpose of sponsorship, for example Telstra dome.

Table 4 A comparison of the commercialisation of sport between the UK and Australia

SOCIAL DETERMINANTS AND EQUALITY IN THE UK AND HOW THESE COMPARE WITH AUSTRALIA

• Discrimination against minority groups in sport is evident both in the UK, for example Asian minorities, and in Australia, for example Aborigine minorities.

• A significant number of UK citizens are denied access to sport participation and the chance to excel at an elite level. By contrast, Australia appears to have been more successful with their inclusion policy. This may be because the Australian population is one-third the size of UK

As in the UK, access to sport in Australia is determined by three factors:

• **Opportunity** is having the chance to take part or to achieve the highest levels in sport. Chance may be determined by time and money.

• **Provision** refers to having the conditions, equipment and facilities to participate or reach the top in sport.

• **Esteem** indicates that confidence is a determining factor in the decision to participate and to strive for the top levels in sport.

The groups that are most likely to suffer from discrimination or social exclusion from sport in the UK and Australia are:

• the elderly
• people with disabilities
• women
• ethnic minorities.

Be aware of three initiatives instigated by the Australian government (ASC) that are designed to address equality and improve access to sport:

• **Indigenous Sport Programme** – developed to encourage indigenous people to be more active and to play sport at all levels

• **Disability Sport Programme** – aims to improve the participation opportunities for people with disability

• **Women and Sport Unit** – The ASC has assigned a department specifically to gender and sport. This department, called The Women and Sport Unit, is in charge of research and programme policy and in 2008 it awarded sports leadership grants to women.

> **Need to know more?** For more information on social determinants and equality in UK Australia see Chapter 7, pages 161–163, in the OCR A2 PE Student Book.

THE SOCIAL VALUES OF UK AND AUSTRALIA

Table 5 displays the social values of both countries side-by-side, although there is not always a direct comparison.

Social values

- The notion of democracy is the basis of the ethos of the UK and Australia but, arguably, both countries in the past have been discriminatory.

- With a commitment to equality of opportunity and multi-culturalism, more people have access to a greater number of sports.
- Increases in sporting opportunity are not only improving health and lifestyle but are helping both countries to improve their international standards in representative sport.

The model on page 80 (Fig 7.2) summarises the cultural forces that stimulate the focus for quality in Physical Education and school sport, the demand for mass participation, the pursuit of excellence and the obsession with sport in Australia.

> **Need to know more?** For more information on the social values of UK and Australia see Chapter 7, pages 164–166, in the OCR A2 PE Student Book.

UK		Australia	
Value	**Explanation**	**Value**	**Explanation**
Democracy	• The right to freedom – it involves the right of free speech and expression.	Impact of egalitarianism	• An egalitarian society is one in which all people are deemed to be equal. • Egalitarianism reflects freedom and democracy. • Australia sport therefore was never subject to a social class divide.
Teamwork	• Working as part of a team has been a traditional British value since the incorporation of team games in the public schools system. • Teamwork was also a feature of the Empire.	Legacy of 'bush culture'	• 'Bush culture' describes the positive approach with which the settlers faced up to hardship. • Bush culture reflected individual courage and enterprise. • Bush culture also inspired teamwork, promoted egalitarianism and eliminated class privilege
Individuality	• The value of the individual is important in the UK and underpins democracy.	Land of the 'fair go'	• The spirit that emerged from the egalitarian ethos and the bush culture was that all people are equal and that all individuals, without prejudice, should have the opportunity to succeed. • This concept is associated with democracy and supports the aspirations of the individual

continued

UK		Australia	
Value	Explanation	Value	Explanation
Competitiveness	• Winning is of increasing importance since the advent of commercial sport and the abolition of traditional friendly fixtures to make way for structured league competition. • The taking part in sport however remains an important UK ethic.	The UK values of competitiveness, fair play and participation are not identified as Australian values in the syllabus. These values are however, closely linked with Australian society. • *Competitiveness:* This was apparent from early colonial settlement and the challenges of 'currency' and 'sterling'. Australia, from this time was a young culture striving for independence and identity. • Success in sport was a benchmark against which national progress could be judged. • *Fair play:* Although Australia is associated with ambition and a competitive spirit a sense of fair play and sportsmanship overrides a win at all cost ethic. • *Participation:* Similar to the UK, Australia places emphasis on participation rather than competitive elitism	
Fair play	• A sense of fair play is central to the British sporting ethos and the participation ethic continues to over ride the 'win at all cost' ethic		
Participation	Emphasis is placed on participation rather than competitive elitism.		
Discrimination	The UK has a tradition of class hierarchy in which the upper classes enjoy great privilege. As a result of imperial rule the UK discriminated against ethnic races. The UK of the twenty-first-century is a cosmopolitan society and is striving to overcome cultural discrimination.	**Social 'melting pot'**	The social melting pot describes the situation in which people from different cultures have blended together to form a unified culture comprising many different strands.
		Commitment to multi-culturalism	In 1971, the Australian government committed to the policy of multi-culturalism which officially recognised that all social groups in society would have equal status. A government apology has been given in the twenty-first-century to the indigenous people who suffered under Imperial expansion and colonial rule.

Table 5 Comparison of UK and Australian social values

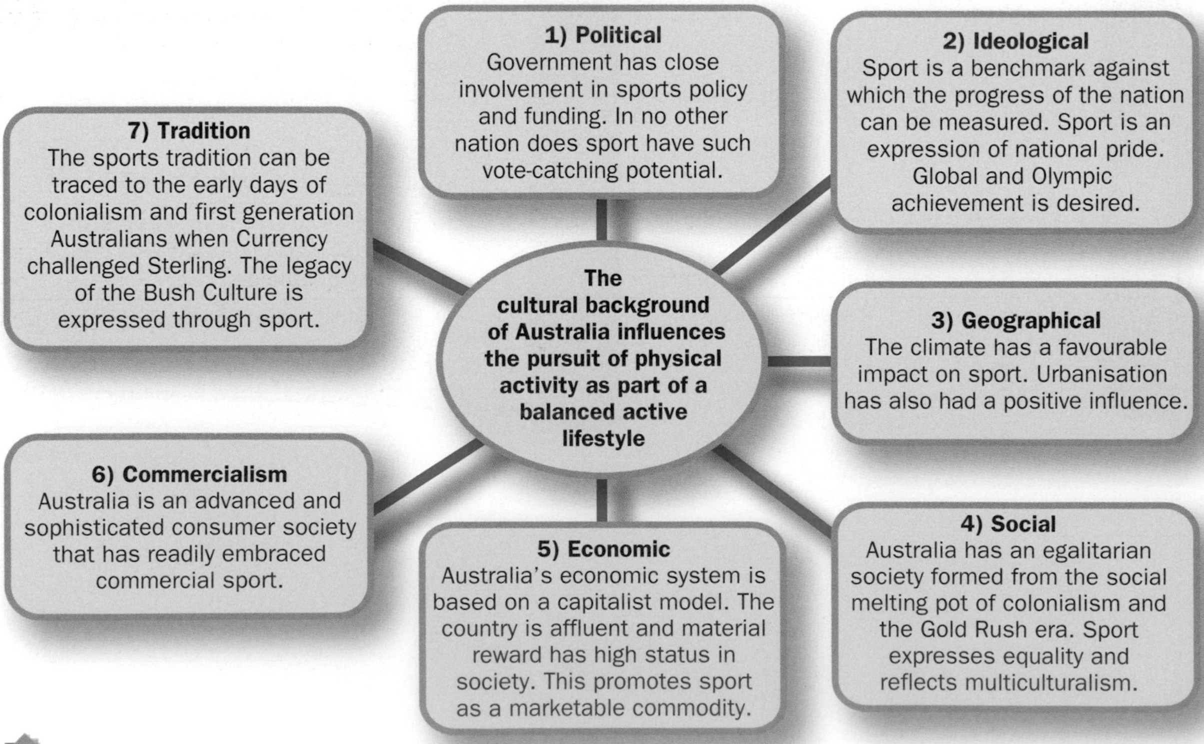

1) Political
Government has close involvement in sports policy and funding. In no other nation does sport have such vote-catching potential.

2) Ideological
Sport is a benchmark against which the progress of the nation can be measured. Sport is an expression of national pride. Global and Olympic achievement is desired.

7) Tradition
The sports tradition can be traced to the early days of colonialism and first generation Australians when Currency challenged Sterling. The legacy of the Bush Culture is expressed through sport.

The cultural background of Australia influences the pursuit of physical activity as part of a balanced active lifestyle

3) Geographical
The climate has a favourable impact on sport. Urbanisation has also had a positive influence.

6) Commercialism
Australia is an advanced and sophisticated consumer society that has readily embraced commercial sport.

5) Economic
Australia's economic system is based on a capitalist model. The country is affluent and material reward has high status in society. This promotes sport as a marketable commodity.

4) Social
Australia has an egalitarian society formed from the social melting pot of colonialism and the Gold Rush era. Sport expresses equality and reflects multiculturalism.

Fig 7.2 The cultural background of Australia and its influence on the pursuit of physical activity

PHYSICAL EDUCATION AND SCHOOL SPORT IN THE UK AND HOW IT COMPARES TO VICTORIA STATE IN AUSTRALIA

UK	Australia
1. Central government has determined a National Curriculum.	1. State and local government determine the programmes for physical activity in schools.
2. Physical Education is compulsory for all pupils up to the age of sixteen.	2. Physical Education is compulsory for all pupils up to the age of sixteen.
3. The priority is to increase participation.	3. The priority is to increase participation.
4. A major reason for increasing participation rates is to encourage lifelong participation and improve the health of young people.	4. A major reason for increasing participation rates is to encourage lifelong participation and improve the health of young people.
5. The UK government is concerned that figures indicating obesity levels for young people are rising.	5. The Victoria government believe that figures indicating obesity levels for young people are stable.

Table 7 A comparison of Physical Education in the UK and Australia

Initiatives to promote Physical Education and school sport in the UK

In addition to the National Curriculum, the UK government has developed a strategy named Physical Education Sport and Young People (PESSYP) in which the government invested 100 million pounds in 2007. The PESSYP strategy comprises nine 'strands' which aim to improve the quality and opportunities for young people in sporting activities (see chapter 6 of this revision guide and page 125 in the OCR A2 PE Student Book).

The Victoria government has established ten strategies to improve the quality and opportunities for young people in sporting activities. Whilst direct comparisons with the UK are not always obvious, there are equivalents and parallels that can be identified across the strategies. The ten Victoria initiatives and UK equivalents are outlined below.

Key term	UK Initiatives	Australia Initiatives
1. Government policy	• National Curriculum • Physical education and School Sport for Young People (PESSYP) • Physical Education and Sport (PESS)	• Sport Education and Physical Education Programme (SEPEP)
2. Professional development	• Teacher training for those already qualified. • INSET programmes.	• Physical and Sport Education (PASE) is a teacher training programme for those already qualified.
3. Specialist provision	• Sports Colleges have a mission to increase sporting opportunities.	• Exemplary Schools share good practice with other schools.
4. Primary Schools	• National curriculum at key stages 1 and 2. • Sporting Playground initiative. • TOPS programmes in primary schools.	• Fundamental Skills Programme
5. Student Leadership	• Step into Sport initiative • Junior Sports leaders Award (JSLA) • Community Sports Leaders Award (CSLA) • Hanson Award	• Sport Leader Programme.

continued

Key term	UK Initiatives	Australia Initiatives
6. Awards for Excellence	• Gifted and Talented scheme	• State Blue Award • De Coubertin Award
7. Sports Personalities	• Sports stars visit schools to be role models.	• Sports Person in Schools Project links sports performers from the Victoria Institute of Sport (VIS) with schools.
8. Links with clubs	• Physical Education and School Sport for Young People (PESSYP) link with clubs.	• Sports Linkage Scheme
9. Targeting sports	• Pessyp aims to introduce students to sports that may have been previously unconsidered.	• Sports Search is a computer programme to match students to suitable sports.
10. Teacher Games	• Informal fixtures may be arranged between staff members on an inter-school basis.	• Teacher Games is a formal initiative that aims to bring the teachers of Victoria together for friendly competition.

Table 7 Initiatives to promote Physical Education and school sport in the UK and Australia

Factor	Comparison
Curriculum administration	Unlike in the UK, there is no National Curriculum or Inspection service in Australia.
Intra-school Sport	In the UK, intra-school sport is played in recreation time or as organised house matches. Intra-school sport in Australia is an integral part of SEPEP.
Inter-school sport	Inter-school sport is organised by a number of agencies in the UK and tends to be extra-curricular. In Australia, the inter-school sports programme is organised through SEPEP and overseen by the national school sport governing body, School Sport Australia (SSA).
Teacher status	The teacher in the UK has high status and is in charge of Physical Education and sport. Although there may be some input from coaches on the Sports Linkage Programme, the situation is the same in Australia.
Ethos	Both countries are committed to a participation ethic and to the development of fair play. The win ethic is not instilled, nor is there an overt attempt to replicate the professional sports scene in either country.
Excellence	Both countries have national schools teams in a variety of sports and have national sports competitions.
Special events	In the UK, although there is a national schools athletics championship, there is not an Australian Schools Pacific Games equivalent.

Table 8 Comparisons of Physical Education and sport in the UK and Australia

Outdoor education

The term outdoor education has the same meaning in Australia as in the UK. This curriculum area relates to the provision of educational experiences in the natural environment.

Although part of the National Curriculum, the experiences that pupils receive during outdoor education in the UK tend to vary. Many factors appear to prevent schools from full engagement in this area. By contrast, outdoor education is strongly supported by Victoria State government

The motives for the promotion of outdoor education are identified in the left column whilst a comparative comment relating to UK is made on the right.

Both countries administer the Duke of Edinburgh Award scheme.

Motives for the promotion of outdoor education in Australia	A comparative UK comment
The climate is favourable for an outdoor lifestyle.	The climate is less conducive to an outdoor lifestyle.
It is associated with a balanced, active and healthy lifestyle, e.g. nearly one million Australians engage in bushwalking.	Backpacking, hiking and walking are popular in the UK and are associated with balanced, active, healthy lifestyles.
The bush or frontier culture can be experienced.	There is no equivalent of bush culture in the UK.
The environment has outstanding natural resources and aesthetic appeal.	The UK has outstanding natural resources and aesthetic appeal but climate and topography limit these areas.
Populated coastal stretches and inland areas of hostile environment mean that survival and safety skills are necessary	Survival skills can be necessary in the mountains, but most of the UK lacks hostile wilderness.
It is perceived as an important area of education and is an examined subject.	Outdoor education varies in the commitment in delivery and is not directly examined.
The Victoria Youth Development Programme (VYDP) is an Outdoor Education programme that incorporates community agencies, for example Army Cadets, Ambulance, Fire and Surf Life Saving services.	Outdoor education in the UK develops skills and provides adventure experiences, but does not directly link with community agencies.

Table 9 Comparisons of outdoor education promotion in Australia and the UK

> **Need to know more?** For more information on PE and school sport or outdoor education in the UK and how they compare to Victoria State in Australia see Chapter 7, pages 166–171, in the OCR A2 PE Student Book.

MASS PARTICIPATION IN THE UK AS IT COMPARES TO AUSTRALIA

Participation rates

- In the UK 72 per cent of young people claim to take part in moderate to vigorous physical activity on most days.
- Recent concern has been expressed by UKSport and Sport England that this trend is beginning to decline.

- In Australia, approximately 70 per cent of boys and girls complete at least 60 minutes of moderate to vigorous physical activity on most days.
- On average boys in Australia devote 2½ hours to exercise while girls average almost 2 hours per day.
- This is significantly higher than UK averages.

Prevalence of overweight and obese children and adolescences in the UK aged 5–17

Recent government statistics for the UK revealed that nearly 30 per cent of young people in the 5–17 category were overweight. Furthermore, 17 per cent of boys and 14 per cent of girls were considered to be obese.

Gender	Percentage overweight but not obese	Percentage obese	Total percent of overweight and obese
Boys			
1995	9.3	1.4	10.7
2005	15.3	4.7	20.0
Girls			
1995	10.6	1.2	11.8
2005	16.0	5.5	21.5

Table 10 Prevalence of overweight and obese Australian children and adolescents aged 5–17 expressed as a percentage

PROMOTION BY THE GOVERNMENT OF REGULAR PARTICIPATION IN PHYSICAL ACTIVITY IN AUSTRALIA

The role of the Australia Sports Commission (ASC) is:

- to promote excellence and to increase mass participation
- to introduce and implement the policy *More Active Australia*
- to increase the active membership of sports clubs across the country through national and State sporting associations by the *More Active Australia* policy.

Adapted games for young people

- In 1986, the government invested in a sports programme for children called Aussie Sport.
- The Aussie Sport initiative set out to modify the rules, reduce the dimensions of the playing environment and introduce child friendly equipment.

- The new simplified games engaged over two million children and by 1995 *Aussie Sport* was implemented by many clubs and 100 per cent of primary schools.
- Aussie Sport Resource Kits introduced 30 modified sports and included guidelines for sporting conduct, available to teachers and coaches.
- Coaching courses and an awards system were established by the ASC and Aussie Sport Coordinators were established in all States and Territories.
- Australia has become the world leader in adapting sport to suit young people and programmes which are modelled on the Aussie Sport system are operated in 16 different countries.
- The term Aussie Sport was changed in 2000 and the initiative is now called The Junior Sport Programme.

Strategy	How it promotes participation in sport
1. Primary and high schools	Ten strategies to ensure that sport and PE are taught to the highest quality in primary and high schools are explained on pages 167–169 in the OCR A2 PE Student Book. School Sport Australia (SSA) coordinates national inter-school competition.
2. School Sport Network	The Network is a support agency for all teachers who are involved in sports activity. It recognises the importance of schools in encouraging and preparing young people for an active life. The Network helps to extend opportunities for sport and physical activities; it can also advise schools on addressing the barriers that prevent participation.
3. Junior Sport Programmes	These promote adapted or modified games for the 5–17 age group and provide resource materials for teachers and coaches. Coaching and the organisation of sports competitions are part of the programmes.

continued

Strategy	How it promotes participation in sport
4. Active After School Communities Programme (AASC)	The AASC provides primary-school children with access to free, structured physical activity programmes after school. The programme is aimed at non-active children and hopes to encourage youngsters to join sports clubs.
5. Local Sporting Champions Programme	Through this programme, the ASC provides financial support to individual youngsters or youth teams. Grants cover equipment, uniforms and travel expenses for young people in the 12–18 age group. In 2008, nearly 2000 individual youngsters received grants of $500 while 200 teams were granted $3000.
6. Bluearth Programme	This is a health and movement education initiative for schools. Specialists in health and movement education work alongside teachers to improve fitness and motor skills. It aims to encourage an active lifetime involvement in sport and exercise.

Table 11 *Examples of strategies designed to promote sports participation in Australia*

Need to know more? For more information on mass participation and adapted games see Chapter 7, pages 171–174, in the OCR A2 PE Student Book.

INSTITUTES OF SPORTS EXCELLENCE OPERATE BOTH IN THE UK AND AUSTRALIA

Both in the UK and Australia, not all sports find it necessary to take advantage of the institutes. There are alternative pathways which access professional sport in both countries. Examples of alternative pathways into professional sport follow.

	Sports Institutes in the UK	Sports Institutes in Australia
Structure	The Sports Institutes of the UK are direct copies of the Australian Institute of Sport (AIS).	
	The Institutes in both countries operate on a decentralised basis.	
	There are four devolved Home Country Sports Institutes that form a network in the UK: • The English Institute of Sport (EIS) • The Sports Institute of Northern Ireland (SINI) • The Scottish Institute of Sport (SIS) • The Welsh Institute of Sport	In Australia there is at least one Institute in each State or Territory, for example: • Victoria Institute of Sport (VIS) Melbourne • South Australia Institute of Sport (SASI) Adelaide • New South Wales Institute of Sport (NSWIS) Sydney • Northern Territories Institute of Sport (NTIS) Darwin
	The whole network of UK sports institute is funded from the National Lottery and government contribution.	In Australia funding is supplied by the government (ASC) and business sponsorship.
	The UK government is not involved with sporting policies.	The ASC is directly involved in policy decisions
	The UK Institutes of Sport and the Australian Institutes of Sport operate in parallel. There is no hierarchy of importance	
	UK Sport is responsible for the strategic direction of the home country institutes.	The Australian Institutes are closely monitored by the National Elite Sports Council.

continued

Sports Institutes in the UK	Sports Institutes in Australia
Function	The Sports Institutes of both countries have similar functions:

- the overall mission is to produce elite sports performers
- world class facilities are made available to all performers
- financial aid and sponsorship are given to athletes
- the highest quality of coaching and technology support is provided
- athletes receive treatment from the sports medical services
- educational and vocational services are provided , for example Athletic Career Education (ACE)
- the provision of national and International competition is facilitated at sports institutes.

Table 12 A comparison of Sports Institutes in the UK and Australia

ALTERNATIVE PATHWAYS INTO PROFESSIONAL SPORT

Not all players find it necessary to be scholarship holders at the sports institute.

The draft system in Australian Rules Football

- The Australian Football League (AFL) is the governing body for Australian Rules Football. The AFL's drafting system recruits players into professional teams.
- The draft allows clubs that finish low down in the league to have the first opportunities to select the best players, not under contract with other clubs.
- The bottom club will have the first pick in the draft. This model follows the American system of the pro draft.
- Each club in the AFL is allowed to have 35 players and drafting takes place from open age State Football Leagues and under 18 State football competitions.
- Players at this level may well be scholarship holders with the AIS.
- Alternatively, they could be talented players who have been developed by the club.

Alternative 'pathways' into professional Rugby League

UK Rugby League	Australia Rugby League
Rugby League does not directly use the UK Sports Institutes to develop talent.	A promising young rugby league player may well be a scholarship holder with the AIS.
Schools and clubs develop talent; good players are selected for town and service area representative teams.	A talented performer could be nurtured through the club academy after selection from school or junior club. AIS support is therefore unnecessary.
Professional clubs have developed 'academies' which tend to select from service area representation.	The Kids to Kangaroos scheme is a new national development plan. it tracks promising junior players through club academies into the professional game
A player could be 'fast-tracked' directly from school or the club into professional rugby.	An under-eighteen competition (the Toyota Cup) has been promoted as a television spectacle and this exposure appears to have 'fast-tracked' some players into professional rugby league.
The draft system does not operate in Rugby League in either country.	

Table 13 A comparison of pathways into professional Rugby League in the UK and Australia

Pathways into professional sport in UK and Australia

- Both countries offer young people with talent alternative pathways into elite levels of sport. This ensures that as many athletes as possible are given the opportunity to achieve.
- Sporting institutes of the UK and Australia also give vocational support to their athletes and this reflects positively on the contemporary culture of both countries.
- The draft system of player recruitment in Australian Rules football is good for teams who finish low in the league tables because they get the first pick of new talent at the opening of the next season.
- The system is open to manipulation, as clubs may be tempted to field weakened teams and accept a low league position knowing the team can be strengthened for the forthcoming season.
- A good cricket player may bypass the sports institute and progress to professional league cricket as an 18-year-old (e.g. Shane Warne).

> **Need to know more?** For more information on sport and the pursuit of excellence in Australia and the UK see Chapter 7, pages 175–180, in the OCR A2 PE Student Book.

CASE STUDIES OF SPORT IN THE UK AND AUSTRALIA

CRICKET	
UK	**Australia**
Cricket originated in England and is closely associated with English tradition, values and social class hierarchy.	Cricket in Australia was a direct copy of the English game. The rules were identical and the format was the same, but there were differences in approach, terminology, and attitudes relating to social class.
The first recorded adult game was in 1611. It was some time later that club cricket became established. Hambledon, a village in Hampshire, became the first to acquire a reputation for success in 1756.	As in the UK the first competitive matches in Australia were arranged challenges between the 'currency lads' and the English military and free settlers. These matches often involved heavy betting.
Cricket thrived in the UK public schools where it was believed to develop character and leadership skills.	From the time of the 'currency' cricket was a game of the people.
Gentleman amateurs and professional players changed in separate rooms, entered the field of play through different gates.	Australia did not incorporate class privilege into cricket.
The captain of England up to the mid-twentieth-century was required to be an amateur. This reflected the English class system.	The captain of Australia was not required to be an amateur.
Today the English select a captain before selecting the national team. This is a legacy of the class system.	The Australians select the national team before choosing a captain. This endorses the absence of class hierarchy.
The Marylebone Cricket Club (MCC) based at Lords Cricket ground soon became the driving force of English and later international cricket.	Australia have replicated the status and tradition of the Lords ground at the Melbourne Cricket Club (MCC).
Defeat against Australia was significant. The operation of the British Empire was, however, the benchmark of national progress.	Victory for Australia in England in 1882 was important as it was seen as a benchmark against which national progress could be measured.
This event marked the beginning of the Ashes mythology. This stimulated greater interest in test cricket. The term Ashes Series in contemporary society helps to market cricket between the two countries as a commercial commodity.	
Limited over cricket was initiated in England in 1963 as a novelty competition at the end of season.	Australia first promoted the shortened version of the game at international level in 1971.
Australian entrepreneur Kerry Packer exploited the commercial potential of this version of the game by staging World Series cricket in 1977. This event changed the image of professional cricket across the world.	

continued

CRICKET	
UK	**Australia**
In the UK twenty20 cricket was introduced in the early twenty-first-century to boost the commercial potential of cricket.	Australia is now following this lead with the same version of the game which they have named twenty20 bash.
Evaluation: It could be argued that although commercialisation has brought extra finance into the game, and that entertainment value might have improved, the traditional sporting values have been lost.	

RUGBY LEAGUE	
UK	**Australia**
In 1895, certain clubs in the North of England broke away from the amateur system adopted by Rugby Union to form the Northern Union. These new professionals were classed as rebels.	In 1907, Australian professionalism followed the northern England 'breakaway' movement where players could be paid for time spent away from work on playing duties.
The Northern Union soon adopted the name Rugby League and changed the format of the game to make it more entertaining for the paying spectators.	Australia followed this lead.
The first international matches between Great Britain and Australia took place in England during the 1908 season. As a direct imitation of cricket, test matches played between these countries are known as Ashes Tests.	
Rugby League in the UK is traditionally associated with the North of England in the former industrial areas of Lancashire, Yorkshire and Cumberland. It is a game with strong working class origins.	The game in Australia is also associated with specific areas, for example Queensland, New South Wales and Capital Territories.
Southern England has never readily accepted the game. This perpetuates the imaginary north/south divide.	The game appears to be established in the east and will not readily expand to the west.
Matches between Lancashire and Yorkshire were marketed as the Battle of the Roses but were a commercial failure.	Matches between Queensland and New South Wales are played as a series marketed as the State of Origin. They are a commercial success
In the late twentieth-century both countries promoted Rugby League as a commercial product and players at the top levels became full time professionals.	
Rugby League in the UK remains less popular and has less commercial potential compared with Rugby Union.	Rugby League in Australia is more popular and has more commercial potential than Rugby Union.
In 1996, the image of the game changed when Australian entrepreneur Rupert Murdoch launched Super League in the UK as a product of BskyB television. The code changed from its traditional winter season to become a summer game.	Super league is a direct copy of the Australia approach and league structure.
Rugby League changed its image to promote itself as a commercial product. Team names have changed, e.g. Wigan became Warriors and Canberra became Raiders. Traditional grounds took on the names of sponsors. Rules were modified and tactical substituting helped to sustain a high level of physical intensity. The UK Grand Final is a copy of the Australian model and is now the showcase commercial event at the end of the UK season. The champion clubs from UK and Australia are matched together in March in an event that opens the season in both hemispheres.	
For the 2009 season, Super League planned to adopt the approach taken to commercial sport in the USA by abolishing relegation and introducing a franchise system to expand its operations to include teams from London, Wales and France.	Australia has expanded Rugby league to all States with a professional team in Victoria. The Australian rugby League will monitor the UK experiment.
Evaluation: Historically, great resentment and bitterness have existed in the UK between the two codes of rugby largely brought about by different social class values. It could be argued that this unpleasant rivalry has inhibited the growth of Rugby League in the south and detracted from the development of Rugby Union in parts of the north. In contrast to the UK – Rugby League in Australia is the stronger code – possibly because of the absence of a rigid class structure	

continued

RUGBY UNION	
UK	**Australia**
The origins of Rugby Union are rooted firmly in the public schools and universities of the UK. There is also a strong tradition of the game in twentieth-century Grammar schools.	In Australia, the elite and exclusively private schools of Queensland and New South Wales play rugby union whilst Catholic schools which cater for students from a different level of society, predominantly play rugby league.
The influence of the schools impacted on the senior game as many clubs were formed as 'Old Boy' associations.	
Rugby Union was firmly rooted as a middle-class game in the UK's hierarchical class structure.	In Australia, as in the UK, Rugby Union is strongly permeated by the middle class amateur ethos.
Although a 'league' competition structure existed in Wales, Rugby Union fixtures were for the most part organised on a 'friendly' basis up until the 1990s.	Fixtures were also organised on a friendly basis in Australia. This system strongly endorsed the amateur ethos.
Both the Australian and the home countries and Australian Rugby Football Unions withstood commercial pressure and remained strictly compliant to the ideals of amateurism until the 1990s.	
After the success of the second World Cup won by the Australians in 1991 (this amateur competition made a profit of $85 million), and as a consequence of increased global television interest, Rugby Union agreed, in what became known as the Paris Declaration of 1995, to break with tradition and adopt professionalism.	
The English RFU was forced to commit to commercialism. This announcement was greeted with astonishment in England where amateurism had remained firmly ingrained and there was no dependence on commercialism.	
A league competition structure was put in place and a sponsored European cup was assigned to increase the commercial potential of the game. Players became full time professionals.	By way of replication, Australian players became professional and the southern hemisphere introduced a 'Super 12' competition.
The laws of the game have, under the suggestion of the home countries RU and the Australian RU, been modified since 1995 in an attempt to make the game more attractive and easier to understand for the casual spectator.	
The advent of professionalism stopped good Rugby Union players from signing up to the rugby league code.	Although in Australia, the flow of junior players from Rugby Union to league has slowed, the defection remains significant
The administration and the structure of the game in the UK has kept pace with professional demands. As a result, Rugby Union in the UK remains the dominant code.	Australia has failed to successfully promote a club, or franchise a league below elite level. As a result, rugby league in Australia remains the dominant code.
UK	**Australia**
ASSOCIATION FOOTBALL	
Until the twenty-first-century football was not popular with the English speaking members of the former Empire, e.g. Australia.	
The Football Association was founded in the UK in 1863 as an amateur organisation. At this time, the amateur ethic was strong as football had its origins in the English public schools.	The organisation was identical in Australia as the sport was directed by colonial english public school graduates.
The FA reluctantly accepted professionalism in 1888 with the formation of the Football League. Association football in the UK quickly became dominated by working class professional players.	Professionalism was difficult to sustain in Australia and football found survival problematic even in working class areas

continued

UK	Australia
ASSOCIATION FOOTBALL	
• The growth of football as a working class game in the latter nineteenth-century was prolific in the UK. • During the early twentieth-century, professional footballers in the UK earned a relatively good wage, for example by 1939 a player earned double the average industrial worker's wage. • In 1961 the Football League abolished the maximum wage. This circumstance changed the culture of football. Football now had to become a commercial business. • TIn 1966 England hosted and won the World Cup. This success endorsed the game as the national sport of England.	• Working class status damaged the reputation of the sport in Australia and the game was marginalised. • Soccer was termed the 'Pommie Game' and was rejected by mainstream culture on the basis of the 'sport space' concept. • The influx of Europeans after 1945 promoted soccer as their main game. Clubs adopted the ethnic names of their former countries. This 'ghetto culture' resulted in racial violence. • Soccer suffered further marginalisation by Australian mainstream culture.
The Broadcasting Act of 1990 allowed BskyB to pay Division One football clubs for the exclusive rights to televise matches.	Association Football in Australia continued to be marginalised and remained unviable as a commercial product until the start of the twenty-first-century.
Division One football clubs broke away from the Football League to form the Premiership.	
Association Football has now entered the realm of 'big business' and remains as well ahead, in terms of contemporary popularity and commercial potential, of other major UK sports.	

Table 14 Case studies of sports in the UK and Australia

Ten factors that have led to a dramatic rise in the popularity of Australian Association Football:

1. **Government:** The Australian government at the turn of the twentieth-century initiated an inquiry into the governance and management of football and this effectively changed the face of football.
2. **Governing Body:** The Football Federation of Australia (FFA) was established as the new governing body with a mission to promote the status of association football as a major Australian game.
3. **Structure:** In 2002, a new National League was established by the FFA.
4. **Ethnicity:** The FFA defused racial problems by enforcing the withdrawal of ethnic team names, for example Sydney Hellas a team with a Greek origin became Sydney Knights.
5. **Media:** The National League competition increased spectator interest and stimulated positive media interests.
6. **Sponsorship:** Increased public and media interest attracted lucrative sponsorship deals to the National League competition.
7. **Success:** Victory against England in 2003, progression in the 2006 World Cup and successful affiliation to the Asian Football Confederation have stimulated excellence and increased popularity.
8. **Excellence:** Excellence has developed further with the creation of a new Youth League, a National competition for women and the inclusion of football as one of the 26 sports supported by the AIS.
9. **Participation:** It is estimated that there are 1 million players in Australia and Australian Football is the fastest growing 'elective' in High Schools.
10. **Ambition:** The FFA is bidding to host the 2018 World Cup. There is great confidence within the FFA that Australia can win the World Cup competition as the host nation.

Australian Rules Football

Australian Football carries a Latin motto *Populo Ludus Populi* which means 'the game of the people for the people'. This description is significant as the game is associated with cultural and ethnic diversity.

> **Need to know more?** For more information on case studies see Chapter 7, pages 180–190, in the OCR A2 PE Student Book. See pages 152–154 OCR A2 PE

Origin	Ethnicity	Class	Gender
It's a combination of an Aboriginal ethnic game and the version of football played in the nineteenth-century in UK public schools. Designed to be manly, but not overly aggressive, its original purpose was to keep cricketers fit in winter.	Australian Football has always been accessible to ethnic groups. The 'cornstalks' brought the aspiring manly image of young Australia to the sport; Irish immigrants exemplified strength and ruggedness; ethnic Europeans were prominent from the 1950s, and from the 1960s the Aborigines demonstrated their great athleticism and are well represented in the game.	For both players and spectators, the game appeals to all classes. It has given skilled players from the working classes a chance to be respected in society. This endorsed the view that Australia is 'the land of the fair go'.	Various governing bodies, such as the Victoria Women's Football League, promote female participation. Even though women have acquired positions as umpires at senior level and some hold salaried promotional positions on club staff, play is dominated by men. There are 10,000 registered female Australian Football players; male participants number 300,000.

Table 15 The wide appeal of Australian Rules Football

CHECK

If you are satisfied with your knowledge and understanding, tick off the sections that you have revised so far. If you are not satisfied then revisit those sections and refer to the pages in the *Need to know more?* features.

☐ Describe the cultural context of Australia

☐ Outline the historical determinants relating to Australia and how they compare with the UK

☐ State the geographical determinants of Australia and how they impact on the opportunities for Physical Education and sport both in Australia and the UK

☐ Describe government policy and the agendas for sport both in Australia and the UK

☐ Explore the commercialisation of sport both in Australia and UK

☐ Describe social determinants relating to Australia and UK to include discrimination against minority groups.

☐ Outline the social values both of Australia and the UK.

TRUE OR FALSE?

1. Australia promotes itself as the 'Motherland' because of its cosmopolitan society.
2. For Australia, victory over England in contemporary sport is important because it expresses national pride and progress.
3. Australian values, such as the 'land of the fair go', and multiculturalism, helped Australia embrace professionalism in sport more readily than the UK.
4. SEPEP is a curriculum framework in Australian schools, but is not a National Curriculum on the same lines as the UK.
5. A 'de Coubertin' award is given to the 'best and fairest' player in the Victoria State school system.
6. PASE is an Australian schools programme that links schools sports departments with local sports clubs.
7. 'More Active Australia' is the slogan used to promote mass participation in Australia.
8. Adapted games for young people is a fitness scheme to promote national fitness levels.
9. The Australian Institute of Sport is supervised by the National Elite Sports Council.
10. Rugby League in Australia operate a draft system to allow young players to enter professional ranks.

EXAM PRACTICE

1. Critically evaluate how historical, geographical and socio-economical factors have influenced the commercial development of sport in the U.K. and Australia.   *(20 marks)*

2. Explain the factors why Outdoor Education is promoted in Australia. Identify one comparative factor that influences the promotion of Outdoor Education in the UK and Australia.   *(5 marks)*

3. Discuss contemporary initiatives to promote Physical Education and school sport in Australia. How does this compare with how PE and sport are promoted in UK schools?   *(20 marks)*

4. In terms of mass participation, women, people with disabilities and ethnic minorities are under-represented in both the UK and Australia.

   Explain the strategies in the UK and Australia that encourage people from these groups to participate in physical recreation or sport.   *(5 marks)*

See page 272 for answers

CHAPTER 8

Individual aspects of performance that influence young people's participation and aspirations

CHAPTER OVERVIEW

By the end of this chapter you should have knowledge and understanding of:

- personality and its importance in producing effective performance and in following a balanced, active and healthy lifestyle
- attitudes and their influence on performance and lifestyle
- achievement motivation and its effect on performance and on following an active and healthy lifestyle
- attribution theory and the impact of attribution on performance and sustaining a balanced, active and healthy lifestyle
- aggression and its impact upon performance and behaviour.

Sports psychology addresses the important mental processes that work together to facilitate effective performance in sport. In this syllabus sports psychology focuses on encouraging and sustaining a balanced, active and healthy lifestyle. This focus is a central theme and will appear on your examination.

EXAM TIP

In your exam, you will need to demonstrate knowledge of personality theories. These theories are based on three very different views or perspectives. Each perspective must be clearly understood.

The three views on personality development are known as:

1. Trait perspective
2. Social learning perspective
3. Interactionist approaches

PERSONALITY

Athletes display their own unique patterns of behaviour while engaged in sports performance and some psychologists believe that quality of performance and participation in sport are determined by personality

TRAIT PERSPECTIVE

- The **trait** view states that all behaviour is innate and **genetically programmed**.
- Traits are thought to be stable, enduring and consistent in all situations.

Trait theory is depicted as:

Behaviour = Function of Personality. B = F(P).

Trait theory – People are born with established personality characteristics.

Trait – a single characteristic of personality that is believed to be a natural force or instinct causing an individual to behave in a predicted way.

Genetically programmed – the personality is inherited through the genes of our parents.

Personality Types

Eysenck identified four primary personality traits or types. These personality types are arranged on a two dimensional model.

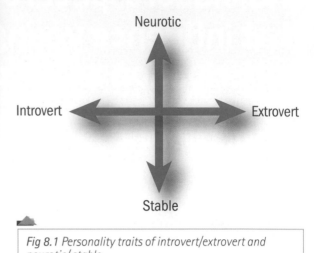

Fig 8.1 Personality traits of introvert/extrovert and neurotic/stable

The drawbacks with the trait approach are:

- it states that behaviour is at all times predictable
- it does not take into account the fact that people adapt their behaviour in response to a particular environmental situation
- it does not consider environmental influences on the shaping of personality.

The two specific theories that belong to the trait perspective of personality are:

- Personality types (Eysenck and Cattell)
- Narrow Band Theory Type A and Type B (Girdano)

Extroverted people perform best in conditions that stimulate high **arousal**. Introverts tend to be more aroused by events than do extroverts. This is due to differences in the individual's **reticular activation system (RAS)**.

Personality type or primary trait	Description of personality type
Extrovert	• Affiliates well to other people • Outgoing, gregarious and sociable • Becomes aroused more slowly than introverts • Has low sensitivity of the reticular activating system (RAS)
Introvert	• Tends to be shy and reserved • Prefers isolation from others • Becomes aroused more quickly than extroverts • Has high sensitivity of the reticular activating system (RAS)
Neurotic	• Displays extreme and unpredictable emotions in the form of mood swings • Their moods are unreliable • They experience high degrees of stress • Their recovery from stress is slow
Stable	• Displays predictable emotions in appropriate situations • Their moods are predictable • They tend not to experience intense stress • Their recovery from stress is rapid

Table 1 Eysenck's four primary personality types

KEY TERMS

Reticular activating system (RAS) – Introverts are more easily aroused than extroverts because of the sensitivity of an area of the brain called the reticular activating system. There is a greater likelihood that with increased stimulation the introvert will become over-aroused.

Arousal – A physical and mental state of preparedness.

Narrow Band Theory

Girdano was also a trait theorist. He proposed that there are two distinct personality types. Type A and Type B:

Type A characteristics	Type B characteristics
Highly competitive	Non-competitive
Works fast	Works more slowly
Strong desire to succeed	Lacking in desire to succeed
Likes control	Does not enjoy control
Prone to suffer stress	Less prone to stress

Table 2 Girdano's Type A and Type B characteristics

EXAM TIP

There is no link between Girdano's personality types and extroversion and introversion.

▶ **Need to know more?** For more information on personality types see Chapter 8, pages 197–200, in the OCR A2 PE Student Book.

SOCIAL LEARNING PERSPECTIVE (BANDURA)

The social learning perspective proposes that all behaviour is learned. Personality is, therefore, not genetically programmed.

Two processes are involved in social learning:

- The behaviour of others is imitated through observation.
- New behaviour is acquired after observation, only when it is endorsed through social reinforcement.

Social learning Theory is depicted as:

Behaviour = Function of Environment (B = F(E) .

▶ **Need to know more?** For more information on trait social learning perspective see Chapter 8, pages 200–201, in the OCR A2 PE Student Book

When observed behaviour is demonstrated by a 'significant' other or role model of high status

The role model is powerful and authoritative

Conditions that support social learning

When the observer wants to adopt the norms and values of a new culture, i.e. after joining a new team or working with different people

The observer and role model are the same gender

Fig 8.2 Conditions that support social learning

INTERACTIONIST APPROACH

The interactionist approach is based on the work of Hollander 1967.

- The Interactionist view combines the trait and social learning perspectives.
- Personality is modified and behaviour is formed when genetically inherited traits are triggered by an environmental circumstance.

Hollander proposed that personality has three levels that interact to form personality:

1. *Psychological core*: this is the most internal of the personality levels. It is thought to be the true self.
2. *Typical responses*: typical responses are changeable and are learned behaviours. They become modified as the person responds to the environment.
3. *Role-related behaviour*: this is the most external of the personality levels. It is the level that is dynamic and most changeable.

Interaction Theory is depicted as:

Behaviour = Function of Personality x Environment B = F (P x E)

- The interactionist view supports the claim that typical responses emerge in accordance with changing environmental situations.
- Behaviour is therefore unpredictable.
- This approach offers an explanation why the personalities of sports performers can change in different situations.

EXAM TIP

Although Hollander is not included on the specification, you should be aware of Hollander's contribution to the interactionist approach to personality.

Need to know more? For more information on interactionist approach see Chapter 8, pages 201–202, in the OCR A2 PE Student Book

THE EFFECTS OF PERSONALITY PROFILING ON THE ADOPTION OF A BALANCED, ACTIVE AND HEALTHY LIFESTYLES

Personality profiling may not be helpful as a predictor of those who are likely to participate in sport or physical activity.

KEY TERM

Personality profiling – A system which classifies an individual into a particular personality type.

While the inclination to participate in sport cannot be predicted by personality profiling, it may be that the identification of traits can be used by a psychologist to recommend participation in sport or physical activity. For example:

- Type A patterns of behaviour that may be linked to stress can be altered through exercise.
- Exercise and increased levels of fitness appear to increase the self-esteem of those individuals who register initially as having low self-esteem. (Biddle *et al* 1995)

Although personality profiling may help a coach to get to know people and provide the motivation for the individual to change behaviour and lifestyle, it must be understood that sport and exercise can not fundamentally change overall personality (Gill 2000).

EXAM TIP

You need to know that personality profiling helps when observing and questioning an individual. Getting to know the individual may help to formulate intervention strategies. Personality profiling has, however, only limited value (see Table 3).

Personality profiling in sport

There are serious limitations to personality profiling in sport. These limitations are listed in Table 3 below.

Key word to identify limitation	Explanation of limitation
Proof	A link between personality types and sport performance cannot be proved. A psychologist named Martens believes that the relationship between sport participation and personality are doubtful.
Evidence	There is no evidence that an ideal sports personality exist, e.g. the most stable and extroverted squad member may not be the best player in the team, or the most appropriate to create team cohesion.
Subjectivity	Profiling results are often subjective. This means that conclusions may be influenced by personal opinions and are not totally supported by scientific evidence.
Invalidity	Profiling results are often inaccurate and invalid. Invalid means that tests do not measure that which they intend to measure.
Modification	The performer may unconsciously modify their behaviour to match up to the profile ascribed to them.
Reliability	Many profiles are calculated by using self-report questionnaire studies. The results of these studies are not always reliable as performers may not answer all questions accurately.
Stereotyping	There is a danger that profiling will stereotype a person.

Table 3 Limitations of personality profiling

EXAM TIP

Explanations of the three personality approaches and the drawbacks of personality profiling in sport are popular examination questions.

▶ **Need to know more?** For more information on the effects of personality profiling see Chapter 8, pages 202–204, in the OCR A2 PE Student Book.

ATTITUDES AND THEIR INFLUENCE ON PERFORMANCE AND LIFESTYLES

- An attitude is a mode of behaviour that is thought to be the typical response of an individual.
- Attitudes are emotional responses that can be enduring but unstable.
- Unstable means that attitudes can be changed.
- An attitude is directed toward an '**attitude object**'.
- A negative attitude towards sport may result in the rejection of physical activity by an individual.
- Long-standing attitudes may adversely influence behaviour causing an individual to be inconsistent in judgement.
- Inconsistencies in behaviour may be revealed in the form of prejudice.
- Prejudice is a pre-judgement arising from an evaluation based on unfounded beliefs or opinions.
- A coach could have a prejudice against an individual performer.

KEY TERM

Attitude object – The people, subject or situation towards which an attitude is directed.

Negative prejudice relates to:

- gender
- race
- age.

Origin of attitudes

Attitudes can originate from a number of sources:

- experience
- **socialisation**
- **peer group**
- the media
- culture.

When an outcome is positively reinforced, worthwhile experiences can encourage favourable attitudes toward physical activity, thus promoting the pursuit of an active healthy and balanced lifestyle.

THE COMPONENTS OF ATTITUDE

The Triadic Model of Attitude

An attitude comprises three components – cognitive, affective and behavioural – as described in Table 4 below.

The cognitive component	Reflects beliefs and knowledge that an individual holds about the attitude object – also known as the information component.
The affective component	Consists of feelings or an emotional response toward an attitude object – known as the emotional component. It is here that an evaluation of an attitude object is made.
The behavioural component	Concerns how a person intends to behave or respond towards an attitude object.

Table 4 The components of attitude

Changing attitudes: Cognitive Dissonance Theory

- By changing one attitude component, a person will experience emotional conflict or dissonance.
- Emotional conflict is the basis of Dissonance Theory.
- Dissonance may cause a negative attitude to be changed.

Attitudes

- Attitudes in general are poor predictors of behaviour and may not necessarily indicate the likelihood of a desirable lifestyle choice.
- An individual's positive attitudes and beliefs relating to the health benefits of exercise do not guarantee that they will commit to an exercise programme.
- When attitudes become more specific, they are more likely to predict behaviour.
- The most accurate predictor of behaviour is when a person makes a clear statement of commitment. This predictor is called Behavioural Intention.

> **Need to know more?** For more information on attitudes see Chapter 8, pages 204–208, in the OCR A2 PE Student Book.

ACHIEVEMENT MOTIVATION

Achievement motivation links personality with the degree of competitiveness shown by an individual.

Atkinson and McClelland (1976) predicted that achievement motivation is generated through a combination of personality and situational factors. They view achievement motivation as a personality trait which is activated by a situation. The situation comprises the probability of success and the incentive value of success:

- *Probability of success*: the extent to which success is likely, for example success is more likely if the task is found to be easy.
- *Incentive value of success*: the intrinsic value experienced by the individual after success has been achieved, for example the harder the task the greater the incentive value will be because the probability of success is reduced.

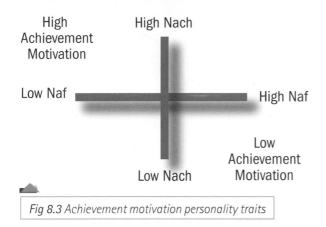

High Achievement Motivation

High Nach

Low Naf

High Naf

Low Nach

Low Achievement Motivation

Fig 8.3 Achievement motivation personality traits

- High achievers, in these circumstances, are likely to display approach behaviour and mastery orientation characteristics.
- The incentive value will be high when the chance of success is evenly balanced.
- Performers showing personality traits that are associated with low achievement motivation would experience greatest anxiety in situations with a 50–50 chance of success.
- In this situation, low achievers are most likely to adopt avoidance behaviour and experience learned helplessness.

EXAM TIP

You need to be aware of a strong link between achievement motivation and attribution.

The Atkinson & McClelland theory of achievement motivation is best at predicting behavioural responses in situations where there is a 50–50 chance of success/failure.

- A situation in which the chance of success or failure is even is likely to trigger the motivation to achieve in performers with high achievement traits.

KEY TERMS

Approach behaviour – Describes behaviour that accepts a challenge.

Avoidance behaviour – Describes behaviour that rejects a challenge.

Mastery orientation – The strong motive to succeed found in the high achiever. This type of person will expect to succeed but will persist when failure is experienced.

Learned helplessness – The belief that failure is inevitable and that the individual has no control over the factors that cause failure.

The characteristics of high and low achievement motivation personality traits	
High Nach personality characteristics	**Low Nach personality characteristics**
High need to achieve	Low need to achieve
Low need to avoid failure	High need to avoid failure
Approach behaviour is adopted	Avoidance behaviour is adopted
Challenge is accepted	Challenge is rejected
Risks are undertaken	Risks are declined
Shows persistence and perseverance when task is difficult	Curtails effort when task is difficult
Success tends to be attributed to internal factors	Success tends to be attributed to external factors
Failure tends to be attributed to external factors	Failure tends to be attributed to internal factors
Failure is seen as a route to success	Failure is seen as the route to further failure
Aspire to mastery orientation	Adopt learned helplessness

Table 5 Achievement motivation and high Nach and low Nach characteristics

▶ **Need to know more?** For more information on Achievement motivation see Chapter 8, pages 208–211, in the OCR A2 PE Student Book.

Sport-specific achievement motivation (competitiveness)

Competitiveness in this context means the motivation to achieve in sport.

ATTRIBUTION THEORY

- Attribution theory looks at the reasons given by coaches and players for success and failure in sport.
- The study of attribution has been shown by Weiner (1971) to have powerful implications for achievement related behaviour.
- There are strong links between attribution and achievement motivation.

With regard to Figure 8.4 above:

- Weiner's model is structured on two dimensions.
- The **locus of causality** dimension indicates whether the attribution relates to factors that are either internal or external to the performer.
- Stability indicates whether attributions are stable or unstable. Stability refers to the degree of permanence associated with an attribution factor.

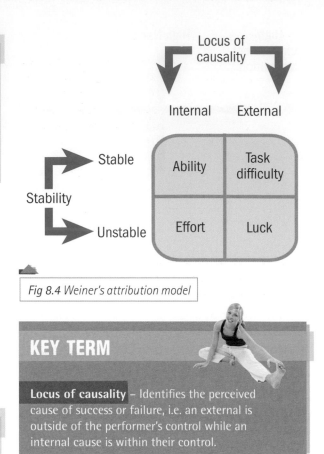

Fig 8.4 *Weiner's attribution model*

Control is a third dimension of the attribution model and this is a key factor in the important process of attribution retraining.

REASONS FOR SUCCESS AND FAILURE

In general, the coach should attribute failure to external causes in order to sustain confidence. Internal attributions should be used to reinforce success.

High achievers

- High achievers, or people who adopt approach behaviour, tend to attribute their success to internal factors, for example high-ability level.
- Failure on the other hand is put down to external factors, for example bad luck.
- Failure, therefore, is seen as a temporary setback.
- This is known as a self-serving bias.
- As a consequence, high achievers tend to remain persistent in the face of failure.
- This is a positive application of attribution.
- Consistent achievement and positive application of attribution would promote mastery orientation. This is likely to encourage a physically active lifestyle.

Low achievers

- Low achievers or people who adopt avoidance behaviour tend to attribute a lack of success to internal factors, for example. a lack of ability.
- Low achievers also tend to attribute success to external factors, for example achievement was the outcome of luck.
- This type of attribution would take away confidence and reduce expectation of future achievement.
- This is negative application of attribution.
- Repeated failure and negative application of attribution would cause the athlete to experience learned helplessness.
- This condition may cause an individual to avoid an activity.

Attribution retraining

Attribution retraining involves changing the performer's perception of the causes of failure. It focuses the reasons for failure onto internal, unstable and controllable factors, for example effort attributions.

The process of attribution retraining:

- raises confidence
- changes avoidance behaviour into approach behaviour
- encourages mastery orientation.

- this will promote the likelihood of lifelong sport participation.

Need to know more? For more information on attribution theory see Chapter 8, pages 212–214, in the OCR A2 PE Student Book.

AGGRESSION

- The prime motive of hostile aggression is to harm an opponent.
- Aggressive actions violate the rules of any game and such indiscretions are dysfunctional in the context of sport.
- Often an aggressive player will disrupt the team's performance and spoil the cohesion of the group.

Aggression needs to be eliminated from sport.

Assertion

Assertion is also known as channelled aggression.

- Assertive behaviour does not attempt to harm and is strictly within the rules and spirit of the game.
- Assertion often involves forceful play, primarily focused upon completing the skill successfully.
- The major aim of assertion is the successful completion of the task.
- Assertion was described by Parens (1987) as non-hostile self-protective mastery behaviour.

Evaluate critically the effects of attribution on performance and on sustaining a balanced, active and healthy lifestyle

	Positive applications of attribution – improve performance and help sustain a balanced lifestyle	Negative applications of attribution – inhibit performance and reduce drive to sustain a balanced lifestyle
Success	Internal attributions given for success help to: • endorse mastery orientation • elevate confidence or self-esteem • develop pride • increase the expectation of success in the future.	External attributions given for success take away: • the pride normally associated with success • the incentive value derived from mastery orientation.
Failure	External attributions given for failure help to: • encourage the pursuit of mastery orientation • sustain confidence or self-esteem • eliminate shame • improve the expectation of success in the future.	Internal attributions given for failure take away: • confidence by highlighting ability incompetence • mastery orientation by leading to learned helplessness.

Table 7 Positive and negative applications of attribution

THEORIES OF AGGRESSION

Theory	Theorist	Summary explanation
Instinct theory	Freud	Aggression is genetically inherited; a trait of violence lies within everyone.
Social learning theory	Bandura	• Aggression is not genetically based but is nurtured through environmental forces. • Aggression can be learned by watching and copying from role models; it becomes an accepted mode of behaviour if reinforced. • Aggression is likely to occur if part of social and cultural norms of a group.
Frustration aggression hypothesis	Dollard	• An interactionist theory – involves an environmental circumstance stimulating a personality gene. • Frustration develops when goal directed behaviour is blocked. • Frustration triggers the aggressive gene.
Aggression cue hypothesis	Berkowitz	• A second interactionist perspective. • Frustration creates a 'readiness' for aggression – only triggered when a provocative environmental cue is present. • Aggressive cues such as perceieved unfairness, the opposition shirt or the nature of the game will trigger aggression in sport if arousal amongst participants is high.

Table 8 *Theories of aggression*

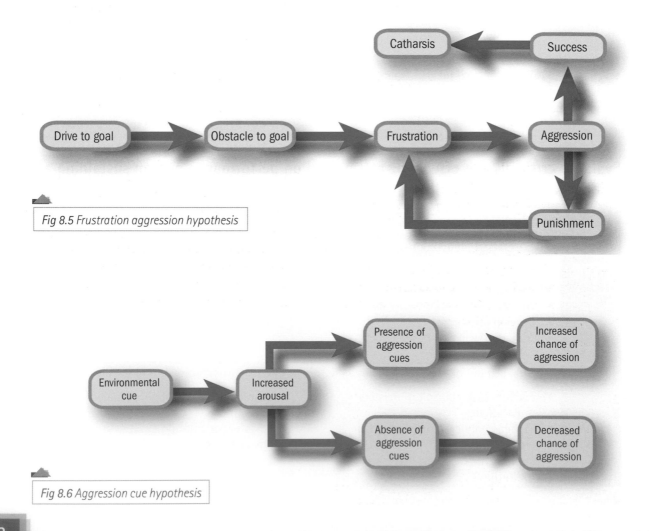

Fig 8.5 *Frustration aggression hypothesis*

Fig 8.6 *Aggression cue hypothesis*

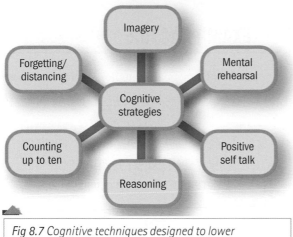

Fig 8.7 Cognitive techniques designed to lower psychological/cognitive arousal

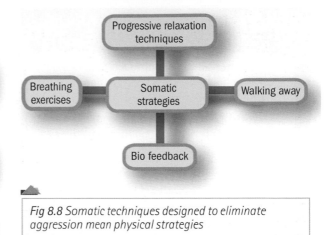

Fig 8.8 Somatic techniques designed to eliminate aggression mean physical strategies

There are a number of methods to eliminate aggression and these come under two headings:

Cognitive techniques: to do with thought processes and involve psychological strategies

Somatic techniques: involve physiological (physical) strategies.

Control of aggression promotes the adoption of active and healthy lifestyles. If unchecked, aggressive behaviour can greatly reduce this possibility.

- Silva (1979) proposed that **hostile aggression**, when demonstrated by an individual, may increase arousal causing reduced concentration and resulting in poor performance. Underachievement can lead to learned helplessness and an inclination to give up.
- Dysfunctional consequences of aggression extend beyond the immediate performance results. Aggressive performers are likely to get injured and run a greater risk of being dismissed from the game.
- Performers with aggressive tendencies tend to feel anger and experience less satisfaction after completing activities and have therefore a reduced motive to continue with the activity.

Need to know more? For more information on aggression and assertion see Chapter 8, pages 215–221, in the OCR A2 PE Student Book.

CHECK

If you are satisfied with your knowledge and understanding, tick off the sections that you have revised so far. If you are not satisfied then revisit those sections and refer to the pages in the *Need to know more?* features.

- ☐ Describe personality and outline its importance in producing effective performance and in following a balanced, active and healthy lifestyle.
- ☐ Discuss attitudes and their influence on performance and lifestyles.
- ☐ Describe achievement motivation and its effect on performance and on following an active and healthy lifestyle.
- ☐ Outline attribution theory and the impact of attribution on performance and sustaining a balanced, active and healthy lifestyle.
- ☐ Consider aggression and its impact upon performance and behaviour.

KEY TERM

Hostile aggression – Aggression is often referred to as hostile aggression if it is defined as deliberate intention to harm or injure another person. Hostile aggression breaks the rules of the game, e.g. a deliberate high tackle in rugby.

1. The inter-actionist approach to personality formation involves a combination of trait and learning perspectives.

2. Type A personalities are determined by the degree of reticular activation and their capacity to work alone.

3. A personality profile gives an accurate prediction as to whether a person will adopt a balanced, healthy and active lifestyle.

4. Attitudes are often formed through socialisation and although they are unstable, they can be enduring.

5. An attitude is unstable but enduring. It comprises of three components: cognitive, affective and behavioural.

6. Sport specific achievement motivation indicates the degree to which an individual is competitive in sport.

7. Attribution theory should never be applied when an individual experiences failure in sport.

8. Attribution retraining involves attributing failure to internal, unstable and controllable factors such as effort.

9. Aggression should be an integral tactic in team strategy and should be reinforced by the coach during performance.

10. Anxiety management techniques may be implemented to eliminate aggression from performance.

EXAM PRACTICE

1. Using practical examples, explain the causes of aggressive behaviour in sport. *(5 marks)*

2. Explain the origins of attitudes and how attitudes can impact upon young people achieving healthy, active and balanced lifestyles. *(5 marks)*

3. Describe the components of attitude and critically evaluate the influence of attitudes when deciding to adopt an active lifestyle. *20 marks)*

4. Describe the use of cognitive strategies by sports performers to eliminate aggression. Explain the effects of these strategies on the adoption of active and healthy lifestyles. *(6 marks)*

See page 278 for answers

CHAPTER 9

Group dynamics of performance

CHAPTER OVERVIEW

By the end of this chapter you should have knowledge and understanding of:

- groups and teams – their impact upon performance and the pursuit of balanced, active and healthy lifestyles
- leadership and the role of a leader in physical activities
- social facilitation and inhibition – the effects of an audience and other participants on performance and lifestyle behaviours.

KEY TERM

Group – "Groups are those social aggregates that involve mutual awareness, a common goal and the potential for interaction" (McGrath 1984).

Properties of groups

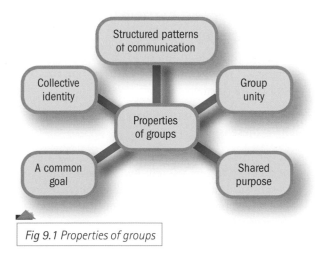

Fig 9.1 Properties of groups

GROUP PERFORMANCE

Steiner's model

Actual Productivity = Potential Productivity – Losses due to faulty processes

AP = PP – FP

- Actual productivity: the team performance at a given time during a game or event and refers to the extent of successful interaction.
- Potential productivity: the maximum capability of the group when cohesiveness appears at its strongest.
- Faulty processes: factors which can go wrong in team performance. They prevent cohesion.

There are two faulty processes that bring about losses in potential productivity:

- *Co-ordination losses (The Ringlemann Effect):* any breakdown in teamwork and the synchronisation of the group is regarded as a co-ordination loss and is termed the Ringlemann Effect.
- *Motivation losses (Social Loafing):* motivational losses relate to an individual who suffers a decrease in motivation during performance and so withdraws effort and 'coasts'. This loss of motivation and subsequent relaxation of effort is called Social Loafing.

Listed below are the negative influences that can cause social loafing and lead to dysfunctional behaviour in the context of group dynamics:

- Feeling that others in the team are not trying.
- Feeling that performances are never watched or valued by the coach.
- Low self-confidence may result in a strategy of social loafing to protect self-esteem.

- Those with negative experiences, e.g. failure, or recipient of negative attribution, tend to 'loaf'.
- Loss of motivation if a task is perceived to be too difficult. This links to 'avoidance behaviour'.

KEY TERMS

Group dynamics – The social processes operating within the group between individual members.

Dysfunctional – A negative process that inhibits or prevents the completion or continuation of a desired operation.

EXAM TIP

- You need to be aware that social loafing is **dysfunctional** behaviour because it prevents effective teamwork. Notice the link between the causes of social loafing, low self-confidence, negative attribution and avoidance behaviour.

Other factors that adversely affect teamwork include:

- Injury can disrupt team strategies and break down coordination.
- A lack of incentive to produce team work will prevent cohesion.
- Vague individual roles inhibit effective teamwork.
- Low sum of the players' overall ability makes team play difficult to achieve.
- Personality can influence team cohesion as people with **low trait confidence** find it difficult to promote group cohesion Carron (1994).
- Inadequate leadership inhibits teamwork.

KEY TERM

Low trait confidence – The general disposition of low confidence. It tends to be both stable and global.

EXAM TIP

- These dysfunctional factors need to be eliminated as they also influence the formation and development of a cohesive group or team.
- An explanation of the strategies that promote teamwork and group cohesion is a popular examination question.

Factors affecting team cohesion

Carron (1993) identified four factors that directly affect team cohesion.

1. **Situational factors:** These include time, the environment and the size of the group.
2. **Individual factors:** Individual factors refer to the characteristics of the team members. The motivation level and the experience of the individual members are examples of individual factors.
3. **Leadership factors:** Leadership factors involve the style of leadership preferred by the group.
4. **Team factors:** Team factors include collective team goals, good communication and a record of shared success.

Factors affecting participation in a group or team

In order to promote group or team cohesion, it is important to encourage the participation of individual performers.

A number of strategies can be implemented to address these issues:

- Clear roles given to each player can help an individual to feel valued. Awareness of the responsibilities of other team members ensures the development of mutual understanding between individuals.
- Participation in team building exercises are good both for task and social cohesion. Spink (1995).
- Evaluating each member's performance effectively reduces social loafing.
- Punishment of non-team or un-cohesive players.
- Selecting team players rather than players only interested in their own performance.

- Team goals help to clarify how team standards encourage effectiveness.
- Rehearsal of set plays during practice facilitates group coordination.
- The reinforcement of team success gives team efficiency as the reason for the achievement of the group.
- Strong leadership encourages group cohesion.

Group and team effects on behaviour

- It has been found (Spink and Carron 1994) that increased levels of group cohesion help an individual to commit to and persist with exercise programmes.
- The group can have a positive influence by providing social support and endorsing the value of a performer's contribution.
- The performer who perceives that their contribution to the team product is valued is likely to experience internal motivation.
- This source of motivation encourages the adoption of a balanced, active and healthy lifestyle.
- The desire to conform to the norms and values of a peer group is particularly strong for a young person. If the consensus of the group favours participation in physical activity, there is a good chance that the individual will follow the trend.
- Tajfel (social identity theory 1978) proposed that the norms and values of the group are looked upon positively by an individual if they are a member of that group.
- If the individual does not belong, the same person will adopt a negative perception of the group ethos.
- This biased perception occurs in order to protect self esteem. Once having become a member, the individual will conform as part of the team to protect the interests of the group.

Need to know more? For more information on group dynamics of performance see Chapter 9, pages 226–231, in the OCR A2 PE Student Book

LEADERSHIP AND THE ROLE OF A LEADER IN PHYSICAL ACTIVITIES

The importance of effective leadership

Successful teams have strong leaders and the importance of this role is evident in all categories of sport and exercise activity groups.

The performance of a leader is very clear in interactive games and at the head of an exercise group. Although less obvious in co-active situations, the leader's contribution to the effectiveness of a team's performance is also influential.

- Leadership may be considered as a behavioural process that influences individuals and groups toward set goals.
- A leader has the dual function of ensuring player satisfaction while steering the individual or group to success.
- Leadership can be a positive influence on lifestyle behaviour.

Fig 9.2 The qualities of an effective leader

Characteristics/styles of leadership

Leader characteristics/styles	Qualities associated with that leader style
Task orientated or autocratic leaders	- Tends to make all of the decisions. - Does not consult the group. - Is motivated to complete the task quickly.
Social, or person, orientated leaders also referred to as democratic leaders	- Will share the decisions with the group. - Believes in consultation. - Is interested in developing inter-personal relationships within the team.
Laissez-faire leaders	- Stands aside and allows the group to make its own independent decisions. - Has severe drawbacks.

Table 1 Characteristics/styles of leadership

The characteristic or style adopted by the leader depends upon the 'favourableness' of the situation.

A highly favourable situation	A highly unfavourable situation
Leader's position is strong	Leader's position is weak
Task is simple with clear structure	Task is complex with vague structure
Warm group and leader relations	Hostile group and leader relations

Table 2 Favourableness of a situation

- Autocratic or task orientated leaders are more effective both in the most favourable and the least favourable situations.
- Democratic or person orientated leaders are more effective in moderately favourable situations.

EXAM TIP

You need to understand that situation favourableness is a major factor in determining leadership style. You also need to be aware of other factors that influence the leader's approach. Some additional factors are identified in Table 3.

Emergent and prescribed leaders

The terms 'emergent' and 'prescribed' leaders refer to the background against which a leader is chosen.

- An emergent leader is selected from within the group.
- A prescribed leader is selected from outside of the group.

There are advantages and disadvantages for both types of leader selection.

> **Need to know more?** For more information on group performance see Chapter 9, pages 227–233, in the OCR A2 PE Student Book

A CRITICAL EVALUATION OF LEADERSHIP THEORIES

Trait approach

- Trait theorists believe that leaders are born with the capacity to take charge.
- Leadership traits are considered to be stable personality dispositions.
- Such traits may include intelligence, assertiveness and self-confidence.
- If this is accurate, a leader should be able to take control of any situation.
- Tough mindedness and independent thinking are traits that may be helpful in leadership but their inheritance and importance cannot be proven.

Autocratic leadership is preferable:	Democratic leadership is preferable:
• when groups are hostile and discipline is needed	• when groups are friendly and relationships are warm
• if groups are large	• if groups are small
• for team players who prefer an instructional approach	• in activities that require interpersonal communication
• in the early or cognitive stage of learning	• when the autonomous stage of learning has been achieved and the performer is expert
• in dangerous situations	• in situations where there is no threat of danger
• when there are time constraints	• when there are no constraints on time
• if the leader's personality is inclined to be authoritarian	• if the leader's personality is inclined to be democratic
• when the leader is male; men prefer an autocratic approach.	• when the leader is female; women prefer a democratic approach.

Table 3 A comparison of democratic and autocratic leadership styles

- Trait theory in general is not a good predictor of behaviour.
- It is unlikely, therefore, that specific dominant traits alone can facilitate successful leadership.

A significant trait theory is the 'great man theory of leadership', which suggests that the necessary qualities of leadership are inherited by sons (not daughters) whose fathers have been successful in this field. This is not a popular theory.

> Like early trait personality research, trait research relating to leadership has been inconclusive.

Social learning theory

Social learning theorists propose that all behaviour is learned:

- Learning comes about through contact with environmental forces.
- The process of imitating the successful behaviour of role models is called vicarious reinforcement.
- The weakness in social learning theory is that it does not take into account the trait perspective.
- It is unlikely that learning alone can facilitate effective leadership.

Interactionist theory

- According to this theory, leadership skills emerge because of a combination of inherited abilities and learned skills.
- Leadership skills are likely to emerge and be acquired when a situation triggers the traits that are of importance to leadership.
- Gill (2000) indicates that in the context of sport and related physical activity, interactionist theories give a more realistic explanation of behaviour.

The multi-dimensional model of leadership (an interactionist theory)

Chelladurai identified three influences that interact to produce effective leadership (Fig.9 4).

With these influences in mind, Chelladurai proposed that the effectiveness of leadership could be judged upon two outcomes:

- The degree of success accomplished during a task
- The extent to which the group experienced satisfaction during the process of achieving the goal.

After taking into account all considerations, Chelladurai presented a multi-dimensional model of leadership (Fig 9.5).

The three influences or antecedents that determine the behaviour adopted by the leader are explained in Table 4.

Situational characteristics are environmental conditions and include:	• the type of activity in which the group members are involved, e.g. interactive or coactive activities • the numbers involved in the team • the time constraints of the play or overall match • considerations about the strengths of the opposition.
Leader characteristics include:	• the skill and experience of the leader • the personality of the leader which may well be inclined either towards a person or a task-orientated style.
Group member characteristics could involve:	• age • gender • motivation • competence • experience.

Table 4 Antecedents that determine the behaviour

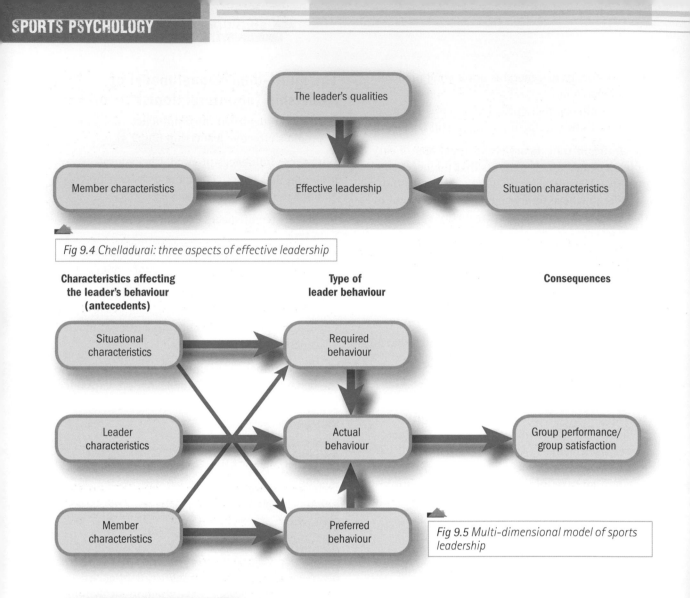

Fig 9.4 *Chelladurai: three aspects of effective leadership*

Characteristics affecting the leader's behaviour (antecedents) · **Type of leader behaviour** · **Consequences**

Fig 9.5 *Multi-dimensional model of sports leadership*

Required behaviour
Required behaviour involves what ought to be done by the leader in certain situations. The leader's behaviour may be dictated by a playing strategy or organisation system.

Actual behaviour
Actual behaviour is what the leader chooses to do as the best course of action in the given situation. Actual behaviour is greatly influenced by the competence of the leader

Preferred behaviour
Preferred behaviour concerns what the group of athletes want the leader to do. The leadership style preferred by the group is usually determined by the member characteristics.

Chelladurai recognised three types of behaviour that impact on the leader. These are termed types of leader behaviour. Types of leader behaviour are guided by the antecedents.

- The key element of the multi dimensional model is that in order for a leader to achieve a positive outcome all three aspects of leader behaviour need to agree.
- An alternative way of describing the agreement or alignment of leader behaviour is to say that the three behaviours need to be congruent (coincide exactly).

Need to know more? For more information on A critical evaluation of leadership theories see Chapter 9, pages 234–237, in the OCR A2 PE Student Book

Fig 9.6 *Three types of leader behaviour*

Leader behaviour		Extent of group performance and satisfaction	
Degree of congruence	Actual leader behaviour is the required behaviour to complete the group task successfully and is also the type of leadership that is preferred by the group. Full congruence in leader behaviours exists.	Outcome	It is predicted that in these circumstances the group will perform effectively and the satisfaction of the group members will be high.
Degree of congruence	Actual leader behaviour is the required behaviour to complete the group task successfully but is not the type of leadership that is preferred by the group. Incongruence in leader behaviours exists.	Outcome	It is predicted that in these circumstances the group will perform effectively but the satisfaction of the group members will be low.
Degree of congruence	Actual leader behaviour is not the required behaviour to complete the group task successfully but is the type of leadership that is preferred by the group. Incongruence in leader behaviours exists.	Outcome	It is predicted that in these circumstances the group will perform ineffectively but the satisfaction of the group members will be high.

Table 5 *Explanation of Multidimensional Leadership Model*

SOCIAL FACILITATION AND INHIBITION

- Most sports or physical activities take place in the company of other people either in the form of spectators or **co-actors**.
- The presence of an audience increases the arousal level of the athlete.
- Increases in arousal can have either a positive or a negative influence on performance. Many factors determine the effects of arousal on performance.
- Social facilitation occurs when arousal enhances performance.
- Social inhibition occurs when arousal inhibits performance.

KEY TERM

Co-actors – Fellow performers in the form of opponents, team mates or people in the same exercise group or Physical Education class.

Much of the current belief relating to audience effects is based around two psychological theories. These theories are:

- Drive theory of social facilitation (Zajonc 1965)
- Evaluation apprehension theory (Cottrell 1968)

Drive theory of social facilitation

In his model of drive theory of social facilitation, Zajonc recognised different types of audience.

The 'mere presence' of other people is sufficient to increase the arousal level of the performer. Zajonc used drive theory to predict the effect of others on performance.

- Drive theory indicates a relationship between arousal and performance.
- Drive theory of social facilitation states that the presence of others is in itself arousing – that arousal enhances production of dominant responses as opposed to subordinate responses.
- Actions that have already been learned are termed 'learned behaviours' and tend to be our dominant responses.
- High arousal is beneficial at the expert stage (autonomous phase of learning) because the performer's dominant behaviour tends towards the correct response.
- At the novice stage (associative stage of learning) the dominant behaviour is likely to be incorrect. High arousal would cause mistakes and inhibit performance.
- High arousal facilitates the performance of simple and ballistic skills that are classified as gross.
- High arousal would benefit an extrovert but would inhibit the performance of an introvert.
- Zajonc's Drive theory of social facilitation is supported by the belief that arousal caused by an audience is a natural (innate) reaction.

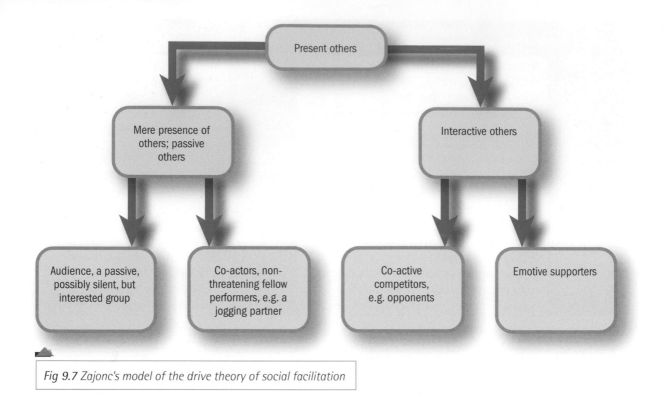

Fig 9.7 *Zajonc's model of the drive theory of social facilitation*

Evaluation apprehension theory

- Cottrell (1968) proposed that the 'mere presence' of others was not sufficiently arousing to produce the social facilitation effect.
- Increases in arousal were only evident when the performer perceived that the audience was assessing or judging a performance.
- Hence, Cottrell's theory was termed 'evaluation apprehension'.
- It could be the case that the perceived evaluation of the audience inhibits performance.
- Some athletes may rely on evaluation to stimulate arousal.

EXAM TIP

The factors that determine the possible influence of arousal on an individual performance are personality, stage of learning, type of skill and level of experience. You might wish to review your AS work on motivation; see Chapter 18 part 1 in OCR AS PE Student Book.

THREE FURTHER THEORIES THAT RELATE TO THE FACILITATION OR THE INHIBITION OF PERFORMANCE DUE TO THE PRESENCE OF AN AUDIENCE

These theories must be considered when helping an athlete to cope with audience effects.

The home advantage effect

Large and supportive home crowds are believed to provide home teams with an advantage.

Proximity effect

Schwartz (1975) proposed that location of the audience in relation to performance was an important factor in social facilitation. The closer the audience, the greater the effect on arousal.

Distraction – conflict theory (Barron)

The limitations of the performer's attentional capacity can explain the effect of an audience. The audience may become additional 'cues' and therefore a distraction overloading the attentional space of the performer.

Strategies to combat the effects of social inhibition in practical activities

It is important that athletes are able cope with the presence of an audience or large crowd.

- Selective attention would narrow the focus of the performer onto the relevant cues.
- Mental rehearsal and imagery could enhance concentration and help block out the audience.
- The athlete would be advised to engage in positive self talk to block out negative thoughts.
- Practice in the presence of an audience would help the athlete to become accustomed to the effects it may have on arousal levels.
- Ensure that skills are overlearned to become dominant behaviours. When arousal increases, dominant responses emerge.
- Confidence building strategies should be implemented to reduce inhibition.
- Positive reinforcement and social support from the coach and team mates will reduce anxiety.
- Confidence could also be increased by appropriate use of attribution.
- The athlete should be made aware of how concentration is maximized when the ideal level of arousal is achieved.

▶ **Need to know more?** For more information on social facilitation and inhibition see Chapter 9, pages 237–242, in the OCR A2 PE Student Book

TRUE OR FALSE?

1. Motivational factors (social loafing) and co-ordination factors (Ringelmann effect) are 'faulty processes that prevent team cohesion'.
2. To allow the 'star' performer to play outside team strategy will increase group satisfaction and promote team cohesion.
3. A player who has had a negative experience (e.g. failure) will tend to 'loaf' during play.
4. Good leadership promotes team cohesion.
5. An autocratic leadership style delegates responsibility to individuals because they want other leaders to emerge from the group.
6. A democratic leadership style should be adopted when the situation is moderately favourable.
7. A prescribed leader is one who has been selected from outside the group.
8. In the multi-dimensional model of leadership it is predicted that group effectiveness and satisfaction will be highest if full agreement in the leader behaviour exists.
9. The presence of an audience always facilitates the best performance in competitive sports situations.
10. Drive theory of social facilitation predicts that as arousal increases due to the presence of an audience, the production of the dominant response is enhanced.

See page 281 for answers.

CHECK

If you are satisfied with your knowledge and understanding, tick off the sections that you have revised so far. If you are not satisfied then revisit those sections and refer to the pages in the *Need to know more?* features.

- ☐ Describe the impact of groups and teams upon performance and the pursuit of balanced, active and healthy lifestyles.

- ☐ Consider leadership and the role of a leader in physical activities.

- ☐ Outline social facilitation and inhibition, including the effects of an audience and other participants on performance and lifestyle behaviours.

EXAM PRACTICE

1. Using psychological theories, explain possible positive and negative effects of an audience on sports performance. Describe the strategies that help prevent social inhibition in physical activities and how these may help the pursuit of a balanced active and healthy lifestyle. *(20 marks)*

2. Describe Chelladurai's multi dimensional model of leadership and explain how leadership can influence performance. *(6 marks)*

3. Social loafing prevents team cohesion. What does social loafing mean and how is it caused? *(4 marks)*

4. Critically evaluate trait, social learning and interactionist theories as they influence the development of leadership skills. *(6 marks)*

See page 281 for answers

CHAPTER 10

Mental preparation for physical activities

CHAPTER OVERVIEW

By the end of this chapter you should be able to demonstrate knowledge and understanding of:

- goal setting as it impacts upon performance and the development and sustaining of a balanced, active and healthy lifestyle
- self-confidence and its impact on performance and participation in physical activity and in raising self-esteem
- attentional control and its impact upon effective performance
- emotional control and its impact upon performance and in sustaining a balanced, active and healthy lifestyle.

GOAL SETTING

- Goal setting can develop positive self-perception and reduce anxiety.
- The correct use of goal setting can improve the confidence and increase the motivation level of an athlete.
- Effective goal setting encourages commitment to an active, healthy and balanced lifestyle.
- As a guide to the correct implementation of goal setting, the SMARTER principle is important.

Identification of the key letter		Explanation of the key word
S	Specific	Goals relate directly to the task, e.g. a netball shooter adopts a goal to improve the rate of success from 60 per cent to 75 per cent. Specific goals are more effective than non-specific or 'do your best' goals e.g. a shooter in netball trying to improve the rate of conversion with no measurable target.
M	Measurable	Goals are evaluated and measured against a previous performance or external standard.
A	Accepted	A goal must be agreed or accepted by the coach and the performer.
R	Realistic	Goals should be challenging but attainable. The attainment of a challenging goal develops confidence and motivates the athlete to aim at the next goal.
T	Timed	Set a time limit to achieve the goal: short, intermediate or long.
E	Exciting	An accepted challenging goal provides excitement which represses boredom.
R	Recorded	Achievement of, or progress toward a target should be recorded ('ink it, don't think it'). This can be exciting and motivating in itself.

Table 1 The SMARTER principle

Goals can be divided into two groups: time-based and activity-based.

Time-based goals

Long-term goals	• An ultimate aim which may take an extended period of time to achieve. • If set on their own, may be daunting to the performer causing increased anxiety. • When set in isolation do not improve performance.
Medium-term goals	• Occur during the short-term goal sequence. • Improve access to long-term goals, endorse short-term goals and are significant improvement indicators.
Short-term goals	• Give immediate success – set at the level of the performer's existing capability. • Set in a sequence that becomes more difficult. • Can provide immediate success.

Table 2 Time-based goals

Activity-based goals

Type of goal	Explanation
Performance goals	Based on judgments of previous performances. e.g. a batter in cricket will try to improve upon last season's runs average.
Process goals	Concerned with improving techniques for a better performance, e.g. the batter in cricket may work upon improving footwork during shot execution.
Product goals	Sometimes called outcome goals. Product goals involve defeating other competitors and are concerned with winning outcomes. Often externally controlled, e.g. winning a tennis tournament.

Table 3 The three types of activity-based goals

A CRITICAL EVALUATION OF GOAL TYPES

- A total focus on product goals can create anxiety during competition as the athlete is required to win in order to achieve the goal.
- Product goals on their own can inhibit performance but should not be discounted. Many sporting activities require the emergence of an obvious winner.
- Performance and process goals give more control to the participant.
- They are good indicators of an athlete's commitment to training and competition.
- Performance goals are better than product goals (Cox 1998).
- A combination of goal types should be incorporated into preparation
- For every product goal there should be a number of performance and process goals set for the athlete (Filby *et al*, 1999).

> **Need to know more?** For more information on goal types see Chapter 10, pages 247–250, in the OCR A2 PE Student Book

Self-confidence

Self-confidence influences motivation and is a factor that determines the decision to participate in a chosen physical activity.

Self-efficacy theory

- Self-efficacy is a specific type of self-confidence and relates to a person's perception of their standard of ability in particular activities and situations.
- Self-efficacy tends to be unstable and is therefore changeable.
- According to Bandura, people with high self-efficacy:
  - adopt approach behaviour
  - seek challenges and persevere with tasks
  - attribute success to internal factors.
- Self-efficacy can exert a powerful influence on performance by raising the performer's expectation of success.
- People with low self-efficacy tend to adopt avoidance behaviour and give up easily.
- By applying the theory of self-efficacy the coach can promote specific confidence and the expectation of success.
- Self-efficacy theory comprises four components or sub-processes (see Table 4).

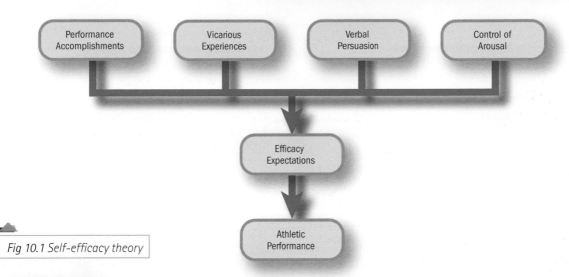

Fig 10.1 Self-efficacy theory

Performance accomplishments	A performer who experiences learned helplessness or a loss of confidence should be reminded of previous successes in the related skill or situation.
Vicarious experiences	The person lacking in confidence watches others of equal ability perform the problematic skill successfully.
Verbal persuasion	Positive communication convinces the athlete that they can perform well.
Control of arousal	The performer evaluates their internal feelings and physiological state. People who develop specific self confidence with regard to performing exercise programmes are more likely to adopt and persist in healthy lifestyles by taking up physical activities.

Table 4 Self-efficacy theory

Application of self-efficacy theory will improve specific self confidence.

SPORTS CONFIDENCE THEORY

Sports confidence theory (Vealey 1986) measures two factors:

- *Trait sports confidence (SC trait)*: innate and described as a natural disposition. Like all personality traits, it is relatively stable.
- *State sports confidence (SC state)*: developed through learning and tends to be unstable and changeable.

State sports confidence operates when a particular skill is to be performed, for example a putt in golf. The degree of state sports confidence is determined by the interaction of three factors.

1. Trait sports confidence.
2. The **objective sports situation**.
3. The performer's **competitive orientation**.

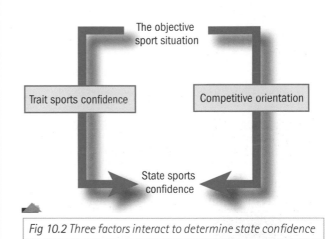

Fig 10.2 Three factors interact to determine state confidence

KEY TERMS

Objective sports situation – The type of skill that is to be performed. This could include the situation in which the skill is to be performed.

Competitive orientation – The extent to which an individual is prepared to compete and whether an individual strives to achieve a performance goal or a product goal.

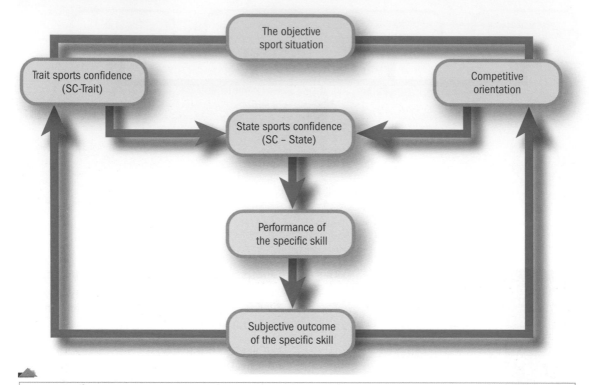

Fig 10.3 Vealey's model of sport confidence shows the formation of state sports confidence and how this type of confidence influences the outcome of a skill

EXAM TIP

Sport specific confidence (competitiveness) links to Vealey's model of sport confidence.

A decrease in SC trait and competitiveness will:	An increase in SC trait and competitiveness will:
1 depress SC state	1 elevate SC State
2 reduce self-efficacy	2 increase self-efficacy
3 make the performer feel less confident	3 make the performer feel more confident
4 cause avoidance behaviour.	4 facilitate approach behaviour.

Table 5 Effects of variation in levels of trait sports confidence (SC trait) and competitiveness orientation

The extent to which the athlete perceives the performance has been successful is termed the subjective outcome. Subjective outcomes produce the following effects:

An outcome perceived to be good will increase:

* trait sports confidence
* competitiveness
* state confidence.

An outcome perceived as poor will decrease:

* trait sports confidence
* competitiveness
* state confidence.

Most importantly, the variations in the levels of trait sports confidence and competitiveness orientation produce the following effects.

Vealey identified strategies to improve state sport confidence (SC state). They are identified in Fig 10.4.

> **Need to know more?** For more information on confidence theories see Chapter 10, pages 250–254, in the OCR A2 PE Student Book

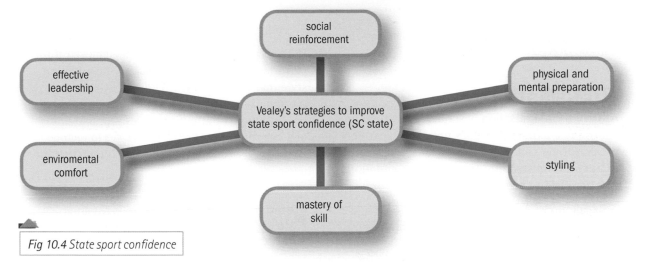

Fig 10.4 *State sport confidence*

ATTENTIONAL CONTROL

Attentional control involves concentration and **selective attention**.

KEY TERM

Selective attention – The process that enables focus to be given to environmental cues.

The Inverted U theory predicts the influence of arousal on the performance of a motor skill.

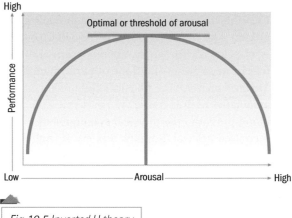

Fig 10.5 *Inverted U theory*

- The Inverted U hypothesis predicts that as arousal increases so does the quality of performance up to an optimal point.
- Arousal levels which are above, or below, this optimal threshold will result in poor performance.
- The reason requires understanding of attentional control and cue utilisation.

Cue utilisation hypothesis

- When arousal is low, the perceptual field of the performer widens excessively and access is given to a wide range of irrelevant environmental cues.
- To focus selective attention onto the most relevant stimuli is difficult. As a result, the information processing system is adversely affected, due to an overload of sensory stimuli.
- As arousal increases up to the optimal level, the perceptual field will adjust and narrow to the ideal width.
- Narrowing allows attention to be given to the most important cues only.
- At this optimal threshold, selective attention is fully operational and the capacity to focus and concentrate is maximised.
- The capacity to focus selectively is termed cue utilisation.
- If arousal increases above the optimal threshold, perceptual focus narrows excessively.
- Excessive narrowing causes relevant data to be missed and the information processing system becomes restricted.
- Under these conditions the performer will experience **hypervigilance**.

KEY TERMS

Cue utilisation – The process that facilitates maximum attentional control, allowing efficient decision making and effective performance to take place

Hypervigilance – A condition of panic that severely impedes selective attention and information processing.

Need to know more? For more information on attentional control see Chapter 10, pages 254–256, in the OCR A2 PE Student Book

ATTENTION STYLES

Although cue utilisation describes how attentional control is maximised, it does not make clear how the performer can adjust the width and direction of attention in response to the varying situations that are encountered in sport.

A psychologist named Nideffer presented a model of attention styles. It is based on two dimensions.

These dimensions are:

1. Broad and narrow focus relating to width of attention.
2. External and internal focus relating to direction of attention.

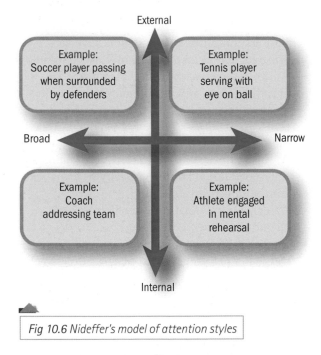

Fig 10.6 Nideffer's model of attention styles

- Broad attention takes in a great deal of environmental information and this includes peripheral cues or stimuli.
- A narrow focus is the required concentration on one or a small number of stimuli.
- The broad and narrow dimension is a continuum depicting a gradual change in the amount of information to be processed.
- An internal focus indicates that the performer's attention has been directed inwards and onto the psychological state.

- External focus enables the athlete to focus on environmental factors.

Optimal performance can only be achieved if the performer has the ability to adopt the attention style that matches the attentional demands of the situation. A good performer can draw upon the full range of attention styles. Optimal arousal and cue utilisation help a performer to change or 'shift' their attention style to match the attentional demands of the situation.

Need to know more? For more information on attention styles see Chapter 10, pages 256–257, in the OCR A2 PE Student Book

EMOTIONAL CONTROL

Anxiety and performance

- Research is now looking at the effect of anxiety on sports performance.
- Anxiety is a negative emotional state associated with feelings of worry and nervousness relating to activation or arousal.
- Confusion arises because it is usual for arousal and anxiety to be discussed together.
- Arousal is not experienced as either pleasant or unpleasant. Anxiety is an unpleasant state of high arousal.

There are two forms of anxiety:

1. *Cognitive anxiety*: the thought component of anxiety and accompanies somatic anxiety. It is associated with worry, apprehension and the fear of negative evaluations of performance.
2. *Somatic anxiety*: the physical component is associated with increases in heart rate and blood pressure, the physical symptoms of increased arousal. Somatic anxiety is triggered by cognitive anxiety.

There is a second dimension relating to the stability of anxiety:

- *State anxiety*: a person's immediate condition of anxiety in any one situation – unstable and often temporary.
- *Trait anxiety*: part of personality – relatively stable.

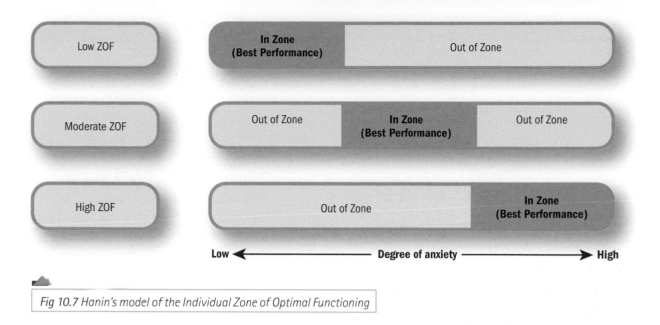

Fig 10.7 *Hanin's model of the Individual Zone of Optimal Functioning*

Individual zone of optimal functioning (IZOF)

- Hanin (1986) proposed that there are differences in the way people respond to anxiety.
- Some performers succeeded when anxiety was low; others achieved success when anxiety was high.
- Each athlete has their own preferred level of anxiety.
- As the facilitator of best performance, the preferred level of anxiety is not shown as a point or threshold as in Inverted U or Catastrophe Theories. It is presented as band width.
- In relation to this 'band' the athlete is neither 'psyching up' to nor are they exceeding a threshold of arousal at any point in time. They are simply either within or outside the zone of anxiety that is their individual preference.
- the athelete who is 'in zone' performs at their best.

Peak flow experience

The characteristics of a performance from an elite athlete who has attained a peak flow state are that skills appear effortless, automatic and fully controlled.

- According to Martens, peak flow experience is most likely to occur when high somatic arousal coincides with low cognitive anxiety.

- Many factors combine to bring about peak flow state. These factors appear to draw most of the Sports Psychology syllabus together.

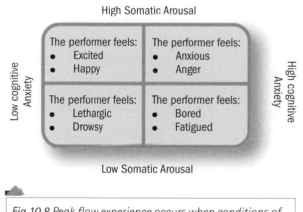

Fig 10.8 *Peak flow experience occurs when conditions of high somatic arousal and low cognitive anxiety converge*

Anxiety management techniques

There are two types of anxiety management techniques.

1 Somatic anxiety management relating to physical processes.
2 Cognitive anxiety management relating to thought processes.

Technique	Description	Critical evaluation of technique
Imagery	Imagery can be used to help relaxation and focus. It can take two forms: 1 External imagery – the athlete pictures performing the task successfully. 2 Internal imagery – mental rehearsal of skills and techniques. It focuses on specific elements without picturing the whole scene, e.g. a pass in football can be rehearsed without envisaging other players.	1 External imagery can be effective if the athlete can form the outside picture. The athlete must be a skilled and experienced performer if the picture is to be of value. 2 Mental rehearsal is thought to stimulate the nervous system and muscles in a way that replicates the real situation. This kinaesthetic experience can help learning and confidence. Mental rehearsal can also desensitise the performer to the anxiety caused by competitive situations. It is most effective for those at the autonomous stage of learning who can associate the correct kinaesthetic feel of the skill to the correct outcome.
Thought stopping	The athlete refuses to think negatively. Any negative inclination is stopped and substituted with a positive thought.	May be more effective if a person is inclined to be confident and extroverted. Individuals with introverted tendencies or prone to learned helplessness may find stopping negative thoughts difficult.
Positive self-talk	The athlete endorses their own ability or progress by talking to him or herself.	Speaking aloud commits the athlete to the task and does much to raise confidence. Is only of value if performers are experienced and of a high standard.
Rational thinking	Anxiety grows from an imbalance of perception between ability and situational demands (Martens, 1975). Rational thinking involves focusing inwardly on the internal and narrow style of attention and evaluating the situation and its possible logical consequences.	Rational thinking works effectively if the athlete has the experience and skill to evaluate a situation realistically. The inexperienced athlete would be unable to make a rational evaluation.

Table 6 Cognitive anxiety techniques

Technique	Description	Critical evaluation of technique
Biofeedback	Physical changes that happen to the body when arousal and anxiety increase, such as heart rate, blood pressure, and skin temperature, are measured when a performer is becoming anxious. Once these changes are being monitored, it is thought that the performer can control the physiological effects of excessive anxiety and adopt a calmer state.	• There is strong evidence that biofeedback is effective in improving performance (Petruzello, 1991). • Physiological indicators of relaxation are different in each individual, so it is necessary to be aware of variations before the extent of arousal can be assessed. • Biofeedback should not be used without knowing if the athlete is over-aroused – there is no need to reduce the arousal of a person who is already relaxed. • Biofeedback takes up time and often requires sophisticated equipment, it may not be practical prior to performance.
Progressive Muscular Relaxation (PMR)	Devised by Jacobson in 1929, the athlete increases the tension of the muscles throughout the body and gradually relaxes each group in turn.	• Many studies have proved that PMR helps relaxation. • PMR may only be successful when used alongside other relaxation techniques (Cox, 1998). • It is time-consuming, taking between 30 and 45 minutes to complete.

Table 7 Somatic anxiety management techniques

▶ **Need to know more?** For more information on emotional control see Chapter 10, pages 257–262, in the OCR A2 PE Student Book

CHECK

If you are satisfied with your knowledge and understanding, tick off the sections that you have revised so far. If you are not satisfied then revisit those sections and refer to the pages in the *Need to know more?* features.

☐ Evaluate goal setting as it impacts upon performance and the development and the sustaining of a balanced, active and healthy lifestyle.

☐ Consider self-confidence and its impact on performance and participation in physical activity and in raising self esteem.

☐ Describe attentional control and its impact upon effective performance.

☐ Outline emotional control and its impact upon performance and in sustaining a balanced, active and healthy lifestyle.

TRUE OR FALSE?

1. The SMARTER principle is a good guide to the correct implementation of goal-setting.

2. The setting of product goals is the best way to promote commitment and participation of an individual in sport.

3. Self-efficacy is a specific type of self confidence and relates to a perception of ability in particular activities or situations.

4. According to Vealey's Sports Confidence Theory, if SC State confidence can be elevated, approach behaviour will be promoted.

5. Attentional control relates to the extent of which the performer can focus awareness onto the most relevant environmental stimuli.

6. The optimal point or threshold of arousal remains constant at all times for all people.

7. The individual zone of Optimal Functioning can only be attained after a catastrophic drop in the quality of performance.

8. Peak Flow experience occurs when high somatic arousal coincides with low cognitive anxiety.

9. If Peak Flow state is achieved the athlete experiences maximum focus and full attentional control.

10. Cognitive anxiety management techniques include Biofeedback and Progressive Muscular Relaxation.

EXAM PRACTICE

1. Nideffer's model of Attentional Styles is presented on two dimensions which are termed broad/narrow and internal/external. Describe broad, narrow internal and external attentional styles, and by referring to sporting examples explain the effect of attentional styles on performance. *(6 marks)*

2. Define cue-utilisation and explain how this process links with arousal. *(6marks)*

3. Evaluate critically the use of goal setting to improve performance and participation in physical activity. *(20 marks)*

4. What is meant by the term self efficacy? Explain how the raising of self-efficacy could enable an individual to sustain a balanced, active and healthy lifestyle. *(6 marks)*

See page 286 for answers

CHAPTER 11
Linear motion in physical activity

CHAPTER OVERVIEW

By the end of this chapter you should have knowledge and understanding of:

- Newton's three laws of motion
- why there can never be motion without force but there can be force without motion
- what is meant by the terms mass, inertia and momentum, and their relevance to sporting performance
- the quantities used to describe linear motion and their relevance to sporting techniques
- how to distinguish between distance and displacement and between speed and velocity
- how to use equations to make simple calculations for speed, velocity and acceleration
- how to plot and interpret information from distance/time and velocity/time graphs.

LINEAR MOTION

Linear motion is where a body's centre of **mass** travels in a straight or curved line, with all its parts moving the same distance in the same direction at the same speed.

Linear motion can be created when an external force is applied through the centre of a body's mass, for example a tobogganist as they come to the final straight to cross the finish line.

▶ **Need to know more?** For more information on linear motion see Chapter 11, pages 277–280, in the OCR A2 PE Student Book

NEWTON'S LAWS OF MOTION

Newton's first law of motion

Newton's first law of motion states that:

'A body continues in a state of rest or uniform velocity unless acted upon by an external/ unbalanced force'.

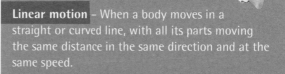

KEY TERMS

Linear motion – When a body moves in a straight or curved line, with all its parts moving the same distance in the same direction and at the same speed.

Centre of mass – The point at which a body is balanced in all directions.

This is also known as the 'Law of inertia'.

Newton's second law of motion

Newton's second law of motion states that:

'A body's rate of change in momentum is proportional to the size of the force applied and acts in the same direction as the force applied'.

- This is also known as the 'Law of **acceleration**'.
- It can be represented by the equation: Force = mass x acceleration (F = ma).

After rearranging the equation F=ma can also be used to calculate acceleration, if the values for force and mass are available.

Newton's third law of motion

Newton's third law of motion states that:

'For every action force applied to a body there is an equal and opposite reaction force'.

- This is also known as the 'Law of reaction'.
- An action force is generated and applied by the athlete to the ground or an object.
- A reaction force is the equal and opposite force generated by the second body back to the athlete.

▶ **Need to know more?** For more information on reaction force see Chapter 11, pages 273–274, in the OCR A2 PE Student Book

Do not confuse mass and weight. Weight is a force measured in Newtons (N) and calculated by mass x gravity.

INERTIA AND MOMEMTUM

Inertia

Inertia is the resistance of a body to change its state of rest or motion.

- It is directly related to mass: the greater the mass the greater the inertia.
- The greater the inertia the greater the force needed to change a state of rest or motion.

For example, a rugby player with a large mass will need to generate a large force to start motion. However, once in motion, it will be very hard to stop their run due to their large inertia. In comparison, a netball centre with a small mass needs little force to create motion, change direction, accelerate or decelerate and therefore can do so very quickly.

KEY TERMS

Inertia – The resistance of a body to change its state of motion, whether at rest or whilst moving.

Mass – The 'quantity of matter of a body', in kilograms (kg).

Momentum – The quantity of motion possessed by a moving body. Momentum = mass x velocity and is measured in $kgms^{-1}$.

Acceleration – The rate of change of velocity. Acceleration = change in velocity/time (ms^{-1}).

You will need to be able to apply Newton's three laws to a single sporting example, practice with actions from several sports.

E.g. a football penalty shot:

- NL1: The football remains at rest on the penalty spot until an external force is applied.
- NL2: The greater the size of the force, the greater the rate of change in momentum and acceleration towards the goal. The ball will travel in the same direction as the force applied.
- NL3: An external action force is applied to the ball from the foot, the ball will apply an equal and opposite reaction force back to the foot to gain kinaesthesis on the penalty shot.

E.g. a track cyclist travelling at constant speed.

- NL1: The cyclist remains travelling at uniform velocity unless the horizontal forces become unbalanced, i.e. friction becomes greater than air resistance generating forward acceleration.
- NL2: The greater the size of the frictional force generated in comparison to air resistance, the greater the change in momentum and forward acceleration.
- NL3: The mass of the cyclist and bike provide an action force acting downwards to the track. The track provides an equal and opposite reaction force upwards to the cyclist.

Momentum

Momentum is the 'quantity of motion possessed by a body'.

- Momentum = mass x velocity (Mo = mv), and is measured in kilogram metres per second (kgms^{-1}).
- The greater the mass or velocity the greater the momentum.
- A rugby player with a mass of 98kg travelling at 8.5ms^{-1} would have a momentum of 98 x 8.5 = 833kgms^{-1}.

DESCRIBING LINEAR MOTION

> **Need to know more?** For more information on mass, inertia and momemtum see Chapter 11, pages 275–276, in the OCR A2 PE Student Book.

EXAM TIP

Make sure you are able to define, calculate and use the correct units for each of the terms below. No units = no mark!

Fig 11.1 Martin Lel set a new World Record at the 2008 Flora London marathon covering a distance of 42.2km (or a displacement of just 10km).

EXAM TIP

- Deceleration is a decrease in velocity over time.
- Zero acceleration is where all forces acting on a body are balanced (net force = 0) and the body is at rest or travelling in uniform velocity.

EXAM TIP

Distance and speed are measures of size only, whereas displacement, velocity and acceleration are measures of size and direction of motion providing a more precise picture.

Distance	Displacement
How far a body has travelled from A to B, measured in metres (m).	The shortest straight-line route from A to B, measured in metres (m).
Speed	**Velocity**
The rate of change of distance, measured in metres per second (ms^{-1}). Speed = distance/time	The rate of change of displacement, measured in metres per second (ms^{-1}). Velocity = displacement/time
Acceleration	
The rate of change of velocity, measured in metres per second per second (ms^{-2}). Acceleration = change in velocity/time	

Table 1 Linear motion

GRAPHS OF MOTION

Distance/time graphs

These indicate the distance travelled by a body over a certain time.

- The gradient of the curve indicates the *speed* of the body and will show whether the body is stationary, in motion with constant speed, accelerating or decelerating.

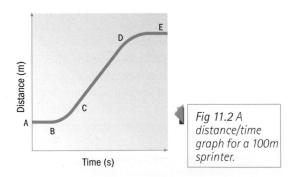

Fig 11.2 A distance/time graph for a 100m sprinter.

For the distance/time graph for a 100m sprinter shown in Fig 11.2 above:

- A-B: horizontal line = no motion (the sprinter waits in the blocks)
- B-C: positive curve = acceleration (a great action force is applied to the blocks and the sprinter accelerates through the first 40m)
- C-D: regular diagonal line = constant speed (the sprinter reaches their maximum speed through 40–100m)

- D-E: negative curve = deceleration (after the finish line the sprinter changes body position and decelerates).

Velocity/time graphs

These indicate the velocity of a body over a certain time.

- The gradient of the curve indicates the *acceleration* of the body and will show whether the body is stationary, in motion with uniform velocity, accelerating or decelerating.

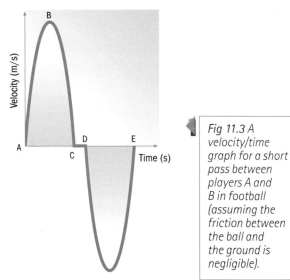

Fig 11.3 A velocity/time graph for a short pass between players A and B in football (assuming the friction between the ball and the ground is negligible).

For a velocity/time graph for a short pass between players A and B as shown in Fig 11.3 above:

- A-B: positive curve = acceleration (an action force is applied to the ball by player A and accelerates towards player B)
- B-C: negative curve = deceleration (the ball is cushioned by player B and decelerates to rest)
- C-D: horizontal line = uniform velocity (the ball is at rest)
- D-E: curve below the x axis = change in direction (player B applies an external force to the ball which accelerates back to player A, who cushions the ball which decelerates to rest).

EXAM TIP

Velocity is a measure of size and direction. Remember, change in velocity/time = acceleration (ms^{-2})

Need to know more? For more information on graphs of motion see Chapter 11, pages 281–284, in the OCR A2 PE Student Book

CHECK

If you are satisfied with your knowledge and understanding, tick off the sections that you have revised so far. If you are not satisfied then revisit those sections and refer to the pages in the *Need to know more?* features.

☐ Describe and apply Newton's three laws of motion to sporting scenarios.

☐ Explain why there can never be motion without force but there can be force without motion.

☐ Explain what is meant by the terms mass, inertia and momentum, and their relevance to sporting performance.

☐ Distinguish the quantities used to describe linear motion and their relevance to sporting techniques.

☐ Explain how to distinguish between distance and displacement and between speed and velocity.

☐ Demonstrate how to use equations to make simple calculations for speed, velocity and acceleration.

☐ Demonstrate how to plot and interpret information from distance/time and velocity/ time graphs.

TRUE OR FALSE?

1. Newton's first law of motion states: 'a body continues in a state of rest or uniform velocity unless acted upon by an external or unbalanced force'.

2. F = m x a is a calculation used to express Newton's third law.

3. There can never be motion without force and there can never be force without motion.

4. Mass is measured in kilograms.

5. The larger the inertia the larger the force required to create motion.

6. There is no difference between distance and displacement. They are both measures of size and the units are metres.

7. Speed = displacement/time (ms^{-1})

8. Acceleration is the rate of change in velocity and calculated by the change in velocity/time (ms^{-2}).

9. A distance/time graph can be used to calculate speed.

10. Momentum is the rate of change in displacement (ms^{-1})

EXAM PRACTICE

1. Using an example, describe linear motion and explain the difference between distance and displacement over a 400m race.   *(4 marks)*

2i.) If Usain Bolt has a mass of 86kg and crosses the 20m line of a 100m sprint in 2.49 seconds calculate his momentum and average speed over the first 20m of the race.

ii.) Using Newton's laws of motion explain how Usain Bolt drives away from the starting blocks.   *(6 marks)*

See page 289 for answers

CHAPTER 12
Force in physical activity

CHAPTER OVERVIEW

By the end of this chapter you should have knowledge and understanding of:

- the definition and measurement of force and the effects of a force on a performer or object
- the concept of net force and balanced and unbalanced forces
- the nature of the vertical forces acting on a sports performer (weight force and reaction force) and an appreciation of the effect they have on the resulting motion of a performer
- the nature of the horizontal forces acting on a sports performer (friction force and air resistance force) and an appreciation of the effect they have on the resulting motion of a performer
- how to sketch simple free body diagrams to identify the type and relative size of the external forces acting on a sports performer at a particular instant in time
- impulse and its relationship to momentum
- how to sketch force/time graphs and appreciate the information that can be gained from them.

NET, BALANCED AND UNBALANCED FORCES

KEY TERMS

Force – A push or pull that alters, or tends to alter, the state of motion of a body, measured in Newtons (N). It is calculated using the equation: Force = mass x acceleration (F = ma).

Net force

Net force is the sum of all forces acting on a body, also termed resultant force. It is the overall force acting on a body (when all individual forces have been considered).

If net force = 0, there is no change in motion.

If a net force is present, the effect on a body is to:

- create motion from a resting position
- cause a moving body to accelerate, decelerate or change direction
- change a body's shape.

EXAM TIP

Make sure you can link the effects of a net force to Newton's laws of motion.

Balanced forces

These occur when two or more forces acting on a body are equal in size and opposite in direction.

- Net force = 0, the body will remain at rest or in motion with uniform velocity (Newton's first law).
- For example, for a gymnast performing an arabesque balance on the beam; weight and reaction force will be equal in size and opposite in direction. Their body will be; static, balanced: net force = 0.

EXAM TIP

A body travelling with uniform velocity will be balanced in both the vertical and horizontal direction.

Unbalanced forces

These occur when two forces are unequal in size and opposite in direction.

- A net force will be present.
- There will be a change in motion in the direction of the net force (Newton's second law).
- For example, the upward reaction force of a basketballer performing a lay-up shot will be greater than the downward weight force. There will be a net force and acceleration in the upward direction. Their body will be: dynamic, unbalanced, vertically accelerating.

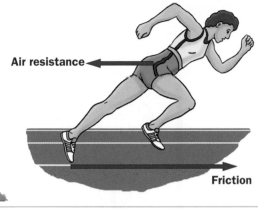

Fig 12.1 *The sprinter accelerates in a forward direction due to the frictional force being greater than the air resistance. Unbalanced force: positive net force in forward direction.*

WEIGHT, REACTION, FRICTION AND AIR RESISTANCE

The external forces acting on a performer in contact with the ground can be divided into:

- *Vertical forces*: weight and reaction force,
- *Horizontal forces*: friction and air resistance.

EXAM TIP

Remember all forces are measured in Newtons (N).

> **Need to know more?** For more information on force see pages 288–308, in the OCR A2 PE Student Book

EXAM TIP

- Normal reaction is the vertical component of ground reaction force.
- Friction is sports specific – it is important to be able to apply the concept of friction to sports that aim to maximise as well as minimise it.
- Remember mass and weight are not the same. Mass is a body's 'quantity of matter', measured in kilograms (kg).
- As air resistance acts in opposition to the direction of motion, always indicate the direction of motion on free body diagrams.

Reaction

- Reaction is the equal and opposite force exerted by a body in response to the action force placed upon it, measured in Newtons (N).
- For example, when a high jumper applies an action force to the ground an equal and opposite reaction force is applied back to the body. If this reaction is greater than weight, an upward force is created – the jumper leaves the ground.
- Reaction force is a result of Newton's third law of motion and will always be present when two bodies are in contact.
- Normal reaction force acts upwards from a point of contact.

Air resistance

- Air resistance is the force that opposes motion, measured in Newtons (N).
- It is affected by:
  - *Velocity*; the greater the velocity the greater the air resistance.
  - *Frontal cross-sectional area*; the greater the frontal cross-sectional area the greater the air resistance.
  - *Shape*; teardrop and aerofoil shapes minimise air resistance.
  - *Surface*; the rougher the surface the greater the air resistance.
- Streamlining is the attempt to create a smoother air flow around a more aerodynamic shape to reduce the air resistance opposing motion, for example the smooth tear-drop helmets and crouched body position adopted by speed cyclists.

Weight

- Weight is the gravitational pull that the Earth exerts on a body, measured in Newtons (N).
- Weight = mass x gravity (W = mg, where acceleration due to gravity is usually assumed to be 10ms^{-2}).
- Weight acts downwards from the centre of mass.

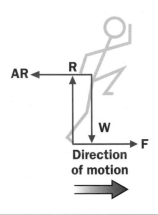

Fig 12.2 Free body diagram of a runner travelling with uniform velocity, where all forces are equal, net force = 0

Friction

- Friction is the force that opposes the movement of one surface over another, measured in Newtons (N). For example, the foot of a sprinter would tend to slip backwards – friction acts forwards.
- Friction acts from the point of contact parallel to the two surfaces in contact.
- Friction is affected by:
  - *Contact and ground surface*; the rougher the surface the greater the frictional force.
  - *Temperature*; for example in motor sports an increase in temperature increases the frictional force.
  - *Normal reaction*; the greater the normal reaction the greater the frictional force.
- To maximise friction, sprinters will wear spikes to increase the roughness of the contact surface, compared to downhill skiers who wax and polish their skis to create a smooth surface and decrease the frictional force.
- This also affects rolling or bouncing balls; clay tennis courts have a rougher surface than grass decelerating the ball on bounce providing a slower game.

FREE BODY DIAGRAMS

A free body diagram is a clearly labelled sketch showing all of the forces acting on a particular object at a particular instant in time.

- These are often used to visualise forces acting on a body.
- A force is represented by an arrow.
- There are three considerations which are useful when describing force;
  - *Point of application:* shown by the point where the arrow begins.
  - *Direction of force:* shown by the direction of the arrow.
  - *Size of the force:* shown by the length of the arrow: the greater the force the longer the arrow.

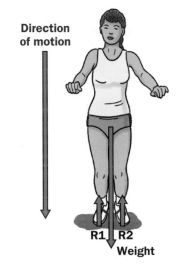

Fig 12.3 On landing R1 + R2< W, forces are unbalanced, net force is present in the downward direction causing the performer to bend their knees.

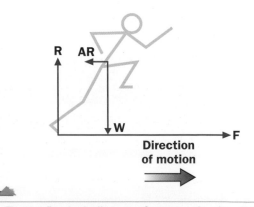

Fig 12.4 Free body diagram of a runner showing all the forces acting when accelerating.
R = W, net force = 0, F >AR, net force = forward acceleration.

	Vertical forces		Horizontal forces	
	Weight (W)	**Reaction (R)**	**Friction (F)**	**Air resistance (AR)**
Point of application	Centre of mass	Point of contact	Point of contact	Centre of mass
Direction of Arrow	Vertically downward	Vertically upward (when considering normal reaction which is perpendicular to the contact surface)	Opposite to the direction of slip (usually with the direction of motion)	Opposite to the direction of motion
Length of arrow	The greater the mass the greater the weight force – the longer the arrow.	Dependant on resultant motion. As a result of Newton's first and second laws if: R = W (net force = 0) arrows are equal and opposite. R >W (net force = upward acceleration) R arrow is longer. R< W (net force = downward acceleration) W arrow is longer.	Dependant on resultant motion. As a result of Newton's first and second laws if: F = AR (net force = 0) arrows are equal and opposite. F >AR (net force = forward acceleration) F arrow is longer. F< AR (net force = deceleration) AR arrow is longer.	

Table 1 Summary of the point of application, direction and length of the four arrows used to represent the forces acting on a body in contact with another surface.

▶ **Need to know more?** For more information on free body diagrams see Chapter 12, pages 297–301, in the OCR A2 PE Student Book

IMPULSE

Impulse is the product of force multiplied by the time for which the force acts. Impulse is measured in Newton seconds (Ns).

Impulse = Force (N) x time (s) (I = Ft)

Impulse is closely related to momentum and can also be calculated by:

Impulse = change in momentum (Ns)

Impulse is important for an athlete and can be increased by:

- increasing the size of the force applied, for example a golf drive compared to putt
- increasing the time the force is applied for, for example a push in hockey compared to a hit.

EXAM TIP

If the body has more than one point of contact there will be more than one reaction/ frictional force. The total length of the force arrows indicates the size of the force. If R = W, but there are two points of contact, the length of the two R arrows must total the same length as the W arrow.

EXAM TIP

When asked to draw a free body diagram, make sure you:

- draw it big enough to read labels and see size of your arrows.
- clearly label your force arrows.
- annotate it with net force at the side.

EXAM TIP

Apply key concepts to sporting examples where possible, for example a high jumper increases impulse to generate maximum momentum and gain greater upward acceleration by leaning back as they plant their foot at take-off. This applies the force to the ground over a longer period of time.

By using a follow through in the recovery phase of a forehand drive in tennis, the effect is to increase the time the force is applied to the ball, which:

- increases the impulse applied to the ball
- increases the outgoing/change in momentum of the ball
- increases the outgoing velocity of the ball
- increases the distance travelled by the ball
- and also gives the player more control over the direction of the ball.

An understanding of impulse is also important for sports performers to prevent injury and maintain lifelong involvement in sport. By increasing the time it takes to stop an object the force applied to the body decreases. For example, netballers bring the ball in to the chest when receiving a chest pass and gymnasts bend their knees when landing a vault increasing control over action.

> ▶ **Need to know more?** For more information on impulse see Chapter 12, pages 301–305, in the OCR A2 PE Student Book

Force/time graphs

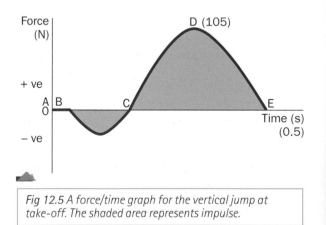

Fig 12.5 A force/time graph for the vertical jump at take-off. The shaded area represents impulse.

EXAM TIP

It is important to be able to draw and interpret force/time graphs. See pages 304–05 in the OCR A2 PE student book.

Vertical jump take-off

Initially the body is stationary; the body then dips downward and finally accelerates upward to leave the ground. There are three phases to the impulse generated whilst in contact with the ground;

- *At rest* (A-B): Impulse = 0, W = R (forces are balanced), therefore no acceleration.
- *Downward phase* (B-C): Impulse is negative, W >R (forces are unbalanced): downward acceleration as the performer flexes the hip and knee.
- *Upward phase* (C-E): Impulse is positive, R >W (forces are unbalanced): upward acceleration from the action force applied to the ground generating a large reaction force. This decreases as the performer extends the hip and knee to move away from the ground.

The area under a force/time curve represents impulse and for the upward phase shown in Fig 12.5 can be calculated by:

Impulse = ½ (150 x 0.5) = 37.5Ns

EXAM TIP

Make sure you also consider the impulse of a 100m sprinter in the acceleration, constant speed and deceleration phases. The area above and below the x axis represent the opposite directions in which force can be applied.

CHECK

If you are satisfied with your knowledge and understanding, tick off the sections that you have revised so far. If you are not satisfied then revisit those sections and refer to the pages in the *Need to know more?* features.

☐ State the definition and measurement of force and the effects of a force on a performer or object.

☐ Define the concept of net force and balanced and unbalanced forces.

☐ Describe the nature of the vertical forces acting on a sports performer (weight force and reaction force) and the effect they have on the resulting motion of a performer.

☐ Outline the nature of the horizontal forces acting on a sports performer (friction force and air resistance force) and the effect they have on the resulting motion of a performer.

☐ Demonstrate how to sketch simple free body diagrams to identify the type and relative size of the external forces acting on a sports performer at a particular instant in time.

☐ Describe impulse and its relationship to momentum.

☐ Demonstrate how to sketch force/time graphs and appreciate the information that can be gained from them.

TRUE OR FALSE?

1. A force is the product of mass multiplied by acceleration.
2. A force is measured in $kgms^{-1}$.
3. A high jumper after take-off lifting towards the bar is an example of balanced forces, net force = 0.
4. Weight is a force measured in Newtons and calculated by mass multiplied by acceleration due to gravity.
5. Frictional force can be minimised by increasing the roughness and temperature of the ground surface.
6. Air resistance acts in opposition to the motion of a body and is affected by velocity, frontal cross-sectional area, shape and the smoothness of the surface.
7. On a free body diagram the weight arrow always starts at centre of mass and extends downwards.
8. If the vertical forces are balanced the weight and reaction arrows on a free body diagram are equal in size but opposite in direction.
9. Increasing impulse increases the rate of change in momentum and therefore velocity as shown by Newton's third law of reaction.
10. Impulse can be represented by the area underneath a force/time graph.

EXAM PRACTICE

1. During a 400m race an athlete will achieve a constant speed. Explain the concept of net force. Describe the horizontal forces acting on this performer and how they maximise forward acceleration. *(6 marks)*

2. When performing a tennis forehand groundstroke the player will follow-through by lifting the racquet over the shoulder. Describe why follow-through is an essential part of good technique. *(5 marks)*

3. A gymnast performs a handstand and holds the position for three seconds. Draw a free body diagram to show the forces acting on the body and describe the net force resulting from this action. *(4 marks)*

See page 290 for answers

CHAPTER 13

Fluid mechanics in physical activity

CHAPTER OVERVIEW

By the end of this chapter you should have knowledge and understanding of:

- the impact of air resistance (drag or fluid friction) on sporting activity and how to apply the concept of reducing drag in certain sports
- how to sketch free body diagrams to identify the forces acting on a projectile in flight and how to use the parallelogram of forces to explain the resultant flight path
- how to explain and apply the Bernoulli principle in a number of different sporting activities
- the three types of spin commonly observed in sporting activities (top spin, back spin and side spin) and their impact on flight path and bounce
- how to sketch detailed diagrams to help explain how the Magnus effect causes spinning projectiles to deviate from their non-spinning flight paths.

▶ **Need to know more?** For more information on fluid mechanics in physical activity see Chapter 13, pages 309–323, in the OCR A2 PE Student Book.

FLUID MECHANICS

- **Fluid mechanics** is the study of a body which travels through a fluid, be it air or water.

KEY TERMS

Fluid mechanics – The study of objects or bodies that travel through a fluid. Fluid mechanics are particularly significant for bodies travelling through water or for those with high velocity travelling through the air, such as projectiles.

Drag/fluid friction – The resistance to motion on a body travelling through fluid. The resistance acts in opposition to the direction of motion and reduces velocity.

- It is important to understand how to minimise air resistance and fluid friction to maximise the velocity of swimmers, cyclists, sprinters, skiers or **projectiles** such as a discus or a javelin.

- **Fluid** friction is the force that opposes motion through a fluid, often referred to as **drag**.
- Projectiles are bodies launched into the air such as a discus or ski jumper.

Air resistance, fluid friction and drag are all forces acting on bodies travelling through fluids, air or water. Therefore, the factors affecting these bodies are the same.

Factors affecting air resistance and fluid friction

Factor	Effect on air resistance and fluid friction (AR/FF)
Velocity	The greater the velocity, the greater the AR/FF.
Frontal cross-sectional area	The greater the frontal cross-sectional area, the greater the AR/FF.
Shape	Teardrop and **aerofoil** shapes minimise AR/FF.
Surface	The rougher the surface, the greater the AR/FF.
Temperature	As air temperature increases, the density of air decreases reducing air resistance.
Altitude	As altitude increases, air density decreases reducing air resistance.

Table 1 Factors affecting air resistance and fluid friction

Streamlining

Streamlining is the attempt to create a smoother air flow around a more aerodynamic shape to reduce the body's frontal cross sectional area and reduce the resistance to motion. An example is the smooth tear-drop helmets and crouched body position adopted by speed cyclists, and the shaved legs and skin tight smooth body suits worn by swimmers.

KEY TERMS

Streamlining – Shaping a body so that it causes the least drag when travelling through a fluid.

Aerofoil – A streamlined shape with a curved upper surface and an under surface that is predominantly flat – like the cross-section of the wing of an aircraft.

EXAM TIP

Make sure you have discussed the factors affecting air resistance and fluid friction for swimmers, sprinters, cyclists and skiers.

PROJECTILES

- A body launched into the air subjected to weight and air resistance forces.
- Projectiles are not in contact with the ground and are not affected by friction or reaction forces during flight.

Once launched, a projectile follows a flight path determined by the relative size of weight and air resistance.

- If weight is the dominant force and air resistance is small, for example a shot in flight, a *parabolic* flight path is followed.
- If air resistance becomes more dominant than weight, for example a hard hit shuttle in flight, a *non-parabolic* flight path is followed.
- Air resistance becomes more dominant than weight when a body travels through the air with high velocity, large frontal cross-sectional area, rough surface or low mass, for example a table tennis ball, shuttlecock or golf ball.

KEY TERM

Parabola – A uniform curve that is symmetrical about its highest point.

Need to know more? For more information on flight paths see Chapter 13, page 312, in the OCR A2 PE Student Book.

Forces acting on a projectile in flight

By using a free body diagram the forces acting on a projectile in flight can be shown.

- There will be three phases of flight – start, middle and end.
- The direction of motion is crucial and should reflect the parabolic or non-parabolic nature of the flight path.
- Air resistance opposes motion and will act from the centre of mass in opposition to the direction flight.
- Weight will act from the centre of mass downwards and be constant through all three stages.
- The greater the velocity, frontal cross-sectional area or roughness of the body, the longer the air resistance arrow.
- The greater the mass of the body, the longer the weight arrow.

EXAM TIP

If there is an additional Bernoulli or Magnus force acting, remember to add it to the free body diagram.

The flight path of a shot put is parabolic throughout flight due to the dominant weight force caused by its great mass. Air resistance is small due to the low velocity, small frontal cross-sectional area and smooth surface (see Fig 13.1).

The flight path of the hard hit shuttle shown in Fig 13.2 is non-parabolic at the start of flight due to the dominant air resistance caused by the high velocity, rough surface and low mass of the shuttle. By the end of flight the flight path has become more parabolic as the shuttle decelerates due to the large air resistance.

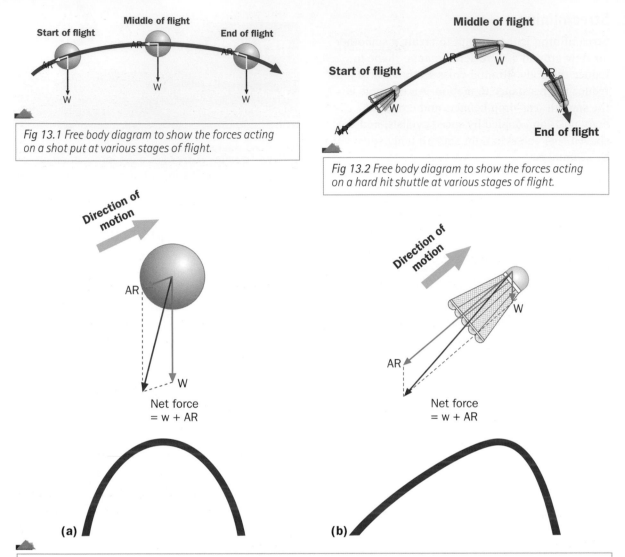

Fig 13.1 Free body diagram to show the forces acting on a shot put at various stages of flight.

Fig 13.2 Free body diagram to show the forces acting on a hard hit shuttle at various stages of flight.

Fig 13.3 A parallelogram of forces used to represent the net force at the start of flight acting on (a) a shot put and (b) a hard hit shuttle.

Parallelogram of forces

A parallelogram of forces is drawn to calculate the net force acting on a body in flight.

- The net force represents the sum of all forces acting on a body.
- The net force represents the acceleration of a body and direction in which it takes place.
- If the net force arrow is closer to the weight arrow, weight will be the dominant force and the flight path will be parabolic.
- If the net force arrow is closer to the air resistance arrow, air resistance will be the dominant factor and the flight path will be non-parabolic.

To sketch a parallelogram of forces:

- show the direction of motion
- air resistance opposes motion from the centre of mass
- weight force will act downwards from the centre of mass
- use a dotted line to complete the parallelogram and a solid diagonal arrow to represent the resultant/net force.

LIFT AND THE BERNOULLI PRINCIPLE

The effect of lift is drawn from the **Bernoulli principle** and will enable a projectile to stay in the air for longer and achieve a greater horizontal distance. This is important in events such as discus, javelin and ski jumping.

- The lift force allows the projectile to stay in the air for longer and travel a greater horizontal distance.

KEY TERMS

Bernoulli principle – Explains how lift is created on a projectile moving through a fluid. Fluid molecules exert less pressure moving at higher velocities.

Lift force – Force that acts perpendicular to the direction of travel for a body moving through a fluid.

Angle of attack – The angle at which a projectile is tilted from the horizontal. Lift force will increase as the angle of attack is increased up to a certain point (usually around 17 degrees).

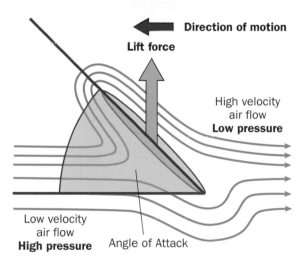

Direction of motion

Lift force

High velocity air flow
Low pressure

Low velocity air flow
High pressure

Angle of Attack

Fig 13.4 An airflow diagram showing the lift force created by the Bernoulli principle.

- A **lift force** is present when projectiles adopt an aerofoil shape.
- The **angle of attack** of the aerofoil will affect the size of the lift force.
- The greater the angle of attack (up to 17 degrees) the greater the lift force.
- Lift force is created by presenting the projectile at the correct angle of attack.
- When this is done, air will travel further over the top of the discus.
- Thus air will travel at a higher velocity over the top of the discus.
- Consequently a low pressure area is created over the top of the discus.
- In this way a pressure gradient is created which applies a lift force to the projectile.

EXAM TIP

Do not confuse the Bernoulli principle of aerofoil shaped projectiles, such as a javelin, with the Magnus effect of rotating projectiles, such as a golf ball.

THEORY INTO PRACTICE

Downforce is maximised by F1 racing cars using the reverse of the Bernoulli principle.

- Rear spoilers are angled to generate downforce and push the car into the track. This generates more friction between the tyres and track surface.
- Downforce is also used by speed skiers and cyclists.

EXAM TIP

Follow two rules when applying the Bernoulli principle:

- Fast flow = pressure low
- All gases move from an area of high pressure to an area of low pressure.

EXAM TIP

When drawing an airflow diagram:

- always draw the direction of motion first – air flow lines will run in opposition
- annotate your diagram with velocity and pressure
- include the lift force from the centre of mass of the projectile.

Need to know more? For more information on the Bernoulli principle see Chapter 13, pages 315–317, in the OCR A2 PE Student Book

SPIN AND THE MAGNUS EFFECT

- Spin is created by applying an eccentric force to the projectile at the point of release.
- This **eccentric force** is off-centre and applied outside the centre of mass to generate a torque.
- Spin and its effects are important in ball sports such as tennis, table tennis, football, golf and cricket.

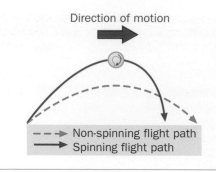

Fig 13.5a – the effect of topspin on the flight path.

KEY TERM

Eccentric force – A force whose line of application passes outside the centre of mass of a body, causing the resulting motion to be angular.

Magnus effect – The Magnus effect explains the deviations in flight paths of spinning balls in sport, especially tennis, golf, football, table tennis and cricket.

Fig 13.5b – the effect of topspin on bounce.

EXAM TIP

Assume that side spin is imparted on the projectile by a right-handed player where:

- hook deviates to the left
- slice deviates to the right.

According to the **Magnus effect** for a ball with topspin:

- Below the ball the airflow travels in the same direction as spin. This accelerates the airflow and creates an area of low pressure.
- Above the ball the airflow travels in opposition to spin. This decelerates the airflow and creates an area of high pressure.
- A pressure gradient forms and the ball deviates towards the area of low pressure.
- The ball 'dips', the flight path is shortened and becomes non-parabolic.

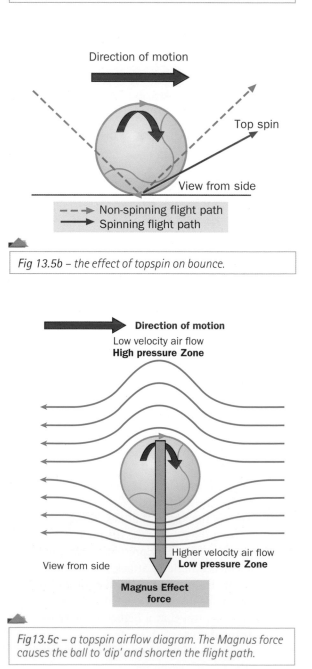

Fig13.5c – a topspin airflow diagram. The Magnus force causes the ball to 'dip' and shorten the flight path.

	Topspin	Backspin	Sidespin
Effect	• Ball 'dips'. • Flight path becomes shorter. • Non-parabolic flight path	• Ball 'floats'. • Flight path becomes longer. • Non-parabolic flight path	• Ball 'swerves'. • Flight path deviates to the left (hook) or right (slice).
View	• View from side.	• View from side.	• View from top.
Bounce	• Friction acts in a forward direction. • Ball will accelerate at a low angle from the ground.	• Friction acts in a backward direction. • Ball will decelerate at a steep angle from the ground.	• Friction acts in the same direction as motion. • Ball will accelerate at a low angle in the direction of swerve.

Table 2 Spin and the Magnus effect

EXAM TIP

Make sure you are able to draw flight path, bounce and airflow diagrams for topspin, backspin, hook and slice.

For flight path and bounce diagrams follow these stages:

- state the type of spin and view of the diagram
- draw the projectile and direction of spin
- label the direction of motion
- sketch the spinning and non-spinning flight path to show the deviation clearly
- write a full explanation to support your diagram.

To illustrate the Magnus effect using an airflow diagram, follow these stages;

- state the type of spin and view of the diagram
- draw the projectile and direction of spin
- label the direction of motion
- draw the airflow lines in opposition to direction of motion
- label the areas of high and low velocity and consequently, high and low pressure
- draw the Magnus force from the centre of mass
- write a full explanation to support your diagram.

Need to know more? For more information on the Magnus effect see pages 318–22 of the OCR A2 PE Student Book.

CHECK

If you are satisfied with your knowledge and understanding, tick off the sections that you have revised so far. If you are not satisfied then revisit those sections and refer to the pages in the *Need to know more?* features.

☐ Describe the impact of air resistance (drag or fluid friction) on sporting activity and how to apply the concept of reducing drag in certain sports.

☐ Demonstrate how to sketch free body diagrams to identify the forces acting on a projectile in flight and how to use the parallelogram of forces to explain the resultant flight path.

☐ Explain and apply the Bernoulli principle in a number of different sporting activities.

☐ Outline the three types of spin commonly observed in sporting activities (top spin, back spin and side spin) and their impact on flight path and bounce.

☐ Demonstrate how to sketch detailed diagrams to help explain how the Magnus effect causes spinning projectiles to deviate from their non-spinning flight paths.

TRUE OR FALSE?

1. Drag and fluid friction in the water are the same as air resistance in the air.

2. Streamlining can be achieved by a sprint cyclist adopting an aerofoil shape.

3. The size of the air resistance is affected by the temperature and roughness of the contact and ground surface.

4. To create spin on a ball the action force is applied through the centre of mass.

5. A parallelogram of forces shows the direction and size of acceleration of a projectile.

6. The Bernoulli principle explains the deviations in flight path of rotating projectiles.

7. The reverse Bernoulli creates downforce assisting F1 cars to corner at high speeds.

8. Side spin to the left is known as 'hook' and sidespin to the right is known as 'slice'.

9. You could be asked to sketch three different diagrams to illustrate the effects of spin.

10. Backspin decelerates the ball causing its angle to increase on bounce.

EXAM PRACTICE

1. A tennis player performs a forehand drive. Sketch and label a diagram showing all the forces acting on the ball at the moment of contact. Describe the forces and state the effects on the flight path and bounce of the ball of applying topspin. *(6 marks)*

2. Describe the concept of air resistance and explain how a speed cyclist can minimise the effects of air resistance. *(5 marks)*

3. Using your knowledge of the Magnus Effect explain the deviation in flight path of a golf ball hit with backspin. *(6 marks)*

See page 292 for answers

CHAPTER 14

Stability and angular motion in physical activity

CHAPTER OVERVIEW

By the end of this chapter you should have knowledge and understanding of:

- centre of mass and its relationship to balance, rotation and efficiency of technique
- the three types of lever system in relation to human movement and the advantages and disadvantages of second and third classes of lever system
- how to define and calculate the units of measurement for the moment of a force
- the three major axes of rotation, giving examples of sporting movements that occur around them
- the quantities used to describe angular motion and their relevance to sporting techniques
- what is meant by the terms 'moment of inertia' and 'angular momentum' and their relevance to sporting performance
- the law of conservation of angular momentum and be able to give examples of how athletes use this principle in a number of sporting activities.

STABILITY AND CENTRE OF MASS

Stability

- Stability is the ability of a body to return to **equilibrium** after being displaced.

- The more stable the body the larger the force needed to create motion, for example a smaller force will be needed to move a gymnast performing a handstand than a bridge although both are in equilibrium.

Performers increase their stability when:

- they lower their centre of mass (on landing flexing the hip and knee)
- they increase the size of the base of support (increase the number of contact points)
- their line of gravity falls within their base of support
- their increase their mass or inertia.

KEY TERM

Equilibrium – A body is in equilibrium (balanced) when the net force = 0.

EXAM TIP

For some performers, e.g. games players who side step, dodge and swerve, it is important to be unstable where the line of gravity will fall outside the base of support; this enables them to change direction at speed.

Fig 14.1 Using the Fosbury Flop technique is more efficient than the scissor kick, it requires less force on take-off to achieve the same height, as the centre of mass passes beneath the bar.

Centre of mass

Centre of mass is the point at which the body is balanced in all directions/the point at which weight appears to act. The centre of mass is moveable and can lie outside of the body – its position depends on the distribution of mass about the body.

The centre of mass of a projectile follows a pre-determined flight path from take off:

- By raising a knee and arm, the centre of mass is raised and overall jump height for a basketballer will be increased.
- By rotating over the bar with the spine fully extended, a high jumper using the Fosbury Flop technique moves their centre of mass outside the body and below the bar, thereby needing less force at take-off to clear the same vertical distance as someone using the scissor-kick technique.

LEVER SYSTEMS AND MOMENT OF FORCE

Lever systems

A lever is a rigid structure which rotates around a fixed point (fulcrum) when two forces unequal in size are applied (effort and load).

In the human body:

- lever is a bone
- fulcrum is a joint (fixed point of rotation about which the lever moves)
- effort is muscular force applied to create the motion of a lever (agonist)
- load is the resistance or weight to be moved (this can be body weight itself).

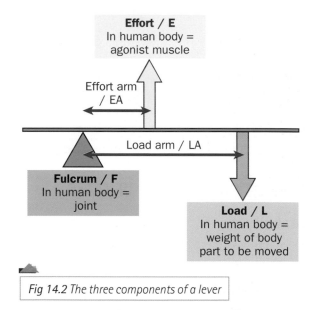

Fig 14.2 The three components of a lever

First-class lever (load – fulcrum – effort)	The fulcrum is located between the load and the effort, for example extension of the neck in preparation for a header in football. Extension of the elbow during an overarm throw in rounders: • load is the weight of the forearm and hand plus the rounders ball • fulcrum is the elbow joint • effort is muscular force exerted by the triceps brachii pulling on the ulna.	*Fig 14.3 A first-class level system: an overarm throw*
Second-class lever (fulcrum – load – effort)	The load is located between the fulcrum and the effort, for example standing on tiptoe or driving up from the ball of the foot against the blocks in a sprint start: • fulcrum is the joint between the metatarsals and phalanges • load is the body weight to be lifted • effort is muscular force exerted by the gastrocnemius pulling the heel upwards.	*Fig 14.4 A second-class level system: standing on tiptoe*
Third-class lever (load – effort – fulcrum)	The effort is located between the load and fulcrum, for example flexion of the elbow joint when performing a bicep curl: • load is the weight of the forearm and hand plus the dumbbell • effort is the muscular force exerted by the biceps brachii pulling the forearm upwards • fulcrum is the elbow joint. This is the most common lever found in the human body.	*Fig 14.5 A third-class level system: flexion of the elbow joint*

Table 1 Types of lever system

Type of lever system	Advantages	Disadvantages
Second-class levers	Has the **mechanical advantage** to move a large load with a small effort: • more efficient than a third class lever • the effort arm is longer than the load arm • the effort is further away from the fulcrum than the load.	Only efficient over a small distance and at the expense of speed and range of movement.
Third-class levers	Can move the load at a high speed of acceleration over a large range of movement.	Has the **mechanical disadvantage** to move only a relatively small load. • Less efficient than a second class lever. • The load arm is longer than the effort arm. • The load is further away from the fulcrum than the effort.

Table 2 Efficiency of second and third types of lever system

MOMENT OF FORCE OR TORQUE

Moment of force, or **torque,** creates a turning effect of the lever about the fulcrum.

Moment of force = force x perpendicular distance from fulcrum.

KEY TERM

Moment of force/torque – The effectiveness of a force to produce rotation about an axis. It is the product of the size of the force multiplied by the distance of the force from the fulcrum. It is measured in Newton metres (Nm).

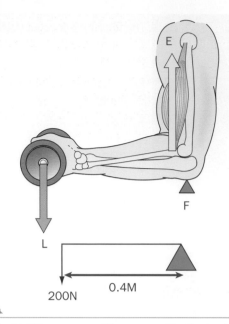

Fig 14.6 The moment of force caused by the dumbbell in the downward phase of a biceps curl.

$$\begin{aligned} \text{Moment of force/torque} &= \text{force x perpendicular} \\ &\quad \text{distance from the} \\ &\quad \text{fulcrum} \\ &= 200N \times 0.4m \\ &= 80Nm \end{aligned}$$

Need to know more? For more information on moment of force see Chapter 14, pages 335–335, in the OCR A2 PE Student Book

To increase the moment of force/torque an athlete can:

- increase the force applied
- increase the distance of the application of force from the fulcrum.

ROTATION

- Rotation or **angular motion** is created by generating a moment of force/torque to a body.
- An eccentric force is applied outside the centre of mass.

KEY TERM

Angular motion – angular motion is when a body or part of a body moves in a circular path about an axis of rotation. It is caused when an eccentric/off-centre force is applied to a body, for example a gymnast on the uneven bars performing somersaults, twists, turns and circles.

The principle of axes of rotation concerns three axes of rotation directed through the centre of mass through which the body can rotate.

Axis of rotation	Definition	Application
Longitudinal	Runs vertically through the body (from top to bottom).	A dancer performing a pirouette or an ice skater performing a spin.
Transverse	Runs horizontally through the body (from left to right).	A gymnast performing a front somersault on the beam.
Frontal	Runs horizontally through the body (from front to back).	A gymnast performing a cartwheel.

Table 3 The three axes of rotation

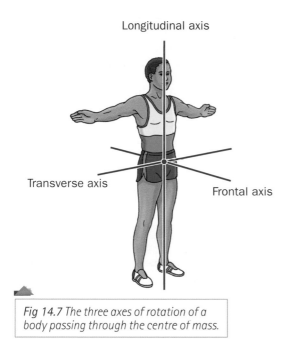

Longitudinal axis

Transverse axis

Frontal axis

Fig 14.7 The three axes of rotation of a body passing through the centre of mass.

KEY TERM

Axis of rotation – An imaginary line or point about which the body, or part of the body, rotates.

DESCRIBING ANGULAR MOTION AND THE ANGULAR ANALOGUE OF NEWTON'S LAWS

EXAM TIP

Make sure you are able to define, calculate and use the correct units for each of the terms below. Remember the key word angular.

Angular Distance - is the angle through which a body has rotated about an axis from A to B, measured in radians.

Angular Displacement - is the smallest angular change about an axis from A to B, measured in radians.

ANGULAR MOTION - when a body or part of a body moves in a circular path about an axis of rotation

Angular Speed - is the rate of change of angular distance (how fast a body rotates or angular distance travelled in a certain time), measured in radians per second (rads⁻¹).
Angular speed (rads⁻¹)= angular distance/time

Angular Velocity - is the rate of change of angular displacement (how fast a body rotates and in which direction), measured in radians per second (rads⁻¹).
Angular velocity (rads⁻¹)= angular displacement/time

Angular Acceleration - is the rate of change of angular velocity, measured in radians per second squared (rads⁻²). Angular Acceleration(rads⁻²)= change in angular velocity/time, e.g. when the angular velocity of a high board diver performing a somersault increases from 6 rads⁻¹ to 14 rads⁻¹ in a time of 0.5 seconds:
Angular acceleration = 14 -6/0.5
= 8/0.5
= 16 rads⁻²

Fig 14.8 Angular motion

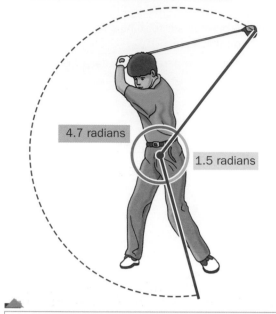

Angular distance = 4.7 radians

Angular displacement = 1.5 radians

4.7 radians

1.5 radians

Angular analogue of Newton's laws

The concept behind the angular analogue's of Newton's laws is exactly the same. Now they are concerned with rotating bodies and so use the term 'torque' instead of force (see Table 4).

MOMENT OF INERTIA

Moment of inertia is the resistance of a rotating body to change its state of angular motion (or the resistance of a body to rotate). Moment of inertia is the rotational equivalent of inertia. The two factors which affect moment of inertia are;

- *The mass of a body*: the greater the mass the greater the moment of inertia.
- The *distribution of the mass from the axis of rotation*: the further the mass is distributed from the axis of rotation the greater the moment of inertia.

Fig 14.9 Angular distance and angular displacement of a golf drive.

Newton's law	Angular analogues of Newton's laws of motion	Application to a rotating body: an ice skater performing a jump with spin
Angular analogue of Newton's first law.	*'A rotating body continues to turn about its axis of rotation with constant angular momentum unless acted upon by an external torque'.*	The spinning ice skater will continue to rotate about the longitudinal axis with constant angular momentum until the ice exerts an external torque on landing.
Angular analogue of Newton's second law.	*'When a torque acts on a body, the rate of change of angular momentum is proportional to the size of the torque applied, and acts in the same direction as the torque applied'.*	On take-off the greater the torque generated by the ice skater from the ice the greater the change in angular momentum experienced. Equally, the direction the torque is applied to the ice skater at take-off will be the direction in which they rotate about their axis.
Angular analogue of Newton's third law.	*'For every torque that is exerted by one body on another there is an equal and opposite torque exerted by the second body back to the first'.*	The ice skater at take-off will apply a downward and right-hand torque to the ice which will generate an upward and left-hand torque to the ice skater who will lift and rotate to the left.

Table 4 Angular analogue of Newton's Laws

Need to know more? For more information on the angular analogues of Newton's laws applied to rotating bodies see Chapter 14, pages 340–341, in the OCR A2 PE Student Book

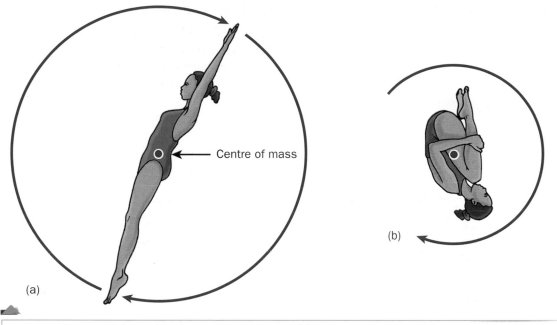

Centre of mass

(a)

(b)

Fig 14.10 The gymnast is rotating about her transverse axis. (a) Moment of inertia is high as the distribution of mass is a long way from the axis of rotation. (b) Moment of inertia is low as the distribution of mass is close to the axis of rotation.

The greater the moment of inertia, the greater the resistance to change state of angular motion (the harder it is to rotate or stop rotating once started).

Moment of inertia can be calculated using:

- MI = $\sum mr^2$ (where m = mass of the body and r = distance from the axis of rotation).
- It is measured in kilogram metres squared (kgm^2).

Moment of inertia can be increased or decreased during rotation:

- To increase the moment of inertia, distribute the mass further from the axis of rotation (straighten the body). This increases the resistance to rotation and angular velocity will decrease (spin slower).
- To decrease the moment of inertia, distribute the mass closer to the axis of rotation (tuck the body). This decreases the resistance to rotation and angular velocity will increase (spin faster).

> **Need to know more?** For more information on the moment of inertia see Chapter 14, pages 341–344, in the OCR A2 PE Student Book

Considering the whole body, a gymnast performing a straight somersault has a high moment of inertia as the distribution of mass is far from the transverse axis of rotation. They will spin slowly (low angular velocity) and complete only one rotation. Whereas, a gymnast performing a tucked front somersault has a low moment of inertia as the distribution of mass is close to the transverse axis of rotation. They will spin quickly (high angular velocity) and complete multiple rotations whilst in the air.

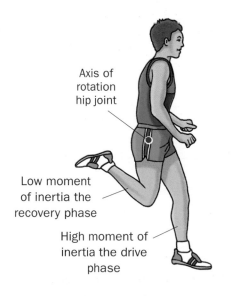

Axis of rotation hip joint

Low moment of inertia the recovery phase

High moment of inertia the drive phase

Fig 14.11 The moment of inertia in the drive and recovery phase of the sprinting action to ensure an efficient action.

Considering only part of a body, a sprinter's drive leg will have a high moment of inertia as the distribution of mass is far from the hip joint. The leg will rotate slowly (low angular velocity) and be in contact with the ground for maximum time, whereas the sprinter's recovery leg will have a low moment of inertia as the mass is distributed close to the hip joint. The leg will rotate quickly (high angular velocity) and be able to start the next drive phase.

ANGULAR MOMENTUM

Angular momentum is the quantity of angular motion possessed by a rotating body:

- To generate angular momentum, a torque must be applied to the body.
- The greater the torque applied, the greater the angular momentum.

Angular momentum = moment of inertia x angular velocity

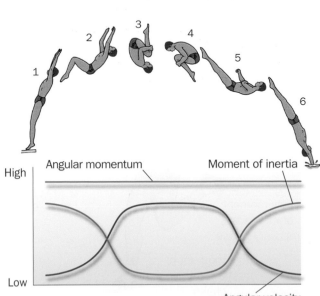

Law of the conservation of angular momentum

Angular momentum generated at take-off is conserved during flight as a result of the angular analogue of Newton's first law:

A rotating body continues to turn about its axis of rotation with constant angular momentum unless acted upon by an external torque.

To maintain constant angular momentum through a sporting technique, such as a front tucked somersault, rotating athletes can:

- decrease their moment of inertia (by distributing the mass close to the axis of rotation – tuck in) to increase their angular velocity (quicker rate of spin)
- increase their moment of inertia (by distributing the mass far from the axis of rotation – straighten out) to decrease their angular velocity (slower rate of spin).

As shown in Fig 14.12, the diver manipulates his body position to maintain a constant angular momentum throughout the dive until entry to the water. The phases of motion are described in Table 5.

Need to know more? For more information on angular momentum see Chapter 14, pages 345–347, in the OCR A2 PE Student Book

At take-off	• A torque is applied to the diver outside the centre of mass to create angular motion about the transverse axis of rotation. • The straight body position ensures a high moment of inertia. • A large angular momentum is generated to enable the one and a half rotations in the time given during flight.
During flight	• To maintain angular momentum the diver tucks in (to distribute his mass closer to the transverse axis of rotation) to lower his moment of inertia. • This increases the angular velocity (rate of spin) to complete the full one-and-a-half rotations.
Prior to landing/ entry to the water	• To control the entry to the water and prevent over-rotation, the diver increases his moment of inertia by straightening his body out to decrease angular velocity.
Landing/entry to the water	• Angular momentum ceases when the diver enters the water, applying an opposite torque passing through the centre of mass to prevent rotation.

Table 5

CHECK

If you are satisfied with your knowledge and understanding, tick off the sections that you have revised so far. If you are not satisfied then revisit those sections and refer to the pages in the *Need to know more?* features.

☐ Define centre of mass and describe its relationship to balance, rotation and efficiency of technique.

☐ Identify the three types of lever system in relation to human movement and the advantages and disadvantages of second and third classes of lever system.

☐ Define and calculate the units of measurement for the moment of a force.

☐ Identify the three major axes of rotation, giving examples of sporting movements that occur around them.

☐ Describe the quantities used to describe angular motion and explain their relevance to sporting techniques.

☐ State what is meant by the terms moment of inertia and angular momentum and their relevance to sporting performance.

☐ Outline the law of conservation of angular momentum and be able to give examples of how athletes use this principle in a number of sporting activities.

TRUE OR FALSE?

1. Centre of mass is the point at which a body is balanced in all directions.
2. To increase stability a performer can widen the base of support and raise the centre of mass.
3. There are four types of lever system in the human body, each consisting of a fulcrum, an effort and a load.
4. Moment of force is the rotational equivalent of force, also known as torque.
5. Moment of force is calculated by moment of inertia multiplied by angular velocity.
6. The longitudinal axis of rotation runs vertically through the body from head to toe.
7. For rotation/angular motion to occur an eccentric/off-centre force must be applied.
8. An athlete can increase their moment of inertia by straightening their body distributing their mass further from the axis of rotation.
9. Increasing moment of inertia increases angular velocity/rate of spin.
10. The law of conservation of angular momentum is the angular analogue of Netwon's first law.

See page 293 for answers

EXAM PRACTICE

1. The figure below shows a lever system for the shoulder during extension of a tennis serve. Identify the class of lever used and calculate the moment of force/torque caused by the load. *(4 marks)*

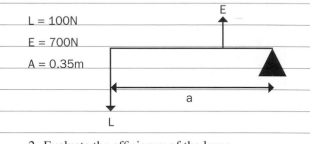

L = 100N
E = 700N
A = 0.35m

2. Evaluate the efficiency of the lever system used during shoulder extension in comparison to the lever used at the ball of the foot to lift the tennis player upwards from the ground. *(5 marks)*

3. A gymnast with a mass of 65kg accelerates upwards and performs a backward somersault before landing, assuming acceleration due to gravity is 10ms-2, calculate the gymnast's weight. Using your knowledge of the angular analogue of Newton's laws of motion and the law of conservation of angular momentum explain the control of this backward rotation. *(20 marks)*

CHAPTER 15

Critical evaluation of the quality, effectiveness and efficacy of performance

CHAPTER OVERVIEW

By the end of this chapter you should have knowledge and understanding of:
- how to review and judge you level of understanding of biomechanical concepts
- how to apply the knowledge you have gained to:
  - running activities such as sprinting, endurance running, swerving, side stepping and dodging in team games.
  - jumping activities such as long jump, high jump, triple jump, simple jumps in trampolining and gymnastics, jumping in team games, ski jumping.
  - throwing activities such as shot put, javelin, discus, throwing, passing and shooting in team games.
  - hitting/kicking activities such as shots in tennis, badminton, golf, cricket, rounders, free kick or corner kicks in football, conversions in rugby.
  - rotating activities such as rotating skills around the principle axes in gymnastics, diving, trampolining, skating, slalom skiing.

EXAM TIP

This is the perfect chapter to get to grips with the 20 mark question. Make sure you can:
- show a detailed knowledge of multiple areas of biomechanics,
- use accurate and specialist vocabulary,
- link theory to practical performance,
- annotate diagrams and use a good level of written communication.

CRITICAL EVALUATION OF RUNNING ACTIVITIES

EXAM TIP

Running activities can include sprinting, endurance running, swerving, side stepping and dodging in team games. Included are varied examples, make sure you consider each activity individually.

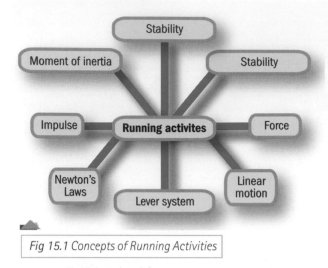

Fig 15.1 Concepts of Running Activities

Newton's Laws

Newton's first law of motion	The sprinter remains stationary until a reaction force is generated from the blocks.
Newton's second law of motion	The greater the reaction generated, the greater the change in momentum and acceleration in the drive phase.
Newton's third law of motion	Down and backward action force is applied to the blocks – equal up and forward reaction force is applied to the sprinter.

Table 1 Newton's laws for a sprint start

Describing linear motion

- A 400m runner completes a *distance* of 400m (how far from A to B) and *displacement* of 0m (shortest straight line route between A to B).
- A sprinter who completes 100m in 10.07s has a *speed* of 9.93ms^{-1} (distance/time) and the first 20m in 2.94s has an average *acceleration* of 2.31ms^{-2} (change in velocity/time).

Graphs of motion

- Speed and acceleration can be calculated from the gradients of distance/time and velocity/time graphs drawn for running activities.
- Gradient of graph = changes in y axis/changes in x axis.

Types of force: Running action

- *Weight* acts from the centre of mass downwards (W = mg).

- *Reaction* acts from the point of contact upwards (Newton's third law).
- *Air resistance* acts from the centre of mass and opposes motion.
- As *velocity* increases, *air resistance* increases. To counteract this, sprinters wear tight, smooth clothing and stay low to reduce frontal cross-sectional area in the drive phase.
- *Friction* acts from the point of contact parallel to the two surfaces in contact. To maximise friction, sprinters wear spikes and rugby players wear studs to increase the roughness of the contact surface.

Free body diagrams

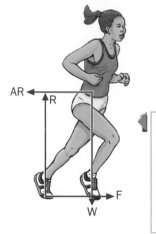

Fig 15.2 Free body diagram for the endurance running stride. W = R: no vertical acceleration. F = AR: constant velocity. Vertical and horizontal forces balanced: net force = 0.

Impulse

Impulse (Ns) = force x time.

Acceleration phase	Positive impulse >negative impulse: net force in forward direction
Maximum speed	Positive impulse = negative impulse: net force = 0
Deceleration phase	Positive impulse< negative impulse: net force in opposite direction

Table 2 Impulse for a sprinting action

Stability for a sprint start

- '*On your marks*': stable (low centre of mass) wide base of support with central line of gravity.
- '*Set*': less stable (centre of mass raised) line of gravity moved forwards.
- '*Go!*': unstable, line of gravity outside base of support.

Lever systems

In the sprint start, a second class lever is used from the ball of the foot to push away from the blocks (E – L – F).

- Effort: force exerted by the gastrocnemius.
- Load: weight of the body.
- Fulcrum: ball of the foot.

As the recovery leg flexes at the hip a third class lever is used (L – E – F).

- Load: weight of the leg.
- Effort: force exerted by the iliopsoas.
- Fulcrum: hip joint.

Moment of inertia for a sprinting action

- Drive leg: high moment of inertia – low angular velocity – maximum contact time with ground.
- Recovery leg: low moment of inertia – high angular velocity – fast leg speed.

CRITICAL EVALUATION OF JUMPING ACTIVITIES

EXAM TIP

Jumping activities can include long jump, high jump, triple jump, simple jumps in trampolining and gymnastics, jumping in team games and ski jumping. Included are varied examples; make sure you consider each activity individually.

Newton's Laws

Newton's first law of motion	Player remains stationary until reaction force generated from the court exceeds weight.
Newton's second law of motion	The greater the reaction generated, the greater the change in momentum and vertical acceleration towards the hoop.
Newton's third law of motion	Downward action force applied to the court – equal upward reaction force applied to the basketball player.

Table 3 Newton's laws for a basketball lay-up shot

Types of force for a triple jumper

- *Weight* acts from the centre of mass downwards (W = mg).
- *Reaction* acts from the point of contact upwards (Newton's second law: the greater the reaction the greater the vertical acceleration).
- *Air resistance* acts from the centre of mass and opposes motion.
- As *velocity* increases, *air resistance* increases. To counteract this the triple jumper wears tight, smooth clothing and stays low in the jump phases to reduce frontal cross-sectional area.
- *Friction* acts from the point of contact parallel to the two surfaces in contact. To maximise friction, triple jumpers wear spikes to increase the roughness of the contact surface and takes off from a rubberised track, thereby increasing the roughness of the ground surface.

Free body diagram

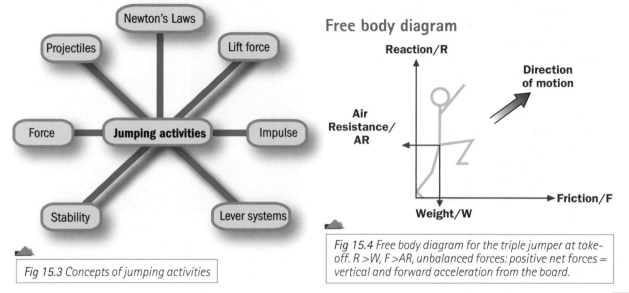

Fig 15.3 Concepts of jumping activities

Fig 15.4 Free body diagram for the triple jumper at take-off. R >W, F >AR, unbalanced forces: positive net forces = vertical and forward acceleration from the board.

Impulse for a triple jumper

- Increase the *time* the force is applied to the board (leaning back, lowering centre of mass).
- Increases the *impulse* applied (Impulse (Ns) = force x time).
- Increases the outgoing/change in *momentum* at take-off.
- Increases the outgoing *velocity* of the triple jumper.
- Increases the *acceleration* and *height* going into the jump.

Projectiles and lift force for a ski–jumper

- During flight, ski-jumper adopts aerofoil shape.
- The greater the angle of attack the greater the lift force (up to 17 degrees).
- Air flows further over the top of the ski jumper. At a higher velocity this creates an area of low pressure.
- Pressure gradient creates a Bernoulli lift force to allow the ski jumper a longer time in flight, achieving a greater horizontal distance.
- Due to the high velocity a large air resistance acts (minimised by streamlining; smooth, skin tight lycra suit, small frontal cross-sectional area).
- Weight force is reduced by the additional lift force.
- AR >W = non-parabolic flight path.

Stability for a basketball lay–up shot

- *Centre of mass* is the point at which the body is balanced in all directions. Position of the centre of mass depends on the distribution of mass.
- Centre of mass follows a predetermined path at take-off.
- Reaction force generated at take-off passes through the centre of mass to prevent rotation.
- At take-off: centre of mass is raised by lifting one knee and arm allowing the basketball player to jump higher.
- During flight: centre of mass is lowered by dropping the knee and arm. This allows the basketball player to return to the ground more quickly to rejoin play.

Lever systems

In the basketball lay-up shot, a second class lever is used from the ball of the foot to push up from the court (E – L – F).

- Effort: force exerted by the gastrocnemius.
- Load: weight of the body.
- Fulcrum: ball of the foot.

CRITICAL EVALUATION OF THROWING ACTIVITIES

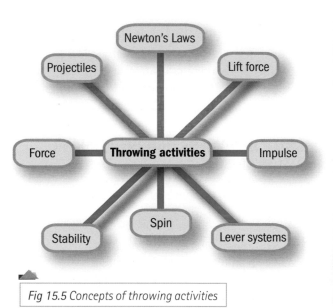

Fig 15.5 Concepts of throwing activities

Newton's laws

Newton's first law of motion	The ball remains stationary in the player's hands until an external force is applied by the player.
Newton's second law of motion	The ball will accelerate towards the hoop proportionally to the size of the action force applied.
Newton's third law of motion	The player applies an action force to the ball and the ball provides an equal and opposite reaction force to the player's hands.

Table 4 Newton's laws for a basketball free throw

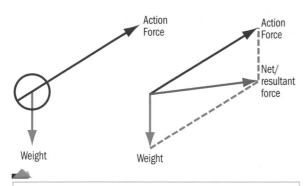

Fig 15.6 *Force diagram showing forces acting on the shot put at the moment of release and parallelogram of forces to show net (resultant) force. The net force represents the size and direction of acceleration of the shot put on release.*

Types of force for a shot put at the moment of release

- *Weight* acts from the centre of mass downwards (W – mg).
- *Action force* is applied to the shot put through the centre of mass in the direction of motion.
- *Air resistance* is negligible at the point of release and is minimised in flight due to the high mass, relatively low velocity, small frontal cross-sectional area and smooth surface.

Impulse for a discus

- Increase the *time* the force is applied to the discus (multiple rotation – *follow through*).
- Increases the *impulse* applied (Impulse (Ns) = force x time (see Fig 15.9 below).
- Increases the outgoing/change in *momentum* at release.
- Increases the outgoing *velocity* of the discus to achieve maximum horizontal *distance*.

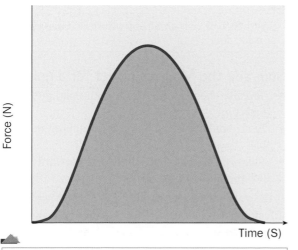

Fig 15.7 *Force/time graph to show the impulse given to a discus by a thrower with good technique at the moment of release*

Projectiles for a shot put

The shot put:

- has high mass
- has small frontal cross-sectional area
- has smooth outer surface
- travels with low velocity
- weight is the dominant force
- has negligible air resistance

W >AR = parabolic/symmetrical flight path

Lift force for a discus

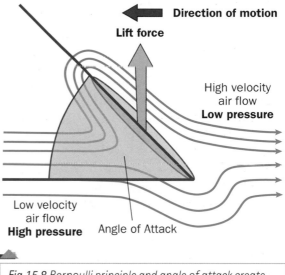

Fig 15.8 *Bernoulli principle and angle of attack create lift force during the flight of the discus. Note: consider aerofoil shape, angle of attack, direction of motion, velocity, pressure, and lift force.*

Spin for a basketball free throw

- Apply an eccentric/off-centre force to impart backspin on the ball.
- Backspin will lead to a softer shot with a high arch.
- As the ball hits the backboard it will decelerate on bounce and rebound towards the hoop.

Lever systems for a netball chest pass

Receiving the netball: third-class lever used as the elbow flexes (L – E – F).

- Load: weight of netball and forearm.
- Effort: force exerted by the biceps brachii.
- Fulcrum: elbow joint.

Execution phase of chest-pass: first-class lever as the elbow extends (L – F – E).

- Load: weight of the netball and forearm.
- Fulcrum: elbow joint.
- Effort: force exerted by the triceps brachii.

CRITICAL EVALUATION OF HITTING AND KICKING ACTIVITIES

EXAM TIP

Hitting and kicking activities can include shots in tennis, badminton, golf, cricket, rounders, free kicks and corner kicks in football and conversions in rugby. Included are varied examples, make sure you consider each activity individually.

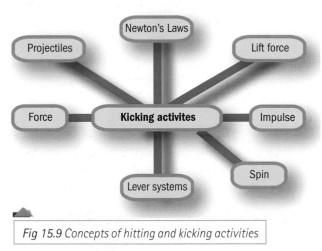

Fig 15.9 Concepts of hitting and kicking activities

Newton's laws

Newton's first law of motion	The football will remain stationary until an external force is applied from the player's foot.
Newton's second law of motion	The football will accelerate proportionally to the size of the external force applied and in the same direction.
Newton's third law of motion	The foot applies an action force to the ball and the ball provides equal and opposite reaction force to the player's foot.

Table 5 Newton's laws for a football free kick

Types of force for a football goal/penalty kick at the moment of contact

- *Weight* acts from the centre of mass downwards (W = mg).
- *Action force* applied to the football in the desired direction of motion.
- Underneath the centre of mass = backspin: lengthen the flight path, for example a goal kick.
- Left or right of the centre of mass = sidespin: swerve the flight path (hook or slice), for example a penalty kick.
- Action force >weight; unbalanced force: positive net force = acceleration in direction of action force.

Impulse for a golf drive with follow through

- Increases the *time* the force acts on the golf ball.
- Increases the *impulse* of force acting on the golf ball (Impulse (Ns) = force x time).
- Increases the outgoing/change in *momentum* and *velocity* of the golf ball.
- Increases the horizontal *distance*, *control* and accuracy of the golf ball's flight path.

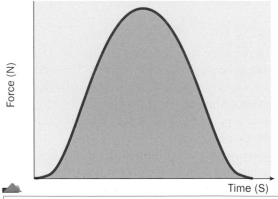

Fig 15.10 Force/time graph to show the impulse imparted on a golf ball.

Spin and the Magnus effect for a golf ball

- *Topspin* shortens the flight path making the ball 'dip'.
- *Backspin* lengthens flight path making the ball 'float'.
- *Sidespin* 'swerves' the flight path towards the left (hook) or right (slice).

If the golf ball is hit with backspin, the Magnus effect creates upward lift force from the centre of mass because:

- above the ball the airflow travels in the same direction as spin, creating high velocity air, and a low pressure area (opposite underneath the ball)

* a pressure gradient forms resulting in the ball deviating towards the area of low pressure, thereby creating 'float'.

Projectiles

Start of flight	• high velocity • low mass • rough surface • air resistance dominant = non-parabolic flight path
End of flight	• deceleration due to high air resistance • weight dominant = parabolic flight path

Table 6 For a hard hit shuttle

Lever systems for a badminton overhead clear

In the preparation phase: Third class lever used as the shoulder extends (L – E – F).

* *Load*: weight of the arm and racquet.
* *Effort*: force exerted by the posterior deltoid.
* *Fulcrum*: shoulder joint.

CRITICAL EVALUATION OF ROTATING ACTIVITIES

EXAM TIP

Rotating activities can include rotation around the principle axes in gymnastics, diving, trampolining, ice skating and slalom skiing. Included are varied examples, make sure you consider each activity individually.

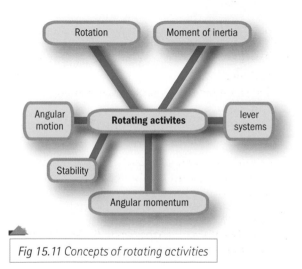

Fig 15.11 Concepts of rotating activities

Preparation phase	Recovery phase
Unstable: • one foot lifted • arms raised lifts centre of mass • body leans forward so line of gravity falls outside the base of support • creates moment of force/torque.	*Stable:* • two feet on beam • low centre of mass due to bent knees on landing • line of gravity from centre of mass falls within base of support • reaction force passes through the centre of mass to prevent rotation.

Table 7 Stability for a gymnast performing a front walkover on the beam

Lever systems for a high board diver

In the preparation phase: Second class lever used to propel the diver into the air from the ball of the foot (E – L – F).

* *Load*: weight of the body.
* *Effort*: force exerted by the gastrocnemius.
* *Fulcrum:* ball of the foot.

The second class lever has the mechanical advantage to move a large load with a small effort, as the effort is further from the fulcrum than the load. However, it is only efficient over a small distance at the expense of speed and range of movement.

Fig 15.12 Preparation for take-off.

Moment of force (Nm) = force x distance from the fulcrum

Force exerted by the gastrocnemius (E) if the load of the body was 650N, 0.05m from the fulcrum would be:

E = 650N x 0.05m

E = 32.5Nm

Describing angular motion for a gymnast performing a full circle about the high bar

The gymnast completes:

- an angular *distance* of 6.28 rad (360° angle rotated about an axis from A to B)
- an angular *displacement* of 0 rad (0°) (smallest angular change between A and B).

If the gymnast completed one full circle in 0.5 seconds, angular speed would be 12.56 rads^{-1} (angular distance/time).

Rotation for a trampolinist performing a straight somersault

- Rotation is created by eccentric/off-centre force.
- This creates a moment of force/torque and generates angular momentum.
- Rotation around the transverse axis.

KEY TERM

Moment of inertia – The resistance of a body to change its state of angular motion. It is dependent on mass and the distribution of mass from the axis of rotation.

Moment of inertia for an ice skater performing a jump with spin (during flight)

- Rotation around the longitudinal axis.
- Arms and legs brought close to the body.
- Reduces moment of inertia.
- Increases angular velocity (rate of spin).

Angular momentum for an ice skater performing a jump with spin

Angular momentum is the amount of angular motion possessed by the ice skater about the longitudinal axis.

Angular momentum = moment of inertia x angular velocity.

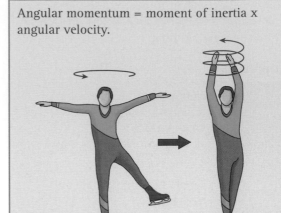

Angular analogue of Newton's first law: 'the ice skater continues to rotate about the longitudinal axis of rotation with constant angular momentum unless acted upon by the ice as they land which provides an external torque'.

At take–off:	• angular motion/torque created as reaction forces pass outside the centre of mass • mass of the arms and legs distributed away from longitudinal axis = large moment of inertia, large angular momentum for flight phase.
During flight:	• mass of the arms and legs distributed close to the longitudinal axis = reduce moment of inertia and increase angular velocity = maintain angular momentum.
Prior to landing:	• mass of the arms and legs moved away from longitudinal axis to increase moment of inertia and lower angular velocity. • increases control and prevents over-rotation on landing.

Table 8 Law of conservation of angular momentum applied to an ice skater performing a jump

▶ **Need to know more?** For more information on critical evaluation of performance see Chapter 15, pages 351–361, in the OCR A2 PE Student Book

CHECK

If you are satisfied with your knowledge and understanding, tick off the sections that you have revised so far. If you are not satisfied then revisit those sections and refer to the pages in the *Need to know more?* features.

- Review and judge your level of understanding of biomechanical concepts.
- Apply the knowledge you have gained to:
  - running activities such as sprinting, endurance running, swerving, side stepping and dodging in team games.
  - jumping activities such as long jump, high jump, triple jump, simple jumps in trampolining and gymnastics, jumping in team games, ski jumping.
  - throwing activities such as shot put, javelin, discus, throwing, passing and shooting in team games.
  - hitting/kicking activities such as shots in tennis, badminton, golf, cricket, rounders, free kick or corner kicks in football, conversions in rugby.
  - rotating activities such as rotating skills around the principle axes in gymnastics, diving, trampolining, skating, slalom skiing.

EXAM PRACTICE

1. Using your knowledge and understanding of force, follow through, and the Bernoulli principle explain how a discus thrower uses efficient technique to increase the distance thrown. *(20 marks)*

2. Explain the concept of moment of inertia and its importance to a gymnast performing a somersault. *(6 marks)*

3. Describe the concept of friction and explain how sports performers in team games of your choice increase and decrease friction to improve the efficiency of their performance. *(6 marks)*

See page 296 for answers

TRUE OR FALSE?

1. Side stepping and dodging in team games is more efficient for performers with a low inertia who can change direction more quickly.

2. The Bernoulli principle should be maximised by a ski jumper adopting an aerofoil shape during flight to increase horizontal distance.

3. The javelin is a good example of an event where the Magnus effect provides an additional lift force.

4. When an action force is applied to a football a reaction force is applied back to the foot following Newton's third law of motion.

5. A gymnast performs a cartwheel on the beam rotating around the transverse axis.

6. In the drive phase of a sprint friction is greater than air resistance and results in forward acceleration as there is a net force present.

7. The Fosbury Flop is not as efficient as the scissor kick technique in the high jump as the centre of mass must be raised above the bar needing a greater force at take-off.

8. At the start, middle and end of flight weight is the dominant force acting on a shot put, therefore the flight path is non-parabolic/asymmetrical.

9. When performing a golf drive an eccentric/off-centre force must be applied to generate backspin causing the ball to 'float' in the air and extend its flight path.

10. When performing a tucked front somersault in trampolining the greater the angular velocity the greater the number of rotations possible in the flight time given.

CHAPTER 16

Energy

CHAPTER OVERVIEW

By the end of this chapter you should have knowledge and understanding of:

- how to define energy, work and power
- the role of ATP; the breakdown and re-synthesis of ATP; coupled reactions and exothermic and endothermic reactions
- the three energy systems: ATP/PC; alactic; the lactic acid and aerobic system
- the contribution of each energy system in relation to the duration/intensity of exercise
- the predominant energy system used related to type of exercise
- the inter-changing between thresholds during an activity, for example the onset of blood lactate accumulation (OBLA), and the effect of level of fitness, availability of oxygen and food fuels, and enzyme control on energy system used
- how the body returns to its pre-exercise state: the oxygen debt/excess post-exercise oxygen consumption (EPOC); the alactacid and lactacid debt components; replenishment of myoglobin stores and fuel stores and the removal of carbon dioxide
- the implications of the recovery process for planning physical activity sessions.

ENERGY CONCEPTS

You need to be able to define and identify the units identified in Table 1 below.

ADENOSINE TRIPHOSPHATE (ATP)

- Adenosine Triphosphate (ATP) is a compound made up of one complex element, Adenosine, and three simple phosphate (P) elements held together by high energy bonds.

Concept	Definition	Measure / units
Energy	• Ability to perform work or put mass into motion	Joules (J)
Work	• Ability to apply force over a distance: Work = force (N) x Distance moved (m) (Force is a pull/push that alters the state of motion of a body)	Joules (J) or Newtons (N)
Power	• Rate at which we can work/work (F x D) divided by time	Watts (W)

Table 1 Definitions of energy, work and power

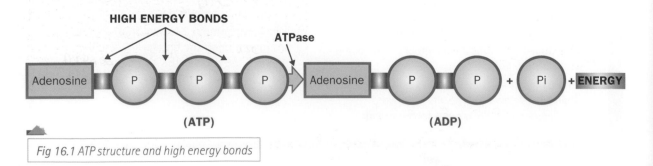

Fig 16.1 ATP structure and high energy bonds

- When broken by the enzyme ATPase, it releases the potential energy stored within for the muscles to apply force as **kinetic energy** (see Fig 16.1).
- This is an **exothermic** reaction as it releases energy and leaves behind a compound called adenosine diphosphate (ADP).

KEY TERMS

Kinetic energy – Energy in the form of muscle contraction/joint movement.

Adenosine triphoshate (ATP) – Chemical energy stored as a high energy compound in the body. It is the only immediately usable source of energy in the human body.

Exothermic – A chemical reaction that releases energy as it progresses.

ATP is the *only* usable source of energy that the body/muscles can utilise for work. It is stored directly within muscles as a simple compound (mixture of elements), so that it can be quickly broken down to supply energy for approximately two to three seconds of muscular work.

ATP resynthesis

- The breakdown of ATP into ADP is a reversible (**endothermic**) reaction.
- This requires energy from one of three energy systems to resynthesise ADP back into ATP.
- The ATP/PC, Lactic Acid and Aerobic systems work together to supply energy to re-synthesise ADP back into ATP via coupled reactions.

Fig 16.2 Break down of PC coupled to the resynthesis of ATP

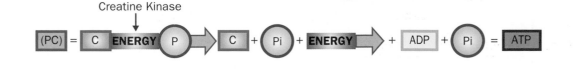

Creatine Kinase
(PC)
=
C
ENERGY
P
C
+
Pi
+
ENERGY
+
ADP
+
Pi
=
ATP

KEY TERMS

Endothermic – A chemical reaction that requires energy to be added for it to progress.

Coupled reactions – When the products from one reaction, such as energy, are then used in another reaction.

EXAM TIP

When answering energy system questions, always ask yourself *Where has the energy come from?* If it is not ATP then it cannot be used for muscular work. It is more likely to be energy that has been released to resynthesise ADP back into ATP as part of a coupled reaction.

THE ATP/PC (ALACTIC) SYSTEM

The information you are required to know for the ATP/PC system is summarised in Tables 2 and 3.

KEY TERMS

Anaerobic – A reaction that can occur without the presence of oxygen.

Coupled reactions – When the products from one reaction, such as energy, are then used in another reaction.

Sarcoplasm – Fluid-like gelatine that fills the spaces within the muscle cells and is a store of glycogen, fat, proteins, enzymes and myoglobin.

Matrix – Intracellular fluid within the mitochondria where oxidation takes place.

Mitochondria – Small sub-unit (membrane) sites of a muscle cell where aerobic respiration takes place.

Cristae – Internal membrane/compartments/fold-like structures within mitochondria.

Energy system	1.Type of reaction	2.Chemical / food fuel	3.Reaction site	4.Controlling enzymes	Process	By-products	Net total ATP
ATP/PC system	Anaerobic	ATP and PC	Muscle cell sarcoplasm	ATPase / creatine Kinase	PC >C+Pi = E	Pi + C	1 ATP
LA system (Anaerobic glycolysis)	Anaerobic	Glycogen / glucose	Muscle cell sarcoplasm	Glycogen phosphorylase PFK LDA	Glycogen to glucose Glucose to pyruvic acid + E Pyruvic acid to lactic acid	LA >Low pH Inhibits enzymes	2 ATP
Aerobic system Three stages (see below)							38 ATP
1. Aerobic glycolysis	Aerobic	Glycogen/ glucose/ FFA's	Muscle cell sarcoplasm	Glycogen phosphorylase PFK	Glycogen to Glucose to Glucose to pyruvic acid + E Pyruvic acid + coenzyme A		2 ATP
2. Krebs	Aerobic	Glycogen/ glucose/ FFA's	Mitochondria matrix	Lipases/Fats	Acetyle Coa + oxaloacetic acid = Citric acid + O_2 =CO_2 + H + E	CO_2	2 ATP
3. ETC	Aerobic	Glycogen/ glucose/ FFA's	Mitochondria cristae		H + O_2 = H_2O + E	H_2O	34 ATP

Table 2 *Energy Systems Summary*
Key = E released from **coupled reactions** *to resynthesise ATP.*

Advantages	Disadvantages
• Does not require oxygen. • PC stored in muscle cell as readily available energy source. • Simple/small compound so very quick reaction/resynthesis of ATP. • Automatically stimulated by a decrease in ATP and increase in ADP. • Provides energy for explosive high-intensity exercise and movements. • No fatiguing by-products. • PC can itself be quickly resynthesised so recovery time quick.	• Only small amounts of ATP and PC stored in muscle cells. • 1 PC resynthesises 1 ATP. • Only provides energy to resynthesise ATP for up to about 8–10 seconds.

Table 3 *Advantages and disadvantages of the ATP/PC system*

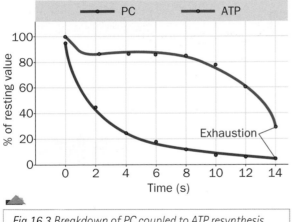

Fig 16.3 Breakdown of PC coupled to ATP resynthesis during sprinting

The energy from the breakdown of PC is not used for muscular work but used to resynthesise ADP back into ATP in a coupled reaction.

Training adaptations

- Anaerobic training overloads the ATP/PC system.
- This increases the body's muscle stores of ATP and PC.
- This in turn delays the **threshold** between the ATP/PC and the lactic acid system.
- Increases the potential duration of high intensity exercise for up to 1–2 seconds.

THE LACTIC ACID SYSTEM

The information you are required to know for the lactic acid system is summarised in Figure 16.4, Table 2 and Table 4.

Advantages	Disadvantages
• Large glycogen store in muscle/liver is readily available as a **potential energy** source. • Resynthesises two molecules of ATP – more than the PC system. • Requires fewer reactions than the aerobic system so provides a quicker supply of energy. • Glycogen phosphorylase and PFK enzyme activation due to a decrease in PC. • Provides energy for high-intensity exercise lasting between 10 and 180 seconds. • Can work aerobically and anaerobically.	• Not as quick as ATP/PC system. • Produces **lactic acid**, which is a fatiguing by-product. • Reduces pH (increased acidity) which inhibits enzyme action. • Stimulates pain receptors. • Net effect is muscle fatigue and pain.

Table 4 Advantages and disadvantages of the LA system

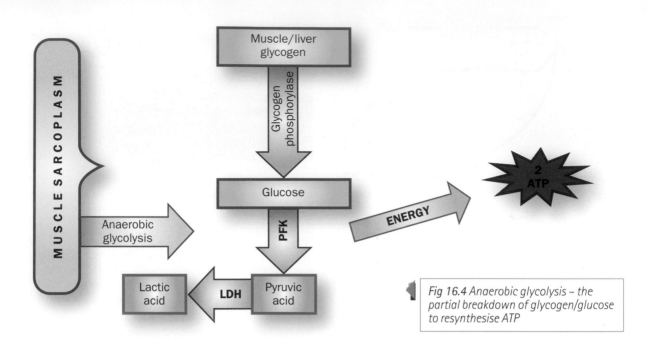

Fig 16.4 *Anaerobic glycolysis – the partial breakdown of glycogen/glucose to resynthesise ATP*

Training adaptations

Anaerobic training:

- overloads the LA system
- increases the body's tolerance to lactic acid
- increases its buffering capacity against high levels of lactic acid
- increases the body's stores of glycogen, delaying the OBLA and prolonging the lactic acid system threshold.

This allows athletes to work at higher intensities for longer periods before muscle fatigue occurs.

THE AEROBIC ENERGY SYSTEM

The information you are required to know for the Aerobic system is summarised in Figure 16.5 (a, b and c), Table 2 (page 164) and Table 5 (page 168).

The total energy produced via the aerobic system is therefore 38 ATP:

- 2 ATP from aerobic glycolysis
- 2 ATP from the Kreb's cycle
- 34 ATP from the electron transport chain (ETC).

EXAM TIP

You should never write in an answer that aerobic glycolysis is the same as anaerobic glycolysis. You must write out the process again but add the changes that occur in the presence of oxygen.

This is summarised by an equation that represents aerobic respiration:

$C_6H_{12}O_6 + 6O_2 = 6CO_2 + 6H_2O +$ energy (for the resynthesis of 38 ATP)
(glucose) + (oxygen) = (carbon dioxide) + (water) + energy

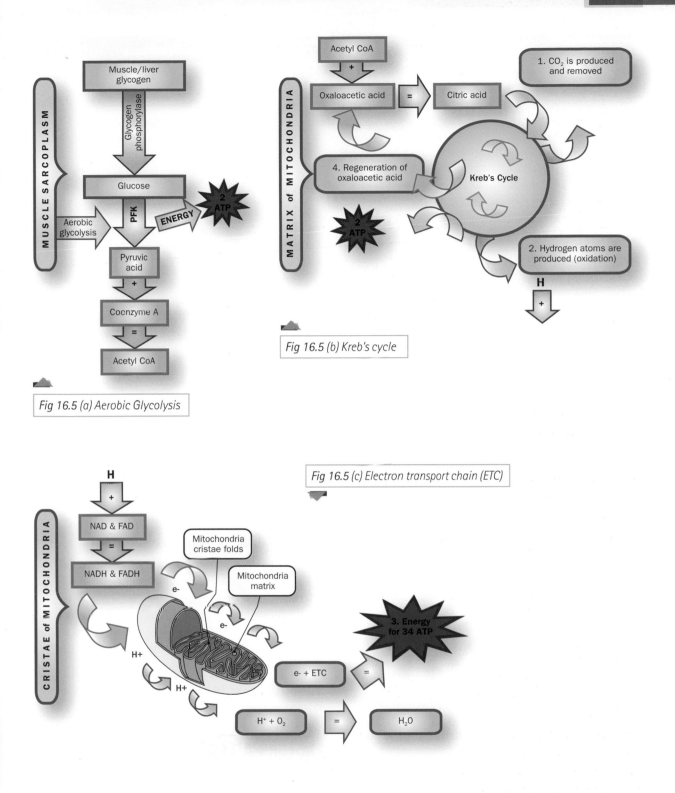

Fig 16.5 (a) Aerobic Glycolysis

Fig 16.5 (b) Kreb's cycle

Fig 16.5 (c) Electron transport chain (ETC)

Although seemingly complex, this equation is simply showing that glucose ($C_6H_{12}O_6$) is completely broken down by oxygen ($6O_2$) in the aerobic system into carbon dioxide ($6CO_2$) and water ($6H_2O$) to release sufficient energy to resynthesise 38 ATP.

EXAM TIP

If the equation for aerobic respiration is too daunting, just remember to describe the process without the complex equation.

Advantages	Disadvantages
• Large potential glycogen and free fatty acids (FFA) stores available as an efficient energy fuel. • Efficient ATP resynthesis when good O_2 supply guarantees breakdown of FFAs. • Large ATP resynthesis: 38 ATP from one molecule of glucose compared to two ATP from LA system and one from ATP/PC. • Provides energy for low/moderate-intensity and high-duration exercise (three minutes to one hour). • No fatiguing by-products; CO_2 and H_2O easily removed.	• Slower rate of ATP resynthesis compared with LA system due to points below. • Requires more O_2 supply (15% more for FFAs). • More complex series of reactions. • Cannot resynthesise ATP at the start of exercise due to initial delay of O_2 from the cardiovascular system. • Limited energy for ATP during high-intensity, short-duration work.

Table 5 The advantages and disadvantages of the aerobic system

Fats

• Triglycerides (fats) are broken down by **enzymes** into free fatty acids (FFA) and glycerol.

• FFA's are used as energy fuel within the aerobic system.
• FFAs are broken down into Acetyl CoA.
• Acetyl CoA enters and is broken down by the Krebs cycle and the ETC in a process termed beta-oxidation.
• FFAs produce more Acetyl CoA and consequently produce far greater energy than the breakdown of glycogen/glucose.
• However, FFAs require approximately 15 per cent more oxygen than that required to break down glucose, and so glycogen/glucose is the preferred energy fuel during moderate or high-intensity activity.
• The energy from the breakdown of glycogen/glucose/fats in the aerobic system is not used for muscular work but used to resynthesise ADP back into ATP in a coupled reaction.

Training effects

Specific 'aerobic' training causes a number of beneficial adaptations which improve the aerobic energy system's efficiency to resynthesise ATP:

• raised storage of muscle liver glycogen
• increased mobilisation of aerobic enzymes
• earlier use of FFAs to conserve glycogen stores.

The net effect of the above adaptations is that they:

• increase/prolong the aerobic threshold
• increase the potential intensity of performance.

This helps delay muscle fatigue by:

• increasing the intensity before OBLA is reached
• improving efficiency to remove lactate during periods of recovery.

ENERGY CONTINUUM

• The energy continuum shows how the energy systems interact to provide energy for the resynthesis of ATP.
• It also highlights the predominance/percentage of each of the three energy systems related to the duration and intensity of the activity (Fig 16.6).

You will be required to explain how all the factors numbered in Fig 16.7 affect which energy system/s is used.

FACTORS AFFECTING THE ENERGY SYSTEMS USED

Intensity and duration of exercise

Fig 16.6 shows that when the exercise intensity is anaerobic (high intensity, short duration) the ATP/PC and LA systems will be the predominant systems, whereas if the intensity is aerobic (medium/low intensity, long duration) the aerobic system will be predominant.

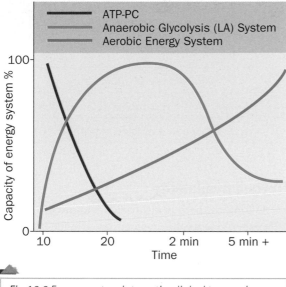

Fig 16.6 *Energy system interaction linked to exercise duration*

Onset of blood lactate accumulation (OBLA)

- During higher intensity exercise, lactate production will start to accumulate above resting levels. This is termed the 'lactate threshold'.
- When blood lactate levels reach 4 mmol/L , the exercise intensity is referred to as 'the onset of blood lactate accumulation' (OBLA) (Fig. 16.8).
- 4 mmol/L is an arbitrary standard value for when OBLA is reached and a point where the production of lactate exceeds the speed of its removal.
- OBLA will continue to increase if this exercise intensity is maintained or increased and causes a series of events, as follows:
  - lower blood pH (increased blood acidity)
  - inhibition of enzyme action
  - stimulation of pain receptors
  - muscle fatigue/pain.

Energy system thresholds

A threshold represents the point at which one energy system is taken over by another as the predominant energy system to provide the energy to resynthesise ATP. It shows the potential duration that each energy system can act as the predominant system and is summarised in Table 6.

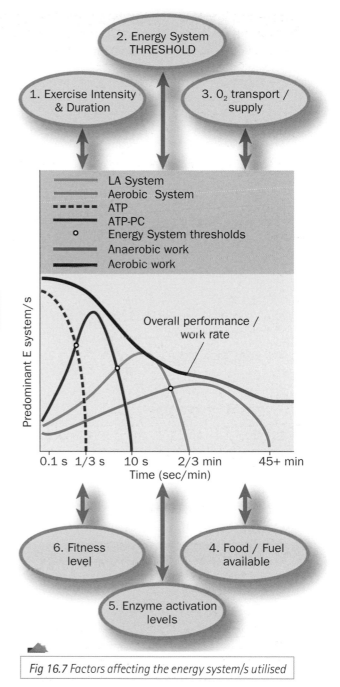

Fig 16.7 *Factors affecting the energy system/s utilised*

EXAM TIP

A common mistake is to think a threshold is when an energy system 'stops' providing energy to resynthesise ATP. If you do use the term 'stop', it is best to word your response as 'stops being the predominant energy system'.

Performance duration	Energy system/s involved (predominant system in *italics*)	Practical example
Less than 10 seconds	*ATP/PC*	Triple jump/100m sprint
10–90 seconds	ATP/PC *LA*	200–400m sprint and 100m swim
90 seconds to 3 minutes	*LA* Aerobic	Boxing (3 minute rounds) 800m/1500m
3+ minutes	*Aerobic system*	Low-impact aerobics and Marathon

Table 6 *Energy system thresholds*

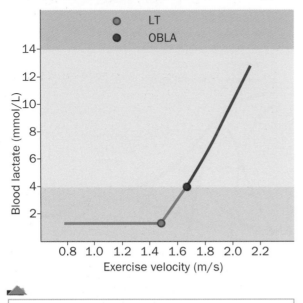

Fig 16.8 *The link between lactate threshold and OBLA*

Oxygen availability

- As long as there is a sufficient supply of oxygen the aerobic system can provide the energy to resynthesise ATP.
- If oxygen supply falls below that demanded for the exercise then the aerobic system threshold is met and the LA system will begin to breakdown glucose anaerobically to resynthesise ATP.
- Oxygen supply also affects which food fuels can be broken down to resynthesise ATP.
- High-intensity, short-duration activity will break down glycogen as the energy fuel.
- Low-intensity, long-duration aerobic activity will break down FFAs and glycogen as energy fuel.

Fuel availability

Fuel	Availability
PC	• With sufficient stores of PC, the body can use the ATP/PC system for very high-intensity, short-duration activity/movements. • PC stores are limited but are available at the start and after recovery during exercise. • If exercise intensity starts too high then PC stores will quickly deplete and continued high-intensity explosive activity cannot be sustained.
Glycogen	• This is the major fuel for the first 20 minutes of exercise, initially because oxygen supplies are limited as it takes 2–3 minutes for the CV systems to supply sufficient oxygen. • Glycogen is readily available in the muscles, requires less oxygen and therefore is quicker/easier to break down than FFAs to allow a higher aerobic intensity of activity.
Fats	• After about 20–45 minutes there is greater breakdown of fats alongside glycogen. • Although FFAs are a more efficient fuel than glycogen, they require about 15 per cent more oxygen to break them down and will result in the athlete having to work at lower intensities. • The greater the liver/muscle glycogen stores, the longer the performer can work aerobically at a higher intensity. • When glycogen stores become almost fully depleted, after about two hours, FFAs have to be used for aerobic energy production. • Unless exercise intensity is reduced it can bring on the sudden onset of fatigue.
Glycogen	• Once OBLA is reached, the body has insufficient oxygen available to burn FFAs. • It therefore has to break down glycogen 'anaerobically' to continue resynthesising ATP.

Table 7 *Fuel availability*

Enzyme activation level

- Enzymes are catalysts that activate the reactions that help break down PC, glycogen/ glucose and FFAs to provide the energy to resynthesise ATP. (Table 8)
- Without enzymes, there would be no reactions and therefore no energy for ATP resynthesis.

Fitness level

- The more aerobically fit the performer, the more efficient their respiratory and cardiovascular systems are to take in, transport and use oxygen to break down glycogen and FFAs aerobically to resynthesise ATP.
- Aerobic athletes have also shown that they can start to use FFAs earlier during sub-maximal exercise and therefore conserve glycogen stores.
- The net effect is that the aerobic threshold in terms of intensity and duration can be increased as the lactate threshold/OBLA would be delayed.
- A typical untrained athlete would reach OBLA at approximately 50–56 per cent of their VO_2 **max**.

> **KEY TERM**
>
> VO_2 **max** – Maximum oxygen consumption attainable during maximal work.

- An aerobic-trained athlete wouldn't reach OBLA until about 85–90 per cent of their VO_2 max.
- In the same way, an anaerobic-trained athlete will increase their ATP/PC, glycogen stores, anaerobic enzymes and tolerance to lactic acid which would increase the threshold of both the ATP/PC and LA systems.

RECOVERY PROCESS

The recovery process is concerned with the events occurring in the body primarily after a performer has completed exercise in order to speed up their recovery in time for their next performance. This could be the same or next day, or even during exercise, to allow the performer to maintain performance, for example repeated sprints during a team game.

The main aim of the recovery process is to restore the body to its pre-exercise state; in other words, to return it to how it was before a performer started exercise.

- After exercise, respiration and heart rate remain elevated during recovery.
- This is the key process of recovery known as the 'excess post-oxygen consumption' (EPOC); formerly termed the oxygen debt.

> **KEY TERM**
>
> **Excess post-exercise oxygen consumption (EPOC)** – The amount of oxygen consumption, above that at a resting level, during recovery, required to restore the body to its pre-exercise state.

Figure 16.9 shows that EPOC is thought to consist of two stages: an initial rapid recovery stage termed 'alactacid' debt and a slower recovery stage termed 'lactacid' debt.

> **KEY TERM**
>
> **Alactacid** – The 'a' before lactacid signifies it is without lactic acid.

Activating factor	Releases controlling enzyme/s	Activating energy system
Increase in ADP and Decrease in ATP	Creatine Kinase	PC
Decrease in PC	PFK	LA system
Increase in adrenalin Decrease in insulin	PFK	Aerobic system

Table 8 Factors affecting enzyme activation for the energy systems

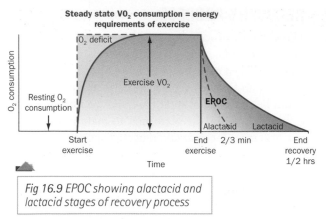

Fig 16.9 EPOC showing alactacid and lactacid stages of recovery process

> **Need to know more?** For more information on the recovery process see Chapter 16, pages 382–388, in the OCR A2 PE Student Book

Alactacid debt (rapid recovery stage)

- Termed the 'restoration of phosphogen stores' as the elevated respiration primarily helps resynthesise the muscles' store of ATP and PC.
- Replenishes the muscle stores of **myoglobin** and haemoglobin with O_2.
- Requires approximately three to four litres of oxygen and takes about three minutes to fully restore ATP/PC stores.
- Approximately 50 per cent are restored within about 30 seconds and about 75 per cent in 60 seconds.

KEY TERM

Myoglobin – Red pigment in muscles that stores oxygen before passing it on to mitochondria for aerobic respiration.

Lactacid debt (slow recovery stage)

The lactacid stage is a slower process primarily responsible for the removal/re-conversion of lactic acid/lactate which is converted into either:

- pyruvic acid, to enter the Kreb's cycle and to be used as a metabolic fuel
- glycogen, glucose or protein.

It is also thought that a significant percentage of EPOC is to support the elevated metabolic functions taking place after exercise, namely:

- high body temperatures remain for several hours after vigorous exercise
- hormones, such as adrenalin, remain in the blood stimulating metabolism
- cardiac output remains high helping to reduce temperature.
- The lactacid stage requires approximately five to eight litres of oxygen and takes between one and 24 hours after exercise, depending upon the exercise intensity and the levels of lactic acid to be removed.

CO$_2$ removal

- An elevated respiration and heart rate helps aids the removal of increased levels of CO_2.
- CO_2 is carried by a combination of:
  - blood plasma, within red blood cells as **carbonic acid** (H_2CO_3)
  - haemogloblin, as $HbCO_2$, to the lungs where it is expired
  - plasma.

KEY TERM

Carbonic acid – ($HbCO_3$) Carbon dioxide (CO_2) combined with water (H_2O).

Glycogen replenishment

- The body's store of muscle and liver glycogen can quickly deplete, and is a major factor in muscle fatigue (Fig. 16.10).
- A large percentage of glycogen can be replaced up to 10 and 12 hours after exercise, but complete recovery can take up to two days.
- Glycogen restoration can be almost completely recovered if a high carbohydrate diet is consumed within the first two hours of recovery.

Implications of the recovery process for planning physical activity sessions/interval training

An understanding of the recovery process provides some guidelines for planning training sessions in respect of optimising both the work intensity and recovery intervals. This is commonly referred to as the work–relief ratio, using a training method termed **interval training**.

Work–relief ratio (same intensity/speed)	Total running distance (m)	Average O_2 uptake (L/min)	Blood lactate level (mg 100 ml blood)
4 minute continuous to exhaustion	1422	5.6	150.0
10 seconds work and 5 seconds relief (20 minutes work in 30-minute session)	7294	5.1	44.0
15 seconds work and 30 seconds relief (10 minutes work in a 30-minute session)	3642	3.6	13.66

Table 9 Total exercise, average O_2 uptake and blood lactate levels during continuous and work–relief training (Source: adapted from Exercise Physiology, D. McArdle, page 139)

Aim of training	
Improving speed using ATP/PC system	The work ratio may be less than 10 seconds and the relief ratio is typically longer (1:3 ratio), to allow time for the ATP and PC stores to fully recover (2–3 minutes).
Improving body's tolerance to lactate to improve speed endurance	Keep the work ratio less than 10 seconds but decrease the duration of the relief ratio (e.g. 1:2 ratio – 30 seconds relief only allows 50% ATP/PC restoration). Alternatively/in addition, increase the duration of the work ratio which both increases lactate production and overloads the lactic acid system.
Improving VO_2 max using the aerobic system	The work interval ratio is normally longer in duration and intensity, just below the anaerobic threshold. The relief ratio is typically shorter (1:1 ratio), which helps reduce the OBLA and delay muscle fatigue and therefore prolong the aerobic system adaptations.

Table 10 Use of work–relief intervals for specific energy system training

Fig 16.10 Muscle glycogen depletion and restoration

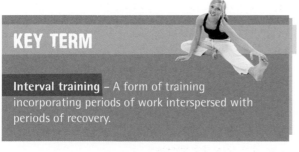

KEY TERM

Interval training – A form of training incorporating periods of work interspersed with periods of recovery.

- Performers training at the same intensity, using work–relief ratios, can train for a longer distance, at a lower average VO_2 max and with a lower blood lactate level compared with continuous work which causes exhaustion after only four to five minutes work (Table 9, row 1).
- Work–relief interval training is more efficient as it increases the quality/intensity of training and consequently improves energy system adaptations.

By altering work-relief intervals the training can target specific energy systems, as Table 10 shows.

GENERAL RECOVERY TRAINING APPLICATIONS

- Complete a warm-up prior to training to increase respiration rate/O_2 supply to reduce the oxygen deficit.
- After anaerobic work, where lactic acid accumulates, perform an active recovery to elevate respiration to speed up lactic acid removal (Fig. 16.11).
- A moderate intensity seems optimal for the active recovery but this can vary, for example 35–45 per cent VO_2 max for cycling and 55–60 per cent VO_2 max for running.

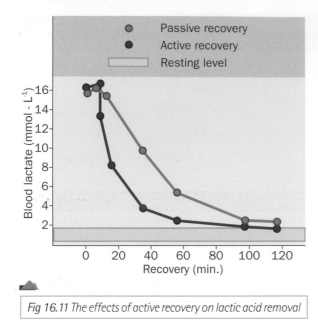

Legend:
○ Passive recovery
● Active recovery
□ Resting level

Y-axis: Blood lactate (mmol · L⁻¹)
X-axis: Recovery (min.)

Fig 16.11 The effects of active recovery on lactic acid removal

- After aerobic exercise, where little lactic acid is produced, a more passive recovery has been shown to speed up recovery more than an active recovery. In this case an active recovery actually elevates metabolism and delays recovery.
- Anaerobic speed/lactate tolerance training will help to increase ATP and PC muscle stores.
- Use all available opportunities, breaks, time-outs, etc., to allow the restoration of ATP, PC and myoglobin O_2 stores during training.
- Use tactics or pacing to control/alter intensity to meet the training objectives.
- Aerobic training will help improve oxygen supply during and after recovery from exercise.
- A mix of anaerobic and aerobic training will help delay the ATP/PC and lactic acid thresholds.
- Use heart rate as an indicator of exercise intensity, OBLA threshold and recovery state, as heart rate mirrors respiratory recovery.

Need to know more? For more information on energy see Chapter 16, pages 365–392, in the OCR A2 PE Student Book

CHECK

If you are satisfied with your knowledge and understanding, tick off the sections that you have revised so far. If you are not satisfied then revisit those sections and refer to the pages in the *Need to know more?* features.

- Define energy, work and power.
- Outline the role of ATP; the breakdown and re-synthesis of ATP; coupled reactions and exothermic and endothermic reactions.
- Identify the three energy systems: ATP/PC; alactic; the lactic acid and aerobic system.
- Describe the contribution of each energy system in relation to the duration/intensity of exercise.
- Indentify the predominant energy system used related to type of exercise.
- Outline the inter-changing between thresholds during an activity, for example the onset of blood lactate accumulation (OBLA), and the effect of level of fitness, availability of oxygen and food fuels, and enzyme control on energy system used.
- Explain how the body returns to its pre-exercise state: the oxygen debt/excess post-exercise oxygen consumption (EPOC); the alactacid and lactacid debt components; replenishment of myoglobin stores and fuel stores and the removal of carbon dioxide.
- Consider the implications of the recovery process for planning physical activity sessions.

TRUE OR FALSE?

1. Power is the rate at which we can work/or work (F x D) divided by time and measured in Joules.

2. ATP, PC and glucose are all usable sources of energy that the body/muscles can directly utilise for work.

3. Cristae are internal membrane/ compartments/fold-like structures within mitochondria, where stage 3, the electron transfer chain takes place.

4. Glycogen is broken down by the enzyme PFK into glucose.

5. OBLA is an abbreviation for the 'Onset of blood lactic acid'

6. The energy continuum shows how the energy systems interact to provide energy for the resynthesis of ATP.

7. 4 mmol/L is an arbitrary standard value for when OBLA is reached and in essence represents a point where the production of lactate exceeds the speed of its removal.

8. EPOC is the amount of oxygen consumption, above that at a resting level, during recovery, required to restore the body to its pre-exercise state.

9. The lactacid stage requires approximately five to eight litres of oxygen

10. The alactacid stage requires approximately three to four litres of oxygen and takes about eight to ten seconds to fully restore ATP/PC stores.

EXAM PRACTICE

1. What is meant by the term energy continuum? Identify a situation in a team game when the ATP/PC system would be predominant. Explain your answer. (5 marks)

2. Compare the relative efficiency of the aerobic system in providing energy to re-synthesise ATP with anaerobic routes. (5 marks)

3. Explain when and how lactic acid is fully removed from the muscles. (5 marks)

See page 298 for answers

CHAPTER 17
Applications of the principles of training

CHAPTER OVERVIEW

By the end of this chapter you should have knowledge and understanding of:
- how to apply the principles of training: moderation, reversibility, specificity, variance, overload and progression
- how to apply knowledge of the principles of training to periodisation
- how to define periodisation and macro, meso and micro cycles
- how to plan a personal health and fitness programme that will promote sustained involvement in a balanced, active and healthy lifestyle; the plan should include the principles of training.

Introduction to principles of training

Effective training follows several basic guidelines that should be applied to all forms of training – these are known as the 'principles of training'. You need understanding of these principles before studying the health components of fitness (in Chapter 18), so that you can apply these principles when planning health and fitness programmes.

EXAM TIP

The principles of training are easier to recall if you can visualise 'Mrs Vopp' who is 'Testing' the 'WC' (toilet):
- 'Mrs' = moderation, reversibility, specificity
- 'Vopp' = variation, overload, progression and periodisation
- 'Testing' = an appropriate test
- 'WC' (toilet) = warm up and cool down.

APPLICATION OF THE PRINCIPLES OF TRAINING

Moderation

- If too much training or exercise (**overload**) is undertaken too quickly, the likely result will be a mixture of overuse injuries to joints

and musculo-skeletal tissues, and physical/mental fatigue (burn out).
- If too little overload (exercise) is undertaken, few training adaptations will be achieved at all.

KEY TERM

Overload – When the body is made to work harder than it normally does, in order to cause adaptation.

Atrophy – Decrease in the size of muscle cells.

Reversibility

- Adaptations to training are reversed if the training is reduced or stops.
- Muscle cell **atrophy** takes place after approximately 48 hours of inactivity.
- The fitness/adaptations gained will be reversed in a third of the time it took to gain them.
- Fast fitness gains/adaptations are quicker to reverse than those gained over a long period.
- Aerobic adaptations reverse quicker than anaerobic adaptations.

Specificity

Specific training elicits specific adaptations critical for a specific sport/activity, and so the choice of training must reflect the demands of the sport/activity.

Specificity can be applied in two ways:

1 *The individual* – each performer has a different rate of adaptation in response to different types of training, primarily due to genetic variations.

2 *The sport/activity* – the predominant energy system/s, the major fitness components, movement patterns, muscle fibre type and muscles/joints used for that particular sport/activity.

Specificity in practice

- Long distance cyclists will undertake predominantly aerobic training on a bike and concentrate on their leg muscles.
- A 50-metre swimmer will undertake predominantly anaerobic training in the pool and concentrate on whole body exercises.

Fig 17.1 Two variations of adaptation/training zone diagrams

Variance

- Varied training ensures the experience is always fresh/motivating.
- Repeated training can lead to boredom and a lack of interest or motivation to continue.
- Variety also helps prevent repetitive strain/ overuse injuries, such as osteoarthritis, stress fractures and shin splints.

Overload

Overload is where the body is working harder than its normal capacity and therefore adapting to the training/work. The point at which adaptations occur in training is termed the **training or adaptation zone** (see Fig 17.1).

KEY TERM

Training/adaptation zone – An area of intensity where adaptations occur in response to training/ overload, i.e. when training occurs in moderation and is neither too high or low an intensity.

Overload is achieved by adjusting/increasing FITT:

- Frequency – how often you train, for example weekly (micro-, meso- and macro-cycles).

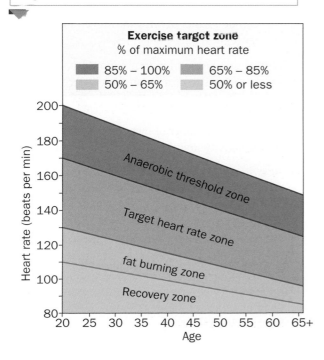

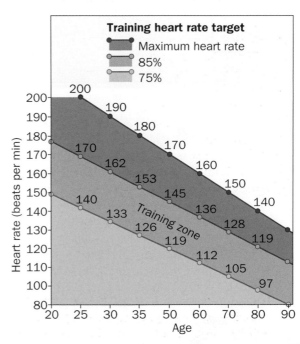

- Intensity – how hard you train, for example faster, heavier, less recovery, etc.
- Time – (duration) how long you train for, for example a 30-minute or 60-minute session.
- Type – aerobic or anaerobic training.

Progression

- As the body adapts to the training overload, its fitness capacity will increase to this level of overload.
- To ensure the body's fitness capacity increases further, the overload (training) needs to be gradually increased to keep the body adapting.
- This is termed progressive overload.
- Fig 17.2 shows that the fitness adaptations are greater earlier in training and slow down as training increases.

Fig 17.2 Progressive overload

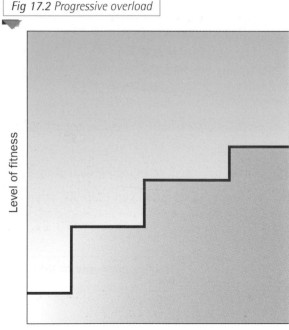

PERIODISATION

- Periodisation is the organised division of training into a number of specific blocks, periods or phases.
- It has the objective of ensuring athletes progressively develop to reach a skill/physiological peak at the correct time for an ultimate sporting target, for example the Olympic Games.
- In its simplest form, periodisation divides the training year into three phases: pre-season, competition season and transition (off)-season (see Fig 17.3), with each phase having its own specific aims.

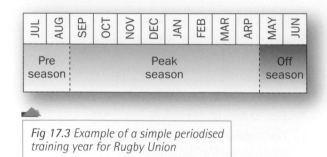

Fig 17.3 Example of a simple periodised training year for Rugby Union

As training has developed, periodisation has become much more complex, but in simple terms you need to apply three basic structures when planning a training programme: macro-cycles, meso-cycles and micro-cycles.

Macro-cycle

- This is a longer-term plan of training aimed at achieving a long-term goal/objective.
- It typically consists of a single-year block of training.
- A mega-cycle is a macro-cycle which may last several years.
- Macro-cycles are made up of a number of meso-cycles.

Meso-cycle

- This is a medium-term plan/goal of training, typically lasting between four and 16 weeks (one to four months).
- Fig 17.4 b) and c) shows how the three pre-season, competition and off-season meso-cycles (b) can be further divided into seven meso-cycles (c).

A typical one-season (winter/summer) training year, characteristic of a team/game activity, is shown in Fig 17.4.

The length and number of meso-cycles is dependent upon the activity and the individual. For example:

- a swimmer or track athlete may have a two-season sport (two competition events in a season)
- a one-season sport like football has a seven to eight month competition season
- there are also all-season sports like road running.

Need to know more? For more information on pre-competition/off-season periodisation, see Chapter 17, pages 399–400, in the OCR A2 PE Student Book

Fig 17.4 The divisions within periodisation: (a) macro-cycle; (b) simple meso-cycle; (c/d) typical meso-cycles; (e) micro-cycles and units (four including game)

a)

Macro-cycle

b)

Pre-season Meso-cycle 1	*Competition* Meso-cycle 2	*Off season* Meso-cycle 3

c)

M1.1	M1.2	M1.3	M2.1	M2.2	M3.1	M3.2

d)

2 weeks	4 weeks	1 week	27 weeks	5 weeks	4 weeks	9 weeks

e)

Monday	*Tuesday*	*Wednesday*	*Thursday*	*Friday*	*Saturday*	*Sunday*
Skill training	Rest	High-intensity training	Rest	Low-intensity aerobic run	Game	Rest

Key: M1 = Meso-cycle 1

Micro-cycle

- This is a short-term plan/goal of training, typically lasting one week (although a micro-cycle can last up to three weeks).
- A micro-cycle is simply a number of training sessions which form a recurrent unit (Fig. 17.4(e)).

The term 'unit' is also used in periodisation and can refer to each individual training session or different parts of an individual session, for example:

- an athlete training three times a week would have a micro-cycle consisting of three units
- one session of training with two aims – flexibility and strength training – may require a session made up of two units.

Benefits of periodisation

Aside from the main aim of ensuring an athlete reaches a peak performance at the correct time for their sporting target, periodisation ensures that many of the principles of training are applied when planning a training programme, as Table 1 shows.

KEY TERM

Unit – A short period/session of training with a specific aim.

TESTING

Testing enables the athlete/coach to monitor whether the training load is correct:

- at the start of training, to ensure the overload is not too high/low
- during training, to assess when it may need increasing to ensure further adaptations or even decreasing to prevent burn out.

The physical fitness tests you are required to describe and apply when planning a health or fitness training programme are shown in Fig 17.5. They demonstrate the need to match an athlete's capacities (test results) with that of the requirements demanded of their activity before any training programme is planned.

Principle of training	Application/benefits via periodisation
Moderation/ reversibility	• Helps prevent overtraining by ensuring adequate recovery but at the same time not allowing time for fitness/skills to decrease.
Specificity	• Each block is designed to prepare a specific performance component, for example sprint-start training can be focused on the needs of the individual performer/ sport-specific.
Variance	• Training is split into smaller units to maintain motivation, avoid boredom and overtraining, and allow recovery.
Overload	• Enables the performer to manipulate training intensity, volume, frequency, and rest.
Progression/testing	Monitoring/testing helps guide the performer when the training overload may require: • stepping up to increase adaptations • decreasing to spot/prevent overtraining and burn out • the tapering down of training intensity and an increase in recovery time.
Warm up/cool down	• Each unit of training should incorporate a warm up and cool down.
Flexible	• Focuses training and the setting of short-term, long-term and time-phased goals. • A double periodisation model allows the performer to peak twice for a number of competitions, for example the qualifying round and the actual championship (this approach is not recommended for endurance sports). • An undulating periodisation model allows the long-season team to perform to best maintain fitness and prevent too much overload/burn out.

Table 1 Benefits of periodisation

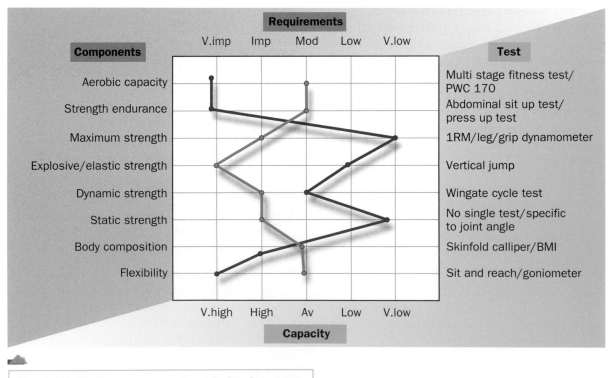

Fig 17.5 Health fitness component matched to fitness tests

WARM UP

- A warm up should precede any activity or training to help prepare the body physically and mentally for the exercise to follow.
- It is unwise to jump into physical activity too quickly (principle of moderation).

A warm up should consist of three phases:

1. *Pulse-raising activities*: aerobic sub-maximal exercise to increase muscle temperature/elasticity and cardiac output (Q), heart rate (HR) and minute ventilation (VE), in order to redistribute blood from organs to muscles (vascular shunt).
2. *Mobility*: controlled joint movements should rehearse activity movement patterns to help mobilise and lubricate joint structures.
3. *Stretching*: active muscles used in the training exercise should be stretched.

> **Need to know more?** For more information on the benefits of a warm up on skeletal muscle tissue and the cardiovascular system see Chapter 17, pages 403-404, in the OCR A2 PE Student Book

The benefits of a warm up include:

- It prepares the cardio-respiratory and musculo-skeletal systems for more intense exercise.
- It increases:
  - muscle temperature thereby increasing oxygen dissociation, nerve impulse conduction and contraction, thereby improving muscle force, speed and reactions
  - enzyme activity required for cellular respiration
  - release of synovial fluid, lubricating joint structures
  - elasticity of muscle/connective tissues
  - redistribution of blood flow (Q) from organs to muscles (vascular shunt).
- It reduces:
  - the risk of injury
  - early onset of anaerobic work, build up of lactic acid and early fatigue.

COOL DOWN

An active cool down should follow any activity/training to help speed up the recovery process to a pre-exercise state. A cool down should consist of two phases:

1. *Pulse lowering activities*: moderate/low-intensity aerobic activity
2. Stretching of active muscles.

> **Need to know more?** For more information on cool down see Chapter 17, page 404, in the OCR A2 PE Student Book

The benefits of a cool down include:

- It maintains venous return (VR), stoke volume (SV), cardiac output (Q), minute ventilation (VE) and blood pressure.
- It gradually reduces muscle temperature.
- Stretching returns muscles to their pre-exercise length.
- It reduces the risk of injury and DOMS.
- It flushes capillaries with oxygenated blood.
- It speeds up removal of lactic acid.
- It prevents blood pooling.

CHECK

If you are satisfied with your knowledge and understanding, tick off the sections that you have revised so far. If you are not satisfied then revisit those sections and refer to the pages in the *Need to know more?* features.

- ☐ Apply the principles of training: moderation, reversibility, specificity, variance, overload and progression.
- ☐ Apply knowledge of the principles of training to periodisation.
- ☐ Define periodisation and macro, meso and micro cycles.
- ☐ Plan a personal health and fitness programme that will promote sustained involvement in a balanced, active and healthy lifestyle; the plan should include the principles of training.

TRUE OR FALSE?

1. Overload is where the body is working harder than its normal capacity and therefore adapting to the training/work.
2. 'Fitness – if you don't use it you lose it' best describes the principle of reversibility.
3. Muscle cell atrophy takes place after approximately 24 hours of inactivity.
4. To ensure progressive overload, training needs to be gradually increased to keep the body adapting.
5. A micro-cycle is a longer-term plan of training aimed at achieving a long-term goal/objective.
6. A macro-cycle is a short-term plan of training, lasting one to three weeks.
7. A meso-cycle is a medium-term plan of training, lasting between four and 16 weeks (one to four months).
8. Periodisation is a short period/session of training with a specific aim.
9. Athletes need to match their capacities (test results) with that of the requirements demanded of their activity before any training programme is planned.
10. A warm up should be performed before any activity and consist of pulse lowering activities and stretching of the active muscles.

See page 282 for answers.

EXAM PRACTICE

1. Periodisation is a training principle that splits training into specific blocks. What are the benefits of using periodisation when designing a training programme? (*5 marks*)

2. Explain how a performer might use periodisation to structure their training programme for one year. (*6 marks*)

See page 300 for answers

CHAPTER 18.1

Health components of physical fitness: Aerobic capacity

CHAPTER OVERVIEW

By the end of this chapter you should have knowledge and understanding of:

- how to define aerobic capacity and explain how a performer's VO₂ max is affected by individual physiological make-up, training, age and sex
- how to describe and apply methods of evaluating aerobic capacity; how to assess your own VO₂ max, comparing your result to the aerobic demands of your chosen activities
- the different types of training used to develop aerobic capacity
- the use of target heart rates as an intensity guide
- the energy system and the food/chemical fuels used during aerobic work
- the physiological adaptations that take place after prolonged periods of aerobic physical activity
- how to plan a programme of aerobic training based on your own assessment of your aerobic capacity and the requirements of your activity.

AEROBIC CAPACITY

Aerobic capacity is the ability to take in, transport and use oxygen to sustain prolonged periods of aerobic/sub-maximal work.

VO₂ MAX

VO₂ max is the highest rate of oxygen consumption attainable during maximal/exhaustive work. An ability to work at a high percentage of VO₂ max (below anaerobic threshold) is thought to be a good indicator of aerobic endurance.

Although a high VO₂ max is typical of aerobic athletes, the ability to work at a high percentage of VO₂ max, hence a higher anaerobic threshold/OBLA, is a better indicator of aerobic performance than is VO₂ max itself.

Sedentary individuals' anaerobic threshold is typically about 50/60 per cent of VO₂ max, whereas elite aerobic athletes may work above 85 per cent of VO₂ max.

A sedentary performer may only be able to use three to four litres of oxygen per minute (L/min) compared with an elite distance runner who can use up to six or seven L/min.

Activity/sport	Male VO₂ max average (ml/kg/min)	Female VO₂ max average (ml/kg/min)
Non-athlete	45–54	36–44
Track athletes	60–85	50–75
Swimming	50–70	40–60
Football	42–64	–
Rugby	55–60	–
Volleyball	50–60	40–56
Cycling	62–74	47–57
Rowing	60–72	58–65
Cross-country skiing	65–94	60–75
Gymnastics	52–58	36–50

Table 1 Typical values for VO₂ max across a variety of activities

Four body systems

Aerobic capacity is dependent upon the efficiency of four body systems:

- respiratory system to consume O_2
- heart to transport O_2
- vascular system to transport O_2
- muscle cells to use O_2.

Heredity

- Heredity/genetics can account for as much as half the variation in VO₂ max, e.g. whether an athlete has a higher percentage of Type I and Type IIa (FOG) oxidative fibres.
- An athlete's individual response to training varies because of genetic variation.
- Heredity only indicates an individual's *potential* to have a high VO₂ max – this is dependent on aerobic training.

Specificity of training

- A specific programme of aerobic training will increase VO₂ max due to the long-term adaptations to aerobic training.
- Links directly to an athlete's individual response to training (see Fig 18.1.1).
- The more specific the aerobic training to the sport performed and the athlete's needs, the greater the potential improvement in that sport.

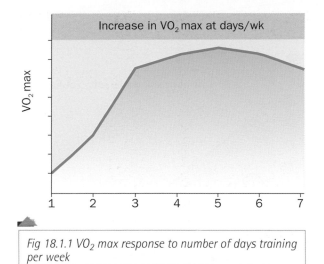

Fig 18.1.1 VO_2 max response to number of days training per week

Age

- VO_2 max decreases approximately one per cent per year due to a decrease in the efficiency of the body systems.
- The limitation in oxygen transport to the muscles and a decreased a-VO_2 diff are the main causes of a reduced VO_2 max.
- The age at which VO_2 max starts to decrease varies with the level of adaptation/training and the individual's response to training, but it is thought to have two main causes:
  - *Cardiovascular* - maximum heart rate (HR), cardiac output (Q), stoke volume (SV) and blood circulation to muscle tissues decreases due to a decreased left ventricular contractility/elasticity.
  - *Respiratory* - lung volumes, for example max VE (minute ventilation), decrease linearly after maturation, again due to a decrease in elasticity of lung tissues and thoracic cavity walls.
- Although VO_2 max decreases with age, this is partly due to decreased activity levels.
- Continued aerobic training with elderly performers will maintain/slow down any decline in VO_2 max.
- High-level aerobic training has an even greater slowing down effect on the rate of VO_2 max decline up to around 50 years of age, but still decreases after this point.

It is therefore important to sustain involvement in physical activity to prolong a balanced, active and healthy lifestyle late into adulthood.

Gender

- VO_2 max values for women are generally 20–25 per cent lower than those for men.
- Women are disadvantaged by having a greater percentage of body fat, since this decreases VO_2 max when measured per kilogram of body mass.
- A woman's lower VO_2 max is primarily due to their smaller body size:
  - a smaller lung volume decreases external respiration and oxygen intake
  - a smaller heart increases resting heart rates, lowering stoke volume (SV) and cardiac output (Q) at maximal rates of work
  - lower blood/haemoglobin levels decrease oxygen transport and blood flow.

KEY TERM

a-VO_2 diff – The difference between the percentage of oxygen (O_2) in the blood consumed and the percentage of oxygen exhaled. An increased a-VO_2 diff reflects a greater percentage of oxygen used and therefore a decrease in the percentage of oxygen exhaled, and vice versa.

▶ **Need to know more?** For more information on factors affecting VO2 max see Chapter 18.1, pages 409-412, in the OCR A2 PE Student Book

MEASUREMENT OF VO₂ MAX

The two tests you are required to know are both 'indirect' tests which estimate/predict a VO_2 max value based on their test results, in contrast to the more accurate direct tests.

PWC 170 Test

- This is a sub-maximal test on a cycle ergometer.
- The performer cycles at three progressive low-to-moderate work intensities (100–115 bpm, 115–130 bpm and 130–145 bpm) and their HR values are recorded.
- As HR increases linearly with work intensity, a line can be drawn through these two points on a graph, which can be extended to predict the intensity level that they would be working at when their HR reaches 170 bpm.
- This figure is chosen as an approximate anaerobic, close to maximal, level of work based on the assumption that VO_2 max is closely linked to maximal HR (see Fig 18.1.2).

Multi-Stage Fitness Test (MSFT)

- This is a progressive and maximal 20-metre shuttle run test.
- The 20-metre distance is timed by a bleep which progressively becomes shorter until the athlete cannot keep up or drops out.
- This provides a level and shuttle number score which is then compared with standardised tables to estimate/predict a VO_2 max value for males and females.

Measuring VO_2 max using gas analysis

- The most valid and accurate direct measurement of VO_2 max is made using expensive, highly complex gas analysis equipment.
- This measures and compares the amount of oxygen inspired and expired as work intensity is progressively increased, either on a raised treadmill or cycle ergometer, until a near exhaustion state is reached.

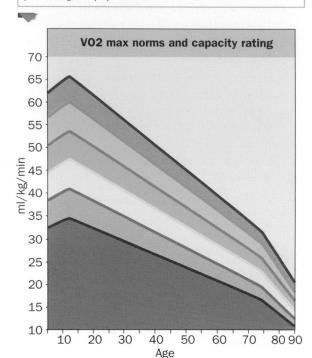

Fig 8.1.3 VO$_2$ max norms and capacity ratings as a percentage of population

CAPACITY RATING	PERCENTAGE OF POPULATION
EXCELLENT	3
VERY GOOD	8
GOOD	22
AVERAGE	34
FAIR	22
POOR	8
VERY POOR	3

- This is not practical unless you are an elite athlete who has access to such testing facilities, which are only found at national centres of excellence or sports universities.

AEROBIC TRAINING

- To enable you to plan a programme of training to develop aerobic capacity, you will be required to describe four types of training:
  - continuous running
  - repetition running
  - fartlek
  - interval training.

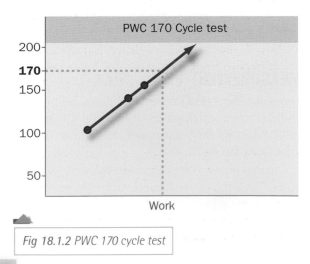

Fig 18.1.2 PWC 170 cycle test

- Irrespective of the type of training being used, and having established the importance of progressive overload and the need to monitor training adaptations, it is essential that you measure the intensity of training to ensure the performer is training within the 'training zone'.
- VO_2 max would be an accurate measure of training intensity, although it is not the most practical measure while training, and for this reason target heart rates are more often used as an intensity guide for training.
- HR needs to be within a percentage of maximum HR to cause any adaptations to occur. Furthermore, any given HR percentage can be equated to an approximate VO_2 max percentage.

A simple formula to calculate the appropriate HR percentage, often termed the critical threshold and based on Karvonen's Principle (220 minus age = max HR), is outlined below.

Critical Threshold = Resting HR + % (max HR – resting HR)

For example, for 60% HR for a 17-year-old with a resting HR of 72:

CT= 72 + (0.60 x 131) 79 = 151 (203 - 72 = 131) = (max HR – resting HR)

- The required HR percentage will vary depending upon the specific adaptations sought by the performer, with general health at the lower end and just below the anaerobic threshold at the top end of the critical threshold (training zone).
- The *American College of Sports Medicine (ACSM)* suggests a HR percentage above 55 per cent max for at least 20–30 minutes three times a week to encourage less fit, sedentary performers for general health benefits.
- Most guidelines suggest a HR percentage above 65 per cent max is required, although the higher the HR percentage the greater the aerobic adaptations will take place in response to training.

Table 2 shows approximate HR percentage training zones linked to varying training objectives.

Training zones (per cent)	Training objectives
60	Fat burning /re-energise glycogen stores
70	Develop oxygen transportation systems
80	Improve lactic acid threshold
85	Lactic threshold
90+	Speed

Table 2 Per cent max HR applied to training objectives

Aerobic training methods

Aerobic training involves whole-body activities like running, cycling, rowing and swimming, and is aimed at overloading the cardio-vascular/respiratory systems to increase aerobic capacity/VO_2 max.

Overload is achieved by applying the FITT principle specifically to aerobic capacity.

- F= Frequency, for example a minimum of 3–5 times a week for a minimum of 12 weeks.
- I = Intensity, measured using HR per cent within the critical threshold/training zone.
- T= Time/duration, for example a minimum of 3–5 minutes to 40+ minutes (elite).
- T= Type: overloading the aerobic energy systems.

Continuous training

- This involves steady state sub-maximal work (running, cycling, swimming, rowing) for prolonged periods (20–30 minutes plus).
- It is more suited to long distance/endurance athletes, when the oxygen demands of the training are met by the supply from the cardio-vascular systems.
- The HR should be above the critical threshold (minimum 55 per cent max), but as already highlighted this may increase depending upon the specific training objectives.

Fartlek training

- Fartlek (speed play) training is continuous steady state training interspersed with varied higher intensity work periods and slow recovery periods.
- It is a mixture of continuous and interval training that adds variation of higher intensity

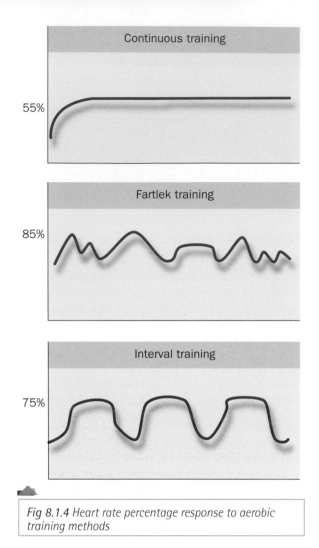

Fig 8.1.4 Heart rate percentage response to aerobic training methods

work, typically being a mixture of sprints, terrain (hills, sand or grass) or any exercises that intersperse the steady state work.

- The HR will remain above the critical threshold and within the training zone to ensure training adaptations occur and will overload both the aerobic and anaerobic energy systems.
- Fartlek training can be formally or informally organised specifically towards the activity, so it is ideal for games players whose matches are

never exactly the same intensity, to improve their VO_2 max and recovery process.

Interval training (repetition running)

- Interval training consists of periods of work interspersed with periods or recovery (relief).
- It can be easily modified for specific training needs by adjusting any of the four components that an interval session contains.

1 *Interval duration* – or distance (for example, three to four minutes or 1000 metres).
2 *Interval intensity* – HR per cent/hill work, etc.
3 *Recovery/relief duration* – increase or decrease in recovery time and whether it is active or passive.
4 *Number of work–relief intervals* – for example, 2 x 2000m and 800m recovery or 4 × 1000m and 400m recovery.

Interval training sessions are often described using a ratio to express the 'work–relief', for example a typical aerobic ratio of 2 : 1 would describe the work interval as being double the recovery; a ratio of 1 : 1 describes the work interval being the same as the relief.

- The work ratio for aerobic training is typically higher, and the relief lower, with a lower number of work–relief intervals.
- In contrast, for anaerobic interval training the work ratio is typically lower and the relief higher to allow a fuller recovery (1 : 3+), and therefore there is an increase in the number of work–relief intervals.

The main advantage of interval training is that it improves the quality/intensity of training by allowing the performer to recover so that each work interval is at a higher intensity than if they performed continuous training.

> **Need to know more?** For more information on aerobic training methods see Chapter 18.1, pages 414-417, in the OCR A2 PE Student Book

Interval training	Aerobic athlete	Anaerobic athlete
Interval duration	3–5+ minutes (longer)	0–90 seconds (shorter)
Interval intensity	Low/moderate = 50–75% VO_2/hr max	High/sprint = 70–95% VO_2/hr max
Interval relief	1 : 1 / 1:½ : – active jog/walk/run	1–90 seconds / 1 : 2 / + – 1 : 2
Ratio of work–relief	1 set of 3–5 repetitions	2–6 sets of 1–10 repetitions
Frequency	3–5 sessions weekly	3–6 sessions weekly
Specificity	Aerobic energy system	ATP/PC/LA energy system

Table 3 Summary of interval training guidelines for aerobic and anaerobic athletes

ENERGY SYSTEM AND FOOD FUELS DURING AEROBIC WORK

Although ATP and PC are the immediate fuels for any aerobic exercise, we will be looking specifically at those that provide energy to resynthesise ATP during aerobic work.

Irrespective of the type of aerobic training used, the energy to resynthesise ATP during aerobic work is supplied from the aerobic system. This will involve all three stages of the aerobic system, namely:

- aerobic glycolysis
- Kreb's cycle
- electron transport chain (ETC).

Aerobic work is fuelled from glycogen/glucose and free fatty acids (FFAs), but this varies depending upon the duration and intensity of the aerobic training and the availability of glycogen and FFAs. A summary of the fuels used during aerobic work is listed below.

- Glycogen/glucose is the major fuel for the first 20–40 minutes of exercise and during mild to more severe muscular effort.
- Greater breakdown of fats alongside glycogen as the energy fuel occurs after 20–45 minutes.
- As exercise duration increases, glycogen stores start to deplete and there is a greater mix of glycogen and fats to fuel aerobic work.
- FFA's provide more energy during prolonged, low-intensity activity, like fell walking.

- When glycogen stores become almost fully depleted (after about two hours) FFAs are used for aerobic energy production.
- If exercise intensity is too high then OBLA is reached and glycogen has to be broken down 'anaerobically' to continue resynthesising ATP.

> **Need to know more?** For more information on the aerobic energy system see Chapter 16, pages 372–376, in the OCR A2 PE Student Book

Aerobic adaptations

The specific adaptations to the four systems of the body in response to aerobic training are summarised in Table 4.

Note: it is the adaptation of the cardio-vascular/respiratory systems along with muscle/metabolism adaptations which collectively improve both the health benefits for an active lifestyle and improved aerobic performance.

EXAM TIP

It may be useful to review your AS anatomy and physiology notes to help refresh your knowledge and understanding of how these structures adapt in response to aerobic training.

Adaptations	Resultant increase/decrease	Net effect
RESPIRATORY SYSTEM		
Respiratory muscles become stronger	Increase in: • efficiency of mechanics of breathing • maximum exercise lung volumes (f x TV = VE) • maximal breathing rate • respiratory fatigue resistance • maximum VE due to increased f x TV. Decrease in: • sub-max breathing rate.	Increased VO_2 max
Increase in active alveoli surface area	Increase in: • external respiration/diffusion • a-VO_2 diff (less O_2 exhaled = more used).	

continued

Table 4 (Contd.)

Adaptations	Resultant increase/decrease	Net effect
CARDIO-VASCULAR SYSTEM: HEART		
Hypertrophy (increase in myocardium size/thickness/volume)	Increase in: • volume EDV (filling capacity) • ventricular stretch and recoil • force of ventricular contraction (emptying) • stroke volume (SV) • HR recovery after exercise. Decrease in: • ESV (volume after contraction) • Resting and sub-maximal HR (<60 = bradycardia).	• Increased blood flow • Increased maximal cardiac output (Q) • Increased O_2 transport
VASCULAR SYSTEM		
Increased elasticity of arterial walls to vasodilate/constrict	Increase in: • vascular shunt efficiency, to redistribute Q from organs to active muscles • BP regulation • exercise systole BP leading to improved blood/O_2 supply. Decrease in: • resting systole/diastole BP.	• Increased circulatory efficiency • Improved O_2/CO_2 transport
Increased number of red blood cells/haemoglobin volume Increased plasma volume	Increase in: • gaseous exchange/O_2 transport • venous return (VR) • stroke volume (SV) and cardiac output (Q). Decrease in: • viscosity during exercise, despite increased water loss (to sweat).	
Increased capillarisation (density) of alveoli and Type I muscle fibre tissues	Increase in: • surface area • a-VO_2 diff • speed for diffusion • removal of CO_2/lactic acid during OBLA. Decrease in: • distance of diffusion	

continued

Table 4 (Contd.)

Adaptations	Resultant increase/decrease	Net effect
MUSCULO-SKELETAL SYSTEM		
Increased Type I and IIa hypertrophy/ efficiency (due to increase in size/strength)	Increase in: • strength and reducing fatigue • skill efficiency. Decrease in: • energy costs.	Increased maximal capacity of muscle fibres to generate ATP aerobically
Increased muscle capillarisation	Increase in O_2/CO_2 transport/diffusion.	
Increased Type IIa fibre ability to work aerobically	Increase in: • fibre type percentage working aerobically • ability to use fuel and O_2. Decrease in: • OBLA.	
Increased myoglobin stores	Increase in O_2 storage and transport to mitochondria.	
Increased aerobic enzymes	Improved: • reliance on metabolism of fat instead of glycogen • aerobic metabolism of glycogen.	
Increased speed/ ability to use fats earlier	• Conserves glycogen stores • Increases amount of ATP from fats	
Increased number of mitochondria	Improved utilisation of O_2/fat for aerobic metabolism	
Increased muscle glycogen/fat stores	Increase in energy fuels to resynthesise ATP	
SKELETAL SYSTEM		
Increased strength of connective tissues	• Increased strength of muscle tendons • Greater thickness/strength of ligaments • Increased thickness/compression of cartilage • Increased calcium content/strength of bones	• Increased strength of musculo-skeletal lever system to endure prolonged activity • Less risk of injury • Reduced rate of ageing
HEALTHY LIFESTYLE		
Reduced body fat composition	Decrease in dead weight leading to an increase in efficiency (Power to weight ratio)	• Improved/healthier body composition • Increase in lean muscle mass • Decrease in fat mass
Energy expenditure	• Increase in calories/Kal • Increase in neutral/negative energy balance	

continued

Table 4 (Contd.)

Adaptations	Resultant increase/decrease	Net effect
HEALTH LIFESTYLE AREAS		
Combined effects	• Increase in the lactate threshold • Delay of OBLA	
Overall net effect: Increase in VO$_2$ max	Increase in: • intensity of aerobic performance • duration of aerobic performance • skill/work efficiency.	
Aerobic metabolism	Increase in: • muscles' ability to use fuels/O$_2$ • ability of body to mobilise/supply fuels and O$_2$ to working muscles. Dependent upon individual fitness at start, but 20–30% improvement possible with sedentary inactive.	• Increase in maximum rate of aerobic work/ endurance. • Decrease in lactate production.

Table 4 Summary of adaptations to aerobic training

▶ **Need to know more?** For more information on aerobic adaptations see Chapter 18.1, pages 418-421, in the OCR A2 PE Student Book

AEROBIC SUMMARY

- All athletes and non-athletes can benefit by improving their aerobic capacity.
- For sedentary individuals, cardio-vascular endurance should be the primary focus of training. By performing regular activity they may gain a marked improvement in endurance.
- A sedentary training programme should be energetic but realistic, permitting individuals to sustain activity for about 20–30 minutes to allow sufficient training effects.
- Even minimum training effects are seen if activity elevates heart rate to 130–140 bpm for 10 minutes on three days a week to achieve a training effect.
- In contrast, athletes will use the FITT principle to ensure their aerobic training lies higher within the training zone to increase the level of aerobic adaptations, so that their aerobic capacity matches the specific requirements of their activity.

▶ **Need to know more?** For more information on aerobic capacity see Chapter 18.1, pages 408-424, in the OCR A2 PE Student Book

CHECK

If you are satisfied with your knowledge and understanding, tick off the sections that you have revised so far. If you are not satisfied then revisit those sections and refer to the pages in the *Need to know more?* features.

☐ Define aerobic capacity and explain how a performer's VO$_2$ max is affected by individual physiological make-up, training, age and sex.

☐ Describe and apply methods of evaluating aerobic capacity; assess your own VO$_2$ max, comparing your result to the aerobic demands of your chosen activities.

☐ Identify the different types of training used to develop aerobic capacity.

☐ Outline the use of target heart rates as an intensity guide.

☐ Identify the energy system and the food/ chemical fuels used during aerobic work.

☐ Describe the physiological adaptations that take place after prolonged periods of aerobic physical activity.

☐ Plan a programme of aerobic training based on your own assessment of your aerobic capacity and the requirements of your activity.

TRUE OR FALSE?

1. Aerobic capacity is the ability to take in, transport and use oxygen to sustain prolonged periods of aerobic/sub-maximal work.

2. Sedentary individuals' anaerobic threshold is typically about 30/45 per cent of VO_2 max, whereas elite aerobic athletes may work above 60 per cent of VO_2 max.

3. A programme of training will increase VO_2 max due to the long-term adaptations to training.

4. The PWC 170 is a maximal test on a cycle ergometer where the performer cycles at three progressive low to maximal work intensities (100–115 bpm, 125–150 bpm and 160-170 bpm) and their HR values are recorded.

5. The American College of Sports Medicine (ACSM) suggests a HR percentage above 55 per cent max for at least 20–30 minutes three times a week to encourage less fit, sedentary performers for general health benefits.

6. Interval training consists of periods of work interspersed with periods or recovery (relief).

7. The work ratio for aerobic training is typically higher and lower for the relief, with a lower number of work–relief intervals.

8. Fartlek training involves steady state sub-maximal work (running, cycling, swimming, rowing) for prolonged periods (20–30 minutes plus).

9. Irrespective of the type of aerobic training used, the energy to resynthesise ATP during aerobic work is supplied from the aerobic system.

10. Glycogen/glucose is the major fuel for the first 20–40 minutes of exercise and during mild to more severe muscular effort. Greater breakdown of fats alongside glycogen as the energy fuel occurs after 20–45 minutes.

EXAM PRACTICE

1. The table below compares VO_2 max and OBLA values for two 18 year old students. One is a top club triathlete and the other a reasonable school team tennis player.

	VO_2 max (ml.min–1. kg–1)	OBLA (as a % of VO_2 max)
Club Triathlete	57	80%
School Tennis player	34	50%

With reference to the efficiency of the vascular system, explain why the triathlete is able to achieve these higher values. (*6 marks*)

2. A trained athlete can perform at a higher percentage of their VO_2 max before reaching OBLA than an untrained person. Describe how an athlete would make use of the principles of training when designing a training programme aimed at delaying OBLA. (*6 marks*)

3. Define interval training and identify the advantages of this type of training. Outline an interval training session that is specific to an aerobic performer. (*6 marks*)

See page 301 for answers.

CHAPTER 18.2
Health components of physical fitness: Strength

CHAPTER OVERVIEW

By the end of this chapter you should have knowledge and understanding of:

- how to define types of strength
- factors that affect strength
- how to describe and apply methods of evaluating each type of strength
- how to describe and evaluate different types of training used to develop strength – use of multi-gym, weights, plyometrics and circuit/interval training
- the energy system and the food/chemical fuels used during each type of strength training
- the physiological adaptations that take place after prolonged periods of physical activity
- how to plan a programme of strength training based on the assessment of a individual's strength and the strength requirements of a chosen activity.

TYPES OF STRENGTH

- Strength describes the application of a force against a resistance.
- The five different types of strength and the respective methods of evaluating them, which you are required to know, are outlined in Table 1.

KEY TERMS

1 RM – The maximal weight an individual can lift just once.

Strength endurance – The ability of a muscle to sustain or withstand repeated muscle contractions or a single static action.

Examples of the different types of strength

- **Static strength:** A gymnast on the rings holding a crucifix position (anaerobic static strength) or a pistol shooter holding their arm up (aerobic static strength). Thus a gymnast would need strength training that involved them holding their body weight out in the crucifix position.
- **Explosive strength:** The triple jump is an excellent example of a sequential series of high intensity movements that reflects explosive strength similar to those in most throwing, sprinting and jumping activities.
- **Dynamic:** Power is a key component of throwing, sprinting and jumping, which are used in all the major invasion/team games and racquet, aquatic and athletic events.
- **Endurance:** A canoeist would have specific **strength endurance** in their arms/upper body compared to their legs.

Strength type	Description	Method of evaluation/test
Maximum	Maximum force the neuromuscular system can exert in a single voluntary muscle contraction.	• 1 RM (1 repetition max) • Leg/Grip dynamometer
Static	Force exerted by the neuromuscular system while the muscle length remains constant/static. Termed an isometric muscle contraction, when a force is applied but there is no change in the muscle length.	• No single, or generic, test for static strength since strength varies and is specific to any given joint angle held.
Explosive / elastic	The ability to expand a maximal amount of energy in one or a series of strong, sudden high-intensity movements or apply a successive and equal force rapidly.	The vertical jump test or broad jump is the most widely used explosive (leg) strength test.
Dynamic	Ability of neuromuscular system to overcome a resistance with a high speed of contraction. More often referred to as 'anaerobic capacity' – the functional application of strength (force × distance) and speed (÷ by time) which represents 'power'.	• Wingate Cycle Test: performer pedals 'all out' for 30 seconds while seated on a cycle ergometer. Measures peak anaerobic power, rate of decline/fatigue and average power output during the whole test. • Comparable running tests such as RAST.
Endurance	Ability of a muscle to sustain or withstand repeated muscle contractions or a single static action.	• Localised tests for differing muscle groups/joints, evaluated by the number of repetitions performed at a percentage of your 1 RM, for example NCF abdominal sit-up test, push-up test (arm and shoulder).

Table 1 Five different types of strength and methods of evaluating them

Although five types of strength are covered in the specification, you can see that three types of strength are most widely applied to physical activity and a healthy lifestyle:

- elastic and **dynamic strength** represents anaerobic strength
- strength endurance represents aerobic strength.

Although maximum and static strength are important in specific activities/movements, **maximum strength** directly correlates with good elastic/dynamic strength, and similarly static strength is important for specific movements in activities like the rings in gymnastics.

KEY TERMS

Maximum strength – The maximum force the neuromuscular system can exert in a single voluntary muscle contraction.

Dynamic strength – The ability of the neuromuscular system to overcome a resistance with a high speed of contraction.

FACTORS AFFECTING STRENGTH

You will have already compared and started to question why there were differences in results across your group/peers when you completed the tests for the different types of strength. You will need to show that you understand the factors that affect strength, which are summarised below.

Muscle composition

The greater the:

- percentage of fast twitch muscle fibres
- cross-sectional area of muscle
- muscle size

the greater the potential force that can be generated or applied.

Gender

There is little gender difference in strength between males and females, except that female strength is generally lower than males because:

- females generally have less muscle mass, cross-sectional area and muscle size
- females have less testosterone than males.

Age

- Female peak strength is reached between the age of 16 and 25 years; for males it occurs around 18–30 years.
- Greatest gains are made between the age of 20 and 30 years for both males and females, when testosterone levels peak.
- Strength generally decreases with increasing age due to a decrease in testosterone leading to less muscle mass and a less efficient neuromuscular system.

Physical Inactivity

Atrophy (decrease in muscle size) starts after approximately 48 hours of inactivity and induces the loss of muscle strength already gained from training (reversibility).

Strength training

Appropriate/specific strength training increases strength/hypertrophy while preventing atrophy.

Joint angle

The weakest point in the range of motion specific to the relative angle of a given joint.

STRENGTH TRAINING TERMINOLOGY/ GUIDELINES (TABLE 2)

Strength training uses a specific terminology, primarily repetition, sets and resistance, which you will be expected to understand and apply when providing guidelines to improve strength.

- Repetitions are the number of times an exercise is repeated, for example ten repetitions.
- The specified number of repetitions along with a rest period then forms an individual set; for example a performer lifting a weight ten times equates to ten repetitions which once completed forms a single set.
- The weight lifted is termed the resistance. A strength training programme is normally expressed as sets multiplied by repetitions at a given resistance (normally in kilograms); for example, 3 x 10 x 50 kg equals three sets of ten repetitions of a 50 kg weight.
- You also need to understand and apply the term repetition max (RM); remember that 1 RM represents the maximum resistance you can lift just once.

- Resistance/load needs to be at least 50 per cent of the maximum capacity for a given muscle/group, while evidence suggests that loads in excess of 80 per cent increase the risk of muscle damage.
- Maximum strength training generally uses low repetitions and higher resistance, whereas endurance strength uses high repetitions and low resistance (see Fig 18.2.1).
- In relation to the development of power the resistance is moderate, thus allowing higher repetitions so that a higher speed of movement can be achieved (see Fig 18.2.2).
- Moderation: general strength conditioning needs to be established before focusing on specific muscle groups to prevent overtraining.
- Exercise large muscle groups before smaller muscle groups prevents the smaller muscles from being fatigued before they act as stabilisers to support larger muscle groups. For example the small wrist muscles stabilise the wrist when lifting a standing bicep curl bar.
- Use periodisation of training to prevent overtraining by varying the volume and intensity of training.
- Allow appropriate recovery between individual exercises and exercise sessions.
- Specificity: training with slow joint movements will increase strength only at slow speeds, whereas faster movements will increase strength at both fast and slow speeds.

TYPES OF STRENGTH TRAINING

The strength training methods you are required to describe and evaluate to develop strength are summarised in Table 3.

All these strength training methods achieve the same aim in that they all require the performer to apply a force against a resistance, which creates the overload to initiate the performance/health adaptations.

Need to know more? For more information on parameters and guidelines identified with interval training see Chapter 18.1, pages 416–417, in the OCR A2 PE Student Book

Fig 18.2.1 *A comparison of repetition/resistance guidelines for endurance and maximum strength*

Fig 18.2.2 *A comparison of repetition/resistance guidelines for maximum and dynamic (power) strength*

Strength endurance (high repetitions but low resistance)

Maximum strength (low repetitions with higher resistance)

Maximum strength (high resistance lower repetitions)

Power (dynamic strength) (**moderate**/high resistance and more repetitions, emphasis on increased **speed** of movement)

Circuit training	Aerobic athlete	Anaerobic athlete
Interval duration	3–5+ minutes/20 minutes (longer)	0–90 seconds (shorter)
Interval intensity	Low/moderate = 50–70%/<speed	High = 70–85%/>speed
Interval relief	Lower: 1 : 1 /jog/walk/jog	Higher: 90 seconds to 3 minutes/1 : 3+
Ratio of work–relief	3–4 circuits; more reps/stations	3–5 circuits of fewer reps/stations
Frequency	3–5 sessions weekly	3–7 sessions weekly (48 hours between sessions if same muscle group)
Specificity	Aerobic energy system	ATP/PC/LA energy system
Resistance training	**Aerobic athlete**	**Anaerobic athlete**
Duration (repetitions)	More reps – 10+ (20+ common)	Fewer reps – 1–10
Intensity (weight)	Low/moderate = 50–70% of 1 RM	High = 70–95% of 1 RM/>speed
Relief/recovery	Lower 1 : 2 (30–60 seconds)	Higher/full 1 : 3+ (2–5 minutes)
Number of work–relief (sets)	Fewer: 3–5 sets of 10+ reps	More: 3–6 sets of 1–10 reps
Frequency	3–5 per week	3–7 sessions weekly (48 hours between sessions if same muscle group)
Specificity	Aerobic system	ATP/PC/LA system (>speed of motion)

Table 2 *Summary of strength training guidelines for aerobic and anaerobic athletes*

Training	Description	Advantages	Disadvantages
Multi-gym	• Series of specialised exercise machines that incorporate a range of resistance exercises with adjustable weight stacks. • Each exercise machine, or station, targets specific groups of muscles. • Examples include a 'super set' and pyramid resistance training.	• Safe training method. • Good for general strength development. • Flexible as the repetitions, sets and resistance can be easily adjusted to suit the specific strength requirements.	• Not always specific to joint/ movement patterns as they occur in actual sporting activities.

continued

Free weights	• Non-mechanical free standing weights. • Each exercise machine or station targets specific groups of muscles. • They require a 'spotter' to assist during heavier resistance training. • Require the less active muscle groups to work isometrically (fixators) as stabilisers.	• Offer improved specificity for joint movement patterns. • Isometric muscle work improves balance and co-ordination specific to actual performance. • Flexible: repetitions, sets and resistance are easily adjusted to suit the specific strength requirements.	• Not as safe as a multi-gym. • Not recommended for the less experienced individual or general strength development for a healthy lifestyle.
Circuit / interval	• Series of exercises (stations) that form one complete circuit which can be repeated a set number of times. • The performer's body weight often acts as the resistance, but a circuit could be completed using a multi-gym. • Stations are normally ordered to alternate muscles/ groups to allow them time to recover.	• Adds flexibility, variation and specificity as the energy system and type of strength developed can be altered by adjusting the four parameters identified. • 'Relief' between stations and circuits can improve the quality/intensity of training by allowing the performer to recover so that each work interval is at a higher intensity.	• If the incorrect guidelines are applied (moderation and overload) to: • *interval intensity* - number of: circuits, stations, repetitions, • *interval duration* • *relief duration* • *number of work/ relief intervals* • the intended strength adaptations will not be gained (specificity).
Plyometrics	• Incorporates jumps, bounds and hop-type exercises. • Involves placing an eccentric stretch on a muscle to initiate the stretch reflex; this recruits increased motor units/muscle fibres, which preloads the elastic/contractile properties of muscle fibres to increase the force of contraction. • Most plyometric exercises are associated with the lower (leg) muscles, but they can also be applied to all skeletal muscles.	• Good for power: explosive, elastic and dynamic strength.	• Increased risk of injury. • Eccentric muscle contractions cause structural damage within muscle tissues leading to the delayed onset of muscular soreness (DOMS). • Good pre-strength is essential before undertaking plyometrics. • Not appropriate for novice sedentary individuals or general strength development. • Moderation, progressive overload and warm-up/ cool-down are also essential to help reduce the effect of injury and DOMS.

Table 3 Summary of strength training methods

THE ENERGY SYSTEM AND FOOD FUELS DURING AEROBIC WORK

A simple way to link energy systems to the different types of strength is to create a pyramid with the three most applicable types of strength and their respective energy systems and food/fuels at each corner (see Fig 18.23).

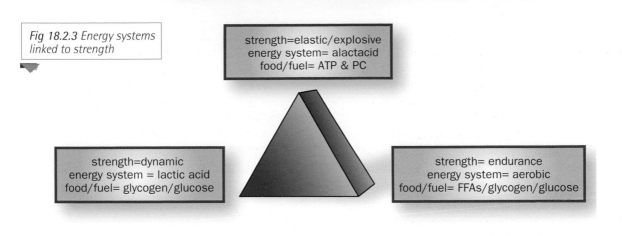

Fig 18.2.3 *Energy systems linked to strength*

strength=elastic/explosive
energy system= alactacid
food/fuel= ATP & PC

strength=dynamic
energy system = lactic acid
food/fuel= glycogen/glucose

strength= endurance
energy system= aerobic
food/fuel= FFAs/glycogen/glucose

- However, in a typical weight training/free weight session with longer relief periods, the total amount of work is small.
- Thus the work does not always raise the heart rate for sufficient time and within the training zone to enable the more aerobic benefits/adaptations to take place.
- This should not undermine the importance of effective general strength development in terms of good body posture/alignment.
- It also reinforces the use of a super set, which does not allow any relief and therefore better maintains heart rate within the training zone for longer than a simple set or pyramid system of weight training.

> **Need to know more?** For more information on energy systems and food fuels see Chapter 16, pages 365-392, in the OCR A2 PE Student Book

STRENGTH ADAPTATIONS

- The effects of strength training are largely confined to muscle adaptations.
- Strength training can produce between 25 and 100 per cent improvement in strength within three to six months, depending upon the starting level of strength.
- Early improvements in strength are reported without any increase in muscle hypertrophy, which can take two to three weeks to adapt.

Explaining early strength gains

Strength improvements are a result of both neural and physiological adaptations (see Fig 18.2.4).

- Short-term early strength gains are primarily due to neural adaptations.
- Long-term gains are largely due to hypertrophy (physiological) changes.

The neural and physiological adaptations leading to greater force production/strength are summarised in Table 4 overleaf.

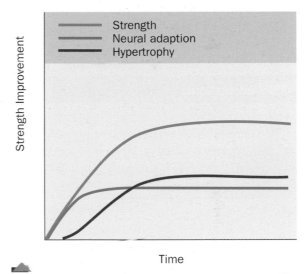

Fig 18.2.4 *Strength improvements as a result of neural and physiological adaptations*

> **EXAM TIP**
>
> You will be expected to explain both the neural and physiological adaptations that take place in response to prolonged periods of physical activity/training.

Cardiovascular adaptations

Cardiovascular adaptations associated with pure strength training need to be considered in relation to a healthy lifestyle. These are:

- hypertrophy of the heart
- increased blood pressure
- slight increase in capillary density
- decreased volume of the left ventricle.

Neural adaptations:	
• Increased recruitment of additional fast twitch muscle fibres • Increased recruitment of motor units • Improved co-ordination and simultaneous stimulation of motor units • Reduction in proprioreceptor/antagonist muscle inhibition allowing the antagonist to stretch further and the agonist to contract with more force	
Physiological adaptations:	
Skeletal muscle	• Hypertrophy – increase in muscle size (predominantly in fast twitch fibres) and/or hyperplasia – increase in muscle fibre number • Increased number/size of contractile protein (width of actin/myosin filaments) • Increased actin/myosin cross-bridges
Metabolic	• Increase in ATP, PC and glycogen stores • Increased buffering capacity/tolerance of fast twitch fibres to work with high levels of lactic acid • Increase efficiency to remove lactic acid • Increased glycolytic enzyme actions: glycogen phosphorylase and PFK • Net effect: increased anaerobic threshold/capacity and recovery of ATP/PC/LA system • Increased intensity/duration of performance and delaying of OBLA/fatigue
Other adaptations:	
• Increased strength of connective tissues – tendons, ligaments and bones (increased calcium production), which helps offset early symptoms of osteoporosis. • Social/psychological: an increased hypertrophic body is often seen as attractive and therefore desirable and may increase an individual's self-esteem and social standing in both sporting and lifestyle contexts.	

Table 4 Neural and physiological adaptations leading to greater force production/strength

The adaptations demonstrate the effects of pure strength training as undertaken by weightlifters and bodybuilders, who lift low repetitions but many sets of very heavy weights very slowly, involving a large percentage of isometric contractions.

- Powerful muscle contractions obstruct arteries passing through active muscles increasing blood pressure and making it harder for the heart to force stroke volume (SV) out.
- This causes the heart to hypertrophy. Heart walls become thicker and stronger and the ventricles can sometimes become smaller in volume to help pump blood against high arterial blood pressure during isometric contractions.
- Larger heart muscle fibres also increase the distance/speed for O_2/CO_2 diffusion, which may limit metabolic functioning and although inconclusive may increase the risk of coronary heart disease.
- Increasing muscle mass (hypertrophy) has to be carried and without any increase in mitochondria it may even decrease aerobic strength endurance.
- Undertaking both strength and endurance training together may hinder strength adaptations.
- The ventricular volume of heavy weight lifters can be similar/smaller than sedentary people, although the mass of the cardiac muscle is significantly greater.
- Isometric resistance training should be avoided by individuals with moderate to high blood pressure (hypertension).

Endurance strength adaptations

- Strength endurance training has little effect on muscle tissue adaptations, except for an increased muscle mitochondria and capillary density.
- In general, strength endurance training increases the metabolic rate by increasing aerobic capacity via the improved efficiency of the cardiovascular/respiratory systems.

STRENGTH TRAINING AND A HEALTHY LIFESTYLE - SOME CONCLUSIONS

- Most of the negative effects of strength training are felt in pure maximum strength training undertaken by weightlifters and bodybuilders who lift low repetitions but many sets of very heavy weights very slowly, involving a large percentage of isometric contractions.
- Power athletes who reduce the resistance to allow them to emphasise the speed of movement do not undergo this large isometric effect.
- Some evidence suggests that strength and endurance training together may hinder strength (power) development. This conflicts with the view that increased cardio-vascular adaptations will allow anaerobic athletes to increase their recovery and removal of the by-products of anaerobic respiration.
- Good strength has a major role to play in sustaining and improving participation in physical activity and maintaining a healthy lifestyle.
- The World Health Organisation (WHO) and the American College of Sports Medicine (ACSM) recommend strength training alongside cardiovascular training to help enhance and maintain muscular strength and bone health.
- The ACSM recommend 8 to 10 strength training exercises of 8 to 12 repetitions of each exercise twice a week.
- An increased muscle mass will increase energy expenditure, which may help achieve a more healthy body composition (reduced fat mass).
- With appropriate resistance, both children and the elderly alongside athletes can benefit from strength training

▶ **Need to know more?** For more information on energy see Chapter 18.2, pages 425-444, in the OCR A2 PE Student Book

CHECK

If you are satisfied with your knowledge and understanding, tick off the sections that you have revised so far. If you are not satisfied then revisit those sections and refer to the pages in the 'Need to know more?' features.

☐ Define types of strength.

☐ Describe the factors that affect strength.

☐ Describe and apply methods of evaluating each type of strength.

☐ Describe and evaluate different types of training used to develop strength – use of multi-gym, weights, plyometrics and circuit/interval training.

☐ Give details of the energy system and the food/chemical fuels used during each type of strength training.

☐ Explain the physiological adaptations that take place after prolonged periods of physical activity.

☐ Plan a programme of strength training based on the assessment of a individual's strength and the strength requirements of a chosen activity.

TRUE OR FALSE?

1. Strength describes the application of a force against a resistance.

2. Static strength is force exerted by the neuromuscular system while the muscle length shortens or lengthens.

3. The triple jump is an excellent example of a sequential series of high intensity movements that reflects explosive strength.

4. Female strength is generally lower than males because females generally have less muscle mass, cross-sectional area and muscle size than males.

5. Free weights are a safe training method but do not offer improved specificity for joint movement patterns.

6. A specified number of repetitions along with a rest period then forms an individual set.

7. Plyometric training involves placing an concentric stretch on a muscle to initiate the stretch reflex.

8. The World Health Organisation (WHO) and the American College of Sports Medicine (ACSM) recommend strength training alongside cardiovascular training to help enhance and maintain muscular strength and bone health.

9. An increased muscle mass will increase energy expenditure, which may help achieve a more healthy body composition (reduced fat mass).

10. Short-term early strength gains are largely due to hypertrophy (physiological) adaptations.

EXAM PRACTICE

1. Identify the type of strength most relevant to a 100 m sprinter. Design a weight training programme to improve this type of strength. *(5 marks)*

2. Sprint type athletes regularly perform strength training programmes to improve their elastic/dynamic strength. Explain the physiological muscular adaptations that will occur after undertaking a prolonged weight training programme to improve elastic/dynamic strength. *(6 marks)*

3. Explain how circuit training can be manipulated to benefit two contrasting types of strength. *(6 marks)*

See page 303 for answers.

CHAPTER 18.3
Health components of physical fitness: Flexibility

CHAPTER OVERVIEW

By the end of this chapter you should have knowledge and understanding of:

- how to define flexibility
- factors that affect flexibility
- how to describe and apply methods of evaluating flexibility
- different types of training used to develop flexibility
- the physiological adaptations that take place after prolonged periods of physical activity
- how to plan a programme of flexibility training based on self-assessment of flexibility
- and the flexibility requirements of your activity.

FLEXIBILITY

Flexibility is the range of motion around a joint (shoulder) or a series of joints (vertebrae).

- Flexibility is joint-specific; for example, someone flexible at the shoulder may have poor flexibility in the vertebrae.
- Flexibility is sport-specific; for example, a rugby player requires less **flexibility** but more strength and stability in the shoulder joint than a gymnast, who requires very good strength, stability and flexibility.
- Flexibility has two components: **static flexibility** and **dynamic flexibility**.

Although not ensuring it, static flexibility is a prerequisite to dynamic flexibility, for example good static adductor flexibility (Fig 18.3.1a) forms the basis for achieving good dynamic flexibility (Fig 18.3.1b).

In respect of the principle of specificity:

- Static flexibility is important to those performers who hold static balances, such as dancers and gymnasts during floor routines.
- Dynamic flexibility is important in high-velocity movement sports like sprinting,

KEY TERMS

Flexibility – The range of motion around a joint or a series of joints.

Static flexibility – The range of motion (RoM) around a joint without accounting for speed.

Dynamic flexibility – The range of motion (RoM) around a joint which occurs in the performance of a physical activity at either normal or rapid speed.

throwing and, again, gymnastics, for example football and netball players require good hip flexion/abduction but need to produce this RoM at high speeds when stretching to tackle or landing under control.

It is also important to differentiate between flexibility and stretching:

- flexibility is the range of movement (RoM)
- stretching is the training method used to increase flexibility.

Fig 18.3.1a Static flexibility. It is the maximum RoM a muscle or connective tissues will allow with an external force, for example holding the adductor stretch at the end of its RoM as shown here.

Fig 18.3.1b Dynamic flexibility. It is the range of motion which takes into account the speed of movement and reflects the joints' (muscle/connective tissues') resistance to movement, as shown by this the straddle jump.

THE IMPORTANCE OF FLEXIBILITY

- Flexibility is probably the most undervalued and neglected health fitness component.
- It is critical for sports participation or to promote a healthy lifestyle.
- If you don't stretch it is only a matter of time before some body tissue will break down leading to injury.
- Most trainers agree that flexibility training should form an integral part of training.

The benefits of flexibility training:

- reduced risk of injury (prevention)
- improved posture, alignment and ergonomics
- reduction of delayed onset of muscular soreness (DOMS)
- performance enhancement:
  - flexible muscles perform better than tight muscles
  - improves range of motion at joints
  - increased range of motion for applying force (power)
  - improved economy of movement (strength endurance/aerobic capacity)
  - improved motor performance/skills.

FACTORS AFFECTING FLEXIBILITY

The factors affecting flexibility are summarised in Table 1.

EXAM TIP

You are required to understand what factors may limit flexibility so that you can account for these when planning a flexibility training programme.

Need to know more? For more information on factors of and the importance of flexibility see Chapter 18.3, pages 446–448, in the OCR A2 PE Student Book

MEASURING FLEXIBILITY

- Since flexibility is joint-specific there is no one single test to measure flexibility. Instead specific tests for specific joints are used.
- The most widely known and used test is the sit and reach test, which is used primarily to measure flexibility of the hip and lower back.

Factor	How it affects flexibility
Type of joint	A ball and socket joint innately has a full RoM; a pivot joint only allows rotation; a hinge joint only allows flexion or extension
Joint shape	The arrangement, shape and alignment of the joints' articulating surfaces/bones dictate RoM, for example the shoulder joint has increased RoM having a shallow joint cavity compared with the hip's deeper cavity which limits RoM but increases stability
Length/elasticity of connective tissues	In and around muscles and joints: the tendons, ligaments, epi/peri/endo-mysium of muscle, fascia and joint capsule all limit RoM
Muscle length/ elasticity	The muscle spindles activation point before it initiates the stretch reflex (when a muscle is rapidly stretched) prevents further RoM
Gender	Generally females are more flexible than males
Age	Flexibility is greater in children and decreases as a person ages due to decrease in elasticity of muscle and connective tissues
Elasticity	The suppleness of skin and adipose tissue
Temperature	Elasticity of muscles and connective tissues is increased as temperature increases by 1–2 degrees Celsius, hence a warm-up should be performed
Muscle mass	Excess muscle mass around a joint restricts joint RoM
Nerves	Nerves pass through the joints; as joints are taken through a full RoM, nerves become stretched or compressed and trigger a stretch reflex within the muscles, increasing their resistance to stretch
Hypermobility	Inherited (double-jointed) or trained factors increasing RoM but can lead to joint instability and increase the risk of injury
Flexibility training	Stretching within a training programme may maintain/increase RoM

Table 1 Factors affecting flexibility

Goniometry

The most valid, accurate and recognised measure of flexibility is goniometry. This uses a double-armed goniometer (angle ruler) to measure the number of degrees from a neutral starting position to the position at the end of a full RoM at specific joints. Fig 18.3.2 shows an example of hip flexion.

> **Need to know more?** For more information on measuring flexibility see Chapter 18.3, pages 448-450, in the OCR A2 PE Student Book

Hip flexion

i. Start position   ii. Finish position

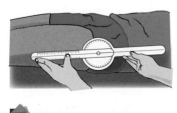

Fig 18.3.2 Measuring RoM at the hip using a goniometer

FLEXIBILITY TRAINING

- Flexibility training is widely incorporated as an integral part of preparation for physical activity.
- The primary role of flexibility training is injury prevention and improved performance.
- Irrespective of the type of stretching undertaken, the aim is to stretch the muscle/connective tissues around a joint just beyond the end point of resistance (RoM), or in some cases further through its extreme point of resistance to cause long-term adaptations in the length of these tissues.

Stretching

Flexibility is either maintained or improved by stretching. Types of stretching include:

- Maintenance stretching is stretching as part of a warm up and cool down. It helps to maintain an individual's current RoM and does not, as often thought, increase RoM.
- Developmental stretching involves whole or part training sessions (a minimum of 10–15 minutes) devoted solely to stretching. This helps to develop RoM.

FITT Principle

In order to stimulate sufficient overload for muscle/connective tissues to adapt and lengthen, the general guidelines use the FITT principle as outlined below:

- F= Frequency, for example two to four times a week depending upon the requirements of the individual's activity and initial flexibility level of the performer.
- I = Intensity, varying from a mild tension (no pain) stretch to a stretch through the extreme point of resistance, depending upon the method being used.
- T= Time/duration, for example hold each stretch for a minimum of 10 and maximum of 30+ seconds and repeat three to six times depending upon the number and type of stretching being performed and the flexibility level of the performer.
- T= Type: static, dynamic, ballistic or PNF stretching.

Specificity

It is essential that the performer identifies the requirements of their activities against their joints' RoM and considers:

- which joints require their RoM increasing, or possibly maintaining or decreasing
- the body position and velocity, or speed, at which these joint(s) are moved through
- the most appropriate type of stretching from those outlined below.

EXAM TIP

Table 2 summarises the four different types of stretching (training) that you need to apply when designing flexibility training programmes, along with recent guidelines regarding flexibility training. However, it is important to understand that there is no single right or wrong way to stretch and that all methods of stretching have some merits.

Type of flexibility training	Description	Considerations, advantages and disadvantages of method
Static (Fig. 18.3.3)	*Active:* Unassisted, the performer actively completes a voluntary static contraction of an agonist muscle to create the force to stretch the antagonist muscle *just beyond* its end point of resistance. The stretch is held still for 6–20 seconds, to increase the RoM at a joint. *Passive:* As above except stretches are assisted by an *external* force, for example gravity, apparatus or a partner, to help move the joint just beyond its end point of resistance in order to stretch the muscle/connective tissues.	• Thought to be the safest method and, despite being the slowest, the most effective form of stretching to increase the length of muscle/connective tissues. • Current research findings question these long-held views, primarily on the grounds that static stretching does not prepare the joints for the more dynamic and powerful RoM that are involved in the actual activity to be performed. • Current research suggests static stretching is most effective/appropriate at the end of a session to help muscle relaxation using: ☐ maintenance stretches to return muscles to their pre-exercise length ☐ developmental stretches to increase RoM (increased FITT). • More appropriate in muscles/connective tissues around joints with poor RoM. • Limit static stretching to less than 20 seconds to prevent loss of subsequent speed, power and strength work.

continued

Ballistic (Fig. 18.3.4)	• Uses momentum to move a joint forcibly through to its extreme end of range or point of resistance. • It involves fast, swinging, active or bouncing movements to complete the joints' full RoM. • Primarily promoted and used by performers whose activities involve similar, fast, dynamic and active RoM of joints.	• Thought to be the least effective method of stretching as it fails to allow adequate time for the tissues to adapt to the stretch, and creates muscle tension making it more difficult to stretch connective tissues. • Greater risk of muscle soreness/ injury. • Thought to produce limited long-term adaptations for increasing muscle length. • Should only be performed by athletes who already have a good RoM in the muscle/ connective tissues being stretched.
Dynamic (Fig. 18.3.4)	• Dynamic stretching involves taking the muscles through a joint's full RoM. • There is muscle tension but with the entry and exit under more control and therefore not the extreme end point of resistance as with ballistic stretching. • Dynamic stretching can be performed actively or passively as with static stretching.	• More controlled version of ballistic stretching or a more technical/intense form of mobility exercises. • Dynamic stretching should only be performed by athletes who already have a good range of flexibility in the muscle/connective tissues being stretched. • Evidence that it develops a more optimum level of 'dynamic' flexibility essential for all activities. • More appropriate for a warm up than static stretches to increase subsequent speed, power, and strength work. • Evolved as a result of the growing research suggesting static stretching impairs the subsequent performance of speed, power and strength work.
Proprioreceptive neuromuscular facilitation (PNF) (Fig. 18.3.5)	The 'contract-relax' is a simple variation of PNF techniques. Put as 'static-contract-relax' it consists of three clear stages: • *Static:* muscle stretch just beyond point of resistance. • *Contract:* isometric muscle contraction held for a minimum of 10 seconds. • *Relax:* muscle relaxed and sequence repeated at least three times. • Requires assistance of a partner to resist the movement of the performer as they isometrically contract the stretched muscle.	• Until dynamic stretching, PNF was thought the most effective, and also the most complex, type of stretching. • PNF is more appropriate in muscles/ connective tissues around joints with poor RoM. • PNF seeks to inhibit this stretch reflex to allow a greater stretch of the muscle/connective tissues. • Isometric contraction inhibits the stretch reflex allowing the muscle to be stretched further in each consecutive PNF stretch. • PNF shown to produce quicker and equal or better flexibility gains than traditional static stretching. • However, PNF is a more complex technique, requiring more time to learn and tolerate the greater discomfort and associated injury risks. • Limit stretching to less than 20 seconds to prevent loss of subsequent speed, power and strength work.

Table 2 Summary of types of stretching and flexibility training guidelines

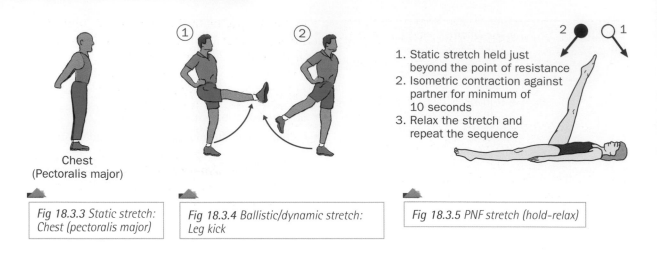

1. Static stretch held just beyond the point of resistance
2. Isometric contraction against partner for minimum of 10 seconds
3. Relax the stretch and repeat the sequence

Chest (Pectoralis major)

Fig 18.3.3 *Static stretch: Chest (pectoralis major)*

Fig 18.3.4 *Ballistic/dynamic stretch: Leg kick*

Fig 18.3.5 *PNF stretch (hold-relax)*

> **Need to know more?** For more information on stretching see Chapter 18.3, pages 453-454 and Chapter 18.2, pages 435–436 in the OCR A2 PE Student Book

The benefits of a warm up

A warm up increases core body temperature which increases RoM and reduces the risk of injuries due to the increased elasticity of muscles, tendons and ligaments. Evidence suggests that if you do not have time to warm up properly, it is arguably better not to stretch at all than attempt to stretch a cold muscle!

> **Need to know more?** For more information on the stretch reflex see Chapter 18.2, pages 435-436 in the OCR A2 PE Student Book

FLEXIBILITY TRAINING ADAPTATIONS AND BENEFITS

The adaptations to stretching are linked directly to an increase in the elasticity of muscle and connective tissues, which limit the RoM around a joint. These adaptations and their associated benefits are summarised below:

- increased elasticity/length of muscle/ connective tissues

- increased resting length of muscle/connective tissues
- **muscle spindles** adapt to the increased length reducing the stimulus to the stretch reflex
- increased RoM at a joint before the stretch reflex is initiated
- increased potential for static and dynamic flexibility (RoM)
- increased distance and efficiency for muscles to create force and acceleration
- increased RoM reduces potential for injury to muscle/connective tissues during dynamic sports movements.

KEY TERM

Muscle spindles – Proprioceptors within muscles which send information on the length and rate of change of muscles to the central nervous system (CNS).

EXAM TIP

Exam questions often refer to the benefits of flexibility training – think of benefits and adaptations as the same thing and you will not misinterpret this type of question.

Examples of the benefits of flexibility

- Increased RoM at the hip joint will allow a runner to increase their stride length.
- A golfer with increased RoM at the hips, shoulder and vertebrae will be able to take the club further back parallel to the target on the backswing. This will create a greater distance for the club head to travel and to apply force on the downswing, thereby increasing club head speed and force at impact, thus increasing the speed/distance the ball travels.

Flexibility, specific to the activity and joints, is critical for sports participation or to promote a healthy lifestyle. Remember: if you don't stretch to maintain your specific flexibility requirements, it is only a matter of time before some body tissue will break down leading to injury.

> **Need to know more?** For more information on flexibility see Chapter 18.3, pages 445-458, in the OCR A2 PE Student Book.

FLEXIBILITY IN RELATION TO POSTURE AND OVERALL HEALTH

The body has a tendency to allow certain muscles/connective tissues to tighten or shorten, and this can affect body posture and may lengthen or weaken the antagonistic muscles. Consequently this may alter an individual's neutral body alignment. Muscles/connective tissues affected include:

- the hamstrings
- rectus femoris
- tensor facia late
- piriformis adductors
- gastrocnemius and quadratus luborium
- pectoralis major
- upper trapezius.

Those listed very often cause postural musculoskeletal pain, the most common being the lower (lumbar) and upper (cervical) regions of the spine.

CHECK

If you are satisfied with your knowledge and understanding, tick off the sections that you have revised so far. If you are not satisfied then revisit those sections and refer to the pages in the *Need to know more?* features.

- [ ] Define flexibility.
- [ ] Outline the factors that affect flexibility.
- [ ] Describe and apply methods of evaluating flexibility.
- [ ] Describe different types of training used to develop flexibility.
- [ ] Consider the physiological adaptations that take place after prolonged periods of physical activity.
- [ ] Plan a programme of flexibility training based on self-assessment of flexibility and the flexibility requirements of your activity.

TRUE OR FALSE?

1. Flexibility is the range of motion around a joint or a series of joints.
2. Flexibility is joint-specific but not sport-specific.
3. Static flexibility is the range of motion (RoM) around a joint which occurs in the performance of a physical activity at either normal or rapid speed.
4. Developmental stretching involves whole/part training sessions (a minimum of 10-15 minutes) devoted solely to stretching and helps to increase/develop RoM.
5. Dynamic stretching uses momentum to move a joint forcibly through to its extreme end of range or point of resistance and involves fast, swinging, active or bouncing movements.
6. Static active stretching is unassisted, when a performer actively completes a voluntary static contraction of an agonist muscle to create the force to stretch the antagonist muscle just beyond its end point of resistance.
7. Flexibility is either maintained or improved by stretching.
8. A warm up increases core body temperature which increases RoM and reduces the risk of injuries due to the increased elasticity of muscles, tendons and ligaments.
9. PNF seeks to increase this stretch reflex to allow a greater stretch of the muscle/connective tissues.
10. Stretching adaptations include; increased elasticity/length of muscle/connective tissues and increased resting length of muscle/connective tissues.

EXAM PRACTICE

1. The purposes of flexibility training is to improve or maintain the range of movement over which muscles can act and joints can operate. Identify and explain three factors which can affect the range of motion around a joint. What are the proposed benefits of flexibility training to a performer?

   (6 marks)

2. Selecting either the hip or shoulder joint, give examples of types of flexibility exercises in an activity of your choice. Describe the types of training that can be used to increase the range of movement in that joint. *(6 marks)*

3. PNF (proprioceptive neuromuscular facilitation) is one type of flexibility training. Describe PNF stretching and explain the theory behind its effectiveness. *(5 marks)*

See page 305 for answers.

CHAPTER 18.4

Health components of physical fitness: Body composition

CHAPTER OVERVIEW

By the end of this chapter you should have knowledge and understanding of:

- what is meant by body composition
- different methods of assessing body composition
- how to calculate a person's body mass index (BMI)
- basal metabolic rate (BMR) and the different energy requirements of different physical activities
- how to estimate your daily calorific requirements based on your BMR and average additional energy consumption
- how to evaluate critically your own diet and calorie consumption
- the health implications of being overweight or obese and how this impacts on involvement in physical activity.

WHAT IS BODY COMPOSITION?

Body composition refers to the chemical make-up of the body. It is split into two components:

- *Fat mass* refers to the percentage of body weight that is stored as fat (within adipose tissue).
- *Lean body mass* is the weight of the rest of the body, i.e. all the body's non-fat tissues including bone, muscle, organs and connective tissues.

Fig 18.4.1 shows that two individuals may have the same weight but their body composition can vary significantly.

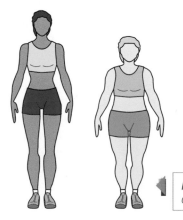

Fig 18.4.1 Height and weight do not always reflect body composition

- The average male has 12-18 per cent body fat, while the average female has 22-28 per cent.
- Typical values for elite athletes are 6-12 per cent for men and 12-20 per cent for women.

Sport	Male	Female
Baseball	12–15%	12–18%
Basketball	6–12%	20–27%
Cycling	5–15%	15–20%
Field Hockey	8–15%	12–18%
Rowing	6–14%	12–18%
Swimming	9–12%	14–24%
Track – Runners	8–10%	12–20%
Track – Jumpers	7–12%	10–18%
Track – Throwers	14–20%	20–28%
Triathlon	5–12%	10–15%
Volleyball	11–14%	16–15%

Table 1 Percentage body fat for male/female athletes in a variety of sports

Size and body composition in relation to sport

- The ideal size for an athlete depends on the sport or event, and sometimes the position they play in their sport, for example:
  - a basketball player needs to be tall, but if their percentage of body fat is too high they will not be able to move their total body weight at the speed and agility required.
  - the traditional high body fat mass of sumo wrestlers has changed to that of a more muscular lean body mass, as the sport has become faster requiring more power and speed.
- Although body size and build are important for athletes, their body composition is of greater concern. Standard ideal weight charts based on height do not provide accurate estimates of what athletes should weigh, as they do not account for body composition.
- Additional weight is not normally a concern if it is lean muscle mass (muscle mass weighs three times more than fat per unit of volume), which contribute towards performance.
- Body composition tends to concentrate more on the percentage of fat tissue than lean body mass, and in most sports the athlete will try to minimise bodyfat, as generally performance is increased the lower the percentage of body fat.

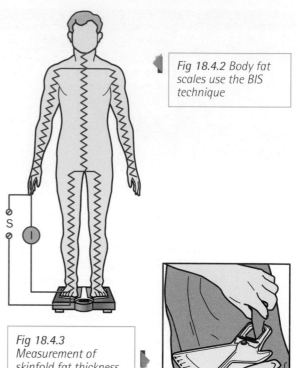

Fig 18.4.2 Body fat scales use the BIS technique

Fig 18.4.3 Measurement of skinfold fat thickness at the triceps using skinfold callipers

EXAM TIP

You need to know the different methods by which body composition is assessed. This will enable you to understand what percentages of fat mass are classified as normal, overweight, obese and typical of different sports performers.

BODY COMPOSITION ASSESSMENT

Table 2 summarises body composition assessment, and the advantages or disadvantages of the assessment.

BODY MASS INDEX (BMI)

Body mass index (BMI) is a measure of an adult's weight in relation to their height, or more specifically their weight in kilograms divided by their height in metres squared.

- The normal acceptable range varies, but 20.1–25.0 for men and 18.5–23.8 for women are norm values.
- BMI does *not* directly measure body fat but is related/correlated to body composition.
- Provides a better estimate of overweight/obesity than standard height/weight tables alone.
- BMI offers a simple measure of 'fatness' to check the risk of weight-related health problems for a particular height.
- Not suitable for: young children, pregnant women, the elderly or athletes.
- Athletes' heavier muscles push their BMI over the normal range, so muscular rugby players, body builders, etc., may have 'obese' BMIs when their body fat actually lies within/below that recommended for good health (Fig. 18.4.4).
- Despite its failings, BMI is now the medical standard used to measure weight and obesity, and used as part of the government's objectives to slow down the trend of increasing obesity rates within the UK.

Method	How it works	Advantages/disadvantages
Hydrostatic weighing	• Athlete is weighed totally immersed in water. • The difference between the athlete's scale weight and underwater weight is the athlete's fat mass percentage. • Fat is less dense and floats in water so the more fat the individual has the greater the difference between the dry and wet weights.	• The most commonly used and accepted measure of body composition. • Although accepted as the most accurate measure, it is not readily available to most. • It only estimates the density of fat-free mass, which varies according to gender, age and race.
Bioelectrical Impedance Spectroscopy (BIS) (Fig. 18.4.2)	• Body fat scales use the Bioelectrical Impedance Spectoscopy (BIS) technique by sending a low, safe electrical current through the body. • This current passes freely through the fluids contained in muscle tissue, but encounters resistance when it passes through fat tissue. This is termed bioelectrical impedance. • When set against a person's height and weight, the scales can then compute their body fat percentage.	• Although reasonably accurate, since BIS relies on the fluid levels of fat-free mass, such as muscle tissue, it is affected by the level of hydration of the performer. • It uses average populations to determine body fat per cent, not appropriate for elite athletes with more lean muscle tissue. • An individual's eating habits (alcohol, caffeine, etc.), the amount of exercise performed, the time of day, etc., cause variations in a person's weight and levels of hydration and therefore affect accuracy readings of body composition.
Skinfold measures: (Fig. 18.4.3)	• Skinfold callipers measure in millimetres the level of subcutaneous fat below the skin from selected sites on the body. • The sum of these skinfolds is used (in an equation) to estimate body fat percentage. • Various skinfold tests are available which measure different sites on the body, but the four most common sites are the triceps, biceps, subscapular and suprailiac. • More detailed tests use up to six sites, some of which are gender specific as body fat is distributed differently between males /females.	• Most widely used method of assessing body composition due to being accessible, cheap and practical to use. • Multiple skinfold fat measurements provide a good estimate of body composition. • Despite its ease of use, testers need to be properly trained and specific sites on the body measured to ensure accuracy.

Table 2 Summary of body composition assessment

BMI	Category	What does your BMI score mean?
Below 18.5	Underweight	You are underweight for your height; this is a health risk.
18.5–24.9	Normal	This is the ideal weight for height range.
25.0–29.9	Overweight	This weight to height ratio is fine if you're a keen athlete with plenty of body muscle, but if the reason for your higher BMI is extra stored fat, check your diet and exercise routine and make small changes to prevent further weight gain.
30.0–34.9	Obese	You are at a much higher risk of developing ill-health due to your weight. You are ten times more likely to get diabetes, and your weight is increasing your risk of arthritis, heart disease and some cancers. Your weight means you have a shorter life expectancy, and weight-related health concerns will reduce your quality of life. Change your diet now.
35.0+	Very obese	Your weight is seriously affecting your health. You're at raised risk of heart disease, stroke and premature death. In addition to making lifestyle changes, you may need the additional support of a health professional.

Table 3 BMI values and meaning

Overweight and obesity

Overweight and **obesity** occur as a result of an imbalance between energy intake (food consumption) and energy expenditure (work/ physical activity).

- If energy intake exceeds expenditure then energy is stored as fat (adipose tissue).
- To lose weight, energy expenditure must exceed intake.

Fig 18.4.4 *Heavier muscles can push the BMI measurement over the normal range*

KEY TERMS

Overweight – Body weight exceeding the normal standard weight based on height/frame size or having a BMI between 25.0 and 29.9.

Obesity – Having a very high amount of body fat (20–25 per cent men and 30–35 per cent women) in relation to lean body mass, or having a BMI over 30.

ENERGY EXPENDITURE

To fully understand how to influence the balance between energy expenditure and energy intake, you need knowledge of:

- basal metabolic rate (BMR)
- energy measurement (METS)
- calorific intake.

Basal metabolic rate (BMR)

- Metabolic rate is the body's rate of energy expenditure.
- Basal metabolic rate is the lowest rate of energy expenditure needed to sustain the body's essential physiological functions while at rest.
- The term 'resting metabolic rate' (RMR) is more often used, to avoid the need to measure sleep.

When calculating the body's total daily energy expenditure:

- RMR accounts for about 60-75 per cent
- physical activity contributes 20-30 per cent
- the energy used in the process of eating, digesting, absorbing and using food, referred to as the 'thermic effect', accounts for the remaining 0-20 per cent (see Fig 18.4.5).

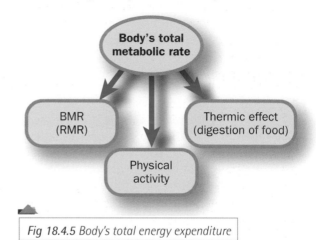

Fig 18.4.5 *Body's total energy expenditure*

BMR/RMR calculation

Numerous equations offer a simple and quick way to calculate your RMR in terms of calories per day/hour, an example of which is shown below:

- For adult males – Multiply the body weight by 10, add double the body weight to this value (i.e. for a 150 lb male, 150 × 10 + 300 = 1,800 cal/day and ÷ 24 = 75 Calories/hr).
- For adult females – Multiply the body weight by 10, add the body weight to this value (i.e. for a 150 lb female, 150 × 10 + 150 = 1,650 cal/day and ÷ 24 = 69 Calories/hr).

This figure represents the amount of Calories you need to consume to sustain your body's energy requirements at rest (RMR).

Metabolic Equivalent Task (METs)

- Metabolic Equivalent Task (METs) use oxygen consumption per unit of body weight per minute (ml O_2/kg/min) to estimate exercise intensity, as oxygen consumption is directly proportional to energy expenditure during activity.
- At rest your body uses approximately 3.5 ml O_2 per kilogram of body weight per minute (3.5 ml/kg/min) and this equates to 0.0175 **kcal**/kg/min.
- Hence, 3.5 ml/kg/min or 0.0175 kcal/kg/min equals 1 MET and equates to your resting VO_2 (volume of oxygen consumed).
- This reflects the resting metabolic rate (RMR), i.e. the energy cost of sitting quietly.

Tables 4 and 5 list the energy costs of specific activities using MET values. They show that a person's calorific consumption can typically be three to six times higher during moderate activity and six times higher when being vigorously active. However, METs are sometimes thought to overestimate energy expenditure.

KEY TERMS

Calorie (cal)/Kilocalorie (kcal) – The amount of heat energy needed to increase the temperature of one kilogram of water by 1 degree Celsius – exactly 1000 small calories, or about 4.184 kilo Joules (kJ). Calorie (cal) and Kilocalorie (kcal/Kcal) are the same and are used interchangeably.

Metabolic Equivalent Task (METs) – To calculate the additional energy expenditure for physical activity you undertake, you need an understanding of Metabolic Equivalent Task (METs). The ratio of a performer's working metabolic rate relative to their resting metabolic rate, for example two or three METs indicates that energy expenditure during activity is 2–3 times the energy expenditure at rest.

METs	Activity/occupation
1.3	Standing
1.5	Reading, talking on telephone
1.8	Sitting in class, studying, note-taking
2.0	Walking on job, at 2 mph (in office or lab area), easy casual
2.0	Light gardening
2.0	Light office work, light use of hand tools (watch repair or micro-assembly, light assembly/repair); standing, light work (bartending, store clerk, assembling, filing)
2.5	Walking downstairs
2.5	Cooking, light housekeeping, shopping
2.5	Somewhat heavier gardening
2.5	Brisk walking: pushing stroller with child, walking dog
3.0	Standing, light/moderate work (assemble/repair heavy parts, welding, auto repair, pack boxes for moving, etc.), patient care (as in nursing); driving heavy tractor, bus, truck
3.0	Washing car or windows, mopping, moderately vigorous playing with children, sweeping outside house, vacuuming, picking fruit or vegetables, scrubbing floors
3.5	Walking on job, 3 mph (one mile every twenty minutes), in office, moderate speed, not carrying anything, or carrying only light articles
4.0	Raking lawn, planting shrubs, weeding garden, heavy yard work or gardening activities
4.0	Masonry, painting, paper hanging, moderately heavy lifting, moderately heavy farm work
5.0	Walking downstairs or standing, carrying objects about 25–49 lb (11–22 kg)
5.0	Digging, spading, vigorous gardening, using heavy power tools; general gardening, mowing lawn (hand mower)
5.0	Painting, carpentry, cleaning gutters, laying carpet, other vigorous activities
5.0	Chopping wood
6.0	Using heavy tools (not power) such as shovel, pick, spade; driving heavy machinery, forestry
6.5	Walking downstairs or standing, carrying objects about 50–74 lb (22.6–33.6 kg)
6.5	Loading and unloading truck (standing); moving heavy objects; heavy farming work
7.5	Walking downstairs or standing, carrying objects about 75–99 lb (34–45 kg)
8.0	Heavy farming

Table 4 METs per hour expended on home and occupational activities

Activity	METS	Activity	METS
Sitting/lying quietly	1.0	Hiking (hilly)	6.5
Walking (less than 3.2 km/hr level surface)	2.0	Aerobic dance, high impact	7.0
Bowling	2.5	Badminton, competitive	7.0
Yoga/stretching	2.5	Backpacking	7.0
Cycling (50 watts, light effort)	3.0	Dancing (vigorous)	7.0
Golf (electric trolley)	3.0	Skating (ice/roller)	7.0
Resistance training (light/)moderate)	3.0	Rowing machine (100 watts, moderate effort)	7.0
Volleyball (recreational)	3.0	Stationary cycling (150 watts, moderate effort)	7.0
Walking (4 km/hr)	3.0	Swimming laps (freestyle, slow, moderate or light effort)	7.0
Horse riding	3.5	Basketball game	8.0
Rowing machine (50 watts, light)	3.5	Circuit training, including some aerobic stations, with minimal rest	8.0
Walking (5.6 km/hr, level surface)	3.8	Football	8.0
Cricket	4.0	Hockey	8.0
Dancing (moderate/fast)	4.0	Outdoor cycling (12–13.9 mph; 19.3–22.4 km/hr)	8.0
Water aerobics, water calisthenics	4.0	Singles tennis, squash, racquet-ball	8.0
Badminton (social singles and doubles)	4.5	Skiing downhill	8.0
Calisthenics	4.5	Running (12 min/mile)	8.5
Golf (carrying/walking)	4.5	Squash	8.5
Table tennis	4.5	Basketball	9.0
Aerobic dance, low impact	5.0	Running (5.2 mph; 3.2 km/hr; 11.5-minute mile)	9.0
Doubles tennis	5.0	Skiing cross-country (vigorous)	9.0
Gymnastics	5.5	Running (6 mph; 9.7 km/hr; 10-minute mile)	10.0
Aerobic dancing	6.0	Swimming laps, freestyle, fast, vigorous effort	10.0
Basketball, non-game	6.0	Stationary cycling, 200 watts, vigorous effort	10.5
Outdoor cycling (16.1–19.2 km/hr)	6.0	Running (6.7 mph; 10.8 km/hr; 9-minute mile)	11.0
Resistance training vigorous	6.0	Rowing machine, 200 watts, very vigorous effort	12.0
Slow jogging	6.0	Running (7.5 mph; 12.1 km/hr; 8-minute mile)	12.5
Swimming (recreational, light)	6.0	Outdoor cycling, more than 20 mph (32.2 km/hr)	16.0
Walking (7.2 km/hr, level surface)	6.3		

Table 5 Approximate METs per hour values for activities

Caloric energy expenditure

To estimate the number of calories (caloric energy expenditure) you use while participating in physical activity, you need to multiply your RMR by the activity's METs value, for example:

- By stating that 0.0175k cal/kg/min is equal to 3.5 ml/kg/min, you can use a more accurate calculation of the energy expenditure into **kilocalories** (kcal) for physical activity using METs. So, for the same performer:

150 lb = 68.1 kg (1 lb = 0.454 kg)
8 METs x 0.0175 = 0.14 kcal/kg/min
(1 MET = 0.0175 kcal/kg/min)
0.14 x 68.1 = 9.534 kcal/min
9.534 x 60 = 572.04 kcal (full duration of
the activity)

An alternative equation, using the same figures and which brings the same results, is shown below.

$$
\begin{aligned}
\text{Total calories burned} &= (\text{METs x 3.5 x your weight in kg}) \\
&\div 200 \text{ x duration in minutes} \\
&= 8.0 \times 3.5 \times 68.1 \\
&= 1906.8 \div 200 \\
&= 9.534 \text{ kcal/min x 60 minutes} \\
&= 572.04 \text{ kcal/hour}
\end{aligned}
$$

- For elite athletes who are training heavily, calculations of energy expenditure are used to indicate their required nutritional intake in terms of calories in order that energy intake equals energy expenditure (neutral energy balance).
- This prevents the danger of athletes not having sufficient energy to fuel the activity demands.
- Similarly, the kcal/min value can be used to calculate how many minutes of exercise (depending upon its METs value) an athlete should undertake in order to ensure they are using equal calories for expenditure as they are for energy intake.
- If energy intake outweighs expenditure, then it will be stored as fat body mass and lead to overweight/obesity-related health problems.

ENERGY INTAKE

Energy intake is the food consumed, or dietary intake.

Recommended daily calorie intake varies from person to person, but there are guidelines for calorie requirements you can use as a starting point. The UK Department of Health Estimated Average Requirements (EAR) give a daily calorie intake of 1940 calories per day for women and 2550 for men, but this can vary greatly depending on lifestyle, age, height, weight, activity and body composition.

A balanced diet should contain:

- approximately 10-15 per cent protein
- no more than 30 per cent fat
- 55-60 per cent carbohydrate (CHO)
- include foods from the main nutrient food groups to ensure vital vitamins, minerals, water and roughage are included. The food groups are:
  - bread, cereal (including breakfast cereals) and potatoes (starchy foods)
  - fruit (including fresh fruit juice) and vegetables
  - meat and fish
  - milk and dairy foods
  - fats and sugar.

- A performer participating in high volume training, especially endurance training, is likely to require an increased percentage (an additional 10-15 per cent) of carbohydrate intake in what's commonly referred to as an 'athlete's diet'.
- Athletes undertaking high volume training (high energy expenditure) will often consume up to 5000 to 6000 kcal a day to refuel the kcal required to maintain their activity/recovery levels (neutral energy balance).

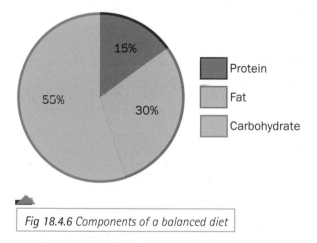

Fig 18.4.6 Components of a balanced diet

Calorie counting

There is not sufficient space to outline all the calorific values of your dietary intake in this book. A more practical method is calorie calculators.

Using calorie calculators

The following calculation is based on the following calorie calculator:

- RMR energy expenditure = 1.3 calories per hour per kg of weight
- Physical activity energy expenditure = 8.5 calories per hour of activity per kg of weight.
  - A male performer weighing 75 kg would have a RMR of 2340 calories a day (75 × 1.3 × 24).
  - 90 minutes of physical activity would produce an energy expenditure of 956 calories a day (75 × 8.5 × 1.5).
  - This equates to a total daily energy expenditure of 3296 calories a day.

Factfile:

Too much fat is associated with:
- increased risk of diabetes
- increased risk of cancers
- long-term stress on cardio-vascular system leading to dangerous medical conditions such as heart disease, deep vein thrombosis, stroke, etc.
- overload of joints which impacts on body posture and alignments. This leads to musculo-skeletal pain/injuries.
- psychological harm from stigma, ridicule, bullying etc.
- under performance in physical and mental work.

This above example provides an indication of what the performer should be consuming in terms of energy intake, depending on whether their target is to achieve a negative, positive or neutral energy balance.

More specifically, we can now apply our recommended percentages for a balanced diet to this total energy expenditure figure to calculate that:

- 1813 (55 per cent of 3296) calories need to come from CHOs
- 989 (30 per cent of 3296) calories need to come from fats
- 494 (15 per cent of 3296) calories from proteins from across the 5 a day food sources.

As you are now probably aware, calorie counting is not a simple task. This is why most elite athletes have a nutritionist to calculate what and how much they should be consuming.

The health implications of being overweight/obese

A positive energy balance, where energy intake is *greater* than energy expenditure, leads to weight/fat gain.

Levels of overweight/obesity are currently of considerable concern in the UK, as the following facts and estimated trends from government and international bodies indicate (Fig 18.4.7):

- There has been an increase in obesity over the last 10 years in the UK. Most adults now considered overweight.
- A sedentary modern lifestyle ensures every generation is heavier than the last – 'passive obesity'.
- Britons are among the heaviest people in Europe.
- Almost two-thirds of adults and a third of children in the UK are either overweight or obese.
- Without action, it is predicted that almost nine in ten adults and two-thirds of children in the UK will be overweight by 2050.
- Associated costs of obesity-related illnesses are forecast to reach £50 billion per year by 2050.

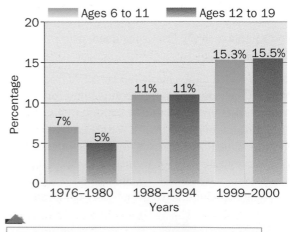

Fig 18.4.7 Increasing trend of childhood obesity, 1976–2000

Need to know more? For more information on body composition see Chapter 18.4, pages 459–486, in the OCR A2 PE Student Book

Performance implications of body weight

- Low body fat is a main characteristic of successful performers (above that required for good health).
- Athletes carry less body fat due to their increased physical activity (energy expenditure).
- This does not necessarily mean a low overall body mass/weight, as heavily muscular athletes will have a high body mass alongside a low fat mass.
- Anaerobic/sprinter-type athletes, such as Asafa Powell, tend to have a heavier body mass (more muscle mass with a low fat mass), while endurance athletes, such as Paula Radcliffe, have a lower body mass (smaller muscle mass with a very low fat mass).
- Low fat mass is more significant in aerobic endurance activity. Any weight not directly linked to metabolism /muscular performance has to be carried for longer, wasting energy which could be used to increase their performance.
- Fat mass reduces the power-to-weight ratio – consider Newton's Second Law: acceleration is inversely proportional to mass of the object.
- Increased weight from muscle mass is fine if it adds power/force specific to the improvement of the activity.

Athletes who participate in high volumes of physical activity are prone to the opposite effect of obesity and can end up with too little body fat, which can lead to other health related problems.

- Body fat less than five per cent in men and 10-15 per cent in women is thought to affect the immune system, thereby increasing the risk of illness. This is typical in elite endurance athletes, resulting in impaired training and performance.
- Female athletes are at further increased risk of irregular menstrual cycles below 18 per cent body fat.
- A low fat mass decreases female oestrogen levels. Alongside a low body mass, this increases the risk of developing osteoporosis, a condition which leads to decreased bone mineral content, decreased bone strength and increased risk of bone fracture, causing problems later in life for post-menopausal women.

Implications of overweight/obesity for involvement in sport

- Overweight and obese individuals participating in any weight-bearing physical activity will have:
  - increased energy expenditure cost, load bearing of joints and risk of injury
  - decreased joint mobility/ flexibility, economy of movement and fatigue resistance.
- Many people who are overweight/obese do not regard physical activity positively.
- There is also the psychological impact of how they may be perceived by themselves and by others due to the associated stigma of being overweight.

EFFECTS OF PHYSICAL ACTIVITY ON BODY COMPOSITION

Inactivity is a major cause of obesity; fat mass does tend to decrease as the volume of training increases and exercise is possibly as important as overeating and an essential part of any weight reduction programme.

Physical activity increases energy expenditure.

- By increasing physical activity the number of calories burned also increases.
- Increased calorie expenditure is incurred post-exercise and this increases the metabolic rate for up to 24 hours after prolonged exhaustive exercise.
- Exercise minimises the loss of muscle mass which burns more calories than fat mass.
- Exercise can increase lean muscle mass thereby burning even more calories.
- Exercise increases the mobilisation/use of fat as an energy fuel.
- All the above factors in turn have the effect of increasing the bodies RMR, so more calories are being burned when the body is at rest.
- Evidence that exercise may suppress appetite so that calorific intake better balances energy intake (this may help decrease energy intake).

Increasing lean muscle mass through exercise

- This highlights the importance of including even the simplest of strength resistance training sessions two to three times a week to help increase lean muscle mass to improve body composition.
- A change in body composition, not just loss of weight is a desirable goal, whether it is for health or performance.

At what intensity should you exercise?

- If the intensity of activity is too long, it takes too long a duration to complete.
- If the intensity of activity is too high, it increases carbohydrate and not fat use.
- Research suggests that to lose body fat and improve body composition, performers should exercise at lower intensities; this increases fat use in preference to carbohydrates.
- This optimum point for burning body fat has been termed either fat zone, fat burning zone or fatmax (see Fig 18.4.8).

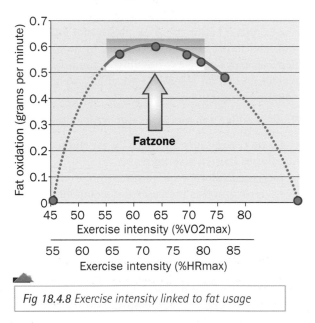

Fig 18.4.8 Exercise intensity linked to fat usage

The effects of dieting on physical composition

The balance between energy expenditure and intake shows exercise alone, like dietary intake, is not a practical prescription for losing weight.

Factfile:

- Decreasing your dietary intake alone may decrease fat mass but is also likely to decrease your lean body mass and RMR, whereas with exercise both are maintained or even increased.
- Although body fat levels may adversely affect performance, reducing fat mass does not guarantee improved performance.
- By simply increasing the energy expenditure of training and decreasing energy intake by restricting your diet, you are more likely to decrease performance due to a lack of energy fuels.

- Exercise increases RMR so we can expect it to lead to weight loss, but it is not that simple.
- Energy expenditure during exercise is dependent upon the intensity of the activity and also on body weight, as more body weight requires more energy to move it.
- In practice, overweight individuals are not capable of carrying out the sufficient intensity of activity required and, due to their lack of fitness, any exercise would initially use carbohydrates as a fuel and not fats.
- Similarly, the normal advice to undertake low-intensity exercise to use more fats may be well-founded, but obese individuals are unlikely to have the time available or be able to endure the duration required to have any real effect.

The effects of ageing on physical composition

Factfile:

- The body's rate of burning calories naturally decreases with age.
- This is partly due to a decrease in muscle mass and increase in fat mass, which is less active in terms of calorie burning.
- At the same time the diet tends to remain the same and over time fat mass continues to increase.
- A more sedentary and inactive lifestyle increases the imbalance between energy intake and expenditure even further.
- Regular physical activity helps reverse this imbalance by increasing/maintaining energy expenditure and RMR.

In conclusion

- Muscles increase calorific expenditure, both during activity and at rest by increasing RMR, which together over time have the effect of decreasing body fat.
- Any weight gain due to physical activity is good weight (lean body mass).
- Exercise, coupled with a reduction in food intake, speeds up weight loss and ensures that more of the lost weight is fat than muscle.

CHECK

If you are satisfied with your knowledge and understanding, tick off the sections that you have revised so far. If you are not satisfied then revisit those sections and refer to the pages in the *Need to know more?* features.

- [ ] Define what is meant by body composition.
- [ ] Describe the different methods of assessing body composition.
- [ ] Calculate a person's body mass index (BMI).
- [ ] Define basal metabolic rate (BMR) and describe the different energy requirements of different physical activities.
- [ ] Estimate your daily calorific requirements based on your BMR and average additional energy consumption.
- [ ] Evaluate critically your own diet and calorie consumption.
- [ ] Consider the health implications of being overweight or obese and how this impacts on involvement in physical activity.

TRUE OR FALSE?

1. Body composition refers to correct height to weight ratio.
2. Body composition is split into two components: Fat mass and Lean body mass.
3. Hydrostatic weighing is the most commonly used and accepted accurate measure of body composition.
4. Body mass index (BMI) is a measure of an adult's weight in relation to their height, or more specifically their weight in kilograms multiplied by their height in metres squared.
5. Obesity can be classed as having a very high amount of body fat in relation to lean body mass, or having a BMI over 30.
6. The UK Department of Health Estimated Average Requirements give a daily calorie intake of 2550 calories per day for women and 1940 for men.
7. A balanced diet should contain: approximately 10 – 15 per cent protein, no more than 30 per cent carbohydrate and 55 – 60 per cent fat.
8. A performer participating in high volume training, especially endurance training, is likely to require an increased percentage (an additional 10–15 per cent) of carbohydrate intake in what's commonly referred to as an 'athlete's diet'.
9. A positive energy balance, where energy intake is greater than energy expenditure, leads to weight/fat gain.
10. Exercise, coupled with a reduction in food intake, speeds up weight loss and ensures that more of the lost weight is fat rather than muscle.

EXAM PRACTICE

1. The UK department of Health's Estimated Average requirements (EAR) suggests a daily calorie intake of around 1940 calories per day for women and 2250 calories for men. The daily calorie intake is recommended to come from 'a balanced diet'

   Outline the contents of a balanced diet and explain how and why you would change this diet when recommending it to an athlete.

   (6 marks)

2. Using examples and average values for body composition, discuss the statement that: 'Two individuals may have the same weight but their body composition can vary significantly. *(5 marks)*

3. Although obesity is not a disease, it is widely recognised as a health hazard. Evaluate the health implications of being overweight/obese and how this may impact on performance and involvement in physical activity.

   (6 marks)

See page 307 for answers

CHAPTER 19
Performance enhancement

CHAPTER OVERVIEW

By the end of this chapter you should have knowledge and understanding of:
- the positive and negative effects of each type of aid, together with the type of
- performer who would benefit from its use
- the legal status of each type of aid
- how to evaluate critically the use of ergogenic aids in order to be able to make
- informed decisions about their use
- the following aids to perfomance:
  - dietary manipulation, pre/post-competition meals/supplements and food/fluid intake during exercise
  - use of creatine supplements; human growth hormone; gene doping; blood doping and recombinant erythropoietin (Rh EPO)
  - use of cooling aids to reduce core temperature and aid recovery
  - use of training aids to increase resistance, for example pulleys and parachutes
  - the effects of alcohol, caffeine and anabolic steroids.

Introduction

- Performance enhancement aids are commonly referred to as ergogenic aids.
- Ergogenic aids is a generic term to describe anything that enhances performance, for example specific footwear or a Speedo LZR swimsuit.
- Most ergogenic aids are legal to use.
- Ergogenic aids have been around a long time: the ancient Greeks took 'magic mushrooms' (hallucinogens) to aid sporting performance, and in the early years of the Tour de France cyclists consumed substances including alcohol and speed (amphetamine).
- With the advent of technology, the practice and use of ergogenic aids has increased to such an extent that the International Olympic Committee (IOC) and World Anti-Doping Agency (WADA) has now produced a list of ergogenic aids that are banned and those that have restrictions.

- Similarly, national and international governing bodies of sport have produced their own codes of practice and lists of banned ergogenic aids, although these vary from one country or governing body to another.

EXAM TIP

For all the aids covered within the specification, make sure you are familiar with:
- the positive and negative effects of each type of ergonomic aid, together with the type of performer who would benefit from its use
- the legal status of each type of aid
- how to evaluate critically the use of ergogenic aids in order to be able to make informed decisions about their use.

- However, the practice of using banned ergogenic aids has not stopped, aided by pharmaceutical technology. New substances, including 'masking' drugs, hide the use of the banned substances.

- The IOC/WADA's banned list and restrictions change and alter as more information is gained.

Tables 1-5 summarise what you are required to know to allow you to evaluate critically the use of ergogenic aids and make informed decisions about their use.

DIETARY MANIPULATION

Performance enhancement aid	Positive performance effects	Negative performance effects	Type of performer benefiting	Legal status
Pre-comp meals / supplements CHO loading (days prior to)	• Increases glycogen stores/ synthesis. • Increases endurance and capacity, delaying fatigue and allowing performance at a higher intensity.	• Can disrupt an athlete's pre-event routine, causing harmful psychological effects, irritability, and depression during depletion stage. • Weight can increase, as more water is needed to store glycogen. • Subject may feel weak after depletion phase.	• Long duration/high endurance aerobic based performers over 60/90 minutes; e.g. middle and long distance/marathon runners.	Legal
Pre-match/ competiton (on the day)	• Increases/tops up liver glycogen stores just prior to actual event on top of that achieved via CHO loading increasing benefits as outlined for CHO.	• Digestive discomfort if CHO volume consumed is too high or ingested 1 hour prior to performance as it may cause rebound hypoglycaemia. • Decreases muscle glucose stores and bring upon the earlier muscle fatigue.	• Benefits any performer fuelled by glycogen/ glucose as the energy source, e.g. both anaerobic and aerobic activity.	Legal
Post competition meals / supplements	• Serves to replenish depleted glycogen/glucose stores increasing recovery from exercise. • Carbohydrate stores used up during short duration exercise can be replenished in a few hours.	• No negative health effects for the performer but not replenishing during exercise will significantly increase glycogen depletion and therefore muscle fatigue.	• Any performer that utilises glycogen/ glucose as a source of energy both aerobic and anaerobic. • Important for next day competition.	Legal
Food intake during	• Replenishes vital glycogen stores delaying fatigue, especially activity of 45+mins.	• No negative health effects, but not consuming a rich CHO intake post exercise will significantly increase the restoration time of glycogen stores and therefore subsequent training days.	• Any performer if activity lasts longer than 45 minutes (football, rugby, marathon).	Legal
Fluid intake during	• Optimises performance by maintaining temperature control by dissipating heat (sweating) and reducing blood viscosity via maintaining plasma volume.	• Significant decrease in performance if dehydration exceeds 2% body weight dehydration also increased blood viscosity and decreasing blood flow (see Fig 19.1).	• All performers for training and competition, especially those in aerobic endurance based activities and in hot conditions.	Legal

Table 1 Dietary manipulation (pre/post/during competition meals/fuels/fluids)

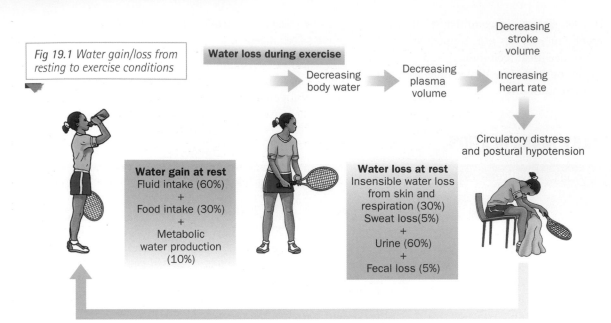

Fig 19.1 Water gain/loss from resting to exercise conditions

Water loss during exercise

Decreasing body water → Decreasing plasma volume → Increasing heart rate

Decreasing stroke volume

Circulatory distress and postural hypotension

Water gain at rest
Fluid intake (60%)
+
Food intake (30%)
+
Metabolic water production (10%)

Water loss at rest
Insensible water loss from skin and respiration (30%)
Sweat loss(5%)
+
Urine (60%)
+
Fecal loss (5%)

Rehydration and recovery = Fluid intake

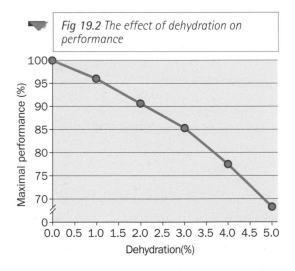

Fig 19.2 The effect of dehydration on performance

Remember that most of the energy from the body's metabolic reactions is given off as heat.

- During exercise, the heat released increases and the body responds by sweating to control body temperature.
- This increases water loss and unless the performer rehydrates, this will result in dehydration and ultimately raise body temperature, which decreases performance.

Need to know more? For more information on dietary manipulation, see Chapter 19, pages 488–491, in the OCR A2 PE Student Book

Performance enhancement aid	Positive performance effects	Negative performance effects	Type of performer benefiting	Legal status
Creatine supplements	• Increases PC stores to prolong ATP/PC energy production • and maintain longer power output. • Aids recovery, increases strength and fat-free body mass, improved quality of training, harder/longer/ volume..	• Increase in body mass and dehydration leads to muscle cramps. • Puts stress on organs such as the heart, kidney and liver, leading to disease.	• Effective for power performers for short-term/high intensity activity, e.g. 100m sprint/hurdles. • Also used by endurance athletes, e.g. middle distance runners.	Legal

continued

Human growth hormone hGH	• Limited/conflicting research but thought to increase fat free mass, blood glucose levels, stimulation of bone growth, capability to heal soft tissues, lipolysis and breakdown of FFAs/decrease fat mass. • Conflicting research regarding muscle mass/strength.	• Hypertrophy of internal organs, muscle and joint weakness, diabetes, hypertension and heart disease, bone thickening/ deformities and glucose intolerance.	• Commonly used by both aerobic and power performers but little research to show it increases strength/ muscle mass. • Good for performers undertaking higher intensity training requiring soft tissue repair.	Banned Very difficult to detect synthetic from natural form in drug testing.
Gene doping	• Future potential improvement in just about all physiological and metabolic functioning of the body.	• Most research in its infancy so risk factors are mostly unknown although they may be less than those from the use of hGH/ anabolic steroids/ rhEPO etc.	• Potentially all performers.	Banned
Blood doping	• Increases total volume of red blood cells which increases haemoglobin levels thus increasing O_2 transportation to the working muscles. • Increases O_2 uptake/VO_2 Max/aerobic capacity. • Increased energy delivery and delayed fatigue for aerobic performance.	• Increased blood viscosity, lower HR/ blood flow can overload the CV system leading to clotting and heart failure/stroke. • Inherent risks of HIV if not using the same blood in the transfusion procedure. • Danger if the body becomes dehydrated, decreasing plasma volume which further increases blood viscosity forcing heart to work harder.	• Endurance/aerobic based performers which relies on the supply of O_2 to the muscles. e.g. distance cycling, running, rowing and swimming.	Banned Tests to show levels of rbc's/Hb over normal values. If too high you are suspended on health grounds.
Recombinant erythropoietin (Rh EPO)	• Same as blood doping above, but can increase red blood cell volume from 45% to as much as 65%. • Therefore significant increase on all the above factors and performance.	• Increased blood viscosity, low HR/ blood flow can overload CV system leading to clotting and heart failure/ stroke. • Danger if body becomes dehydrated, decreasing plasma volume which further increases blood viscosity forcing the heart to work harder.	• Endurance/aerobic performers who rely on the supply of O_2 to the muscles, e.g. distance cycling, running, rowing and swimming. • Cyclists mainly caught using it.	Banned Tests to show levels of rbcs/Hb over norm values. Suspension if too high on health grounds.

Table 2 Other aids to performance

Need to know more? For more information on other aids to performance see Chapter 19, pages 491–494, in the OCR A2 PE Student Book

Enhancing performance in practice

- Body builders are thought to use high doses of HGH as it promotes an increase in fat-free weight, a decrease in fat mass, proposed muscle growth and strength, and aids recovery/repair from training/injuries.
- Endurance cyclists are common users of Rh EPO.

Need to know more? For more information on cooling aids see Chapter 19, pages 494–496, in the OCR A2 PE Student Book

RICE

RICE should be the immediate response when you suffer a soft tissue injury:

- *Ice* – apply up to a maximum of 10 minutes as soon after the injury as possible and repeat every 2 hours during the first two days after injury. Do not apply ice directly to the skin.
- *Compression* – after ice, apply a compression bandage/wrap to help minimise the swelling to the tissues.

KEY TERMS

Human growth hormones (HGH) Hormone – produced naturally in the body to aid growth and development. HGH can also be made synthetically for use in sport. Its use in sport is illegal.

Blood doping – Any means by which a person's total volume of red blood cells is increased.

Erythropoietin (EPO) – Naturally occurring hormone which increases the body's ability to manufacture red blood cells.

Rh EPO – An artificial synthetic copy of erythropoietin.

- *Elevation* – raise the injured part to limit blood flow and prevent use of muscles in the injured part.
- *Rest* – rest the injured part as much as possible to allow the healing of damaged tissues.

Need to know more? For more information on resistance aids see Chapter 19, page 497, in the OCR A2 PE Student Book

Performance enhancement aid	Positive performance effects	Negative performance effects	Type of performer benefiting	Legal status
Cooling aids; ice baths; ice vests; RICE	• Reduce core temperature pre-exercise to improve performance; • Prevent, ease, treat pain or injury. • Post exercise • constricts blood vessels and helps remove lactic acid and flushes dilated capillaries with O_2 rich blood. • Reduces muscle damage and decreases soreness from DOMS.	• Some ice/cold is immediately painful. • Used on chest region it may cause muscle reaction causing angina pain from constriction of coronary arteries. • Ice may hide or will complicate nerve impingement injuries. • Do not use with hypertensive's as vasoconstriction may increase Bp. • Decreased efficiency of vasoconstriction /dilation in the elderly. • Ice burns if placed directly onto skin. • Tissue/vascular impairment if kept on for too long.	• All performers who have soft tissue injuries, DOMS, undertaking contact type activities and performers wishing to speed up the recovery process after exercise.	Legal

Table 3 Use of cooling aids to reduce core temperature and aid recovery

Performance enhancement aid	Positive performance effects	Negative performance effects	Type of performer benefiting	Legal status
Pulleys/parachutes (resistance aids)	• Increased specificity and variety of resistance training • Add variation and motivation.	• No negative health risks but still not 100% specific to activity.	• Most performers for specificity in running, swimming, throwing events.	Legal

Table 4 Use of training aids to increase resistance: Pulleys and parachutes

Performance enhancement aid	Positive performance effects	Negative performance effects	Type of performer benefiting	Legal status
Alcohol	• Provides a form of CHO energy and initially dulls pain sensation, reduces anxiety and adds self-confidence.	• A depressant that can lead to dehydration • Impairs psychomotor function, concentration and motor skill production. • No effect on power, strength, endurance.	• Was common with snooker, darts players but now little used.	Legal
Caffeine	• Increases CNS stimulation, mental awareness and concentration. • Breakdown of FFA's saving glycogen stores. • Decreased fatigue/ perceived effort.	• Diuretic and can increase dehydration, Bp, heat exhaustion. • Can cause nervousness, tremors, shaking, addictive.	• Mostly used by endurance performers but now also used by more anaerobic performers.	Legal
Anabolic steroids	• Increase muscle mass and therefore strength and power. Are also believed to promote recovery. • Increase ability to train harder for longer and aid in the recovery of strain and injury. • Used for medical reasons of rehabilitation. • Increased aggressiveness may be beneficial in some activities.	• Risks of permanent liver damage and liver cancer, raised Bp, raised LDH (bad) cholesterol and lower HDL (good) cholesterol leading to cardiovascular and coronary heart diseases. • Males: shrinking of testicles, reduced sperm count, impotence, baldness, enlargement of prostate gland, breast enlargement, pain urinating. • Females: facial hair, deepening voice, enlargement of genitals, breast reduction, menstrual cycle disruption.	• Mostly high intensity, short duration performers such as weightlifters, sprinters and throwers but also power positions like wingers in rugby. • Also used by any injured performers to speed up injury, muscle repair recovery.	BANNED

Table 5 Effects of alcohol, caffeine and anabolic steroids

> **Need to know more?** For more information on alcohol, caffeine and anabolic steroids as performance enhancement aids see Chapter 19, pages 497-498, in the OCR A2 PE Student Book

> **Need to know more?** For more information on performance enhancement, see Chapter 19, pages 487-501, in the OCR A2 PE Student Book

KEY TERMS

Anabolic steroids – Synthetic derivatives of the naturally produced hormone testosterone which promotes bone maturation and development of muscle mass. Their use in sport is illegal.

CHECK

If you are satisfied with your knowledge and understanding, tick off the sections that you have revised so far. If you are not satisfied then revisit those sections and refer to the pages in the *Need to know more?* features:

☐ Describe the positive and negative effects of each type of ergonomic aid, together with the type of performer who would benefit from its use.

☐ Outline the legal status of each type of aid.

☐ Evaluate critically the use of ergogenic aids in order to be able to make informed decisions about their use.

☐ Discuss the following aids to performance:
  – dietary manipulation, pre/post-competition meals/supplements and food/fluid intake during exercise
  – use of creatine supplements; human growth hormone; gene doping; blood doping and recombinant erythropoietin (Rh EPO)
  – use of cooling aids to reduce core temperature and aid recovery
  – use of training aids to increase resistance, for example pulleys and parachutes
  – the effects of alcohol, caffeine and anabolic steroids.

TRUE OR FALSE?

1. Ergogenic aids is a generic term for illegal aids that enhance performance.
2. Carboloading is a dietary strategy aimed at increasing an athlete's glycogen/glucose stores.
3. Creatine supplements increase PC stores to prolong ATP/PC energy production but are presently illegal.
4. Endurance cyclists are common users of rhEPO.
5. Erythropoietin (EPO) is a naturally occurring enzyme which increases the body's ability to manufacture red blood cells.
6. (HGH) is produced naturally in the body to aid growth and development.
7. Caffeine was previously on the WADA watch list but due to misuse it is now banned above 12mm.
8. Cooling Aids aim to reduce core temperature pre-exercise to improve performance and prevent/ease/treat pain/injury post exercise.
9. Ergogenic aids have increased to such an extent that the International Olympic Committee (IOC) and World Anti-Doping Agency (WADA) have now produced a list of ergogenic aids that are banned and those that have restrictions.
10. Gene doping research is in its infancy, so risk factors are mostly unknown although they may be less than those from the use of hGH/anabolic steroids/rhEPO.

EXAM PRACTICE

1. Performers may use the ATP-PC system during short explosive movements. Name two performance enhancement aids, excluding gene doping, that might affect performance in explosive activities. Describe the physiological effects of each aid. *(6 marks)*

2. Pulleys and parachutes are two types of ergogenic aid. Discuss the effects of using pulleys and parachutes referring to the following:
   - the theory behind their use
   - the type of performer benefitting
   - the performance enhancing qualities
   - the associated side effects. *(5 marks)*

3. An ergogenic aid is any substance that enhances performance. Critically evaluate the use of the following as aids and, using examples, identify the type of performer/s who may benefit from their use:
   - the use of dietary manipulation
   - pre-competition meals
   - post competition meals. *(20 marks)*

See page 309 for answers

CHAPTER 20

Improvement of effective performance and the critical evaluation of practical activities in Physical Education

CHAPTER OVERVIEW

By the end of this chapter you should have knowledge and understanding of:

- which practical activity you can choose to be assessed in
- the roles you can choose to be assessed in
- how you will be assessed in each of these roles
- the terms 'standardisation' and 'moderation'
- how you can improve your performance, coaching or officiating.

INTRODUCTION

In this chapter we will explore the opportunities that you have within Advanced level PE to be assessed in practical activities and in different roles, as well as ways in which you can improve the marks you can achieve.

At A2 level you will be assessed in your activity in the 'normal' environment in which the activity takes place.

You will find useful information in this chapter, but to improve your practical performance there is no substitute for actual practice which can be performed both in and outside your centre.

THE IMPROVEMENT OF EFFECTIVE PERFORMANCE AND THE CRITICAL EVALUATION OF PRACTICAL ACTIVITIES IN PHYSICAL EDUCATION

Module content

Candidates are assessed in one of three pathways:

1. Performance in one activity.
2. Coaching/Leading in one activity.
3. Officiating in one activity.

In additon, candidates are assessed by oral response in evaluation, appreciation and the improvement of performance.

In performing, coaching/leading and officiating you will be assessed out of 40 marks. Evaluating and planning for improvement response is assessed out of 20 marks. This enables you to score a maximum of 60 marks in this coursework unit. This is 30 per cent of your A2 marks.

Officiating is only available in:

- Association football
- Basketball
- Field hockey
- Gaelic football
- Hurling
- Netball
- Rugby League
- Rugby Union
- Handball
- Hurling

> **Need to know more?** More information on the OCR website can be found in 'Teacher Support – Coursework Guidance'.

Choice of activities

You must select one of the two activities in which you were assessed at AS for your A2 assessment. You can, however, change the role in which you are assessed, for example if you have been assessed coaching netball at AS you can be assessed performing netball at A2.

EXAM TIP

Remember that you have to select an activity in which you were assessed at AS.

KEY TERMS

Moderation – The process by which OCR ensures that all candidates have been fairly and accurately assessed. If selected to attend it is compulsory.

EXAM TIP

If you are selected to attend moderation make sure that you can perform at the standard you were assessed at. You should ensure that you can perform well in terms of skills and fitness.

Assessment

Your teacher will assess you throughout your practical activity course rather than during just one assessment session towards the end of the course. This will enable more accurate assessment and ensure that if you are injured there will be marks on which to base your assessment.

The final assessed marks have to be sent to the exam board by 31 March. You will probably be videoed doing your practical activity. This is to provide OCR with evidence of your performance.

Standardisation

- The teachers in your centre consult with each other to check that activities are all assessed at the same standard.
- Standardisation is particularly important for activities which cannot be done in your centre and are taught by coaches based at clubs.
- In cases such as these, the PE teacher responsible for A-level will liaise with the coach to ensure that they are aware of what you need to do in your activity. This teacher will assess you with the help and advice of the coach.

Moderation

- Between Easter and late May, some students in your centre will be chosen to perform their practical activities alongside students from other centres in your area at a **moderation**.
- A moderator from the exam board will look at all these performances to check they have been assessed correctly and that marks awarded by different centres are all at the same level.
- The moderator knows the correct levels and standards of performance and ensures that all candidates have been treated fairly.
- Moderation is part of the examination process so if the moderator asks you to attend the moderation you must do so.

1. PERFORMING AN ACTIVITY

You can be assessed in performing a practical activity.

What are the assessment criteria?

There are several key areas that your teacher will be looking at:

- level of acquired and developed skills
- selection and application of advanced techniques
- use of appropriate advanced strategies
- level of overall performance
- level of physical and mental fitness
- level of physical endeavour, sportsmanship and flair
- understanding and application of rules/regulations
- level of representation.

Your teacher will use these criteria to put you into one of five bands (33–40; 25–32; 17–24; 9–16; 0–8) before he or she finally decides the exact mark to give you out of 40.

The OCR specification indicates that the focus of your activities will be on the 'the selection, application and improved performance of skills in an open environment'. These skills will be performed in the situation in which the activity normally takes place.

Preparation	• Try to get someone to video one of your performances so that you can analyse it yourself, probably with the help of your teacher or coach. • This analysis should identify the good aspects of your performance together with the weaknesses. It should cover skills, tactics and fitness. • It will enable you to structure an action plan to improve your performance.

Physical fitness	• This is an important aspect in any practical activity and will be a key part of your preparation for your performance activity.
	• Different activities have different fitness requirements and through your training, and by talking to your teacher/coach, you should be able to identify which of the four main fitness components below are important in your activity.
	  o strength
	  o speed
	  o stamina
	  o suppleness
	• You will be able to use your knowledge from your physiology studies to help you appreciate how you can improve your fitness.
	• You will be able to use fitness tests to measure your fitness and any improvement.
	• If you can increase your levels of fitness in the relevant components then you will undoubtedly improve the standard of your performance and therefore your marks.

Mental fitness	You should work on improving the following aspects of your performance: • using tactics, strategies or compostional ideas • concentration and ability to focus on the important aspects • being at your optimum level of arousal – 'in the zone' • being confident in your performance • enjoying your performance!
Improving the quality and range of your skills	You can achieve a wide range of skills and a high level of performance by practising, developing and perfecting your skills. Your knowledge of acquiring movement skills will help you to plan the focus and structure of your practices. • First, consult the coaching manuals to identify both the basic and advanced skills that are required for your activity and the appropriate practices to develop them. • Your teachers and coaches are valuable sources of information. They will identify the coaching points you will need to concentrate on in each of the skills. • This information is essential for you to have, and to remember, as you will need it for your evaluating, appreciation and the improvement of performance response. • Valuable additional and specific information can be found in coaching books which are normally published by the governing or organising body. Consult these for ideas and information on improving your performance.
Developing your skills	• You should start your learning by practising each skill in its simplest form. • The practice situation should allow you to concentrate on the coaching points and getting the skill right. • Once you have mastered this simple skill, make the practice a little more difficult and bring in further coaching points. • As the skill practices get more difficult they should also get more 'open', bringing in more decision making and opposition.
Feedback from your teachers and coaches	• A critical part of the practice of skills is feedback. It is important that you receive this from your teacher and coach, listen to and act upon it. This will improve the quality and rate of your learning. • Progressive practices will not only help you to improve your basic skills but also to learn advanced skills.

Table 1 How to improve your performance

How can I improve my practical activity performances?

You should now be aware of how and when you will be assessed as well as the focus for your assessment. This will help you to plan how to use your time to improve your performances in your practical activities and increase the marks you are awarded.

It is useful if you identify the skills you need to develop and organise them into groups, these being:

- preparation/organisation
- physical and mental fitness
- improving the quality and range of your skills
- feedback from your teachers and coaches.

Analysing skills

You should also refer to OCR's coursework guidance booklet, which identifies the movement

> **EXAM TIP**
>
> You should work on improving the quality and range of your basic and advanced skills. Know the coaching points and progressive practices to develop the skills of your activity.

phases through which the skills will be analysed for assessment purposes. These phases may also help you in improving and extending your range of skills.

Structuring and implementing your practices

- Your skill practices can be done in a variety of ways but it is unlikely that there will be enough time in your lessons for you to perfect your skills.
- You must therefore look for additional opportunities to practise.
- Within your centre there will be clubs and teams which will offer valuable opportunities to improve your skills.
- Other opportunities may be found by joining a local club where you will receive coaching and performing experience.
- It is important that you and your teacher talk to the coaches to make them aware of exactly what you have to do in your practical activity and how you will be assessed.

> **EXAM TIP**
>
> Make sure that you join a club for your performance activity in order that you can practise and improve. You will need this time and practise in addition to any that you get as part of your course if you are to get good marks in your coursework.

2. COACHING/LEADING AN ACTIVITY

The OCR specification indicates that the focus of the assessment of your coaching/leading is on a range of applied and acquired skills, abilities and qualities. These skills will be assessed while you lead safe, purposeful and enjoyable activities. A suitable arena for these activities could be with secondary school pupils or youth groups.

- You may, within your centre, undertake the British Sports Trust Higher Sports Leader's Award. Successfully completing this award may allow you to develop many of the skills on which your assessment will be based.
- Alternatively you could undertake a Governing/Organising Body coaching/ Leading award.

As with your performance you will need to practise your coaching/leading if you are to improve. You will also need someone to observe you and give you feedback on your performances.

There may be opportunities for practice created by your centre, but you may have to seek opportunities with local clubs or with your local sports development officer.

What are the assessment criteria?

The focus of your assessments will be on:

- ability to apply coaching/leading skills in delivering sessions
- organisational and planning skills
- use of a range of coaching/leading strategies
- overall performance in coaching/leading
- awareness of health and safety
- implementation of risk assessments
- awareness of child protection
- awareness of the fitness and health benefits of the activity

- organisational skills in planning and delivering sessions
- knowledge of the rules/regulations of the activity
- evaluative skills.

Your teacher will use these criteria to put you into one of five bands (33–40; 25–32; 17–24; 9–16; 0–8) before he or she finally decides the exact mark to give you out of 40.

Producing evidence for your assessment

In order to produce evidence for your assessment you will have to keep a comprehensive log which contains the following detailed information:

- record of coaching/leading over 12 months
- scheme of work with ten hours of session plans and evaluations
- video record of 40 minutes coaching/leading
- details of health and safety issues and risk assessments
- details of child protection procedures and evidence of CRB clearance
- evidence of first aid qualification
- details of health and fitness benefits of the activity.

EXAM TIP

You will need to complete the log as you do your coaching, particularly in keeping the record of your coaching sessions and their evaluations. You should not leave it to the end, near the final date for the submission of assessments, before you put your log together.

▶ **Need to know more?** For more information on the assessment criteria descriptors, access the OCR website – Teachers' Support: Coursework Guidance

The level of success of their basic and advanced skills together with their strategic awareness will be based on:

- planning and organisation
- delivery
- evaluation and reflection
- technical knowledge
- production of a detailed log.

How can I improve my coaching/leading?

You should now be aware of how and when you will be assessed, as well as the focus for your assessment. This will help you plan how you should use your time to practise and improve your coaching/leading and thereby improve the marks you are awarded.

It is useful if you identify the skills you need to develop and organise them into groups, these being:

- planning/organisation
- delivery
- evaluative
- technical knowledge.

Planning and organisational skills

- These mainly concern things that you will do before your sessions and help to ensure that your sessions have a good chance of being safe, enjoyable and successful:
- produce a scheme of work - what you plan to do; aims; how you are going to achieve those aims; how you are going to evaluate those aims.
- facilities – suitability; availability; booking; cost; safety; accessibility; rules of usage
- equipment - availability; suitability; quality; quantity; storage; access; maintenance; distribution in sessions
- participants – numbers; age; gender; ability; experience
- consider health and safety issues - first aid availability; emergency procedures
- completing risk assessments - what are the possible hazards?
- child protection details.

EXAM TIP

You need to ensure that you produce a detailed plan for each of your sessions.

Delivery

When focusing on your delivery you should think about:

- your appearance, which should be clean, neat, tidy and set an example
- your 'presence' and personality
- giving clear simple instructions
- giving good clear, correct demonstrations

- how you are going to control the group, for example with a whistle
- encouraging, motivating and praising participants
- being enthusiastic and positive
- variation in the tone of your voice
- building a positive relationship with the participants
- treating all participants equally and fairly
- including all participants
- timekeeping, ensuring that you keep to your planned timings.

Evaluation

During and after your session you will need to apply your evaluative skills. You will need to identify the strengths and weaknesses of:

- the participants' performances
- your own performance
- the session itself.

These evaluations enable you to decide what is good about a performance, what is weak and what needs to be improved. It is important that you do the session evaluation as soon as possible after your session so that things are fresh in your mind.

Technical knowledge

Another area of skills that you need to concentrate on is your technical knowledge of the activity you coach/lead. You will need to know:

- the correct technical models for the skills of the activity
- the phases they break down into
- the coaching points
- the progressive practices to develop them
- tactics/compositional ideas

You can learn these from the sessions you take part in as part of your A-level Physical Education course, or you can find them in the coaching manuals which most governing bodies produce.

EXAM TIP

Watching other coaches/leaders is a good way of improving your own coaching/leading. Observe how they approach situations and see the practices they use for different skills. Use the good parts of these sessions in your own coaching and avoid the mistakes that you see them make!

3. OFFICIATING AN ACTIVITY

Candidates are assessed in their ability to officiate in safe purposeful activities, whilst exhibiting responsibility, control and confidence.

The level of success of their basic and advanced skills together with their strategic awareness will be based on:

- planning and organisation
- officiating
- evaluation and reflection
- technical knowledge
- production of a detailed log.

What are the assessment criteria?

The focus of your assessment will be on your:

- ability to apply your officiating skills in sessions
- organisational and planning skills
- use of a range of officiating strategies
- overall performance in officiating
- awareness of health and safety
- implementation of risk assessments
- awareness of child protection procedures
- knowledge of the rules and regulations/ conventions of the activity
- evaluative skills
- awareness of the fitness and health benefits of the activity.

Your teacher will use these criteria to put you into one of five bands (33–40; 25–32; 17–24; 9–16; 0–8) before he or she finally decides the exact mark to give you out of 40.

Practice

- You will need to practise your officiating if you are to improve.
- You will also need someone to observe you to give you feedback as to what you have done well and areas you need to improve on.
- While there may be opportunities for practice in your centre, you may have to seek opportunities for practice in your local clubs or through your local sports development officer.

Producing evidence for your assessment

You will need to keep a detailed log which contains evidence for your assessment. The log needs the following detailed information:

- record of officiating over twelve months
- four evaluated sessions by qualified assessors

- evidence of risk assessments
- video record of 40 minutes officiating
- details of health and safety issues
- details of child protection procedures
- details of health & safety benefits of the activity.

You should complete your log as you officiate rather than leaving it until your final assessment. It is far easier to put together information relating to your officiating sessions as you do them than to wait until your log is due to be assessed by your teacher.

EXAM TIP

Put your evidence log together as you do your officiating sessions rather than leaving it to the submission date. Make sure it has all the detail required.

How can I improve my officiating skills?

You should now be aware of how and when you will be assessed as well as the focus of your assessment. This understanding will help you plan how you should use your time to practise and improve your officiating and therefore increase the marks you get in your assessment.

It is useful if you identify the skills you need to develop and organise them into groups, these being:

- planning and organisation
- officiating
- evaluative
- technical knowledge.

Planning and organisation skills

You will need to complete your planning and organising prior to your officiating sessions in order to officiate successfully. You should develop routines that you go through prior to officiating. The areas you are looking at are as follows:

- knowledge of participants
- knowledge of rules of the competition
- knowledge of venue/facility
- health and safety
- risk assessment
- child protection
- preparation of equipment.

Officiating

In officiating your sessions, you will need to:

- be decisive
- communicate your decisions to participants
- be fair and consistent
- be in control
- keep up with play be in the right position
- work with other officials who are involved.

Evaluation

Once you have officiated your session you will need to evaluate your performance. You will need to identify the strengths and weaknesses of your performance in terms of:

- planning and organisation
- officiating
- technical knowledge.

Technical Knowledge

When you are officiating you will need to:

- have an excellent, up to date knowledge of the rules
- be physically fit enough to keep up with play throughout the whole session.

EXAM TIP

Get an up-to-date copy of your activity's rules and regulations from the governing body.

CHECK

If you are satisfied with your knowledge and understanding, tick off the sections that you have revised so far. If you are not satisfied then revisit those sections and refer to the pages in the *Need to know more?* features:

- ☐ Identify which practical activity you can choose to be assessed in.
- ☐ Outline the roles you can choose to be assessed in.
- ☐ Describe how you will be assessed in each of these roles.
- ☐ Explain the terms 'standardisation' and 'moderation'.
- ☐ Identify how you can improve your performance, coaching or officiating.

TRUE OR FALSE?

1. I can be assessed in any approved activity at A2.
2. If I was assessed performing football at AS then I can only be assessed performing football at A2.
3. I can be assessed officiating in any approved activity.
4. I can be assessed coaching any approved activity.
5. In performing, coaching or officiating I will be assessed out of 40 marks.
6. I will need to be assessed by 31 May.
7. If I am assessed in coaching or officiating I need to produce a log.
8. If I am assessed in performing I do not need to produce a log.
9. Logs are not really important.
10. If I don't want to go to a moderation, I don't have to.

See page 313 for answers.

CHAPTER 21

Evaluation and appreciation of performance

CHAPTER OVERVIEW

By the end of this chapter you should have knowledge and understanding of:
- the evaluation, appreciation and improvement of performance aspect of your assessment
- how to structure your oral response
- how to successfully complete your response
- how you will be assessed
- how you can improve your evaluation and appreciation of performance.

Introduction

Candidates are assessed in their ability to:

- evaluate a performance
- create a viable action plan to improve that performance
- support evaluative and appreciative comments and their strategy with the application of relevant knowledge.

This element of your practical assessment is part of your synoptic assessment and represents 10 per cent of your A2 mark. In your response you are expected to apply relevant theoretical concepts to the performance you are observing. The focus will be a fellow student's performance of the activity even if you have been assessed coaching/leading or officiating.

WHAT DO I HAVE TO DO IN MY EVALUATION AND APPRECIATION OF PERFORMANCE?

You will observe a fellow student's performance in the activity in which you have been assessed. You will:

- make an oral response
- make notes as you observe the performance (but cannot refer to pre-prepared notes)
- observe and immediately respond (it must be a continuous process).

The response should cover the following areas:

1. Describe the strengths of the performance in relation to:
   - skills,
   - tactics and strategies/compositional ideas
   - fitness.

2. Describe the weaknesses of the performance in relation to:
   - skills
   - tactics and strategies/compositional ideas,
   - fitness.

3. Prioritise a major weakness of the performance needing improvement and create a detailed action plan for the major fault identified to include:
   - detailed coaching points
   - detailed progressive practices
   - timescale.

4. Justify evaluative comments and the action plan by applying relevant theoretical knowledge from:
   - physiology
   - psychology
   - socio-cultural disciplines.

You should therefore have a clear structure to their response:

- describe strengths and weaknesses
- create a viable action plan – coaching points. progressive practices, timescale

- apply relevant physiological knowledge to support their evaluative comments and their action plan
- apply relevant psychological knowledge to support their evaluative comments and their action plan
- apply relevant socio-cultural knowledge to support their evaluative comments and their action plan.

How do I do this?

You will do this by talking to your teacher.

Evaluation

You have already experienced the process of evaluation when you identified the strengths and weaknesses of a performance in your oral response at AS. This time you are going to carry out the same process but also apply relevant theory to support your evaluative comments and your action plan. You are going to identify what is:

- good about the performance – the strengths
- poor about the performance – the weaknesses.

As you did in your AS response, you must focus on the following areas:

- skills
- tactics/strategies/compositional ideas
- fitness.

To help you do this you may refer to the phases that are used to analyse the activity and its skills (refer to the OCR's Teacher Support – Coursework Guidance booklet).

Action planning

Initially you have to identify the major weaknesses you have observed in your evaluation and select one of these to be the focus of your action plan. This should be one that you think is important to improve first. Having selected the focus, your action plan should have the following:

- a clear realistic goal – improving the major weakness you have identified
- a timescale
- a method for achieving the goal – detailed coaching points and detailed practices together with a timescale.

Apply theory

This involves using relevant theoretical concepts to support and justify your evaluation and action plan. This should include concepts from the three main theory areas:

- anatomical and physiological aspects
- psychological aspects
- socio-cultural aspects

Structure of your response

You now have a clear structure or plan of what it is that you have to do. This can be identified as follows:

- Accurately identify and describe the major strengths of the performance.
- Accurately identify and describe the major weaknesses of the performance.
- Prioritise the major weaknesses and select one to focus on.
- Construct a viable action plan to remedy this major weakness.
- Apply relevant theory from physiological, psychological, socio-cultural aspects to support and justify the evaluation and action plan.

Need to know more? For more information on the oral response see Chapter 21, pages 520-529, in the OCR A2 PE Student Book

HOW CAN I IMPROVE MY EVALUATION AND APPRECIATION OF PERFORMANCE?

Like your practical performance, this aspect of your assessment is a skill. To improve it you need to practise it and receive feedback. Like other skills, it can be broken down into parts for you to practise.

Analytical phases

It is helpful to know the movement phases that are used to analyse the activity. If you know these phases and their coaching points for the skills of your activity, they will help you to identify what is good about the performance and what aspects are poor.

> **Need to know more?** For more information on the movement phases that are used to analyse the activity can be found in OCR's Teacher Support – Coursework Guidance, which are found on the OCR website.

Identification and description of strengths

Start by splitting the activity into the analytical movement phases and identifying strengths in each of these phases. You must focus on the following three aspects:

- skills
- tactics and strategies/compositional ideas
- fitness.

You are going to talk about the positive aspects of the performance as detailed in Table 1 below.

Skills	• These skills will be performed under pressure.
	• You must be aware of the 'technical' models to which you are comparing the performance you are observing; they can be found in the relevant governing or organising body coaching manuals.
	• Knowledge of how the skill should be performed enables you to judge how good it is and to justify your evaluation by identifying why it is good.
	• You will also use this knowledge when you are identifying weaknesses and constructing your action plan.
	• You will have to describe the coaching points you are going to give to the performer in your action plan; these will come from the technical model.
	• You may use analytical phases to help you, e.g. if you are observing a swimming stroke you would use the analytical phases of: body position, arm action, leg action, breathing, overall efficiency.
Tactics and strategies/ compositional ideas	• You will need to have a good understanding of the major tactics and strategies used in the activity to be able to evaluate the performer you are observing.
	• This understanding will be gained from your own involvement in the activity but should be further improved by watching others perform your activity as well as reading the appropriate coaching manuals and talking to coaches.
	• You will be comparing the performer you are looking at to what you know they should be doing. This will enable you to identify what they are doing correctly.
	• If the performer is part of a team, you will probably want to comment on the team's effective use of strategies as well as the individual's contribution.
	• Tactics may include the formations that teams adopt and an individual player's role in that formation; for example, how players defend. It could also include how a player copes with their own weakness or how they adapt their play to focus on opponents' weaknesses. In net/wall games it may be about the player utilising their strengths and manoeuvring their opponent to pressurise weaknesses.

continued

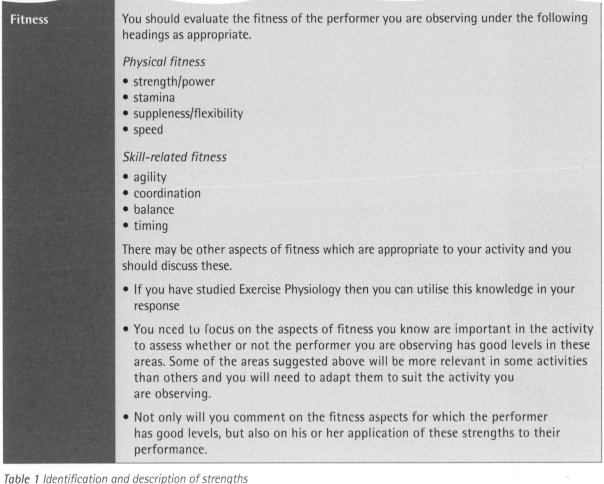

Fitness	You should evaluate the fitness of the performer you are observing under the following headings as appropriate.

Physical fitness
- strength/power
- stamina
- suppleness/flexibility
- speed

Skill-related fitness
- agility
- coordination
- balance
- timing

There may be other aspects of fitness which are appropriate to your activity and you should discuss these.

- If you have studied Exercise Physiology then you can utilise this knowledge in your response

- You need to focus on the aspects of fitness you know are important in the activity to assess whether or not the performer you are observing has good levels in these areas. Some of the areas suggested above will be more relevant in some activities than others and you will need to adapt them to suit the activity you are observing.

- Not only will you comment on the fitness aspects for which the performer has good levels, but also on his or her application of these strengths to their performance.

Table 1 Identification and description of strengths

Identification and description of weaknesses

- Start by splitting the activity into the analytical movement phases and identifying weaknesses in each of these phases.

- This aspect will follow the same structure as the identification of strengths. You are identifying major weaknesses and those for which you can construct a viable action plan.

- You do not want to be too negative by identifying every small weakness, particularly those that do not significantly affect the performance.

- You must also place the weaknesses you identify in a rank order (prioritise) to show which you consider to be the most important for you to rectify.

- The areas to focus on should be the same as those looked at when identifying strengths:
  - skills
  - tactics and strategies/compositional ideas
  - fitness.

It should have become apparent to you by now that in identifying strengths and weaknesses you are using the same information to determine both aspects. You should, however, ensure that you identify the strengths before the weaknesses, as it is easy to overlook them!

Skills	• Focus on the skills which, when under pressure, the performer either executes poorly or chooses not to use at all.
	• You will be able to identify those performed poorly by comparing them to the correct technical models and the coaching points as well as the level of success.
	• When under pressure some performers will be very inconsistent in some aspects of their skill production.
	• When under pressure do they choose not to perform advanced skills indicating they are unsure or lack confidence in them?
Tactics and strategies/ compositional ideas	• These will vary a great deal from activity to activity.
	• They will focus on attempting to outwit the opposition or the environment.
	• In individual activities, tactics and strategies will be different, particularly those activities which are not games-based. They might involve the order in which skills are placed in a sequence to ensure that the skills are performed successfully.
	• In a group activity tactics and strategies could involve capitalising on each individual's strengths and teamwork.
	• Compare what your performer does against what you know to be good tactics and strategies for that situation. This may be focused on the individual you are observing or the team in general.
Fitness	• Using the areas of fitness you have determined are important for the activity, identify those areas in which, in your opinion, the performer has weaknesses or in which you consider he or she could perform better by having increased levels of fitness.
	• Remember that you will only be observing the performer for approximately ten minutes, and therefore you may find it difficult to identify weaknesses in some aspects of fitness, such as stamina.

Table 2 Identification and description of weaknesses

EXAM TIP

Ensure that you cover skills, tactics and strategies/choreographic and compositional ideas in both strengths and weaknesses, not only identifying them but explaining why they are strong or weak.

Prioritise the major weaknesses

You will need to identify what you consider to be the major weaknesses that you have recognised in your evaluation of skills, tactics/compositional ideas and fitness.

Construct a viable action plan to improve a major weakness

Select one of the major weaknesses you have identified and create a plan to remedy it, thereby improving the performance as a whole. Your action plan has to include the following aspects:

• clear, achievable, realistic goal or goals
• timescale
• method for achieving the goals – detailed coaching points and detailed practices.

These must be covered in detail in your **action plan**.

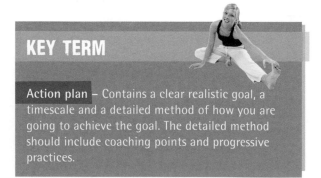

KEY TERM

Action plan – Contains a clear realistic goal, a timescale and a detailed method of how you are going to achieve the goal. The detailed method should include coaching points and progressive practices.

Set a clear, realistic goal

• The goals you set will be to remedy a major fault you have identified and thereby improve the performance.

- All you have to do is select one of the major faults you have identified and which you think is important to be rectified first.
- You may, in addition, identify more specific goals, for example to achieve a 75 per cent success rate for first serves in tennis if you have identified a major fault as being the first serve.
- When choosing the fault you should ensure you are able to suggest ways in which you will be able to remedy it; that is, to construct an action plan. Sometimes it is easier to focus on weaknesses within a skill or fitness area, as these are easier for creating action plans.

Remember that your action plan must:

- relate to the person you have observed
- be intended to help improve one of the major faults you have observed in their performance

If your action plan is for:

- A skill: it must include coaching points and progressive practices to develop the skill.
- An aspect of fitness: it should include details for the regimes you will use to improve it, including coaching points and progression.

KEY TERM

Progressive practices – A practice that starts with a skill in its simplest, closed situation and goes through a series of stages to practice the same skill in its natural, open situation.

Timescale

- You need to identify how long your action plan is designed to take, how often the practices or training will be and so on.
- Different action plans will have different timescales. Those designed to develop aspects of fitness will usually be over a longer period than those to develop skills.
- You should give an indication of the overall length of the action plan – that is, the number of weeks or months together with the frequency of the sessions (for example, number of times a week).
- You should also include the length of each of the sessions.

Method for achieving the goals

- Detail the practices and drills you will suggest that the performer does to remedy the weakness in detail. This should include the coaching points for the skills you wish to be improved as well as each of the practices you will use.
- As in your AS oral response, the practices you identify should show progression going from simple to complex and closed to open.
- Take care to be realistic, starting the practices at a level that is appropriate to the performer you are observing.
- Demonstrate your knowledge of training by identifying exactly the aspects of fitness you are going to focus on together with their relevance and application in the activity.
- Describe in detail the fitness regimes you would prescribe to improve these aspects of fitness, including coaching points where relevant.
- You might also include details of tests you would apply to see if they have improved.

Application of theoretical knowledge

You will need to explain, or justify, your evaluative comments and your action plan by applying relevant theory from the physiological, psychological and socio-cultural subject areas.

This is not as difficult as it first appears, but needs to be practised. You should:

- Identify theory areas from each of the three subject areas which you can apply to your activity.
- Start off with a small list and see how you can apply these to your activity.
- You could begin with the points identified in Table 3. Write these down and use your list to remind you when you practise.
- Once you are able to apply these theory areas to your activity, you should add to the list, gradually building up the theory you are able to apply to support your observations.
- You should then identify other theory areas from your course notes.
- By doing this you will build up your 'bank' of theory areas you know how to apply.

Physiological	• What are the important joints and their movements involved in the activity/skill?
	• What are the major muscles/important muscle groups involved?
	• What are the physical fitness requirements of the activity?
	• What are the energy systems used in the activity?
	• What are the health benefits of the activity?
Psychological	• Classification of the skills involved – is the activity gross/fine, closed/open and so on?
	• Identification of the underpinning abilities – which are important to the activity/skill?
	• Information-processing demands – is there a lot of interpretation of information and are there decisions to be made?
	• What types of practices and guidance are used in your action plan?
Socio-cultural	• What is the performer's position on the performance pyramid; what level is the performer at?
	• Is there local support for the activity from the governing or organising body? What facilities or opportunities are there for those involved in the activity?
	• What is the role of the media in the activity – is there good coverage of the activity? Are there role models to relate to?

Table 3 *Application of theoretical knowledge*

Need to know more? For more information on the application of relevant theory see Chapter 21, pages 526–527, in the OCR A2 PE Student Book

Need to know more? For more information on or examples of other theory areas that are suggested as being relevant to apply to your observations, refer to OCR's Teacher Support – Coursework Guidance booklet. Remember that they are only suggestions, so you should not think that you will be able or required to apply them all!

EXAM TIP

- When you are being assessed in your Evaluation and Appreciation of Performance, you may not be able to apply all the theory areas you have learned and practised in the performance you are observing, as they may not be relevant to that particular performance. You should aim at applying three or four concepts from each of the three theory areas, but remember that they must be relevant to the evaluation and action plan of the performance you have observed.
- In the socio-cultural area you may be able to use information from your AS oral response in relation to opportunities for participation and progression in the activity. Obviously it must be the same activity as you are observing at A2!
- You may decide to apply relevant theory as you go through your response, i.e. as you describe strengths and weaknesses and within your action plan. This is a good method but equally you may decide to evaluate and action plan and then apply theory. This is just as acceptable and effective.
- You should ensure that the theory you talk about is relevant to and applied to the performance you have observed.
- You may, when you are assessed, want to use your clip board and blank paper to write down your list of theory topics that you will try to apply to the performance you observe.

Practising your evaluation and planning for improvement

You should practise your Evaluation and Appreciation of Performance as many times as you can. Like any skill, you should break it down to its simplest form, practise this, then move on to practise the next stage until you have mastered the complete skill. At each stage you should add that stage on to those you have already mastered.

The following stages would be appropriate for you to practise.

- Identifying the strengths in each of the movement phases.
- Identifying the weaknesses in each of the movement phases.
- Prioritise the major weaknesses.
- Select one major weakness and create a viable action plan to remedy it and improve the performance.
- Applying two to three concepts from each of the three theoretical areas.
- Increasing the number of concepts applied.

It may be that you can practise by looking at a video of the activity you are focusing on. You can also record your response on tape, so that you can listen to it and evaluate your oral response.

What will happen when I am assessed?

- Your teacher will ask you to watch one of your fellow students performing the activity. They will ask you to focus on particular aspects of the performance or particular performers.
- You will observe a performance you have not seen before. After you have watched the performance for some time, your teacher will ask you to comment on it.

- When you have started your response, you may be able to look at the performance again to refresh your memory.
- When you have observed the performance, the teacher will say something like: 'You have just observed the effective performance of Alex. Describe the strengths and weaknesses of the performance and create an action plan to improve a major weakness of the performance. You should apply your knowledge from physiology, psychology and socio-cultural areas to support your comments and action plan.'

The teacher will expect you to go through the stages already identified (as follows).

1. Identify and describe the strengths of the performance.

2. Identify and describe the weaknesses of the performance.

3. Identify the major weaknesses and select one for your action plan.

4. Create a viable action plan on which you:

   a) have clear, realistic, achievable goals
   b) identify a timescale
   c) describe the detailed coaching points you will use
   d) describe the detailed practices you will use.

5. Apply theory to support your observations from:

   e) physiological areas
   f) psychological areas
   g) socio-cultural areas.

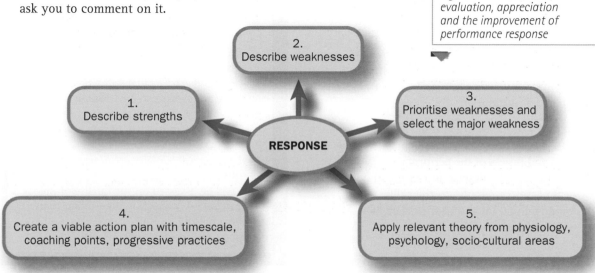

Fig 21.1 Structure of evaluation, appreciation and the improvement of performance response

- If you get stuck or miss out a stage, the teacher will probably ask questions to help direct you.
- These questions should be the type that will guide you to think about a particular stage or area, rather than needing a specific answer.
- Examples of these questions could include the following.
  - What were the good elements of the performance you have just seen?
  - What are the causes of the faults/ weaknesses?
  - If you were Alex's coach, what would you do in order to improve one of the major weaknesses which you have identified?

Remember

- This is your opportunity to tell your teacher how much you know and understand by applying it to the performance you observe.
- Take your time. Don't start to talk before you have had sufficient opportunity to observe the performance.
- Make notes and refer to them. You might forget to talk about some of the points you have seen.
- Try to apply theory throughout your response, i.e. apply theory to help explain why aspects of the performance are strong or weak, and to justify why you are using certain types of practice for particular skills, etc.

Assessment criteria

Your teacher will use the following criteria to assess you and put you into one of four bands: 16–20, 11–15, 6–10, 0–5.

- Accuracy of the description of the major strengths in relation to the skills, tactics/compositional ideas and fitness of the performance.
- Accuracy of the description of the major weaknesses in relation to the skills, tactics/compositional ideas and fitness of the performance.
- Accuracy of the prioritising of the major areas of the performance which need improvement.

- Creating a viable action plan which contains all the detailed coaching points, a range of detailed progressive practices together with a timescale.
- Justification of the evaluative comments and their action plan with the appropriate application of a range of relevant physiological, psychological and socio-cultural knowledge and concepts.

Your teacher will then give you a definite mark out of 20 within the band.

ANSWERS TO TRUE OR FALSE AND EXAM PRACTICE QUESTIONS

CHAPTER 1

Popular recreation in pre-industrial Britain

True or False?

1. True
2. True
3. False. They are associated with the lower or peasant class.
4. True
5. False. They were occasional, with simple unwritten rules and were rural.

6. True
7. False. It was a two class society, upper- and lower-class (or peasant).
8. True
9. True
10. True

Exam practice

1. Describe and explain two characteristics of popular recreation. To what extent are these characteristics evident in physical activity today? *(4 marks)*

One mark for each description with explanation (both needed). One mark for each relevant/acceptable link to today.

Characteristic	Explanation	To what extent are these characteristics evident in physical activity today?
		Accept any suitable comparative point that argues for, or against, the continued existence of the characteristic. The following examples should be acceptable for one mark.
Local	Limited transport and communications.	• Transport still affects opportunity to participate in physical activity (as part of provision).
With simple unwritten rules	Widespread illiteracy/the lack of NGBs.	• Literacy is now widespread and most sports and games have written rules. • Informal games still have made-up local rules.
Cruel/violent	Reflect the harshness of pre-industrial rural life.	• Accept any example of activities today that show cruelty/violence. • Accept reference to the fact that most activities are now 'civilised' and socially acceptable though some crowd behaviour associated with them is not.
Occasional	Due to the amount and nature of free time, based on Holy Days and annual holidays.	• Accept reference to pressures of work limiting opportunities for participation. • Continued significance of Bank Holidays etc.
Divided by class (courtly and popular)	Because Britain was a two-class society (based on the feudal system).	• Some activities today are still divisive by class (accept any suitable example such as polo).

continued

Rural	They occurred before the industrial revolution when Britain was an agricultural society.	• Britain is now mainly urbanised with many sporting and recreation opportunities in towns and cities. • Surviving ethnic sports continue (mainly in rural areas), e.g. Gloucestershire cheese rolling.
Occupational	Work often became the basis of sport, e.g. for a pedestrian race walker/ runner.	• Today it is the opposite. Excellence in sport and physical recreation gives opportunities for the elite to become professional.
Wagering	It was a chance for the poor to make money and for the rich to show their status/position in society.	• Wagering still exists (reference to betting shops).

2. Explain how two pre-industrial societal factors impacted on the characteristics of popular recreation and the extent to which your two chosen factors impact on participation and performance in physical activity today.

(4 marks)

One mark awarded for societal factor and its impact, up to a sub-mark of two. Only the first two responses are marked. Two more marks available for the extent to which societal factor/s impact on participation and performance in physical activity today.

Accept reference to factors listed below and other relevant factors that candidates may make.

Societal factor	Characteristic impacted on	Extent to which it impacts on participation and performance in physical activity today.
Seasonal time/free time on Holy Days or annual holidays	Occasional	Unemployment/shorter working week/Bank Holidays. More regular due to regular working patterns.
Pre-industrial Britain a two-class society.	Courtly/popular	Different today/middle-class influence/merging of classes in 21st century.
Rural society	Rurally located	Urbanisation means impact of physical activity, opportunity and provision.
Work often became the basis of play/sport/a living	Occupational	Sport can be a job for the elite few e.g. professional tennis players.
Opportunity for poor to make money, rich to show status.	Linked with wagering	Betting still popular/betting shops/evidence of deviance/match fixing
Lack of technology/purpose built facilities/funding.	Natural/simple	Modern sport is highly technical with technological products prevalent
Limited transport/ communications	Locally significant	Widespread, modern transport systems make travel easier.
Widespread illiteracy/impact of public schools not yet felt	Simple unwritten rules	Thorough rules by NGBs/rules updated regularly/ illiteracy does not impact on rules.
Society was harsh/brutal	Cruel/violent	Society allegedly more civilized/evidence of violence and deviance in some modern professional sports eg Rugby Union or boxing.

CHAPTER 2

Rational recreation in post-industrial Britain

True or False?

1. False. By the early nineteenth-century industrialisation was evident, however rational recreation is associated with the late, not early nineteenth-century.

2. True

3. True

4. True

5. False. For the first half of the century the new working class had very little opportunity and provision.

6. False. Rational recreation and the development of public school athleticism were parallel processes which ideally should be seen as reflections of each other.

7. False. The railways had a hugely significant impact.

8. False. Both the early closing movement and Saturday half day had a great impact on the spread of sports and recreations.

9. True. Usually class decided your status as an amateur or a professional.

10. True. Working-class women had no opportunity or provision for leisure activities. It could be argued that this is the same or different today.

Exam practice

1. Contrast *three* characteristics of popular recreation with *three* characteristics of rational recreation and explain why the change occurred. Take one societal factor and explain the extent to which it continues to impact on participation in sport and physical activity today. *(6 marks)*

One mark for each contrasting characteristic plus explanation, up to a maximum of four marks (all three items of information are needed for one mark).

Characteristic of popular recreation	Characteristic of rational recreation	Explanation of why change occurred
Local	• Regional, national or international.	• Improved transport communications
Simple unwritten rules	• Written (NGB) rules.	• Business and administrative skills • Ex-public schoolboys • Improved literacy
Cruel/violent	• Refined and respectable. • Fair play and sportsmanship.	• Middle class influence • Impact of public schools
Occasional	• Regular	• Increased and more regulated free time • Improved transport
Divided by class (courtly & popular)	• Divided by status (amateur and professional).	• Social class gender status/discrimination
Rural	• Urban or suburban.	• The industrial, agrarian and urban revolutions
Simple/natural facilities	• Purpose built facilities.	• Advances in technology
Courtly/popular	• Amateur/professional.	• Class structure and professionalism
Wagering	• Less wagering/control on gambling.	• Increased law and order

continued

2 marks maximum for the following contemporary societal factor/s:

Contemporary societal factor	Impact on participation in sport and physical activity today. (Accept any suitable/ relevant example such as those below.)
Transport and communications	• Huge impact. Urban transport systems are widespread and accessible. • Most homes now own a car (some more than one).
Business and administrative skills	• Impact of contemporary communication, e.g. email and text on organising sporting and recreational gatherings easily.
Free time	• Pressure of work may limit spare time. • Unemployment may offer spare time but limited funds.
Social class and gender discrimination	• Opportunity and provision based on class still exists, e.g. funding needed for private gym membership.
Where you live (rural/ urban)	• Quantity and type of provision is still linked to rural or urban environments, e.g. opportunity for water sports in Cornwall and other coastal areas compared to artificial inland facilities.
Modern technology	• Modern media methods and TV time devoted to sport can influence both participation (e.g. influenced by an advertising campaign, or Wimbledon coverage) and lack of participation (spectating rather than taking part).
Betting/gambling	• Still a key factor, linked mainly to national rather than local sporting events, e.g. the Grand National.

2. Describe and explain two characteristics of rational recreation. To what extent are these rational characteristics evident in physical activity today? *(4 marks)*

Need description (characteristic) and explanation (societal influence) in order to achieve each mark. Second two marks are awarded for the extent to which each chosen characteristic is evident in physical activity today.

Description of rational recreation/characteristic	Explanation of characteristic	Extent to which characteristic evident in physical activity today
Regional/national/international	Improved transport	An even greater extent today
Codification/administration	Increased literacy/business and administrative skills	An even greater extent today
Respectable with fair play	Public school and middle-class influence	This could be argued both ways
Regular	Increased free time, improved transport and communications	An even greater extent today
Exclusive/elitist	Social class and gender discrimination	This could be argued both ways
Urban/suburban	Industrial, urban and agrarian revolutions	An even greater extent today
Control of wagering/gambling	Due to increased law and order	This could be argued both ways
Purpose built facilities	Technological advancement	An even greater extent today
Amateurism/professionalism	Class structure/working class opportunities to make a living through sport	An even greater extent today

3. Contrast *three* societal factors that that impacted on popular recreation with the equivalent factors that impacted on rational recreation. Take *two* post-industrial factors and explain the extent to which each of them continues to impact on participation in sport and recreation today. *(5 marks)*

One mark for each contrast (i.e. one popular plus one rational factor = 1 mark) up to a max of three marks.

Mark first three responses only.

Two marks max for how post-industrial factors continue to impact on participation in sport and recreation today.

Socio-cultural factors influencing popular recreation	Corresponding factors influencing rational recreation	Explanation of factors continuing to impact on participation in physical activity today.
Limited transport and communications	Improved transport and communications	Provision or ownership of transport is still a key factor (give a suitable example)
Widespread illiteracy	Improved literacy	Literacy linked to income and social deprivation is a key factor (give a suitable example)
Two class society	Emergence of middle class	Class linked to income is still a key factor (give a suitable example)
Seasonal time	Machine time	Availability of spare time is still a key factor (give a suitable example)
Harsh society	More civilised society	Sportsmanship associated with rational recreation still associated with modern day participation.
Pre-industrial	Post-industrial	Provision of and access to community facilities is still a key factor (give a suitable example)
Limited law and order	Improved law and order	Reference to police and security presence in modern day sport (or other suitable/relevant example).

CHAPTER 3

Nineteenth-century public schools and their impact on the development of physical activities and young people

True or False?

1. True. They were also expanding, non-local, controlled by trustees, endowed and for gentry boys.

2. False. The Clarendon Report was published in 1864 and was an account of all aspects of public school life.

3. False – his doctorate was in theology not medicine. He was an ordained clergyman and was headmaster of Rugby School between 1828-1842.

4. True. Bullying and brutality, social control and athleticism.

5. False. Along with the technical development of games and the values they could instil in boys, the social relationships within the schools changed greatly in this 100-year period.

6. False. Teams games took a while to get organised – though recreational swimming would have taken place during stage one.

7. True.

8. True.

9. False. They had a significant influence as (for example) army officers, industrialists and teachers.

10. True.

Exam practice

1. Explain the delay in the development of athleticism in girls' public schools during stage three of athleticism. Comment on the comparative status of sport for males and females in schools today. *(5 marks)*

Maximum of four marks for explanation of delay:

- Due to the traditional role of (middle-class) women to be dainty rather than vigorous.
- Prevailing social attitudes which deemed it unladylike to be athletic.
- There was social concern about females wearing revealing clothing.
- Medics believed it to be unhealthy, or even dangerous for women to be too physically active and that it would inhibit child bearing capabilities.
- Many believed that girls would not be able to cope with over exertion, physical activity. There was a perceived physical inferiority.
- Females had lower status than males. It was not thought necessary to give girls the same opportunities as boys.
- Girls schools concentrated on other things such as music and dancing.
- There were fewer leading female reformers than in boys' schools.
- Lack of female role models.

Maximum of one mark for comments on comparative status of sport for males and females in schools today (other suitable comparative comments should be accepted):

- Generally equal status today of sport for males and females in schools.
- Some schools may still have inequality.
- Any inequality may be because less female staff who teach academic subjects are available for extra-curricular activities.
- There may be a difference in status in independent vs. state school.
- Other relevant/accurate comments on comparative status of sport today should be accepted.

2. Explain the status and organisation of a striking game other than lawn tennis in Public Schools during stage three of development. Explain why lawn tennis was more popular in society at large than in the boys' public schools at that time. *(5 marks)*

One mark for explanation and one mark for organisation.

Fives	Raquets/squash
• Accepted as a recreational game/hugely popular in public schools but failed to become national game of any repute/boys and masters would play against each other/ house competitions had high status.	• More formal/sophisticated than fives and with higher status/squash had fairly high status as a more compact and less expensive game than racquets.
• Organised with purpose built courts/different styles of court in different schools (e.g. Eton or Winchester fives).	• Highly or well organised/professional racquets coaches in many schools/purpose built courts for racquets and/or squash.

Max of three marks for explanation of popularity of lawn tennis in society:

- Tennis in society was important as an experience rather than for the development of qualities or values
- Tennis was an important vehicle for the emancipation of women, so not seen as manly or useful for developing other qualities/values
- In public schools tennis took up a large amount of space for few boys
- Games such as football or cricket demanded more physicality or manliness
- Cricket and football were already established in the schools, tennis had to fight for its place/for status
- It was a new invention and treated with some suspicion in public schools

3. Nineteenth-century public schools were mainly for *gentry boys* and were *Spartan*. Explain the impact of these *three* characteristics on the development of games in nineteenth-century public schools and the extent to which *two* of these characteristics impact on young people in schools today. *(5 marks)*

One mark for each explanation of impact of characteristics on development of games. Two marks (one mark each) for extent to which two characteristics impact on young people in schools today. (Other accurate explanation for impact on young people in schools today should be considered and credited) .

Characteristic	Impact of characteristic on the development of games in public schools
Gentry	Influential families brought status and money and influenced the types of activities brought into the schools
Boys	Great energy and enthusiasm channelled into games
Spartan	Harsh treatment and living conditions prepared boys for the rigours of competitive sport and adult life
Characteristic	**Impact of characteristic on young people in schools today**
Gentry	Less, limited or no impact in terms of activities brought to schools by upper class. *Credit should be given for reference to independent or state school provision which might be influenced by class e.g. independent school may have squash, fives or racquets courts which state schools are unlikely to have.*
Boys	It could be argued that boys' energy/enthusiasm still channelled into games and sports
Spartan	No impact today

CHAPTER 4

Case Studies

True or False?

1. False. Each case study must also be studied today with reference to participation, barriers to participation, and factors impacting on performance or excellence.

2. True. It was also important for the initial development of competitive swimming.

3. True.

4. False. Although pedestrianism was mainly local, occasional, rural and associated with wagering, cheating and match fixing were common and there was violence among the crowd. Also, early rules were established by the organisers.

5. False. The Amateur Athletics Association, set up by middle-class members, was desperate to dissociate respectable modern athletics from the old corrupted professional form. It adopted the 'exclusion clause' (1866) which banned manual workers.

6. False. The correct term was 'broken-time' payments which also lead to the split between Rugby Union and Rugby League.

7. False. There are barriers associated with opportunity, provision and esteem as well as more specific social changes such as less 'street football'.

8. False. Early cricket was quite unusual in that both classes played together.

9. True.

10. True.

Exam practice

1. Discuss the development of athletics from its early pre-industrial roots to the present day. Your answer should include pre-industrial factors; athletics in the public schools; the emergence of amateur athletics as a rational recreation, as well as factors that have helped to develop athletics in the UK today. *(20 marks)*

20-mark questions are marked with a 'levels of response' mark scheme. See page vii in the Exam Strategies section at the front of this book.

Indicative content: candidates are likely to include some of the following (other relevant points not identified below will be considered and, if deemed accepted, credited):

Pre-industrial factors:

- community events
- rural sports
- festivals
- commercial fairs and/or wakes
- reference to the views of the church
- pedestrianism – its nature status and development.

Athletics in the public schools:

- Hare and hounds and steeplechase as adapted activities.
- Athletics sports days.
- Reference to values and status of athletics in the public schools.
- Influence of Exeter College, Oxford.

The emergence of amateur athletics as a rational recreation:

- Opportunities for working class participation.
- Amateurism and professionalism.
- The exclusion clause.

Factors that have helped to develop athletics in the UK today: credit accurate inclusion of points relating to general factors linked with opportunity, provision and esteem:

- Technology, for example tracks, clothing, titanium for javelins and so on.
- Sports hall athletics: indoor athletics for young people.
- Playground athletics. Similar to above with a teacher pack for schools.
- Adequate media coverage to promote role models and to make a difference.
- Competition organisers and development officers who work for county councils and run the sports hall athletics programmes in some areas.
- Passion of individual teachers and club members.
- In September 2008, former Olympic champion Sally Gunnell launched McCain 'Track & Field', a nationwide campaign aiming to make athletics more accessible to more people.
- Sponsorship (e.g. McCain announced a sponsorship deal with UK Athletics).
- Lottery funding and prize money has meant that the elite can now be career athletes.

2. Discuss the development of public baths in late nineteenth-century Britain and how factors continue to impact on participation and performance in swimming today. *(20 marks)*

20-mark questions are marked with a 'levels of response' mark scheme. See page vii in the Exam Strategies section at the front of this book.

Indicative content: relevant points other than those below should be considered and given credit

Development of public baths in urban industrial communities

Late nineteenth–century	Impact today
• Rivers were polluted/unsuitable for washing	• Blue flags or cleaner beaches
• Local authorities built public baths as washing facilities	• Swimming as part of healthy balanced lifestyle to combat obesity
• Cholera/disease reduced	• Most towns have swimming facilities
• Towns grew due to industrialisation	• Fashionable health spas.
• Public baths safer than rivers	• Swimming part of National Curriculum
• Working class did not have washing facilities/bathrooms at home	• Very limited or no impact today
• Plunge baths for recreation/ middle class influence	• Impact of NGB awards/initiatives/campaigns for both participation and performance
• ASA established (1884)/clubs and galas	• Some towns have prestigious facilities which draw people from surrounding areas
• Baths reflected status of town	• Government aims for free swimming for all
	• Opportunity – money/ability/time, choice/access/quite expensive family activity/(govt supported) free swimming (for under 16s and over 60s)
	• Provision –availability of facilities/coaching/courses/transport/ health clubs/limited school provision
	• Cultural factors, including ethnicity
	• Role models/impact of Olympic Games (e.g. Rebecca Adlington)
	• Technology - hoists for disabled/teaching aids/leisure pools/ wave machines
	• Status of ante-natal swimming/aqua aerobics/parent and child sessions
	• Increasing popularity of triathlon

CHAPTER 5

Drill, physical training and Physical Education in state schools

True or False?

1. True.
2. True.
3. False. It was delivered by Army NCOs (non-commissioned officers).
4. False. It was brought in due to Britain's poor performance in the War, not for the loss of the war.
5. True.
6. False. Group work was encouraged.
7. True.
8. True.
9. False. The industrial action that had this effect was in the 1970s and 1980s.
10. False. You need to critically evaluate the impact of the National Curriculum which means that potential negative impact must also be considered.

Exam practice

1. Compare the objectives of the 1950s curriculum for Physical Education in State Schools with the objectives of Physical Education in Sate Schools today. *(4 marks)*

Two linked comparative points (1950s and today) needed for each mark.

The 1950s	PE in State Schools today
• Physical, social and cognitive development/holistic aims.	• Same or similar today, as well as learning, thinking and analytical skills. • Also creativity, innovation, enterprise and fair play.
• Variety of experiences.	• Same today. • Increasing emphasis on fundamental skills at lower ages.
• Enjoyment.	• Same today. • The development of healthy balanced lifestyles. • The start of lifelong involvement in physical activity.
• Personal satisfaction and sense of achievement.	• Same today.
• Increased involvement for all concerned.	• Same today.
• National standards not (so clearly) identified.	• The achievement of national standards.
• Limited - no national demands or curriculum.	• Consistent opportunity and content for all wherever they go to school via National curriculum.
• Aims of risk not (so clearly) identified.	• Helps students to manage risk and cope with difficulty.

2. Identify **two** differences between the 1902 Model Course and Physical Education in State Schools today. Explain why the Model Course was replaced and the how the 1933 course was different in terms of objectives and content. *(6 marks)*

Two marks for outlining two differences between 1902 and today (accept first two responses only). Two marks for why Model Course was replaced and up to two marks for how 1933 course was different in terms of objectives and content.

Model Course 1902	PE in State Schools today
Imposed by war office.	National Curriculum.
For fitness for military service or war/training in handling weapons.	For physical, persona, preparatory or qualitative outcomes (ref contemporary studies AS work).
For discipline.	
Trained in military drill, marching, weapons training, staves, deep breathing.	Reference national curriculum activity groupings: gymnastics, athletics, dance etc.
Centralised/in ranks/no individuality/command-response e.g. 'attention'.	Decentralised/variety of teaching styles.
Command style/taught by army NCOs	Specialist PE teachers
Explain why the Model Course was replaced ...	
Because it had been imposed by the war office.	
Teachers objected to army non-commissioned officers (NCOs) in schools and wanted PT to be their responsibility.	
Due to influence of Dr George Newman.	
Educationalists demanded a healthier approach, linked to good posture and therapeutic exercises with children being allowed to play rather than being treated as soldiers.	
Military drill with its command style was now considered unsuitable for young children.	
... and the how the 1933 course was different in terms of objectives and content.	
1933's different objectives: Physical fitness, health, therapeutic outcomes rather than military fitness; good physique stressed; holistic aims (mind and body); discipline of working class not a major objective.	
1933's different content: Athletics, gymnastics, games skills rather than military drill, static exercises, weapons training or breathing exercises; group work rather than working as an individual.	

3. Identify two possible positive and two possible negative impacts of the National Curriculum for PE in state schools today and explain the impact on sport and PE of the 1970s and 1980s teachers' industrial action.

(6 marks)

Two marks for positive impacts, and two marks for negative aspects.

Possible positive impacts of National Curriculum

- Higher standards.
- Consistent experience in all areas of country so easy transfer between schools.
- A balanced/varied PE experience increases likelihood of lifelong participation.
- Learners gain the right to learn particular things.
- Schools can adapt curriculum to suit strengths.
- Thinking, analytical or social skills developed.
- Examples of skills or values such as fair play, integrity, independence or problem solving.

Possible negative impacts of the National Curriculum

- Administrative overload.
- Lack of experience and difficulty with assessment notably by non-specialist (PE) teachers.
- Some teachers may feel constrained.
- Lack of support and training, especially for teachers at lower key stages.
- Pressure on facilities e.g. lack of tennis courts.
- Teachers may stick to what they like most e.g. avoid gymnastics if they prefer games.

Explain the impact on sport and PE of the 1970s and 1980s teachers' industrial action

Two marks for outlining the impact of industrial action.

- Increased community or club participation.
- Fewer non-specialist staff helping with extra-curricular programm.
- Impact on lifelong involvement (in physical activity).
- Reduced extra-curricular activity or reduced participation by young people in schools)/fewer weekend fixtures.

CHAPTER 6

Comparative study of the USA and the UK

True or False?

1. True	3. True	5. True	7. False	9. False
2. False	4. False	6. False	8. True	10. True

Exam practice

1. Evaluate the development of one case study sport from the UK and one from the USA. Your answer should include cultural and commercial factors. *(20 marks)*

20-mark questions are marked with a 'levels of response' mark scheme. See page vii in the Exam Strategies section at the front of this book.

Key word	UK Case Study Game	USA Case Study Game
	Cricket	**Baseball**
Cultural factors		
Historical determinants	• originated in England • associated with traditional English values and social class hierarchy • thrived in Public Schools • believed to develop character/leadership skills • County Cricket was established before the mid nineteenth century (1839) • Gentleman amateurs and professional players identified but played in the same teams • the English class system was reflected in amateur and professional status	• originated in the USA • associated with the inner city working classes • thrived in the back streets and open field sites of the city • The National Association of Baseball Players assembled during the mid nineteenth century (1858) to organise leagues. • professional players played as one group • professional leagues were formed • class system was less strict therefore professionalism was accepted
Evaluation		
The English amateur ethic would be inclined to support the concept of fair play whereas the professional approach of the USA may have fostered gamesmanship and the adoption of the Lombardian ethic in sport		

Historical determinants	• Due to the English class system, up to the mid-twentieth century, the captain of England had to be an amateur • Today, the English select a captain before selecting the national team. This is a legacy of the class system • Seen to endorse the values of the empire, it was played across it.	• The professional captained the clubs in the professional league • The game was played in the USA and endorsed the policy of Isolation
Evaluation		
Cricket helped to establish traditional British values across the Empire and this confirmed superiority over the colonies. Conversely Baseball helped to establish the new culture of the USA and give identity to a developing cosmopolitan nation		
Historical determinants	• Major Cricket-playing nations of today are part of the Commonwealth or are former Empire countries. • This rivalry has stimulated traditional contests e.g. the Ashes (England v Australia)	• USA remain the dominant force in Baseball • No other country can compete with USA
Commercialism	• Traditional rivalry has promoted twenty-first-century commercialised cricket	• The World Series promoted the commercialisation of baseball in the early twentieth century (1903)
Evaluation		
The International rivalry of cricketing nations in the 21st century may have greater potential to generate a wider commercial market than a competition confined to one country albeit the richest country in the world		
Geographical determinants.	Growth of both cricket and baseball was aided by the expansion of the railways in each country.	
Social determinants	• Discrimination has never been officially imposed • Increasing opportunities are given to minority groups	• African American players were officially excluded from major leagues until the mid twentieth-century (1947). • Increasing opportunities are given to minority groups
Values	• Cricket is fundamentally a team game but at times, allows the player to operate as an individual.	• Baseball is fundamentally a team game but there is greater opportunity to operate as an individual.
	• Discrimination on the basis of class, race, gender and ability is addressed	• Discrimination on the basis of class, race, gender and ability is addressed
Evaluation		
The powerful influence of the UK upper classes and the domination in the USA of the WASP group was possibly necessary to enhance the early development of both sports. The growth of Cricket and Baseball as 21st century commercial businesses however, depends upon inclusion of groups which previously suffered from discrimination.		
Nature of the game		
Duration	Traditional Cricket is played over an extended period e.g. Test Cricket is five days	Baseball is played in a short period of time e.g. one evening
Pace	The game in traditional Cricket may progress slowly	The game progresses quickly

Result	A draw can be a good result	There are no draws
Nature (bowler)	The ball is bowled at the batter allowing for variations of flight, movement and speed	The ball is pitched (thrown) at the batter Movement of the ball can be induced but emphasis is on speed of pitch
Nature (batter)	Batter defends and the bowler attacks	Batter attacks pitcher defends
Aggression	Opportunity for aggression can arise but the game is essentially non-violent	The game can become aggressive and violent
Playing surface	The nature of the pitch/wicket/bowling area between bowler and batter is a key factor in the game	The nature of the area between bowler and batter is not a factor in the game/the pitcher does not bounce the ball
Ritual	The game has elements of ritual e.g. lunch and tea intervals e.g. players wear caps and the captains wear blazers for the toss	The game does not display ritualistic traditions
Uniform	The traditional colour for playing kit is white	Coloured uniforms are worn
Fielding positions	There are numerous fielding positions requiring thought from captain before placement	Outfield positions are set / largely pre determined requiring little thought from captain

Evaluation

It could be argued that five day cricket is a more subtly complex game than baseball, offering greater opportunity for tactical application over an extended period. This traditional approach was previously enjoyed by the UK public. Cricket today, in order to satisfy the demand for instant entertainment is required to adopt some of the sensationalism found in USA Baseball. (This is an example of 'cultural borrowing).

Commercial factors

Golden Triangle	There is a strong link between Cricket, the media and sponsorship	There is a strong link between Baseball, the media and sponsorship
Development	A faster/shorter game has been developed to attract audiences, media and sponsorship e.g. Twenty20	Traditional Baseball has the potential to attract audiences, media and sponsorship
Entertainment	Twenty20 is a variation of traditional cricket designed to have immediate entertainment appeal	Baseball has no commercial variations/ has always had immediate entertainment appeal

Evaluation

Whilst it is good that a talented player can make a living from professional engagement it is a drawback that as sport has become an entertainment spectacle it may have lost its original values of sportsmanship.

Outcome	A winner is now produced/no draws this increases entertainment potential	A winner has always been produced/ no draws this increases entertainment potential
Uniform	Coloured clothing improves T.V. appeal/ can be sold as merchandise	Baseball players have always worn coloured/team kit/uniforms/coloured kit enhances spectacle

Audience accessibility	The shorter game can be played under floodlights to appeal to a wider audience/ game can be played in the evening so more people can watch/accessibility to audience has improved	Baseball has always been suited to floodlit presentation/accessibility to audience has always been evident
Corporate development	Corporate entertainment is now a part of the cricket scene at the highest level	Corporate entertainment has been a long standing feature of baseball
TV coverage	• Television channels have copied the USA approach of presenting sport as entertainment to attract a wider audience • Television channels can now bid to secure the exclusive 'rights' to televise cricket	• From the mid twentieth century, television displayed sport as entertainment/ a show to attract a wider audience • Television networks have always bid for the exclusive 'rights' to televise Baseball

Key word	UK Case Study Game	USA Case Study Game
	Rugby Union	**Grid Iron Football**
Cultural factors		
Historical determinants Origin	• The origins of rugby union are rooted firmly in the Public Schools and Universities of the UK. • There is also a strong tradition of the game in twentieth century Grammar schools. • The influence of the schools impacted on the senior game as many clubs were formed as 'Old Boy' associations.	• American grid iron football was adapted from English rugby football • The origin of American football lies in the American Universities /Ivy League Colleges e.g. Princeton, Colombia, Harvard and Yale. • The game was adopted by the High Schools • High Schools later impacted on the professional game.
Historical determinants Tradition	• Schools prepared players for the amateur game	• Schools prepared for the professional game/ reflected the professional game
Evaluation		
It could be argued that preparation for the amateur game encourages participation and from an education viewpoint is ethically sound. Conversely coaching players to a professional standard may instil a 'win at all cost' ethos which has no place in education		
Historical determinants – Tradition	Rugby Union fixtures were for the most part, organised on a 'friendly' basis up until the 1990s.	A tradition of league rivalry from the nineteenth century/rivalry began in the American Universities/Ivy League Colleges
Historical determinants – Social	Rugby Union was firmly rooted as a middle class game in the UK's hierarchical class structure	American Grid Iron Football was not influenced by a rigid class structure

Historical determinants – Boundaries	Played traditionally by countries in the former Empire	An American game that endorsed policy of isolation
Historical determinants – Boundaries	Endorsed values of UK society/Empire	Reflection of frontierism
Historical determinants – Amateurism	• No professional coaching during development/little coaching at club level until the 1960s. • The Rugby Football Union (RFU) resisted the move towards commercialism. • RFU strictly compliant to the ideals of amateurism until the 1990s.	• Professional coaches were employed by Universities • American Grid Iron Football readily accepted commercialisation/saw commercialism as progression/desirable • Grid Iron embraced professionalism

Evaluation		
Professionalism may have encouraged gamesmanship and corruption, however standards of play have improved.		
Geographical	The growth of both cricket and baseball was aided by the expansion of the railway in each country.	

Nature of the Game		
Physical	Both games involve an emphasis on physical contact.	
Violence	Rules restrict aggressive/violent play.	Rules encourage physical confrontation. Play tends to be aggressive.
Equipment	Limitations on padding/helmets/protection restrict physical confrontation/contact.	Pads/helmets/protection promotes physical confrontation/contact.
Substitutions	Restriction on substitutions.	Unrestricted substitutions.
Skill	Rugby Union Football emphasises skill – less impact/confrontation.	American Grid Iron Football emphasizes high impact/collision.

Evaluation		
The emphasis on collision may explain why amateur participation in American Grid Iron Football is low whilst less emphasis on impact has helped Rugby Union to enjoy relatively high participation outside the professional game		
Scoring	High scoring **does not** determine quality/ excitement/ entertainment.	High scoring **does** determine quality/ excitement/ entertainment.
Ethos	Ethos does not encourage sensationalism.	Ethos encourages sensationalism/games relies on sensationalism.
Ethos	Winning increasingly important.	Notion of zero sum/'Win at all cost' has been a feature at all levels.
Amateur traditions	Tradition of amateur clubs.	No tradition of amateur clubs.
Participation	Game played at a social level and encourages broad range of ability.	Game is for elite players.

Evaluation		
It is good that Rugby Union at amateur level can be played at a social level and by all abilities, but it may be argued that a level of elitism, such as that found in American Grid Iron Football, is essential if the game is to progress and be taken seriously as a competitive sport.		
Commercial factors		
Golden Triangle	There is a strong link between both these sports and the media and sponsorship.	
Professionalism	Players became full time professionals in the late 20th century (1995).	Tradition of professionalism.
Competition	A league competition structure was put in place and the European cup increased the commercial potential of the game.	The show piece event of American football in the 21st century is the 'Super bowl' – the championship game of the National Football League (NFL).
Laws	The laws of the game have been modified since 1995 to make the game more attractive.	Laws were designed to promote sensationalism/entertainment/spectator attraction/appeal.
Rivalry	The advent of professionalism stopped good rugby union players from signing up to the rugby league code.	Rival codes/alternative codes do not exist.
Sponsorship & business	The administration and the structure of the game has adapted to professional demands e.g. sponsorship from multi-national companies	Grid Iron has always been administered as a business/business cartel/a franchised organisation/sponsorship from multi-national companies
Business	A growing business, still behind Premiership Football League in the UK.	As a business enterprise the NFL is more lucrative than the Premiership Football League in the UK.
Location	Aspiring to be a global game e.g. World Cup.	Remains as an American game/difficult to spread.
Evaluation		
It is possible that the Rugby Union believes that commercial growth can be increased if the game is played globally. By contrast, it seems that the NFL achieved full commercial potential by operating as a business cartel in the USA.		

USA Case Study
Basketball
Cultural factors
Origin	Rooted in white educational institutions (e.g. schools and colleges), it was invented in the college system by James Naismith at Springfield YMCA Training School and was instantly successful.
Isolation	The game endorsed the USA policy of isolation
Marginalisation	Basketball (as with all of the 'big four' sports) contributed to the marginalization of UK sports

Social determinants	Played predominately by African Americans, white Americans have withdrawn (white flight).
Minority groups	The game has helped ethnic minorities to achieve the American Dream.
Social opportunity	Ethnic minorities have enjoyed increased provision, opportunity and esteem in relation to basketball.
Community participation	Midnight League organization has given Basketball inner city appeal.
Community participation	The game caters for children through Little League competition. Biddy Basketball organises Little League basketball.
Community participation	The Midnight Basketball League is funded entirely by the local business community and staffed by volunteers.
Values	The Lombardian ethos is displayed in basketball.

Nature of the game

Speed	The game moves quickly from defence to offence/end to end action.
Intensity	The small number of players makes action intense.
Time out breaks	The inclusion of 'time out' periods/tactical substitutions increases the intensity.
Sensationalism	Sensation is evident in quick passing movements and shooting.
Scoring	Scoring is high and frequent.
Outcome	• There are no drawn games/always a winner. • Basketball is reflective of a zero – sum ethos.

Commercial factors

Golden Triangle	The game is linked to the Golden Triangle.
Media	Basketball is fast, exciting and easy to understand it has therefore considerable media appeal.
Advertising	Commercial advertising fits easily into the many breaks.
Sponsorship	Sponsorship is attracted to this spectacle.
Business cartel	National Basketball Association (NBA) is organised as a business cartel.
Franchise	Basketball operates a franchise system. Basketball teams make up 13% of franchised sport in America.
Profit making	The sole purpose of professional basketball is to make profit, e.g. the Chicago Bulls now has a team value of $500 million with annual revenue of approximately $140 million.
Entertainment industry	Basketball (like all 'big four' sports) has adapted to become part of the sports entertainment industry.

USA Case Study

Ice Hockey

Cultural factors

Origin	• Ice hockey was adapted from 'ice hurly' by British soldiers serving in Canada in 1850. • Its contemporary form has origins in the Collegiate system/American Universities
Isolation	Adoption by USA (1893) endorsed the policy of isolation.
Marginalisation	Ice Hockey (as with all 'big four' sports) contributed to the marginalization of UK sports.
Frontierism	Ice Hockey reflects the frontier image.

Social opportunity	The sport is a way through which an individual can achieve the American Dream.
Minority groups	The game is not favoured by ethnic minority groups.
Community participation	• Limited community participation: game is played at professional level/College level. Some High Schools have Ice Hockey provision. • No amateur club provision/no tradition of amateur club. • Little League opportunities are not as well developed as the other three major sports
Values	The Lombardian ethos is displayed in Ice Hockey
Commercial factors	
Golden Triangle	The game is linked to the Golden Triangle
Franchise	Ice Hockey joined the 'big three' (in the late 1960s) when the 'franchise market' enabled the major Canadian teams to relocate to America.
Olympic success	Spectator appeal/popularity were stimulated by the 1980 Gold medal Olympic success.
Media	Ice Hockey is fast, exciting and easy to understand it has therefore considerable media appeal.
Advertising	Commercial advertising fits easily into the many breaks.
Sponsorship	Sponsorship is attracted to this spectacle.
Business cartel	National Hockey League (NHL) is organised as a business cartel.
Profit making	The sole purpose of professional Ice Hockey is to make profit, e.g. the Carolina Hurricanes was bought for $48 million in 1994 and has a team value of $144 million.
Entertainment industry	Ice Hockey (like all 'big four' sports) adapted to become part of the sports entertainment industry.
Commercial and Cultural factors relating to the nature of the game	
Contact	Ice Hockey is a high impact collision game.
Confrontation	The rules encourage physical confrontation
Aggression	Play tends to be aggressive/violent
Playing area	The confined playing areas increase physical contact.
Speed	The ice rink encourages high speeds
Equipment	Helmet and padding dehumanizes the players, this combined with the hockey stick as a weapon encourages aggressive play.
Sensationalism	The action is sensational/ intense.
Intensity	The inclusion of 'time out' periods and tactical substitutions increases the intensity.
Scoring	Scoring is high/frequent
Outcome	There are no drawn games

UK Case Study	
Association Football	
Cultural factors	
Origin	Association Football origins in the (nineteenth century) English Public Schools.
Origin Amateurism	The Football Association (FA) was founded in the nineteenth century (1863) as an amateur organisation.
Origin Professionalism	The FA reluctantly accepted professionalism (in 1888) with the formation of the Football League.

Origin Social	Association football in the UK became dominated by working class professional players. The growth of football as a working class game in the nineteenth-century was prolific.
Tradition	• Amateur and professional football exists under one governing body (FA). • No divide between amateurism and professionalism, (contrasting to Rugby Football e.g. Rugby Union and League)
Boundaries	A global game, but less popular in English speaking parts of the former British Empire e.g. New Zealand.
Contemporary popularity	Contemporary popularity in the UK is high (national sport of England).
Social	Played by all social groups/ popular with all classes/ethnic groups/gender/ages
Geographical (transport)	The growth of Football was aided by the expansion of the railway network (circa 1850 onwards)
Geographical (population)	Nineteenth-century development of professional Football was in densely populated industrial areas (north and midland areas of England).
Geographical (urbanisation)	Close proximity of towns/cities have generated strong rivalry/support/passion/pride/ parochialism.
Commercial factors	
Tradition	Professional Football clubs have been organised as businesses since the nineteenth century.
Wages	Traditionally, footballers earned more than the average working class wage.
Maximum wage	The abolition of the maximum wage (1961) emphasised importance of profit making.
Broadcasting 'rights'	• The Broadcasting Act (of 1990) allowed BskyB to pay Division One football clubs for the exclusive rights to televise matches. • Television channels now bid for the 'rights' to televise sport
Entertainment	Television began to market Football as entertainment.
Improved presentation	The presentation of Football on television made more exciting (e.g. more camera angles. Television presentation in the UK began to follow the USA lead)
Premiership Football	Division one football clubs then broke away from the Football League to form the Premiership.
Business reliance	Association Football had now became reliant on/orientated toward business
Status	The game is the dominant commercial sports business in the UK/the only commercial sports business in the UK to match the USA 'big four'
Golden Triangle	The game is linked to the Golden Triangle.
Merchandise	Club merchandise is sold (globally).
Contemporary popularity	English football is televised globally/clubs have global fan base.
Commercial and cultural factors relating to the nature of the game	
Skill	A game of skill rather than collision/impact/force/aggression
Rules	Rules discourage aggression/violence
Specialism	Individual skills/specialist skills are essential/diverse skills are necessary
Teamwork	Teamwork is a high priority

Positions	Positions are set, but flexible. Field positions allow creativity, innovation and individuality.
Speed	Fast, exciting and can be spontaneous. Principles are simple to understand

UK Case Study	
Rugby League	
Cultural factors	
Origin (breakaway)	In the late nineteenth century (1895), certain clubs in the North of England broke away from the Rugby Union to form the Northern Union.
Origin (purpose)	The purpose of the breakaway was to allow professionalism/break away from the amateur tradition of the Rugby Union.
Origin (Location)	The industrial north of England.
Origin (title)	The Northern Union soon adopted the name Rugby League.
Funding	The game needed to entertain spectators in order to survive and so the rules were changed to make it more entertaining for the paying spectators and to support professionalism.
Social	It is a game with strong working class origins/background/roots.
Boundaries (UK)	Strong northern roots/never fully accepted in south of England, the spread of the game is difficult to achieve.
Boundaries (Global)	Not considered as a global game. (A major Australian game but minor in New Zealand and France).
Geographical (transport)	Initially rail transport aided the development of Rugby League (RL) but post 1895 road transport was more important.
Geographical (urbanisation)	Development was helped by (relative) close proximity of industrial areas. (There were 'outposts' e.g. Barrow and Hull)
Commercial Factors	
Full time professionalism	In the late 20th century players at the top levels became full time professionals for the first time. Only the top teams could be full time professionals.
Commercial acceptance	Rugby League readily accepted the move towards commercialism/professionalism.
Image	In 1996, the image of the game changed with the advent of 'Super League'.
Commodity	The RL engaged in a policy of aggressive marketing to sell itself as a consumer product.
Golden Triangle	The game is linked to the Golden Triangle
Television	Super League became a product of BskyB television.
Season	The code changed from its traditional winter season to become a summer game to be commercially viable
Team names	Teams changed their names to increase media appeal e.g. the traditional name Bradford Northern changed to Bradford Bulls.
Rules	Rules changed to allow the game to be more entertaining e.g. the scrum became a way to restart the game and is now non-competitive.

Competitions	New competitions were designed to raise the profile of the game e.g. the Grand Final.
Franchise	For the 2009 season, Super League planned to adopt the approach taken to commercial sport in the USA by abolishing relegation and introducing a franchise system.
Expansion	The RL has a policy to expand the spectator base e.g. to expand its operations to include teams from London, Wales and France.
Commercial and cultural factors relating to the nature of the game	
Confrontation	Physical contact/physical confrontation is the major feature
Aggression	Aggression/violence is minimised by a strict application of the rules and high player respect for the referee.
Skills	Specialist skills required e.g. passing, evasion and tackling
Rules	Rules have encouraged fast, open play
Continuity	Continuous play is a major feature of the game
Substitutions	Tactical/interchangeable/rolling substitutions are intended to intensify the play
Positions	Positions are set but are flexible. Field positions allow creativity, innovation and individuality.
Teamwork	Teamwork is an essential requirement of good play

2. The UK and the USA strategies are in place to improve national fitness levels of young people by increasing participation in sport and physical activity.

Outline the opportunities in the USA that enable young people to participate in sport and physical activity.

State one similar opportunity in the UK   *(4 marks)*

*There a maximum of **three marks** available for outlining the opportunities in the USA:*

- Intra/Inter mural sports in schools and colleges.
- Improved approach to Physical Education through (PEP).
- The Amateur Athletic Union organises sports leagues and competitions.
- Little League organisation of junior sports.
- National Youth Fitness programmes (part of the Presidents Challenge).
- Midnight Leagues/ sports on inner city asphalt playgrounds e.g. basketball.
- Health club/gym club membership.

*There is only **one mark** available for the UK:*

- Inter House/ Form and School/College fixtures.
- National curriculum Physical Education.
- Sport England promotes mass participation.
- 12 National Governing Bodies provide competitions to encourage participation.
- Strong tradition of amateur club involvement.
- Outdoor activity centres/ outdoor assault course/ Duke of Edinburgh Scheme.
- Evening competitions at leisure centres/ Sport for All Centres (e.g. Five a Side).
- Health Club membership has risen sharply.

3. Compare the provision for inter-school sport in the UK and in the USA. Your comparison should include the organisation, status and ethos as well as an evaluation of provision of school sport in both countries.

(20 marks)

20-mark questions are marked with a 'levels of response' mark scheme. See page vii in the Exam Strategies section at the front of this book.

The information below details the content that should be discussed in your answer. Read through it and check it against what you have written to make sure you have covered all relevant areas:

UK organisation:

- Competitions and leagues administered by several agencies e.g. teachers, local school leagues, NGB competitions.
- Extra-curricular activities after school.
- Occurs on school premises/national curriculum facilities.
- There may be some grants or donations from former pupils but schools tend not to be reliant on them.
- Gate money is not taken and is not a source of income.
- Some sponsorship from businesses may be available but sponsorship is not widespread.
- The PE teacher often is in charge of the organisation and coaching of teams.

US organisation:

- The State High School Athletic Association (SHSAA) has branches in each state and controls Inter-mural athletic competition.
- Takes place in the evenings to attract spectators.
- Played in the High school stadium
- Alumni donation (financial support from former pupils) helps to finance teams.
- 'Gate money' is an important source of revenue.
- Heavy reliance on sponsorship and Alumni donation.
- The coach is in charge although they may operate below the status of the Athletic Director.

Evaluation

Playing in a school stadium in the USA can help prepare a player for professional sport, however some players may experience anxiety and drop out of the system. School sport in the UK doesn't attract spectators and this may encourage those of lesser ability to participate.

Large crowds in the USA bring revenue and enable Inter-mural High School sport to reflect the professional sports scene. A reliance on gate money may force the coach and players to focus on entertainment rather than the values of playing the game. Inter-school sport in the UK is not supported by fee paying crowds. This may have preserved the traditional values of school sport

Having a PE teacher in charge of sport in the UK means that important educational values can be conveyed to the pupils. Many UK PE teachers have a little knowledge of many sports but no specialism. On the other hand USA High School coaches have considerable expertise in one sport but may focus more intently on winning and compromise the educational value.

UK Status:

- Some schools and colleges have developed academies of sport but these tend to be associated with professional sports clubs.
- Physical Education is considered to be of higher status than sport.
- Some University scholarships are awarded but it is not common in UK.
- School sport is not organised to reflect the professional sports scene.
- Little media attention.
- Sport in UK schools does not aspire to become a business.

USA Status:

- USA High Schools are perceived as Centres of Sporting Excellence.
- Sport has high status and is more important than Physical Education.
- The best players are awarded scholarships from Colleges (Universities).
- School sport is a direct reflection of the professional sports scene.
- Considerable media attention.
- Sport is very expensive with media, sponsorship and large crowds. High School sport is organised as a business.

Evaluation

College scholarships in the USA allow student athletes and those lacking academic qualification to enrol by 'Special Admit Programmes'. Scholarship holders may however, be exploited and made to give excessive commitment to support the commercial sporting interests of the college. In the UK entry into University is restricted to those who are academically qualified but, as sport is not commercialised at this level, students with sporting interests are not exploited.

UK Ethos:

- Participation is considered more important than winning.
- The teacher is employed on what is usually a permanent contract.
- Sport tends to be inclusive and available to all children.

USA Ethos:

- The Lombardian 'win at all cost' ethic prevails
- The coach is employed on a temporary contract that is termed 'hire and fire'.
- Sport tends to be exclusive and elitist.

Evaluation

While the UK participation ethic may promote lifelong sporting involvement, it may not instil the hard competitive ethos seen in USA High Schools that is necessary for sporting success at professional level.

4. The UK followed the USA in making professional sport into a commercial business.

By referring to historical and social factors, explain why the commercialisation of professional sport was quicker to develop in the USA than in UK. *(6 marks)*

You will achieve a maximum of two marks for making a 'stand alone' answer on just the UK or the USA. To gain the other marks, you must make direct comparisons.

UK	USA
Nineteenth-century Public Schools:	**Ivy League Colleges:**
• The greatest influence on UK sport came from the reformed English Public School system.	• Universities had a great impact on sports development.
	• Sports e.g. Grid Iron Football were aggressive/ violent.
• Public Schools codified sports.	• Development of the 'cult of manliness'.
• Public School system instilled the notion of amateurism.	• New sports suited the developing culture of the USA.
	Organisation of nineteenth-century society:
Nineteenth-century notion of amateurism and professionalism:	• 'A New World' culture was developing which did not have clear class boundaries.
• The English 'gentleman' amateur belonged to the upper classes.	• Hereditary privilege did not exist in America.
• Amateurs did not compete for extrinsic reward – a 'win at all cost' ethos was against the spirit of sportsmanship.	• Frontierism was a factor that prevented a social class structure.
	Promotion of 'big four' sports:
	• This 'New World' culture stimulated the adoption of four major sports.
Organisation of nineteenth-century society:	• These sports were to become highly commercialised during the 20th century.
• Clearly defined class system based on hereditary privilege.	• Win at all cost was the dominant ethic.
• A hierarchical class structure.	**Marginalisation of UK sports:**
• Class determined income, lifestyle and most significantly, sporting opportunities.	• The USA began to reject UK sports.
	• Society in the USA demanded its own brand of sport, compatible with a competitive, diverse and dynamic 'New World' culture e.g. baseball rather than cricket.
Importance of Empire:	
• The power and prestige of Imperial ownership influenced traditions and class structure of UK society.	**Frontierism:**
• The Empire influenced the development of sport in the UK and across the world.	• Frontierism refers to the spirit of toughness, ruggedness and independence.
• The values of sport reflected the British class system and the English ideal.	• This spirit has been an underpinning factor that has shaped the USA society and is evident in sport today e.g. sport is termed the last frontier.
	Policy of isolation:
	• A policy of isolation separated the USA from influences and traditions of the UK and Europe.
	• Isolation is one of the major factors that shaped modern sport in the USA and made it different in terms of the nature, appearance and ethos to sports in the UK.

5. Compare the status and value of Physical Education in the UK and USA. (5 marks)

See Table 6 on page 62 for a comparison of physical education in the UK and USA.

You can achieve a maximum of one mark for making a 'stand alone' answer on the UK or the USA. All other marks require a direct comparison. Read through your answer and make sure you have made enough points and comparisons.

CHAPTER 7

Comparative study of Australia and the UK

True or False?

1. False	3. True	5. False	7. True	9. True
2. True	4. True	6. False	8. False	10. False

Exam practice

1. Critically evaluate how historical, geographical and socio-economical factors have influenced the commercial development of sport in the U.K. and Australia. *(20 marks)*

20-mark questions are marked with a 'levels of response' mark scheme. See page vi in the Exam Strategies section at the front of this book.

Historical factors:

UK:

- Origin of sport in 19th century Public Schools.
- Amateur /participation ethos was of great importance.
- Professionalism was considered ungentlemanly.
- Strict rigid class structure that determined the sports played.
- Class structure based on privilege/ ideals of Empire.
- Ruling classes perpetuated amateurism e.g. promotion of rugby union.
- Traditional approach to sports participation prevailed e.g. the Sporting Governing Bodies dictated the promotion of sport.

Australia:

- Adopted sports of the Motherland.
- Origin of sport lies in Currency (convict) Sterling (Colonial) competition.
- Winning was important to the Currency.
- Professionalism was acceptable.
- Less rigid class structure therefore class did not restrict access to sport.
- Society organised on basis of social 'melting pot' creating 'Bush Culture'.
- Egalitarianism/ 'Land of the Fair' ethos more lenient to professionalism e.g. promotion of rugby league.
- Encouragement of entrepreneurialism helped to stimulate commercial sport.

continued

UK :	Australia:
• Tradition of terrestrial television e.g. the BBC had exclusive rights to televise the most popular sports events.	• Private television channels e.g. Channel 9 promoted commercial sport.
• Murdoch established Super League (rugby league) in England (1996).	• Media business magnates e.g. Packer (cricket)/ Murdoch (rugby league) were innovators of commercial sport.
	• Packer cricket 'circus' 1977 was an early forerunner of commercial sport.

Evaluation:

It could be argued that the amateur ethos promoted all that was good about sport e.g. sportsmanship. However, professionalism may have encouraged gamesmanship and deviance

In the UK, rugby union resisted professionalism (and those who 'turned' to professional rugby league) until the 1990s. It could be argued this is an example of the rigid class structure that promoted the amateur culture. In Australia, rugby league is more popular than rugby union. This preference shows acceptance of professionalism and supports the 'land of the fair go' ethos.

Kerry Packer's defiance of the traditional values of the cricket Governing Body could be considered the beginning of commercialised sport in countries other than the USA (Big Four sports).

Geographical factors:

For a direct comparison of geographical factors in the UK and Australia as they relate to commercialisation, see Table 4 on page 78. Below is an example explanation of these factors:

Evaluation:

The growth of commercial sport is dependent on urbanisation e.g. association football in England became professional in 1888 and therefore became a business. The major areas of professional soccer were the heavily populated industrial north and midlands. Good transport links to venues promote spectator attendance and increases popularity of the sport.

Socio-economic factors:

• Both the UK and Australia are affluent countries.
• People in both countries have disposable income to spend on sport.
For a direct comparison of socio-economic factors in the UK and Australia, see Table 4 on page 78. Below is an example explanation of these factors:

Evaluation:

It may be considered that all countries have economic systems which are inclined either toward a capitalist or a socialist model. Australia is inclined further towards an extreme capitalist model than the UK. This may have further stimulated the growth of commercial sport.

It could be argued that as commercial sport has become a consumer commodity it must increasingly become a spectacle of entertainment controlled by the media. The original sporting values of the gentleman amateurs will therefore disappear.

2. Explain the factors why Outdoor Education is promoted in Australia. Identify one comparative factor that influences the promotion of Outdoor Education in the UK and Australia.

(5 marks)

*There are a maximum of **four** marks for factors relating to Australia and **one** mark for comparison between UK and Australia.*

Both countries promote Outdoor Education as a way to teach skills, provide adventure experiences and enhance physical and cognitive development.

UK:

- A mild climate means outdoor activities are possible for most of the year.
- Outdoor experiences are promoted in areas of outstanding natural beauty.
- Activities such as backpacking and walking are promoted as healthy pursuits and are popular.
- There is no equivalent of 'Bush culture' in the UK.
- The UK has outstanding natural resources and aesthetic appeal. Climate and topography limit these areas.
- A safe environment encourages promotion of outdoor education.
- Outdoor Education is part of national curriculum but is not directly examined.
- Outdoor Education in the UK does not directly link with community agencies.
- Duke of Edinburgh scheme promotes outdoor experiences but is not compulsory.

Australia:

- The climate promotes outdoor education.
- Outdoor experiences are part of the national culture (links with history and tourist promotion).
- Outdoor activities are associated with a balanced, active and healthy lifestyle.
- The 'Bush' or 'Frontier' culture can be experienced through Outdoor Education.
- The environment has outstanding and extensive natural resources and aesthetic appeal.
- Survival and safety skills are necessary in a country with genuine wilderness areas.
- Outdoor experience is perceived as an important area of education and is an examined subject.
- Outdoor Education has important community links e.g. Army Cadets, Ambulance, Fire, Surf Life Saving services.
- The Victoria Youth Development Programme (VYDP) is a Government scheme to promote Outdoor Education.

3. Discuss contemporary initiatives to promote Physical Education and school sport in Australia. How does this compare with how PE and sport are promoted in UK schools? *(20 marks)*

20-mark questions are marked with a 'levels of response' mark scheme. See page vi in the Exam Strategies section at the front of this book.

The table below outlines the content that your answer should include. Read through and make sure you are including the right information in your work.

UK Initiatives	Australian Initiatives
• UK has a National Curriculum. • In addition to the National Curriculum, the UK government has developed a strategy named Physical Education Sport and Young People (PESSYP). • The PESSYP initiative comprises nine 'strands' which aim to improve the quality and opportunities for young people in sporting activities. • PESSYP operates within the framework of National Curriculum	• A National Curriculum does not exist in Australia • Victoria State responded to a government inquiry into declining standards in Physical Education and school sport by establishing a specialist department called The Victoria School Sport Unit. • This department implemented ten initiatives to promote physical activity in schools

Evaluation			
A National Curriculum may be a good policy because it is designed to give all pupils the same high quality education experience. The absence of a prescribed curriculum however, may encourage a PE department to be innovative and provide experiences for pupils that specific to their needs			
Government initiatives	• National curriculum. • High quality Physical Education and School Sport. (PESS) • PESS involves guidance as to how a school can improve the quality of Physical Education.	Sport Education and Physical Education Programme (SEPEP)	• SEPEP is a curriculum equivalent. • SEPEP comprises 100 minutes of Sport Education and 100 minutes of Physical Education per week. • The Sport Education programme focuses on teaching game strategies and incorporates both intra and inter-school games. • The Physical Education programme is concerned with teaching basic motor skills. • The aim of SEPEP is to ensure skills are well learned in order to increase the likelihood of lifelong participation.
Professional Development	• Professional Development of teachers and coaches involves providing teachers with training to improve the quality of their lesson delivery.	Physical and Sport Education (PASE)	• PASE is training programme for non-specialist teachers. • Primary teachers tend to take courses in Physical Education. • Secondary teachers tend to focus on Sport Education.
Sports Colleges School Sports Partnerships (SSPs) Kitemarking	• Sports Colleges receive additional government funding to increase the opportunities for young people to become involved in sport. • Sports Colleges link with other local schools to form School Sports Partnerships. • SSPs is the name of the scheme involving the work of the Sports College in collaboration with a group or a 'cluster' of schools.	Exemplary Schools	• Exemplary Schools are schools with outstanding sports and Physical Education departments. • Teachers from Exemplary Schools are selected to deliver Professional Development to neighbouring institutions called cluster schools. • Government grants for Exemplary Schools could be seen as the equivalent of Kitemarking in the UK

National Curriculum Sporting Playgrounds TOP Programmes	• Basic skills for sport are addressed in National Curriculum at Key Stages 1 and 2. • Involves the development of Primary school playgrounds to promote play and physical activity. • TOPs programmes in UK Primary schools teaches basic skills.	Fundamental Skills Programme (FSP)	• The Fundamental Skills programme is a compulsory Physical Education programme for Primary children. • The focus of FSP is to increase competence in eleven fundamental motor skills.
Evaluation			
The school initiatives both in UK and Australia give priority to the ethos of participation to encourage active lifestyles. This approach appears to contrast with USA High Schools who seem to emphasise elitism.			
Step into Sport Junior and Community Sports Leaders Award	• This strategy provides a clear framework to enable young people (14 -19) to be involved with sports leadership. • The Junior Sport Leaders Award (JSLA) and the Community Sports Leaders Award in the UK are the equivalent of Sport Leader Programme in Australia.	Sports Leader Programme	• A Sports Leader is usually a senior pupil who can elect to become involved in administration, refereeing and coaching. • In this capacity, they may help a senior coach to deliver a Sport Education lesson enabling the teacher to take up a coordinator's role. • The leader is facilitating sporting opportunities for others and this may later develop into a career in sports development.
Evaluation			
Both countries recognise the importance of developing the leadership and coaching skills of young people. This priority may help to produce high quality professional coaches for the future. It could be argued however, that the most valuable contribution made by junior leadership programmes is to produce coaching skills in those who will later volunteer their service to increasing opportunity in mass participation.			
Gifted and Talented	• Gifted and Talented is a scheme to help young people with identified ability to develop core skills that are the basis of all sports.	State Award Schemes	• A 'State Blue' is awarded for attainment and fair play whilst engaged in school sport. • The De Coubertin awards are presented to students who have made outstanding contributions to administration, coaching and other important non-playing roles.
		Sport Linkage Scheme.	• The Sport Linkage Scheme involves an alliance between schools and sports clubs. • Sharing facilities on a dual use basis. • Teachers and coaches may interchange.

Sports Personalities	• This is not an official strand of the PESSYP initiative but in the UK sports celebrities may visit schools some are involved in coaching. • Visiting sports personalities is not an initiative /condition of the English Institute of Sport. • Some professional clubs may send personalities into schools to coach / enhance community relations e.g. Wigan warriors Rugby League coaching scheme.	Sport Person in Schools Project.	• This project involves engaging a sport performer from the Victoria Institute of Sport (VIS) as a teaching assistant in schools. • The VIS athlete may be an international performer who will coach all children and raise the profile of sport. • Visiting personalities is a condition/obligation of the sports institutes.

Evaluation

Visiting personalities who are national sporting celebrities serve as inspiring role models but it may be that acclaimed sports stars need to become involved with coaching before they can make a significant impact on the development of young people.

The overall aims of PESSYP	• The principle aims of PESSYP and in particular the initiative SSPs are to develop a wide range of sporting opportunities and to increase participation.	Sports Search	• Sports Search is a computer programme into which students can enter their sporting interests and any relevant statistical information. • The programme will then advise students regarding the sports to which they would best be suited.
• Informal inter-school staff fixtures	• Informal fixtures on a friendly basis may be organised by some schools but there is not an equivalent of the Teacher Games as they occur in Australia.	Teacher Games	• The Teacher Games are residential competitive sport experiences for Victoria teachers. • By electing to take part in the games, teachers have an opportunity to raise their own profiles as role models.

Evaluation

Informal sports fixtures for staff in the UK may be good for morale but they do not have professional aims. The residential Teacher Games in Australia are designed to enhance professional development as they help to develop the participation philosophy and provide network opportunities for teachers.

---

4. In terms of mass participation women, people with disabilities and ethnic minorities are under-represented in both the UK and Australia.

Explain the strategies in the UK and Australia that encourage people from these groups to participate in physical recreation or sport.

(5 marks)

Sub max of three marks for:

UK:

Government: The government promotes mass participation through Sport England.

Disability: Disability Sport England promotes sport for people with disabilities by promoting positive images, improving access, providing specialist sports centres and providing financial help.

Women: Special Interest Groups and promotion of positive sporting female role models aim to attract women into sport.

Ethnic groups: Commission for Racial Equality applies to sport and initiatives such as Let's Kick Racism out of Football aim to encourage multiracial participation.

Sub max of three marks for:

Australia:

Government: The government promotes mass participation through the Australian Sports Commission (ASC) and More Active Australia.

Disability: Disability Sport Programme aims to improve the participation opportunities for people with disabilities. It enables coaches, teachers and organisers of sports to access resources to enhance practical teaching.

Women: Women's Sport Unit is an ASC initiative to promote women's sport.

Ethnic groups: The Indigenous Sport programme encourages indigenous people to be more active and to play sport at all levels. It works to increase the opportunities for indigenous people to learn the skills needed to organise, deliver and manage community based sport.

CHAPTER 8

Individual aspects of performance that influence young people's participation and aspirations

True or False?

1. True	3. False	5. True	7. False	9. False
2. False	4. True	6. True	8. True	10. True

1. Using practical examples, explain the causes of aggressive behaviour in sport. *(5 marks)*

Make sure you use examples in your answer to achieve full marks. If you don't, you can only achieve a maximum of three.

- A major cause of aggression in sport is perceived or actual unfairness during play e.g. a poor decision given by the referee.
- Frustration could arise through poor performance or losing a game.
- Displaced aggression or an influence outside of sport is a significant cause e.g. a player in football may be disenchanted by a managerial policy.
- A player may respond aggressively if placed under excessive pressure to win.
- Retaliation to an incident or copying the actions of others may stimulate aggression.

- Aggressive play could well be an expected team or a group norm.
- The nature of a game is a major cause of aggression e.g. ice-hockey is a collision game played at a fast pace.
- Players with an innate tendency toward aggression may react instinctively in a hostile situation e.g., offensive crowd chants might stimulate aggression.
- A wide score margin may well stimulate the losing side to be aggressive.
- A local derby game or a game in which there has been previous ill-feeling may induce violent reactions.

2. Explain the origins of attitudes and how attitudes can impact upon young people achieving healthy, active and balanced lifestyles. *(5 marks)*

You can only achieve up to four marks if you do not make reference to a healthy, active and balanced lifestyle.

Key term	Explanation
Experience	A good experience of PE promotes a positive attitude towards sport.
Socialisation	• Interaction with others who show a positive attitude towards active lifestyles. • Copying the behaviour of positive role models.
The media	If sport and physical activity is portrayed attractively in the media, it is likely to be copied.
Peer group	If a group of friends participates enthusiastically it is likely that, in an effort to conform to group norms a reluctant individual may join in.
Culture	Race, religion and class are influential attitudes. E.g. race and religion may exclude individuals from certain activities; class may influence the choice of sport.
Personality	• Extroverted people enjoy performing in the presence of others, and may adopt positive attitudes towards group participation. Introverts may experience high anxiety in the same situation. • People with a high need to achieve are likely to show approach behaviours and therefore positive attitudes to active participation. • Individuals with a high need to avoid failure will adopt avoidance behaviours and therefore show negative attitudes to participation
Lifestyle	All factors can influence a person to engage in physical activity thus promoting an active, healthy and balanced lifestyle.

3. Describe the components of attitude and critically evaluate the influence of attitudes when deciding to adopt an active lifestyle. *(20 marks)*

20-mark questions are marked with a 'levels of response' mark scheme. See page vii in the Exam Strategies section at the front of this book.

Components:

- The cognitive component represents the knowledge and belief that the individual has toward the attitude object, e.g. volleyball training makes the performer a better team player.
- The affective element is the feelings of the individual and relates to an evaluation of the attitude object, e.g. the performer has positive feelings towards volley training and enjoys it.
- The behavioural component represents the behaviour demonstrated towards training, e.g. a player attends volleyball training and demonstrates high levels of effort, persistence and commitment.

Attitudes:

Attitudes are poor predictors of behaviour and may not necessarily indicate the likelihood of a desirable lifestyle choice.

- A person may have a very positive attitude toward physical fitness but this alone will not guarantee that they will attend sport/activity sessions.
- An individual's positive attitudes and beliefs relating to the health benefits of exercise do not guarantee that they will commit to an exercise programme.
- Social/ situational factors can intervene to significantly influence actual behaviour even when an attitude is well established.
- When attitudes become more specific, they are more likely to predict behaviour, e.g. the student who is positive about fitness activities but specifically enjoys circuit training is more likely to attend a session.
- The most accurate predictor of behaviour is when a person makes a clear commitment of intent, e.g. a student making the statement that they will definitely attend the extra football session arranged for after school (Behavioural Intention).
- Behavioural Intention arises when a positive attitude is reinforced by significant others.
- Social processes impact strongly on attitude formation e.g. peer group pressure and this has implications when making lifestyle choices.
- Attitudes are unstable and can be changed.
- Changing an attitude can bring about lifestyle choices e.g. to give up smoking.
- By changing one attitude component, components can be made to oppose each other resulting in the individual experiencing emotional discomfort (dissonance).
- If one attitude component can be changed to bring about cognitive dissonance there is an increased possibility of changing the whole attitude.
- By changing the cognitive component e.g. smoking damages health conflict is set against the affective component e.g. smoking is pleasurable.
- By providing a person with new and positive experiences, the affective component can be modified, e.g. a student who has a negative experience through excessive physical contact in rugby may enjoy the indoor 'tag' version of the game and change their attitude towards participation in that sport.
- If a skill is simplified or if some form of guidance is used to make execution easier, the behavioural component of the attitude can be changed, e.g. fitting the novice skier with short skis would give more control and reduce apprehension.
- Persuasive communication could be applied within cognitive dissonance as an additional technique in changing attitude.

4. Describe the use of cognitive strategies by sports performers to eliminate aggression. Explain the effects of these strategies on the adoption of active and healthy lifestyles. *(6 marks)*

Up to four marks are available for strategies:

- Cognitive strategies are to do with thought processes and are designed to lower psychological/ cognitive arousal.
- Imagery focuses on achieving a calm state of mind.

- Mental rehearsal involves formulating an image of one's own movements during performance.
- Positive self talk and concentrating on repeated words or phrases can also lower an inclination to be aggressive.
- Counting up to ten will give the opportunity to regain composure.
- Forgetting or distancing oneself from aggressive cues can prevent aggression.
- Reasoning with oneself that aggression is wrong and that punishment is the likely result is a good preventative measure.
- Rational thinking/ logical thinking.

Up to four marks are available for effect on healthy lifestyle:
- Aggression may increase arousal causing reduced concentration resulting in poor performance and reduce the motive to engage in activity.
- Underachievement can lead to learned helplessness (inclination to give up).
- The dysfunctional consequences of aggression may result in the aggressor becoming injured and forced to give up.
- Performers with aggressive tendencies tend to feel frustration/anger during sporting activities.
- Minimal satisfaction would reduce the inclination to adopt an active lifestyle.
- Aggressive people tend to experience less satisfaction after activities and so have a reduced motive to continue.
- An aggressive person may be forced out of a group inclined to active and healthy lifestyles.
- Aggression is often the result of stress and so detrimental to healthy lifestyle.

CHAPTER 9

Group dynamics of performance

True or False?

1. True	3. True	5. False	7. True	9. True
2. False	4. True	6. True	8. True	10. False

1. Using psychological theories, explain possible positive and negative effects of an audience on sports performance.
   Describe the strategies that help prevent social inhibition in physical activities and how these may help the pursuit of a balanced active and healthy lifestyle. *(20 marks)*
20-mark questions are marked with a 'levels of response' mark scheme. See page vii in the Exam Strategies section at the front of this book.
- The presence of a crowd causes an increase in arousal.
- The Drive Theory of Social Facilitation states that as arousal increases there is a greater likelihood of the performer's dominant response emerging.

- If the performer is at the autonomous stage of learning the dominant response will be of high quality / the motor programme will run automatically.
- At the associative stage the dominant response or habit of a novice is likely to be incorrect.
- An increase of arousal at the associative stage would stimulate an undesired response.

Evaluation

An increase in arousal can facilitate a person's best performance, however under certain conditions (e.g. execution of fine skills) high arousal levels may cause performance to deteriorate. Successful control of arousal can lead to a higher chance of participation and the consequent benefits of a balanced, active and healthy lifestyle.

- Evaluation Apprehension Theory states that the performer learns to associate high arousal with the presence of a crowd.
- This theory predicts that it is only when the athlete perceives that the crowd is assessing performance that arousal increases e.g. during a goal kick in rugby.
- Extrovert personalities perform better under conditions of high arousal because of a subdued/ low level Reticular Activation System (RAS).
- This is predicted by Inverted U Hypothesis.

Evaluation

While it is possible that extrovert personalities perform best when an audience is present, it is difficult to predict the extent to which extroversion is the dominant personality trait. Personality profiling has serious limitations as people of all personality types participate in sport and therefore benefit from balanced, active and healthy lifestyles.

- The introvert performs best when arousal is low because of a RAS that operates at a higher level of intensity.
- The performance of gross skills benefits from high arousal e.g. the long jumper encourages the crowd to help mental preparation.
- Fine skills require a lower optimal arousal level e.g. the spin bowler in cricket would block out the crowd during performance.
- The experienced player would benefit from the presence of an audience.
- The novice should be encouraged to focus away from the crowd.
- The player at the autonomous stage of learning performs better under conditions of high arousal.
- Optimal arousal ensures maximum concentration/facilitates the process of Cue Utilisation/the performer has an increased capacity to select the most important cue from the environmental display.
- A combination of high somatic arousal and high cognitive arousal causes an abrupt drop in performance/ catastrophe theory.
- The audience may induce excessive cognitive anxiety preventing the athlete from achieving Individual Zone of Optimal Functioning.

Evaluation

Anxiety is perceived as a negative emotion but individuals respond differently to degrees of anxiety. Some perform best under conditions of high anxiety. These people are said to have a high Zone of Optimal Functioning.

- The presence of an audience may facilitate/ prevent entry to peak flow state.
- Peak flow state is the interaction of high somatic arousal and low cognitive anxiety.
- An external and broad attention style may allow the crowd to become a distracting influence.
- Experienced players are less likely to be distracted by the crowd predicted by Distraction Conflict Theory.
- Experienced players have the skill to narrow their attentional style onto specific cues e.g. Nideffer identifies this focus as narrow and external.
- This attention style filters out unwanted information such as an audience.
- Homefield Advantage Theory predicts that away teams are disadvantaged as crowds at away venues may be perceived as hostile.
- Proximity Effect states that the closer the crowd is to the play the greater influence it has on arousal levels e.g. in Ice Hockey the crowd is close to the rink.

Strategies that help prevent social inhibition

Evaluation

Most sports or physical activities take place in the company of other people either in the form of spectators or co-actors. With this in mind it is important to prevent the negative effects of social inhibition in order to encourage people to participate and pursue an active, healthy and balanced lifestyle.

Selective attention would narrow the focus of the performer onto the relevant cues.

- Mental rehearsal and imagery could enhance concentration and help to block out the audience which can be the source of inhibition.
- Development of a narrow and internal attentional style would help to focus away from the audience.

Evaluation

While mental rehearsal can help the performer to internalise and focus away from the audience, a person experiencing an exercise programme for the first time should not be in a situation in which they can be observed by others as they could be discouraged from further active participation.

- The athlete would be advised to engage in positive self talk to block out negative thoughts that may have been induced by the presence of an audience.
- Practice could be undertaken in the presence of an audience.

Evaluation

Practice undertaken in front of an audience would help the athlete to become accustomed to the effects spectators may have on arousal levels. The audience however must be perceived by the performer to be supportive and non-evaluative. In this way, active participation will be more likely to be enjoyed and continued.

- The performer should ensure that skills are overlearned to become dominant behaviours. It must be remembered that when arousal increases, dominant responses emerge.
- Confidence building strategies should be implemented as high self efficacy will reduce inhibition.

Evaluation

If confidence is increased, an individual is more likely to feel comfortable in the performance environment and commit to following a balanced, active and healthy lifestyle.

- Positive reinforcement and social support from the coach and team mates will reduce anxiety.
- The athlete should be made aware of how concentration is maximized when the ideal level of arousal is achieved.

Evaluation

Prevention of social inhibition is achieved by controlling the increased arousal often experienced when performing before an audience. It must be remembered however that extroverted people with high ability levels may well be attracted to sport and physical activities because they enjoy the excitement induced by the presence of an audience. This sustains involvement in a balanced and active lifestyle.

2. Describe Chelladurai's multi dimensional model of leadership and explain how leadership can influence performance.   *(6 marks)*

There is a sub max of four marks for description of multi dimensional model:

- **Interaction:** The multi dimensional model operates on the interaction between the characteristics affecting leader behaviour, and the type of behaviour chosen by the leader.
- **Factors affecting leader behaviour:** Situation, leader and members characteristics.
- **Type of chosen leader behaviour:** Required behaviour to complete the task, preferred behaviour desired by the group and the actual behaviour adopted by the leader.
- **Optimal group performance:** Optimal performance and group satisfaction occurs when the leader's behaviour is appropriate for the situation and suits the preference of the group.

There are a sub max of four marks available for explanation of the influence of leadership on performance:

- Success of leadership depends on the compatibility of actual leader behaviour and the leadership style preferred by the group members
- Best performance and satisfaction is achieved if high compatibility occurs between the leadership that matches the situational demands and preference of group.
- Effective group performance, but low satisfaction to members is caused by leadership suiting the situational demand but not the preference of the group.
- Ineffective group performance, but high satisfaction to members is caused when leadership does not match the situational demand but is preferred by the group.

3. Social loafing prevents team cohesion. What does social loafing mean and how is it caused?   *(4 marks)*

You will achieve one mark for defining the meaning of social loafing:

Social loafing refers to loss of personal responsibility or motivation. An individual player withdraws effort in a team game situation. The 'loafing' player is coasting and relying upon the efforts of others.

There are three marks available for outlining the causes of social loafing:

- A lack of accountability.
- The player not having an identifiable role.
- The performer does not feel valued by the team or coach.
- Low efficacy (specific self confidence).
- High level of anxiety.
- Learned helplessness can cause a withdrawal of effort.
- Other people not trying.
- Loafing is most prevalent in team games with high numbers e.g. Rugby.

4. Critically evaluate trait, social learning and interactionist theories as they influence the development of leadership skills. *(6 marks)*

There are a maximum of two marks available for each part of the answer:

Trait perspective:

- Leadership traits are innate/stable. They emerge in a given situation e.g. intelligence, assertiveness and self-confidence.
- It is unlikely that specific dominant traits alone can facilitate successful leadership.
- Some traits (e.g. tough mindedness) may be helpful in leadership, but their inheritance and importance cannot be proven.
- Trait theory in general is not a good predictor of behaviour.
- Trait approach does not take account of learning/ vicarious processes.

Social Learning perspective:

- Social learning theorists propose that behaviour relating to leadership is learned.
- Leadership skills can be learnt through experience, role modelling, and advice.
- It is unlikely that learning alone can facilitate effective leadership.
- The weakness in social learning theory is that it does not take into account the trait perspective.

Interactionist approach:

- Leadership skills are a combination of inherited abilities and learned skills.
- Leadership skills emerge and are acquired when a situation triggers the traits that are of importance to leadership.
- Interactionist theories give a more realistic explanation of leadership behaviour.

CHAPTER 10

Mental preparation for physical activities

True or False?

1. True	3. True	5. True	7. False	9. True
2. False	4. False	6. False	8. True	10. False

1. Nideffer's model of Attentional Styles is presented on two dimensions which are termed broad/narrow and internal/external.

Describe broad, narrow internal and external attentional styles, and by referring to sporting examples explain the effect of attentional styles on performance. *(6 marks)*

There are up to four marks available for description:

- **Broad attention:** takes into account a great deal of information /peripheral stimuli and is required in an open skill situation like dribbling the ball in basketball.
- **Narrow focus**: concentration on one, or a small number of stimuli. e.g. the ball during a tennis serve.
- **External focus**: is on an environmental stimulus e.g. the ball when a performer is making a catch in rounders.
- **Internal focus**: the performer focuses inwardly on themselves (their emotions and thoughts). By focusing on their psychological state, a performer is able to control arousal levels, enter the zone of optimal function and attain a peak flow experience.
- **External focus**: enables the athlete to focus on outside factors such as the position of an opponent in badminton. It can a useful distraction from physical pain or fatigue.

There are also up to four marks available for explanation:

- Optimal psychological states can optimise concentration and attentional control.
- The correct attention style can help a performer to deal with distractions e.g. a narrow focus is required when taking a rugby goal kick; the crowd needs to be 'blocked out'.
- Effective attention will serve to prevent negative feelings and enable the performer to make positive attributions during performance e.g. the successful vault was executed because the gymnast has high ability levels.
- A good performer can draw upon a range of attention styles, e.g. before passing in open play, a rugby player would require broad and external attention; catching a high ball would require a style which is both narrow and external.
- If the rugby player is the captain, a team talk would be helped by a strong internal and broad attention style.

2. Define cue-utilisation and explain how this process links with arousal. *(6 marks)*

There is one mark available for the definition:

Cue-utilisation is the realisation that not all information is important. Performers select and pay specific attention to a selected number of cues.

There are five marks on available for links to arousal. This is broken down in the following way:

Up to two marks from:	*Up to two marks from:*	*Up to two marks from:*
When arousal levels are low (sub-optimal):	**When over aroused:**	**At optimal arousal:**
• The perceptual field widens excessively.	• The perceptual field narrows excessively.	• The perceptual field adjusts to the correct/ideal width.
• Arousal-irrelevant cues are given attention.	• Relevant cue is missed/ information processing channel is restricted.	• The most relevant cues are detected and selective attention is in operation.
• Selective attention does not operate.	• Panic/hyper-vigilence will result and performance will deteriorate.	• Performance is maximised due to the efficiency of information processing.
• Information overload is induced.	• Selective attention does not operate (if not used in under arousal).	

3. Evaluate critically the use of goal setting to improve performance and participation in physical activity.

(20 marks)

20-mark questions are marked with a 'levels of response' mark scheme. See page vii in the Exam Strategies section at the front of this book.

For comparisons and definitions of time-based and activity-based goals see Tables 2 and 3 on page 116.

Check against your own answer to ensure you have understood the terms correctly.

Below are example evaluations of each:

Time-based goals:

Short term goals: are beneficial as they form a link between the athlete's initial capability and the long term goal of achievement. It has been said (Jarvis 2006) that the most effective goals are short term because they can provide immediate success.

Medium term goals are beneficial because they improve access to long term goals, endorse the effectiveness of short term goals and are significant improvement indicators.

Long term goals: It is good to have an overall aim because long term ambition can be motivating. When set on their own however, long term goals may appear as unachievable targets to the performer and tend to cause increased anxiety.

Activity-based goals:

Performance and process goals: Performance and process goals give more control to the participant and are good indicators of an athlete's commitment to training and competition.

A most effective way to improve performance /commitment to participation is to set both performance and process goals. Goals that give control to the performer are more likely to improve self efficacy.

Performance goals encourage persistence because improvement is measured against self. External assessment required in product goal setting may result in obvious failure causing the athlete to withdraw. Under such circumstances performance goals would be better than product goals (Cox 1998).

Product goals: A total focus on product goals can create anxiety during competition as the athlete is required to win in order to achieve the goal.

Product goals are not always detrimental; the outcomes of many sporting activities require the emergence of an obvious winner. They should always be included for high-level performers.

Evaluation of goal setting:
- For every product goal there should be a number of performance and process goals set for the athlete.
- It would appear that the most effective way to improve performance and commitment to participation is to set both performance and process goals.
- Effective goal setting can be achieved only when feedback accompanies the outcome.
- Application of the SMARTER principle improves motivation, participation, persistence and performance.
- When positive attributions are given for the achievement of any goal type, the promotion of mastery orientation/approach behaviour will occur.
- Goals that can be measured objectively have a stronger influence on the performer than subjectively measured goals/objective measurement of goals is more effective than 'do your best' goals.

4. What is meant by the term self efficacy? Explain how the raising of self-efficacy could enable an individual to sustain a balanced, active and healthy lifestyle. *(6 marks)*

There is one mark given for the definition:
Self-efficacy is specific self-confidence, i.e. the confidence shown by an individual in a given situation.
Make sure your explanation refers to a balanced, active and healthy lifestyle, otherwise you will only achieve a maximum of two marks for it.
- Raising self-efficacy involves reminding the individual of previous accomplishments e.g. the discipline of taking regular exercise, adopting good sleep patterns etc.
- A vicarious experience involves learning from, or copying a role model.
- Vicarious experiences show successful role models who have similar abilities to the individual lacking in confidence.
- Those previously low in self confidence become role models because they have chosen a healthy lifestyle of exercise/diet.

- Talking positively to those of low self efficacy will increase confidence e.g. exercise is important to improve health/image/appearance.
- Control the emotional state /control of arousal/anxiety.
- Anxiety management techniques will control feelings of anxiety/nervousness/ apprehension that often accompanies low confidence e.g. adopt a positive image of oneself when engaging in physical activity.
- Attribution retraining can give those people lacking in self efficacy the feeling of control.
- Make people aware that self efficacy is the major motivating factor that encourages engagement in fitness activities.
- Raise awareness that people who develop high efficacy expectations in relation to exercise programmes are more likely to adopt and persist in healthy lifestyles by taking up physical activities.

CHAPTER 11

Linear motion in physical activity

True or False?

1. True.
2. False. F = m x a is used to express Newton's second law of acceleration (Force = mass x acceleration).
3. False. There can never be motion without force – according to Newton's first law of motion however, there can be force without motion (if all forces are balanced in size and opposite in direction) net force = 0.
4. True.
5. True.
6. False. Distance is 'how far a body moves from A to B' compared to displacement 'the shortest straight-line route from A to B'. They are both measured in metres however, displacement is a measure of size and direction.
7. False. Speed = distance/time (ms^{-1})
8. True.
9. True.
10. False. Momentum is the 'quantity of motion possessed by a body' and calculated by mass x velocity ($kgms^{-1}$).

Exam practice

1. Using an example, describe linear motion and explain the difference between distance and displacement over a 400m race. *(4 marks)*
- Linear motion is where a body's centre of mass travels in a straight/curved line, with all its parts moving the same distance, in the same direction, at the same speed + any relevant specific example.
- Linear motion is created by an external force passing through the centre of mass.
- Distance is how far a body travels from A to B (in metres) + distance = 400m.
- Prevents rotation.
- Displacement is the shortest straight-line route from A to B (in metres) + displacement = 0m.

2i. If Usain Bolt has a mass of 86kg and crosses the 20m line of a 100m sprint in 2.49 seconds calculate his momentum and average speed over the first 20m of the race.

- Momentum = mass x velocity, 86 x (20/2.49)
- Momentum = 690.76kgms^{-1}
- (Average) Speed = distance/time, 20/2.49
- (Average) Speed = 8.03ms^{-1}

ii. Using Newton's laws of motion explain how Usain Bolt drives away from the starting blocks.   *(6 marks)*

- Usain Bolt will remain at rest in the starting blocks until an external force is applied from the blocks to his body (which is greater than his weight).
- The greater the size of the force generated by Usain Bolt the greater the change in momentum and acceleration from the blocks,
- Acceleration will take place in the same direction as the force applied.
- An action force is applied by Usain Bolt to the starting blocks and an equal and opposite reaction force is applied from the blocks to Usain Bolt.

CHAPTER 12

Force in physical activity

True or False?

1. True. F = ma
2. False. Force is measured in Newtons (N). Momentum is measured in kgms^{-2}.
3. False. There is resultant motion as the high jumper lifts from the floor and accelerates towards the bar. Forces are unbalanced, positive net force in the upward direction as R > W.
4. True. W = mg.
5. False. The rougher and warmer the ground surface the greater the friction.
6. True.
7. True.
8. True.
9. False. Newton's second law of motion shows that increasing impulse increases the rate of change in momentum and therefore subsequent velocity.
10. True.

Exam practice

1. During a 400m race an athlete will achieve a constant speed. Explain the concept of net force. Describe the horizontal forces acting on this performer and how they maximise forward acceleration.   *(6 marks)*

Sub-max 2 marks:

- Net force is the sum of all forces acting on the body/result of all forces acting on the body,
- 400m: (vertical and horizontal) forces are balanced when in constant speed,
- 400m: net force = 0/the 400m runner experiences no change in state of motion.

Sub-max 5 marks:

- Horizontal forces: Friction and Air resistance
- Friction is the force that opposes the movement/tendency to move/slide of one surface over another,
- Air resistance is the force that opposes motion.

Forward acceleration maximised by (must include sporting application to the 400m):

- Increasing roughness of contact surface: 400m runner wears spikes,
- Increasing roughness of ground surface: rubberised athletics track (or equivalent),
- Increase normal reaction: the greater the normal reaction the 400m runner generates the greater the friction.

2. When performing a tennis forehand groundstroke the player will follow-through by lifting the racquet over the shoulder. Describe why follow-through is an essential part of good technique. *(5 marks)*

- (Follow through) increases the time the force acts on the ball.
- (Follow through) increases the impulse of force acting on the ball.
- (Follow through) increases the outgoing/change in momentum of the ball.
- (Follow through) increases the outgoing velocity of the ball.
- This increases the distance the ball travels.
- This increases the control/accuracy over the ball.

3. A gymnast performs a handstand and holds the position for three seconds. Draw a free body diagram to show the forces acting on the body and describe the net force resulting from this action. *(4 marks)*

Weight acts downwards from the centre of mass (or diagram equivalent),

- Reaction acts upwards from the point of contact (or diagram equivalent),
- W = R, net force = 0,
- Forces are balanced there is no change in state of motion.

CHAPTER 13

Fluid mechanics in physical activity

True or False?

1. True.
2. True.
3. False. Friction is affected by the roughness and temperature of the contact and ground surface. Air resistance is affected by velocity, frontal cross-sectional area, shape and smoothness of surface.
4. False. To create spin/angular motion an eccentric force/off centre force is applied.
5. True.
6. False. It is the Magnus effect that explains the deviations in flight path of rotating projectiles.
7. True.
8. True.
9. False. There are five possible diagrams regarding spin. A free body diagram representing the forces acting on the projectile, a parallelogram to show the resultant/net force, an air flow diagram explaining the Magnus force, a flight path diagram showing the spinning compared to non-spinning flight paths and a bounce diagram showing the effect of spin on bounce.
10. True.

Exam practice

1. A tennis player performs a forehand drive. Sketch and label a diagram showing all the forces acting on the ball at the moment of contact. Describe the forces and state the effects on the flight path and bounce of the ball of applying topspin. *(6 marks)*

Diagram must show appropriate labels (sub-max two marks):

- Eccentric force/off-centre action force/F (from the edge of the ball outside centre of mass).
- Weight/W (from the centre of mass).
- Force arrow must be longer than the Weight arrow.

Eccentric force/action force/F

Weight

Description:

- Eccentric/off-centre action force creates torque/angular motion/causes spin.
- Weight acts from the centre of mass downwards/is the effect of acceleration due to gravity on mass.

Flight path:

- (Topspin) creates an additional Magnus force acting downwards (or equivalent diagram).
- (Topspin) shortens the flight path/causes the ball to dip (or equivalent diagram).

Bounce:

- (Topspin) accelerates the ball on bounce/decreases the angle of bounce/bounces at a shallower angle.

2. Describe the concept of air resistance and explain how a speed cyclist can minimise the effects of air resistance. *(5 marks)*

- Air resistance acts in opposition to motion (of a body moving through the air).
- Air resistance reduces velocity/speed.
- The greater the velocity the greater the air resistance.
- Cyclist tucks in to reduce the frontal cross sectional area (reducing AR).
- Cyclist wears a skin-tight lycra suit to create a smooth surface (reducing AR).
- Cyclist streamlines their body shape to minimise AR.

3. Using your knowledge of the Magnus Effect explain the deviation in flight path of a golf ball hit with backspin. *(6 marks)*

- Flight path becomes non-parabolic/asymmetrical/lengthens (or equivalent diagram).
- Magnus effect reduces the effects of gravity/provides a lift force (or equivalent diagram).
- Creates 'float'/increases the distance travelled.
- Air travels at a higher velocity above the ball/lower velocity below the ball (or equivalent diagram).
- Area of low pressure is created above the ball/area of high pressure is created below the ball.
- Magnus force is created from high to low pressure gradient.
- Air flow lines closer together above the ball (airflow diagram only).
- Resultant force shows the size and direction of acceleration of the golf ball/Newton's second law (or equivalent diagram).

CHAPTER 14

Stability and angular motion in physical activity

True or False?

1. True.

2. False. Widening the base of support does increase stability. Raising the centre of mass decreases stability.

3. False. There are three types of lever system in the human body, each consisting of a fulcrum, effort and load.

4. True.

5. False. Moment of force is calculated by force multiplied by the perpendicular distance from the fulcrum.

6. True.

7. True.

8. True.

9. False. Increasing the moment of inertia increases the resistance to change state of rotation.

10. True.

Exam practice

1. The figure shows a lever system for the shoulder during extension of a tennis serve. Identify the class of lever used and calculate the moment of force/torque caused by the load. *(4 marks)*

- 3rd class lever.
- Moment of force/torque = force x (perpendicular) distance from the fulcrum/L x a
- Moment of force/torque = 100N x 0.35m.
- Moment of force/torque = 35Nm.

2. Evaluate the efficiency of the lever system used during shoulder extension in comparison to the lever used at the ball of the foot to lift the tennis player upwards from the ground. *(5 marks)*

- 3rd class lever used to lift the tennis player upwards from the ground.
- 2nd class levers are efficient (compared to) 3rd class levers.
- 2nd class levers have the mechanical advantage (compared to) 3rd class levers which have the mechanical disadvantage.
- 2nd class levers can move a large load with little effort (compared to) 3rd class levers which take more effort to move an equivalent load.
- (Due to) 2nd class levers effort is further from the fulcrum/ball of the foot (compared to) 3rd class levers effort is closer to the fulcrum/shoulder joint.
- (However) 3rd class levers can move the load at speed over a large range of movement (compared to) 2nd class levers produce considerable force at the expense of speed and range of movement.
-

3. A gymnast with a mass of 65kg accelerates upwards and performs a backward somersault before landing, assuming acceleration due to gravity is $10ms^{-2}$, calculate the gymnast's weight. Using your knowledge of the angular analogue of Newton's laws of motion and the law of conservation of angular momentum explain the control of this backward rotation. *(20 marks)*

20-mark questions are marked with a 'levels of response' mark scheme. See page vii in the Exam Strategies section at the front of this book.

Indicative answer:

Calculation:

- Weight = mass x gravity
- Weight = 65kg x $10ms^{-2}$
- Weight = 650N

Angular analogues:

- (Newton 1) Gymnast will continue to rotate with constant angular momentum unless acted upon by an external torque/moment of force/the ground on landing.
- (Newton 2) The rate of change of angular momentum experienced by the gymnast is proportional to the size of the torque/moment of force acting upon them.
- And takes place in the same direction in which the torque acts.
- (Newton 3) For every torque/moment of force that is exerted by the gymnast to the ground there is an equal and opposite torque exerted by the ground to the gymnast.

Creation of rotation:

- Transverse axis (of rotation).
- Eccentric force/off-centre force/force applied outside the centre of mass.
- Torque/moment of force applied to the body.
- Generates angular momentum.

Law of the conservation of angular momentum:

- Angular momentum = moment of inertia x angular velocity.
- Moment of inertia is the gymnast's resistance to rotate/change state of angular motion.
- Angular velocity is the rate of change in angular displacement/rate of spin/rate of change of the angle of the gymnast.

Take-off:

- Mass distributed far from the axis of rotation/straight body position.
- Large moment of inertia.
- Low angular velocity/rate of spin.

During flight:

- Mass distributed close to axis of rotation/tucked body position.
- Decreases moment of inertia.
- Increases angular velocity/rate of spin.

Prior to landing/landing:

- Mass moved away from the axis of rotation/straight body position/raise moment of inertia.
- Reduces angular velocity/rate of spin.
- Landing controlled.
- Torque applied on landing reduces angular motion/passes through the centre of mass to prevent over rotation.

CHAPTER 15

Critical evaluation of the quality, effectiveness and efficacy of performance

True or False?

1. True.
2. True.
3. False. The Magnus effect applies to projectiles which spin during flight only.
4. True.
5. False. A cartwheel rotates about the frontal axis.
6. True.
7. False. The Fosbury Flop is more efficient as the centre of mass moves outside of the body and below the bar needing less force to generate the same height as the scissor kick technique.
8. False. If weight is the dominant force the resulting flight path will be parabolic/ symmetrical.
9. True.
10. True.

Exam practice

1. Using your knowledge and understanding of force, follow through, and the Bernoulli principle explain how a discus thrower uses efficient technique to increase the distance thrown. *(20 marks)*

20-mark questions are marked with a 'levels of response' mark scheme. See page vii in the Exam Strategies section at the front of this book.

Indicative answer:

Force:

On release:

- Angular motion is created (when a body or part of a body moves in a circular path about an axis of rotation).
- An eccentric/off-centre force is applied to the discus (or equivalent diagram).
- Generates torque/moment of force.

During flight:

- Weight acts from the centre of mass downwards.
- Weight = mass x (acceleration due to) gravity.
- Air resistance opposes motion of the discus.
- Force diagram: W acting downward from the centre of mass + AR acting from the centre of mass in opposition to the direction of motion. AR arrow must be longer than the W arrow.
- Air resistance is high due to high speed of the discus.
- At the end of flight: air resistance becomes negligible as velocity decreases/weight becomes dominant force.
- Flight path is non-parabolic/asymmetrical (or equivalent diagram).
- Resultant force shows the size and direction of acceleration of the discus/Newton's second law (or equivalent parallelogram diagram).

Follow through:

- Discus thrower uses multiple rotations.
- Increases the time the force acts on the discus.
- Increases the impulse of force acting on the discus (or equivalent force/time graph).
- Increases the outgoing/change in momentum of the discus.
- Increases the outgoing velocity of the discus.
- This increases the distance the discus travels.
- This increases the control over the release of the discus.

Bernoulli principle:

- Bernoulli principle provides a lift force/reduces the effects of gravity (or equivalent force diagram).
- Creates 'float'/increases the distance travelled.
- Discus adopts an aerofoil shape.
- Discus thrown at an angle of attack/increase the angle of attack to increase the lift force (up to 17 degrees) .
- Air travels further over the top of the discus/air travels at a higher velocity above the discus/lower velocity below the discus (or equivalent air flow diagram).
- Area of low pressure is created above the discus/area of high pressure is created below the discus.
- Bernoulli principle and lift force from the pressure gradient (from high to low pressure).
- Air flow lines closer together above the discus (airflow diagram only).

2. Explain the concept of moment of inertia and its importance to a gymnast performing a somersault.
(6 marks)

- Rotational equivalent of inertia.
- Gymnast's resistance to change their state of rotation/change their state of angular motion.
- Dependant on the mass of the gymnast/the greater the mass the greater the moment of inertia.
- (application) Gymnasts have a relatively low mass to ensure efficient changes in state of rotation.
- Dependant on the distribution of mass from the axis of rotation/further the distribution of mass from the axis of rotation the greater the moment of inertia.
- (application) Gymnasts have a high moment of inertia at take-off/straight body position/to generate angular momentum.
- (application) Gymnasts have a low moment of inertia during flight/tucked body position/to increase angular velocity/increase the rate of spin.(application) Gymnasts have a high moment of inertia prior to landing/straighten body position/to decrease angular velocity and increase control for landing.
- $I = \sum mr^2$

3. Describe the concept of friction and explain how sports performers in team games of your choice increase and decrease friction to improve the efficiency of their performance. *(6 marks)*

Friction

- Friction occurs when two surfaces slide/have a tendency to slide across one another.
- Friction opposes motion.
- Friction occurs parallel to the two surfaces in contact.

Increase friction

- Relevant sporting example (team game): rugby, football, hockey (or equivalent).
- Increase the roughness of the ground/contact surface (for example, studded boots for a rugby player).
- Increase the surface temperature (for example, rubber crumb Astroturf on a warm day).
- Increase the normal reaction/downforce (for example, applying a large action force to the ground to change direction).

Decrease friction

- Relevant sporting example (team game): ice hockey (or equivalent).
- Increase the smoothness of the ground/contact surface (for example, polished ice).
- Decrease the normal reaction/downforce (for example, 'lifting' to turn quickly).

CHAPTER 16

Energy

True or False?

1. False. Power is the rate at which we can work/work (F x D) divided by time but is measured in WATTS NOT joules
2. False. ATP is the only usable source of energy that the body/muscles can directly utilise for work.
3. True.
4. False. Glycogen is broken down by the enzyme Glycogen phosphorylase into glucose.
5. False. OBLA is an abbreviation for the 'Onset of blood lactate accumulation'
6. True.
7. True.
8. True.
9. True.
10. False. The alactacid stage requires approximately 3–4 litres of oxygen and takes about three minutes to fully restore ATP/PC stores.

Exam practice

1. What is meant by the term energy continuum? Identify a situation in a team game when the ATP/PC system would be predominant. Explain your answer. *(5 marks)*

Two marks are available for definition:

Energy continuum

- describes the relative contribution of the three energy systems/aerobic and anaerobic work/the continual movement between and combination of the energy systems;
- to supply energy to resynthesise (ADP back into) ATP
- depends on the intensity/duration of exercise

There is also one mark for an example and two marks for an explanation. You can use any relevant example and explanation that is consistent to ATP/PC system.

	ATP–PC
Example (e.g. netball) (guideline only)	(Used to sprint into the centre third to receive the centre pass)
Intensity	(Very) high
Duration	0–10 seconds/2/3–10 seconds
PC stores	Sufficient PC stores available

2. Compare the relative efficiency of the aerobic system in providing energy to resynthesise ATP with anaerobic routes. *(5 marks)*

*Remember, to obtain marks you must **compare**.*

Maximum of five marks from:

- Aerobic route is 18-19 times more efficient than LA/ATP/PC;
- 36-38 ATP produced compared with 2 lactic acid/1 PC;
- Anaerobic production is the incomplete breakdown of one molecule of glucose into LA whereas aerobic production is complete break down;
- Aerobic releases all potential energy so higher energy yield whereas LA system only releases 2 ATP.
- Aerobic (and ATP/PC) have no fatiguing by-products/lasts longer whereas LA system produces Lactic acid leading to muscle fatigue.
- Aerobic = CO_2/H_2O , ATP/PC = Pi +C and but LA in LA system
- Aerobic system of ATP production slower but lasts longer whereas LA and ATP/PC faster but shorter
- Aerobic system can use fats as fuel as well as glycogen/ LA only glycogen/both can use glycogen as food fuel
- In absence of O_2 anaerobic systems are used instead.

3. Explain when and how lactic acid is fully removed from the muscles. *(6 marks)*

There are two marks available for 'when' lactic acid is removed:

- at the end of exercise recovery period, active cool down, and partial removal during breaks and intervals
- during the lactacid, slow recovery phase component.

There are four marks available for 'how' it is removed:

- using oxygen/aerobic respiration/oxidation
- through elevated respiratory rates
- lactic acid is converted to pyruvic acid
- and metabolised to carbon dioxide and water (and energy) in Krebs cycle
- lactic acid is converted to protein
- lactic acid is converted to glycogen/glucose/Cori cycle

CHAPTER 17

Application of the principles of training

True or False?

1. True.
2. True.
3. False. Muscle cell atrophy takes place after approximately 48 hours of inactivity.
4. True.
5. False. A macro=cycle is a longer-term plan of training aimed at achieving a long-term goal/objective.
6. False. A micro-cycle is a short-term plan/goal of training, typically lasting one to three weeks

7. True.
8. False. A UNIT is a short period/session of training with a specific aim.
9. True.
10. False. A warm up should be performed before any activity and consist of pulse raising activities, mobility and stretching of the active muscles/joints.

Exam practice

1. Periodisation is a training principle that splits training into specific blocks. What are the benefits of using periodisation when designing a training programme? *(5 marks)*

Five marks available from:

- Timing/peaking for event helps to ensure that an optimal physiological peak is reached at the correct time for an important competition e.g. Olympics/World Cup etc.
- Focuses training and the setting of short-term, long-term and time-phased goals.
- Enables the performer to manipulate training intensity, volume, frequency and rest
- Each block is designed to prepare a specific performance component, e.g. sprint-start training can be focused on the needs of the individual performer/sport-specific.
- Variance training is split into smaller units to maintain motivation, avoid boredom and overtraining, and allow recovery.
- A double periodisation model allows the performer to peak twice for a qualifying round and the championships (this approach is not recommended for endurance sports).
- An undulating periodisation model allows the long-season team to perform to best maintain fitness and prevent too much overload/burn out.
- Moderation/reversibility helps prevent overtraining by ensuring adequate recovery, while ensuring time for fitness/skills does not decrease.

2. Explain how a performer might use periodisation to structure their training programme for one year. *(6 marks)*

- Split year into macrocycles, mesocycles and microcycles.
- Macrocycle as the long term/one year training block.
- Long-term objective, plus example, e.g. to achieve the national team qualifying time.

- Mesocycle as the intermediate training block (between one and four months)
- Medium-term objective, plus example, e.g. increase strength/power/endurance
- Microcycle as the short term training block (One week up to three weeks)
- Short-term objective, plus example, e.g. resistance training each week to ensure sufficient recovery and develop endurance.
- A Unit (a short period/session) of training with a specific aim.
- An athlete training three times a week would have a micro-cycle consisting of 3 units
- session of training with two aims – flexibility & strength training.
- Split year into seasons: off-season, pre-season and competitive season.
- In off-season phase performer will build a training base and develop general fitness, e.g. aerobic capacity, muscular endurance, flexibility.
- In pre-season phase performer will develop more specific fitness. Taining sessions will increase in intensity. Focus on the fitness components important for the event. e.g. develop speed/appropriate energy system/techniques/skills

CHAPTER 18.1

Health components of physical fitness: Aerobic capacity

True or False?

1. True.
2. False. Sedentary individuals' anaerobic threshold is typically about 50/60 per cent of VO_2 max, whereas elite aerobic athletes may work above 85 per cent of VO_2 max.
3. False. No, a programme of aerobic training will increase VO_2 max due to the long-term adaptations to aerobic training. This is specificity.
4. False. The PWC 170 is a sub-maximal test on a cycle ergometer where the performer cycles at three progressive low to moderate work intensities (100–115 bpm, 115–130 bpm and 130–145 bpm) and their HR values are recorded.
5. True.
6. True.
7. True.
8. False. Continuous training involves steady state sub-maximal work (running, cycling, swimming, rowing) for prolonged periods (20–30 minutes plus).
9. True.
10. True.

Exam practice

1. The table below compares VO2 max and OBLA values for two 18 year old students. One is a top club triathlete and the other a reasonable school team tennis player.

   With reference to the efficiency of the vascular system, explain why the triathlete is able to achieve these higher values.   *(6 marks)*

   One sub-max mark for capillarisation (eight and ten), one sub-max mark for gas exchange (seven and nine).

Due to aerobic training, the triathlete has:

- better oxygen carrying capacity in the blood/more oxygen transported
- (due to) increased number of red blood cells/more haemoglobin
- decrease in blood viscosity/enhanced ease of blood flow
- (due to) an increase in blood plasma/the water component of the blood
- more efficient vascular shunt mechanism
- (due to) improved elasticity/stronger arteriole/artery walls
- improved gaseous exchange at the alveolar × capillary membrane
- (due to) capillarisation on the alveoli wall/lungs
- improved gaseous exchange at the tissue-capillary membrane
- (due to) capillarisation in the muscle (cell)
- increased tolerance/blood buffering to Lactic Acid
- raised anaerobic/lactate threshold
- (due to) improved removal of lactic acid/CO_2.

2. A trained athlete can perform at a higher percentage of their VO2 max before reaching OBLA than an untrained person. Describe how an athlete would make use of the principles of training when designing a training programme aimed at delaying OBLA. *(6 marks)*

You must explain the principle and apply aerobic trig where possible in order to achieve full marks.

- (overload) body must be put under stress/made to work harder/longer/more often (6)
- (F = frequency): at least 3 times a week
- (I = intensity): 50 per cent – 75 percent of VO2 max/low/moderate intensity
- (T = time): at least 20 minutes (3-5+ minutes for interval/circuits)
- Work /relief ratio: 1 : 1/ **1 :□** : – active jog/walk/run
- (T = type): aerobic (and anaerobic) training/continuous/interval/fartlek/circuit
- (progression:) as the body adapts further increases in frequency/ intensity/time must follow to ensure continued improvements
- (specificity:) training should be relevant/specific to the sport and the individual
- athlete must train the aerobic system/SO/FOG muscle fibres
- (reversibility:) athlete must train consistently to avoid a deterioration in performance
- (moderation:) need for realistic targets that do not put too much stress on the body too soon/avoid overtraining/risking injury
- (variance:) include a number of diff training methods to maintain interest/ enthusiasm/ avoid boredom
- (warms ups/cool downs:) avoid injury and minimise the risk of muscle soreness/DOMS

3. Define interval training and identify the advantages of this type of training. Outline an interval training session that is specific to an aerobic performer. *(6 marks)*

One mark for definition.

Interval training :

- a form of training in which periods of work are interspersed with periods of recovery

Three marks for the advantages:

- very versatile/can be used for practically any sport/performer/flexible trig methods
- can improve both aerobic and anaerobic capacity
- specificity/performer can train relevant energy system
- allows performer to train at higher intensities without undue fatigue
- allows for quicker gains in aerobic capacity.

*Three marks for outlining the **interval training session**:*

For aerobic performer:

- (duration of interval) 3+ minutes
- (intensity of interval) low to medium/55 per cent to 75 per cent VO2 max/HR max
- (work : relief ration/duration of recovery period) 1:1/ 1:□
- (number of work/relief intervals) 1 set of 3/4 reps

CHAPTER 18.2

Health components of physical fitness: Strength

True or False?

1. True.
2. False. Static strength is when the force exerted by the neuromuscular system while the muscle length remains constant/ static
3. True.
4. True.
5. False. Free weights are a less safe training method and DO offer improved specificity for joint movement patterns.
6. True.
7. False. Plyometric training involves placing an eccentric stretch on a muscle to initiate the stretch reflex;
8. True.
9. True.
10. False. Short-term early strength gains are primarily due to neural adaptations and Long-term gains are largely due to hypertrophy (physiological) changes.

Exam practice

1. Explosive/elastic strength is important for anaerobic athletes such as sprinters whereas strength endurance is important for aerobic athletes like a marathon runner.

Compare and apply the relevant guidelines that need to be considered in order to develop explosive and endurance strength to one strength weight training session. *(6 marks)*

Sub-max three marks if there's no comparison . Sub-max three marks from any of the sections below:

Principle of specificity

- Both emphasise major muscle groups of the legs involved in sprinting/running
- Sprinting uses more fast twitch muscle fibres whereas marathon uses ST fibres
- Sprinter = ATP/PC/alactacid energy system & lactic acid/anaerobic glycolysis whereas marathon = aerobic energy system

Principle of overload

- weight/resistance) heavy/high resistance /70% □100% of 1 RM V's aerobic = low/mod weight resistance 50 % - 75% 1RM
- (reps) sprint = 1 □10 aerobic = 10+
- (sets) sprint = more 3 □6 aerobic = fewer/3-5
- (Frequency) sprint = more/3 □7 week aerobic = less/3-5 (recovery)
- sprint = 1:3 ratio/ full recovery between sets/2-5 minutes aerobic = 1:2 ratio/0-60secs/less recovery
- sprint allow for full recovery between sessions - 48 hours

2. Sprinters perform strength training programmes to improve their elastic/dynamic strength.
Explain the physiological muscular adaptations that will occur after completing a prolonged weight training programme to improve elastic/dynamic strength. *(6 marks)*

Only anaerobic muscular physiological responses will be accepted. Six marks available for any six of the following:

Physiological adaptations

- Muscle hypertrophy/the muscle fibre will increase in size.
- Hyperplasia /increase in number of muscle fibre number.
- Increased number/size of contractile protein (actin/myosin filaments) .
- Increased actin/myosin cross-bridges increase in glycogen stores.
- Anaerobic respiration more efficient.
- Increase in tolerance/buffering capacity of FT fibres to lactic acid enabling the athlete to work for longer in the lactic acid system.
- Increased efficiency to remove lactic acid more quickly/recover faster.
- Increased strength of ligaments/tendons/connective tissues.
- Increase in anaerobic (glycolytic) enzyme activity/ glycogen phosphorylase/PFK (making the energy release quicker).
- Increased ATP/PC stores (increased efficiency of ATP/PC system).
- Net effect: increased anaerobic threshold/capacity and recovery of ATP/PC/LA system.
- Increased intensity/duration of performance and delaying of OBLA/fatigue.

3. Explain how circuit training can be manipulated to benefit two contrasting types of strength. *(6 marks)*

There's one mark for naming two types of strength, and one mark if the two components contrast. You can get four marks for man manipulation of circuit training to suit both athletes. (sub-max of two for each circuit)

Endurance athlete

- Interval duration: longer, 3–5 minutes up to 20 minutes, or more.
- Interval intensity: low/moderate, 50 per cent to 75 per cent less emphasis on speed
- Ratio/number of work-relief: more stations but fewer circuits
- Interval relief: lower or no active relief between stations/circuits1:1.
- Frequency: three to five sessions a week

Power athlete

- Interval duration: shorter, 0-90secs, fewer Stations but more circuits
- Interval intensity: higher, 70 per cent to 90 per cent more emphasis on speed
- Ratio/number of work-relief: less stations but more circuits
- Interval relief: higher rest between stations/circuits/1:3
- Frequency: three to seven sessions a week

CHAPTER 18.3

Health components of physical fitness: Flexibility

True or False?

1. True.
2. False. Flexibility is both joint and sport-specific.
3. False. Dynamic flexibility is the range of motion (RoM) around a joint which occurs in the performance of a physical activity at either normal or rapid speed.
4. True.
5. False. Ballistic stretching uses momentum to move a joint forcibly through to its extreme end of range or point of resistance and involves fast, swinging, active or bouncing movements.
6. True.
7. True.
8. True.
9. False. PNF seeks to inhibit the stretch reflex to allow a greater stretch of the muscle/connective tissues.
10. True.

Exam practice

1. The purposes of flexibility training is to improve or maintain the range of movement over which muscles can act and joints can operate. Identify and explain **three** factors which can affect the range of motion around a joint. What are the proposed benefits of flexibility training to a performer? *(6 marks)*

Factors affecting RoM

*Only your first three responses are accepted, and the factors affecting RoM must be identified **and explained** in order to win the mark.*

Identify	Explanation
Type of joint	E.g. A ball and socket joint innately has a full RoM; a pivot joint only allows rotation; a hinge joint only allows flexion or extension, + any equiv'
Joint shape	The arrangement, shape and alignment of the joints' articulating surfaces/bones dictate RoM, e.g. shoulder joint has increased RoM having a shallow joint cavity, hip's deeper cavity limiting RoM but increases stability
Length/elasticity of connective tissues	In and around muscles and joints: the tendons, ligaments, epi/peri/endo-mysium of muscle, fascia and joint capsule all limit RoM
Muscle length/ elasticity	The muscle spindles activation point before it initiates the stretch reflex (when a muscle is rapidly stretched) prevents further RoM
Gender	Generally females are more flexible than males/accept opposite

continued

Age	Flexibility is greater in children and decreases as a person ages due to decrease in elasticity of muscle and connective tissues
Elasticity	The suppleness of skin and adipose tissue
Temperature	Elasticity of muscles and connective tissues is increased as temperature increases by 1–2 degrees Celsius, hence a warm-up should be performed
Muscle mass	Excess muscle mass around a joint restricts joint RoM
Nerves	Nerves pass through the joints; as joints are taken through a full RoM, nerves become stretched or compressed and trigger a stretch reflex within the muscles, increasing their resistance to stretch
Hypermobility	Inherited (double-jointed) or trained factors increasing RoM but can lead to joint instability and increase the risk of injury
Flexibility training	Stretching within a training programme may maintain/increase RoM

Benefits of flexibility training

(Sub-max 3 marks)

- increased **resting** length of muscle/connective tissues
- due to increased elasticity/length of muscle/connective tissues
- muscle spindles adapt to the increased length reducing the stimulus to the stretch reflex
- increased ROM at a joint before the stretch reflex is initiated
- increased potential for static and dynamic flexibility (ROM)
- increased distance/efficiency for muscles to create force and acceleration
- increased ROM reduces potential for injury during dynamic sports movements

2. Selecting either the hip **or** shoulder joint, give examples of types of flexibility exercises in an activity of your choice. Describe the types of training that can be used to increase the range of movement in that joint. *(6 marks)*

One mark for types of flexibility exercises:

- Any appropriate stretches for muscles around the shoulder or hip joint (at least two examples).

Five marks for types of flexibility training (must name more than one type for full five marks.

- static stretching/active
- **athlete** moves into a position that takes the joint just beyond its point of resistance
- passive stretching
- **partner** moves athlete into a position that takes the joint just beyond its point of resistance
- soft tissue around joint is lengthened
- position held for minimum of 6 seconds
- ballistic stretching/dynamic
- athlete uses momentum to move a body part through its extreme range of movements/ under control for dynamic
- (e.g.) using swinging leg/arm movements
- ballistic stretching should only be done by athletes who are already flexible

- PNF (Proprioceptive Neuromuscular Facilitation) stretching
- the muscle undergoes an isometric contraction then muscle is relaxed
- seeks to inhibit the stretch reflex mechanism
- so that a greater stretch can be performed next time
- stretches should be repeated during session
- for maximum benefit at least three times a week
- better performed when muscles are warm/ during warm up/cool down

3. PNF (proprioceptive neuromuscular facilitation) is one type of flexibility training. Describe PNF stretching and explain the theory behind its effectiveness.   *(5 marks)*

Three marks for a description of PNF:

- Performer/partner moves a joint/muscle to just beyond its resistance point/normal range.
- Performer performs an isometric contraction against resistance.
- Performer holds the stretch for six to 10 seconds.
- Performer relaxes muscle and stretches again.
- Performer usually achieves a greater RoM in each consecutive stretch.

Three marks for an explanation of PNF theory:

- Muscle spindles stimulate the CNS/spinal cord when a muscle is being stretched.
- Stimulates stretch reflex, muscle contracts to protect from being overstretched
- PNF isometric contraction inhibits the stretch reflex.
- Allowing a greater stretch of the muscle/connective tissues.

CHAPTER 18.4

Health components of physical fitness: Body composition

True or False?

1. False. Body composition refers to the chemical make-up of the body.
2. True.
3. True.
4. False. Body mass index (BMI) is a measure of an adult's weight in relation to their height, or more specifically their weight in kilograms divided by their height in metres squared.
5. True.
6. False. The UK Department of Health Estimated Average Requirements give a daily calorie intake of 1940 calories per day for women and 2550 for men.
7. False. The UK Department of Health Estimated Average Requirements give a daily calorie intake of 1940 calories per day for women and 2550 for men.
8. True.
9. True.
10. True.

Exam practice

1. The UK Department of Health's Estimated Average Requirements (EAR) suggests a daily calorie intake of around 1940 calories per day for women and 2550 calories for men. The daily calorie intake is recommended to come from what is termed a balanced diet.

Outline the contents of a balanced diet and explain how and why you would change this diet when recommending what is termed an 'athletes diet'. *(6 marks)*

Three marks for outlining what a balanced diet should contain:

- approximately 10 -15 per cent protein
- no more than 30 per cent fat
- 55 - 60 per cent carbohydrate (CHO)
- foods from the '5 nutrient food groups to ensure vital vitamins, minerals, water and roughage are included.

One mark for highlighting the changes of an athlete's diet:

- an additional 10–15 per cent of carbohydrate intake
- up to 5000 to 6000 kcal a day.

One mark for explaining Why

- to refuel the kcal/calories required to maintain their activity/recovery levels (neutral energy balance).

2. Using examples and average values for body composition discuss the statement that 'Two individuals may have the same weight but their body composition can vary significantly'. *(5 marks)*

You'll get one mark for an for an example, e.g.:

- appropriate muscular athlete may weigh the same as an obese/overweight individual who has greater fat mass s-max

There are four marks available from the body composition information below:

- Body composition refers to the chemical make-up of the body split into two components
- *Fat mass* refers to the percentage of body weight that is stored as fat (within adipose tissue).
- *Lean body mass* is the weight of the rest of the body/ all the body's non-fat tissues including bone, muscle, organs and connective tissues.
- Height and weight do not always reflect body composition.
- Muscle weighs more than fat mass.
- BMI/ideal height weight tables do not account for muscle weight

Two marks available for average values from:

- The average male has 12–18 per cent body fat,
- The average female has 22–28 per cent.
- Appropriate average value for elite athletes: 6 -12% for men and 12-20% for women.

3. Although obesity is not a disease, it is widely recognised as a health hazard. Evaluate the health implications of being overweight/obese and how this may impact on performance and involvement in physical activity. *(6 marks)*

Four marks are available from:

- An increased risk of diabetes/cancers.
- Long-term stress on the cardio-vascular systems leading to coronary heart disease, angina, varicose veins, deep vein thrombosis, increased blood lipids, atherosclerosis (disease of arteries), high blood pressure, stroke, poor temperature regulation, low fatigue resistance, renal/gall bladder disease, respiratory problems, lethargy, and surgical operations at much higher risk
- Overload of joints, especially lower body joints, which impacts on body posture, alignment and consequently leads to musculo-skeletal pain.

Four marks are available from explaining the impact on:

Involvement

- Increased (real/perceived) energy expenditure/effort/load bearing of joints and risk of injury
- Psychological harm due to the associated stigma, ridicule, staring, bullying, etc.
- Less likely to be involved in physical activity

Performance

- under performance in both physical and mental work, such as education.
- Low body fat is a main characteristic of successful performers.
- Athletes generally carry less body fat due to their increased physical activity (energy expenditure).
- does not necessarily mean a low overall body mass/weight, as heavily muscular athletes will have a high body mass alongside a low fat mass.
- Anaerobic/sprinter-type athletes tend to have a heavier body mass (more muscle mass with a low fat mass).
- Endurance athletes have a lower body mass (smaller muscle mass with a very low fat mass).
- Low fat mass is more significant in endurance activity.
- Any weight not directly linked to metabolism /muscular performance has to be carried for longer, wasting energy which could be used to increase their performance.
- Fat mass reduces the power-to-weight ratio.
- Increased weight from muscle mass is fine if it adds power/force specific to the improvement of the activity.

CHAPTER 19

Performance enhancement

True or False?

1. False. Ergogenic aids is a generic term to describe anything that enhances performance.
2. True.
3. False. Creatine supplements increase PC stores to prolong ATP/PC energy production and are presently legal.
4. True.
5. False. RhEPO is an artificial synthetic copy of EPO, a naturally occurring hormone which increases the body's ability to manufacture red blood cells.
6. True.
7. False. Caffeine was previously banned above 12mm but is now on the WADA watch list
8. True.
9. True.
10. True.

Exam practice

1. Performers may use the ATP-PC system during short explosive movements. Name **two** performance enhancement aids, excluding gene doping, that might affect performance in explosive activities. Describe the physiological effects of **each** aid. *(6 marks)*

There's one mark for each of the points listed, but two aids must be discussed for maximum marks.

Caffeine:

- is a CNS (central nervous system stimulant), it increases blood pressure/heart rate/alertness/focus
- is weaker, but similar in action to amphetamines/stimulant
- combats/delays fatigue and increases energy levels
- acts as a diuretic, increases the risk of dehydration and heat exhaustion
- can be physically addictive
- elevates level of blood Free Fatty Acids.

Anabolic Steroids:

- increase development of bone maturation, muscle mass, strength, fat free body mass and power
- facilitate recovery and muscle repair from high intensity training
- allow athletes to train harder, more frequently
- cause hormonal disturbances in males and females: males – testes shrinking, reduced sperm count, impotence, breast enlargement; females – facial hair, deepening voice, breast reduction, enlarged genatalia
- cause liver damage/cancers
- cause musculoskeletal damage, weakened tendons.

- reduces HDL cholesterol levels, increases risk of heart disease (CHD), heart attack and increase blood pressure.

Human growth hormone:

- aids muscle growth/increases muscle mass
- gives overall decrease in body fat
- enhances healing after musculoskeletal injuries
- increases blood glucose levels/lipases for FFA (fat) breakdown
- increases possibility of abnormal growth/acromegaly/bone thickening which causes broadening of hands, feet, face, skin thickening and abnormalities
- causes enlargement of internal organs/sort tissue growth
- causes muscle and joint weakness
- causes heart disease
- causes glucose intolerance/diabetes
- causes hypertension/high blood pressure.

Creatine supplements:

- elevate levels of stored PC
- speed up the recovery process
- enhances ATP resynthesis
- increases stress on the heart/liver
- works longer at higher intensity/increased alactic threshold.

2. Pulleys and parachutes are two types of ergogenic aid. Discuss the effects of using pulleys and parachutes referring to the following:

- the theory behind their use
- the type of performer benefiting
- the performance enhancing qualities
- the associated side effects *(5 marks)*

There are five marks for discussing five from the table below. You need one from each section to get full marks.

	Pulleys/Parachutes
Theory	Another form of resistance training. Resistance to apply a force against to develop strength, in the same way as body weight in circuit training and weights on the multi-gym.
Type of performer	Most performers for specificity in running/swimming/throwing events but mostly explosive activities **Pulleys:** most performers and heavily used by swimmers. **parachutes** increase the resistance to apply a force against while maintaining the specificity of movement and are used predominantly in sprint type running activities and they can provide fun and variety from routine training.
Performance enhancing qualities	Increased SPECIFICITY and variety of resistance training effect therefore better motor skill development more closely match the actual movement pattern that is used in the performance activity. they can provide fun and variety from routine training.
Associated side effects	No negative health risks but still not 100% specific to activity

3. An ergogenic aid is any substance that enhances performance. Using examples, critically evaluate the use of the following as aids to enhance performance and identify the type of performer/s who may benefit from their use.

- the use of dietary manipulation

- pre competition meals

- post competition meals *(20 marks)*

20-mark questions are marked with a 'levels of response' mark scheme. See page vii in the Exam Strategies section at the front of this book.

Indicative content: *Answers are likely to include (some of) the following:*

Dietary manipulation:

- Dietary strategies should be part/alongside a balanced diet of CHO.Fat,Protein
  - o athletes diet/higher % CHO's
  - o affect on body composition/energy intake/balance/expenditure
- Use of carbohydrate/glycogen loading
- Glycogen stores are depleted a week before competition
- By heavy training/eating a diet rich in protein/fats/low in carbohydrates
- 3–4 days prior to competition training is tapered/reduced/performer eats a diet rich in carbohydrate
- The body compensates for its previous lack of carbohydrate
  - o Storing more glycogen than before/increasing glycogen levels
  - o Alternative models of carboloading –Astrand/Shermans/others EQ's
- Fluid intake /hydration/rehydration, alongside CHO loading
- Benefits endurance/aerobic athletes/games players
- (Negative effect) is quality of training may be compromised/feelings of weakness during glycogen depletion stage

- (Negative effect) is possible weight increase/water retention/muscle stiffness/ soreness
- (Negative effect) could be possible depression/irritability during thedepletion phase

Pre-competition meal

- These should be eaten 2–4 hours before competition
- To ensure that glycogen stores are high
- Glucose can also be eaten immediately before competition
  - Fluid intake /hydration/rehydration, pre-exercise
- Benefits any performer who relies on the breakdown of glycogen for energy e.g. aerobic performer/ games player
- (Negative effect) if consumes too close to competition can have detrimental effect
- (Negative effect) high blood glucose levels will stimulate the release of insulin that will remove glucose from the blood stream/
  - Reactive/rebound hypoglycaemia if too close to exercise(under 2 hrs and immediately before) causing early fatigue

Post competition meal

- The optimal time is within 2 hours of end of exercise
- As rate of muscle glycogen replacement is at its quickest
- Eat a carbohydrate rich meal (within 2 hours)
  - Fluid intake /hydration/rehydration, post-exercise/rehydration
- Benefits any performer who has used glycogen as their fuel for exercise e.g. aerobic performer/games player

Performers that would benefit

Examples may be covered within three area headings above but separated below for clarity

- CHO loading = Aerobic/endurance athletes, eg.g marathon/cycling
- Pre-comp meals = Any athlete reliant on glycogen within anaerobic/aerobic energy systems e.g. Team/ invasion/racquet game activities eg, football/hockey/net/B-ball
- Post exercise = Any athlete reliant on glycogen as fuel source
- CHO loading/pre-comp/post comp = Any athletes involved in all day tournaments reliant on glycogen
- Prolonged anaerobic training/activity reliant upon glycogen.

CHAPTER 20

Improvement of effective performance and the critical evaluation of practical activities in Physical Education

True or False?

1. False – you must be assessed in one of the activities you were in at AS.
2. False – if you were assesses in football at AS you can be assessed in performing, coaching or officiating football at A2.
3. False – there are only ten activities you can be assessed officiating in.
4. True
5. True
6. False – assessments are submitted by 31 March.
7. True
8. False – some activities require you to produce a log (e.g. circuit training).
9. False – when a log is part of the assessment criteria the quality of it will affect the mark you are given.
10. False – if the moderator asks you to attend moderation then, unless you have another exam, you must go as part of the examination.

CHAPTER 21

EVALUATION AND APPRECIATION OF PERFORMANCE

True or False?

1. True – it is worth 10 per cent of your A2 marks and can make a significant difference to your grade.
2. False – you are allowed to bring a blank piece of paper and a clipboard on which to make notes as you observe.
3. False – you can only bring a blank piece of paper to make notes on.
4. True – students who just look at one strength and one weakness in each of those areas will not get into the top bands.
5. False – your action plan must be for a weakness you have seen in the performance you have observed.
6. False – your action plan should be for one of the major weaknesses you have identified in the performance. It must also cover coaching points and progressive practices.
7. True – you have to apply theory from your physiological, psychological and socio-cultural areas. This can AS or A2.
8. False – the theory you talk about must be relevant and applied to support your evaluation of the performance and your action plan.
9. False – your teacher will decide which performer you are to observe.
10. True – however your response must cover everything that is required.

INDEX

INDEX